WELL-BEING AND MORALITY

Essays in Honour of James Griffin

Well-Being and Morality

Essays in Honour of James Griffin

Edited by

ROGER CRISP

and

BRAD HOOKER

CLARENDON PRESS · OXFORD

Great Clarendon Street, Oxford OX2 6DP

Oxford University Press is a department of the University of Oxford.
It furthers the University's objective of excellence in research, scholarship,
and education by publishing worldwide in

Oxford New York

Athens Auckland Bangkok Bogotá Buenos Aires Calcutta
Cape Town Chennai Dar es Salaam Delhi Florence Hong Kong Istanbul
Karachi Kuala Lumpur Madrid Melbourne Mexico City Mumbai
Nairobi Paris São Paulo Singapore Taipei Tokyo Toronto Warsaw

and associated companies in Berlin Ibadan

Oxford is a registered trade mark of Oxford University Press
in the UK and certain other countries

Published in the United States
by Oxford University Press Inc., New York

British Library Cataloguing in Publication Data

Data available

Library of Congress Cataloging in Publication Data

Well-being and morality: essays in honour of James Griffin / edited by Roger Crisp and Brad Hooker.
Includes bibliographical references and index.
1. Ethics. I. Griffin, James, 1993– II. Crisp, Roger, 1961– III. Hooker, Brad, 1957–
BJ1012.W42 1999   17–dc2   99-045060
ISBN 0-19-823584-4

1 3 5 7 9 10 8 6 4 2

Typeset by Best-set Typesetter Ltd., Hong Kong
Printed in Great Britain
on acid-free paper by
T. J. International Ltd
Padstow, Cornwall

Preface

These essays are offered to James Griffin by friends, colleagues, and students in recognition of his significant and lasting contribution to moral philosophy, and in particular to mark his appointment to the White's Chair of Moral Philosophy at the University of Oxford.

Griffin was born in 1933. He was a graduate student at Oxford, supervised first by Gilbert Ryle and later by B. F. McGuinness, but taught also by G. E. L. Owen, David Pears, and Iris Murdoch. In 1966 he took up a Tutorial Fellowship in Philosophy at Keble College, Oxford, and was in 1990 appointed to a Readership in Philosophy. He became White's Professor in 1996. His first book, *Wittgenstein's Logical Atomism*, is still read by those interested in the *Tractatus*, but it is primarily for his work in ethics that Griffin is now celebrated.

Griffin's *Well-Being: Its Meaning, Measurement and Moral Importance* (Oxford, 1986) was largely responsible for the reintroduction of the ancient question of the nature of the human good, and its relation to morality, into moral philosophy. To that ancient question, Griffin offered an answer with ancient resonances: well-being consists in certain goods, instantiated in a life. But his awareness of the important role of the notion of desire in any plausible account of value explains partly why Samuel Scheffler felt able to describe Griffin's position as a 'more sensitive and less doctrinaire utilitarianism than many have thought possible'.

Griffin himself, however, would be unhappy to be labelled as utilitarian, or indeed as a member of any philosophical school. He is doubtful about many of the distinctions on which modern ethics has relied. Nevertheless, his understanding of the motivations for these distinctions, and his sensitive reconstructions and revisions, have led many to see certain areas of moral philosophy in an entirely new way, or at least to take seriously the idea that they may so be seen. Griffin's constructively questioning approach resulted in *Value Judgement: Improving our Ethical Beliefs* (Oxford, 1996). The richness and suggestiveness of Griffin's arguments in that book are striking, and emerge further as he spells out and develops his position in the important 'Replies' in this volume.

Many of the articles in this book are on Griffin's own work, and all are on areas in ethics that have been transformed by his presence. Our hope is that, through their arguments, they will serve both to honour Griffin and to continue the debates to which he has made, and continues to make, such an invaluable contribution.

Roger Crisp
Brad Hooker

Contents

Notes on Contributors

JOHN BROOME is Professor of Philosophy at the University of St Andrews, and was previously Professor of Economics at the University of Bristol. His books include *Weighing Goods* and *Ethics Out of Economics*. He edits the journal *Economics and Philosophy*.

ROGER CRISP is Fellow and Tutor in Philosophy, St Anne's College, Oxford. He is the author of *Mill on Utilitarianism*, editor of *Utilitas*, and a member of the Analysis Committee.

JONATHAN DANCY is Professor of Philosophy at the University of Reading. He is author of *Moral Reasons* and has published many articles on epistemology and moral theory. His *Practical Reality* will appear in 2000.

JONATHAN GLOVER is Professor of Ethics and Director of the Centre of Medical Law and Ethics at King's College London. He is author of *Humanity—A Moral History of the Twentieth Century*.

BRAD HOOKER teaches at the University of Reading. He edited *Truth in Ethics* and *Rationality, Rules, and Utility*. Forthcoming work includes *Ideal Code, Real World: A Rule-Consequentialist Theory of Morality*.

S. L. HURLEY is Professor of Political and Ethical Theory at the University of Warwick, and was formerly a Fellow of All Souls College, Oxford. She is author of *Natural Reasons* and *Consciousness in Action*, as well as various articles, and is co-editor of *Foundations of Decision Theory* and *On Human Rights*.

ANDREW MOORE is Senior Lecturer in Philosophy at the University of Otago, Dunedin, New Zealand. He has published papers in *Utilitas*, the *Australasian Journal of Philosophy*, and *Bioethics*, and is currently working on a manuscript for a book on well-being.

PETER RAILTON is Professor of Philosophy at the University of Michigan, Ann Arbor. He has written numerous articles in ethics and the philosophy of science, and is co-editor (with Stephen Darwall and Allan Gibbard) of *Moral Discourse and Practice*.

JOSEPH RAZ is Professor of the Philosophy of Law at Oxford University and Fellow of Balliol College. His publications include *The Authority of Law, Practical Reason and Norms, The Morality of Freedom*, and *Ethics in the Public Domain*.

AMÉLIE OKSENBERG RORTY is Professor of the History of Ideas at Brandeis University, author of *Mind in Action*, and editor of *Essays on Aristotle's Ethics, Explaining Emotions, Essays on Aristotle's Rhetoric*, and *Philosophers on Education*. She has written numerous articles on the philosophy of mind and on the history of moral psychology.

JOHN SKORUPSKI is Professor of Moral Philosophy at the University of St Andrews. His most recent book was *English-Language Philosophy 1750–1945*. A volume of his essays on ethics, *Ethical Explorations*, will be published in 1999.

MICHAEL SMITH is Professor of Philosophy at the Research School of Social Sciences, Australian National University. He is the author of *The Moral Problem* and the editor of *Meta-Ethics*.

L. W. SUMNER is Professor in the Department of Philosophy and the Faculty of Law at the University of Toronto. He is the author of *Abortion and Moral Theory, The Moral Foundation of Rights*, and *Welfare, Happiness, and Ethics*, as well as numerous articles in ethics, political philosophy, and philosophy of law.

LARRY S. TEMKIN is Professor of Philosophy at Rice University, and Director of the Rice University Lecture Series on Ethics, Politics, and Society. Recent honours include outstanding teaching awards, and Visiting Fellowships at Harvard and All Souls College, Oxford. The author of *Inequality*, Temkin is currently exploring the good, moral ideals, and practical reasoning.

Abbreviations

ATM   J. Griffin, 'Against the Taste Model', in Jon Elster and John E. Roemer
        (eds.), *Interpersonal Comparisons of Well-Being* (Cambridge: Cam-
        bridge University Press, 1991), 45–69

DB   J. Griffin, 'Dan Brock: Quality of Life Measures in Health Care and
        Medical Ethics', in Martha Nussbaum and Amartya Sen (eds.), *The
        Quality of Life* (Oxford: Clarendon Press, 1993), 133–9

HG   J. Griffin, 'The Human Good and the Ambitions of Consequen-
        tialism', in E. Paul, F. Miller, and J. Paul (eds.), *The Good Life and
        the Human Good* (Cambridge: Cambridge University Press, 1992),
        118–32

IV   J. Griffin, 'Are there Incommensurable Values?', *Philosophy and
        Public Affairs*, 7 (1977), 39–59

I   J. Griffin, 'Incommensurability: What's the Problem?', in Ruth
        Chang (ed.), *Incommensurability, Incomparability, and Practical
        Reason* (Cambridge, Mass.: Harvard University Press, 1997), 35–51

ME   H. Sidgwick, *The Methods of Ethics* (7th edn., London: Macmillan,
        1907)

MV   J. Griffin, 'Mixing Values', *Proceedings of the Aristotelian Society*,
        suppl. vol. 65 (1991), 101–8

NE   *Nicomachean Ethics*

V   J. Griffin, 'Values: Reduction, Supervenience, and Explanation by
        Ascent', in David Charles and Kathleen Lennon (eds.), *Reduction,
        Explanation, and Realism* (Oxford: Clarendon Press, 1992), 297–321

VJ   J. Griffin, *Value Judgement: Improving our Ethical Beliefs* (Oxford:
        Clarendon Press, 1996)

WB   J. Griffin, *Well-Being: Its Meaning, Measurement, and Moral Impor-
        tance* (Oxford: Clarendon Press, 1986)

WR   J. Griffin, 'On the Winding Road from Good to Right', in R. Frey
        and C. Morris (eds.), *Value, Welfare, and Morality* (Cambridge:
        Cambridge University Press, 1993), 158–79

1

Something in Between

L. W. Sumner

Mental state accounts are too narrow, desire accounts too broad. We ought to look in between.

(*WB* 18)

In the first sentence of his excellent book *Well-Being,* Jim Griffin announces that he intends to offer answers to three questions: 'What is the best way to understand "well-being"? Can it be measured? Where does it fit in moral and political philosophy?' Although all three questions are of obvious importance, and although the answers he develops to all of them have been deservedly influential, I intend in this discussion to focus exclusively on the first. As Griffin comes to define this project more precisely, it takes the form of seeking the best formal account of well-being or (as the utilitarians would have it) 'utility'. By calling such an account 'formal', Griffin means to distinguish it from the classical utilitarian view on which 'utility' was the supreme substantive prudential (and ethical) value. By contrast, on the account he defends ' "utility". . . is not to be seen as the single over-arching value, in fact not as a substantive value at all, but instead as a formal analysis of what it is for something to be prudentially valuable to some person' (*WB* 31–2).

The distinction Griffin is drawing here—between a formal account of the nature of prudential value and substantive prudential values—is very important. It has its analogue in metaphysical theories about the nature of natural phenomena such as causation or substance. The task of a philosophical theory of causation, for example, is to tell us *what it is* for one event or state of affairs to cause another. That is to say, it must complete the formula '*x* causes *y* if and only if *x* stands in relation *R* to *y*' by proposing some value for *R*. It would be a mistake for such a theory to confuse the conditions that constitute the relation of causal efficacy (the value for *R*) with any of the particular things capable of being causally efficacious (the values for *x*).

An account of the nature of causation is one thing, an inventory of causes quite another.

Likewise, a theory about the nature of well-being must tell us, as Griffin says, *what it is* for something (anything) to be prudentially valuable for someone. In order to do so it must provide the appropriate relation to complete such formulas as 'x is prudentially valuable for y if and only if x stands in relation R to y'. It would also be a mistake for such a theory to confuse the conditions that constitute the relation of prudential value (the value for R) with any of the particular things capable of being prudentially valuable (the values for x). An account of the nature of well-being is one thing, a list of its sources or ingredients quite another.[1]

The distinction is important, because it offers the possibility that well-being may be unified in its nature though diverse in its sources or ingredients. I interpret Griffin's argument in *Well-Being* as taking up this possibility by defending both a unified theory about the nature of well-being and 'a strong form of pluralism about [prudential] values' themselves (*WB* 31). The pluralism shows itself in Griffin's own list of such values (*WB* 67–8): accomplishment, the 'components of human existence' (autonomy, basic capabilities, liberty), understanding, enjoyment, and deep personal relations. The particular items Griffin enumerates here are unsurprising: they are similar to those featured in most so-called objective-list theories. We should expect any plausible formal theory of well-being to yield a similar inventory of substantive (human) values; doing so is a large part of what would make it plausible. What is distinctive in Griffin's approach is the particular formal theory he defends.

That theory treats well-being, or utility, as 'the fulfilment of informed desires, the stronger the desires, the greater the utility' (*WB* 14). In explicating his account, Griffin tells us that 'desiring something is, in the right circumstances, going for it, or not avoiding or being indifferent to getting it'. A desire is informed when it is 'formed by appreciation of the nature of its object'. It is fulfilled 'in the sense in which a clause in a contract is fulfilled: namely, what was agreed (desired) comes about'. Finally, the strength of a desire is its 'rank in a cool preference ordering, an ordering that reflects appreciation of the nature of the objects of desire' (*WB* 14–15).

I take Griffin's articulation and defence of this kind of account of prudential value to be one of the central projects, and also one of the great accomplishments, of *Well-Being*. However, before getting on with my discussion of it, I have to acknowledge that it may not any longer be one of Griffin's central

---

[1] By 'sources' or 'ingredients' of well-being I shall mean throughout those conditions or states of affairs that make us better off directly or intrinsically, as opposed to indirectly or instrumentally.

projects. Since *Well-Being* was published in 1986, Griffin has continued to write about prudential value (and prudential values). Nowhere, as far as I know, has he actually renounced the desire account. But nowhere, again as far as I know, has he actually reaffirmed it either. There is considerable discussion in some of his later writings of the complex interrelationships, and relative priorities, between desire and value: are prudential goods valuable because desired or desired because valuable (see e.g. ATM)? These discussions continue, and develop, the much briefer treatment of this issue in *Well-Being* (*WB* 26–31), but, unlike this earlier treatment, they do not occur within the framework of the desire theory (or of any other formal theory). Rather, what seems to have happened is that the entire project of developing a formal theory of the nature of prudential value has receded into the background, not so much officially abandoned as bypassed or superseded.

This impression is reinforced by a reading of Griffin's recent book *Value Judgement*. In it we find much discussion of prudential value(s), but no appearance by the desire theory as such. In this book, which brings together much of Griffin's work since 1986, I detect two themes, each of which tends to distance Griffin somewhat from the project of the earlier book. One is an association, more implicit than explicit, between the desire theory and one particular model of the desire–value relationship: what Griffin calls the 'taste model', according to which things become (prudentially) valuable by virtue of being desired. The alternative direction of argument is affirmed by (again what he calls) the 'perception model': we recognize that certain things are valuable, independently of our attitudes towards them, and then come to desire them for that reason. One of Griffin's main themes, which he introduced in the earlier book and has greatly developed in the later, is that both of these models give one-sided pictures of the ground of prudential values by virtue of distorting the relationship between reason and desire. In *Well-Being* his treatment of this theme consists, in part, of resisting the idea that acceptance of the desire theory implies a commitment to (what he later came to call) the taste model. But in this argument Griffin relies primarily on the requirement that desires be informed: 'It is the strength of the notion of "informed desire" that it straddles—that is, does not accept any sharp form of—the divide between reason and desire' (*WB* 30). The discussion ends with a reaffirmation of the desire theory:

The advantages of the informed desire account, therefore, seem to me to be these. It provides the materials needed to encompass the complexity of prudential value. It has the advantages of scope and flexibility over explanations of 'well-being' in terms of desirability features. It has scope, because all prudential values, from objects of simple varying tastes to objects of universal informed agreement, register somewhere in informed preferences. It has flexibility, because not everyone's well-being is affected in the same way by a certain desirability feature, and we want a notion sensitive to these individual differences. We want to know not only that something is valuable, but how valuable it is, and how valuable to different persons.   (*WB* 30–1)

No such endorsement appears anywhere in *Value Judgement*, and I surmise that Griffin would no longer feel comfortable writing one. Instead, in his more recent work he seems to rely much more directly on the desirability features of prudential goods: 'To see anything as prudentially valuable, then, we must see it as an instance of something generally intelligible as valuable and, fur-thermore, as valuable for any (normal) human' (*VJ* 29). What immediately follows this 'general profile of prudential values' (as he calls it) is the same list of substantive goods Griffin presented in *Well-Being*. What is conspicuously absent is the formal theory.

This leads me to the second theme I discern in *Value Judgement*—namely, an impatience with, and distrust of, value theories in general. The most obvious instance of this deflationary tendency is Griffin's critique of the main contemporary ethical theories—utilitarianism, deontology, virtue theory—which are dismissed as both overly ambitious and not really necessary for (in the words of the book's subtitle) 'improving our ethical beliefs'. Instead, Griffin practises a more modest, low-level methodology that begins by identifying a few core beliefs of 'high reliability' and then expands outwards from there by (to cut a long story short) a process of critical reflection. 'If one sees one's moral outlook as an assemblage of norms arrived at in a piecemeal fashion,' he says, 'then one is much less likely to call it a "theory" ' (*VJ* 132). He would, I think, say the same about our prudential beliefs: they too 'seem to arise in different ways to meet different needs, without any overarching background consideration, either substantive or formal, generating and sanctioning them' (*VJ* 132). Here too there may be no real work to be done by a theory, including the desire theory.

So the aspect of Griffin's work that I am addressing in this discussion may now be ancient history for him. I persist regardless for three reasons: because I still believe in the project of developing a general theory about the nature of well-being, because the desire theory is the dominant contemporary form of such a theory, and because the version of the desire theory that Griffin defended a decade ago in *Well-Being* remains both the strongest and the most influential. His case in favour of the desire account emerges initially out of his critique of mental-state accounts of well-being, exemplified by the hedonism of the classical utilitarians. Against such accounts he deploys two powerful objections (*WB* 7–10). The first consists in arguing that there is no single positive feeling such that having more of it necessarily makes us better off, and no negative feeling such that having more of that must make us worse off. He gives the example of Freud who, when terminally ill, refused all drugs except aspirin, preferring to think in torment rather than not to be able to think clearly. As Griffin asks, 'can we find a single feeling or mental state present in both of Freud's options in virtue of which he ranked them as he did?' Less dramatic instances occur in our ordinary lives whenever we choose between heterogeneous activities or pursuits. There is a recognizable feeling tone to sexual arousal that is quite different from the relief of finally completing a long-standing task or the tranquillity of a walk in the woods. If these are your options for the next hour, you might have a decided preference for one over the others (on purely prudential grounds). But it would be difficult for you to locate any particular felt quality, common to all three experiences, that you expect your preferred choice to maximize.

Of the classical utilitarians, Bentham was the most clearly committed to the homogeneity of all pleasures, and all pains. Both Mill and Sidgwick, however, seemed to recognize that the mental states we call pleasures are a mixed bag as far as their phenomenal properties are concerned.[2] On their view what pleasures have in common is not something internal to them—their peculiar feeling tone, or whatever—but something about us—the fact that we like them, enjoy them, value them, find them satisfying, seek them, wish to prolong them, and so on. Griffin's first objection to hedonistic theories is, therefore, not decisive. When confronted with the case of Freud, the hedonist can say that he chose the option that, despite the greater suffering involved, he found on balance to be the more satisfying or fulfilling. And that seems roughly right.[3]

Against this form of hedonism, however, Griffin brings a second objection:

The trouble with this eclectic account is that we do seem to desire things other than states of mind, even independently of the states of mind they produce. . . . I prefer, in important areas of my life, bitter truth to comfortable delusion. Even if I were surrounded by consummate actors able to give me sweet simulacra of love and affection, I should prefer the relatively bitter diet of their authentic reactions. And I should prefer it not because it would be morally better, or aesthetically better, or more noble, but because it would make for a better life for me to live.   (*WB* 9)

It is undeniable that, offered a choice between bitter truth and comfortable delusion, at least sometimes we opt for the former. Not all the time—that would be too strong a claim. When we find reality hard enough to face, the comfort afforded by the appropriate delusion may be irresistible. There is, of course, an epistemic problem here: a delusion has no power to comfort unless

---

[2] For a discussion of the classical utilitarians' conceptions of pleasure and pain (and of well-being) see my *Welfare, Happiness, and Ethics* (Oxford: Clarendon Press, 1996), §4.1.

[3] Griffin says that in Sidgwick's account desire unifies the several mental states that count as pleasures (*WB* 9). This sets up the transition to his own desire theory, once the reference to the states themselves is discarded as redundant. But it is at least as plausible to point to the fact that they are all liked or enjoyed or found fulfilling. This is not the same as saying that they are desired—*au contraire*, it identifies the most obvious reason for desiring them.

it is accepted as real, in which case how can we be said to prefer it *as a delusion*? After all, the problem is that *from the inside* delusion and reality may be indistinguishable. However, we do often have an inkling that our carefully safeguarded belief structure is fragile and we can collude in protecting it against damaging counter-evidence; deception then shades into self-deception. Furthermore, like Griffin, we can express a standing preference, one way or the other, about specified areas of our lives: 'I don't want to know', or 'I would like to be told'.

Most of us will surely agree with Griffin in preferring reality to illusion in some key sectors of our lives. And we will agree that, in those sectors, being in touch with reality makes for a better life. Since there are many ways in which a life may have value, the question remains open whether, when we get the truth we seek, our lives are *prudentially* better. Certainly the opposite can seem to be the case, if we are shattered or decentred by the knowledge we gain. Griffin claims that he prefers truth to delusion 'not because it would be morally better, or aesthetically better, or more noble, but because it would make for a better life for me to live'. But a life of greater moral or aesthetic or perfectionist value is also, in that respect, a better life for him to live, so we have not yet succeeded in isolating the prudential question.[4] Nor can we easily discount the influence of these other ideals. Could our judgement not sometimes be that a life filled with illusion or deception, while it may be going very nicely for its subject, is none the less unworthy of a human being? If so, then the lesson may be, not that mental-state theories are deficient as accounts of the nature of welfare, but that prudential value is only one dimension of the value of a life.

After all, it is a commonplace that we care about, and are motivated by, many considerations other than our own interest—considerations to which we are prepared to sacrifice our interest, if necessary. Defenders of mental-state theories can try to hold the line here, arguing that every choice of bitter truth over comforting delusion is a case in which we allow our well-being to be overridden by some rival dimension of value. Upon reflection, however, this is difficult to accept. If what you have treasured as an important ingredient of your well-being—your accomplishments, say, or your deep personal relations—turns out to have been an elaborate deception, you are likely to feel hurt and betrayed. How else to explain this, except to say that, at least in this area of your life, what mattered to you was not merely how things seemed but how they actually were? Your reaction to the deception certainly looks, and feels, like a reassessment, in the light of your own priorities, of how well your life has been going for you. And that seems to place it squarely within the domain of prudential value.

---

[4] For a distinction among aesthetic, perfectionist, and prudential value, see Sumner, *Welfare, Happiness, and Ethics*, §1.3.

So I am prepared to join Griffin in rejecting mental-state theories of well-being. As he himself recognizes, the alternative he offers—a desire theory—is also open to objection: 'The trouble is that one's desires spread themselves so widely over the world that their objects extend far outside the bound of what, with any plausibility, one could take as touching one's own well-being' (*WB* 17). This problem arises because desires, like beliefs, are intentional (even propositional) attitudes. Just as beliefs can be verified or falsified, desires can be satisfied or frustrated. A belief is verified by the existence of the state of affairs (or the truth of the proposition) that is its intentional object; a desire is satisfied by the existence of the state of affairs (or the truth of the proposition) that is *its* intentional object. Like beliefs, desires can take spatially and/or temporally remote states of the world as their intentional objects. As a result, your desire for something can be satisfied without your knowing it (just as your belief about something can be true without your knowing it). All that is required is that whatever you want actually come to exist. Carl Sagan wants us to establish contact with extraterrestrial beings. Suppose that, twenty thousand years from now, some intelligent alien civilization encounters one of our probes in deep space and deciphers the messages that it carries. Sagan's desire will then have been satisfied, though he will know nothing of it. (Maybe it has been satisfied already.)

The intentionality of desire is an awkward feature for a theory of prudential value. According to the desire theory, something makes me better off when it satisfies some (informed) desire on my part. Since my desires can range over spatially and temporally remote states of affairs, it follows that the satisfaction of many of them will occur at times or places too distant from me to have any discernible effect on me. In such cases it is difficult to see how having my desire satisfied could possibly benefit me.

Sometimes the absence of feedback into my life is due to contingent circumstances. Suppose that my brother suffers from some debilitating disease that I very much want to be cured. Having unsuccessfully sought medical treatment at home, he moves to Papua New Guinea where a promising new treatment is available. After his arrival he breaks off contact with me, and I receive no further news of his fate. Two years later the treatment succeeds and his disorder is completely cured. At this time my desire that he be cured (which I continue to hold) has been satisfied. Because I care deeply about his well-being, if I knew of this I would be greatly cheered. Since I never know of it, how can the cure make me better off?

All of us have many desires that, unbeknownst to us, will come to be satisfied during our lifetime. Like Carl Sagan, we also have many desires that will be satisfied, if ever, only after we are dead and gone. Sometimes the posthumous satisfaction of a desire is itself due to contingent circumstances, as when I want my daughter eventually to attend university but die before she is able to do so. In this case it is just unlucky for me that my desire is satisfied only after my demise. In other cases this outcome is ensured by the temporal location of the desired state of affairs. Nearly everyone wants the ecosystem of the planet to be in a healthy state two centuries from now, but no one alive now will be alive then. In still other cases, such as your wish to be remembered by your lover after your demise, if the desire is ever satisfied then this must (logically) occur posthumously. In any of these cases, if the desired state of affairs eventually comes about, does it make our life go better? If so, *when* does it go better? When our desire is satisfied? But how can the quality of our life be improved after it has ended? Retroactively, at the time we held the desire? But how can what happens *then* affect us for better or worse *now*?

Sometimes it can seem to. Griffin offers the following example:

It would not have been at all absurd for Bertrand Russell to have thought that if his work for nuclear disarmament had, after his death, actually reduced the risk of nuclear war, his last years would have been more worthwhile, and his life altogether more valuable, than if it all proved futile. True, if Russell had indeed succeeded, his life clearly would have been more valuable to others. But Russell could also have considered it more valuable from the point of view of his own self-interest.   (*WB* 23)

However, on closer examination claims of posthumous benefits always seem to rest on conflating different modes of value. If Russell's work had turned out to contribute to eventual nuclear disarmament, then this would, of course, have shown, retrospectively, that his life had enormous instrumental value; but this, as Griffin recognizes, is not the question at issue. Somewhat closer to the mark, accomplishment might be a perfectionist value—that is, it might make someone's life a better specimen of its kind, a better human life, independently of its prudential pay-off for that person. In that case, posthumous accomplishment might retroactively increase the perfectionist value of a life, and Russell might well have considered his life more valuable from that point of view. But from the standpoint of his own self-interest? That certainly does not follow, and seems much less plausible. It also seems an unlikely interpretation of Russell's own (imagined) evaluation. He can think that a more successful life is a better life, without thinking that he is made better off by it.

The issue of whether posthumously satisfied desires can benefit their erstwhile holders is a hotly debated one. Some people find it just obvious that the dead can be neither benefited nor harmed, while others find it equally obvious that lives are capable of retroactive prudential improvement.[5] I confess that I belong to the former camp. Dying has precious few consolations, but surely one of them is that we are thereafter safe from any further misfortunes. Whatever may befall the living after our demise, nothing can ever again go badly (or, alas, well) for us. That death is the end, prudentially speaking, has always

---

[5] Griffin feels the pull of both sides of the question (see *WB* 317–18).

been the principal attraction of suicide for those whose lives appear to have gone into irreversible decline. Where might we seek our comfort if adversity could pursue us even beyond the grave?

Given the division of opinion on this question, I do not think it is fair to treat the fact that an account of prudential value entails the possibility of posthumous harms and benefits as a sufficient reason for rejecting it. However, the posthumous cases are merely the most dramatic instances in which the fulfilment of a desire fails to benefit us because it has no impact, direct or indirect, on our experience. The obvious remedy is to impose on the desire theory what Griffin has called an *experience requirement* (*WB* 13), which would stipulate that a state of affairs can be prudentially valuable for me only if it somehow enters or affects my experience. A version of the desire theory that incorporated such a requirement might look like this: x is prudentially valuable for me just in case (*a*) I desire x, (*b*) x occurs, and (*c*) I am at least aware of x's occurrence.

As his handling of the Russell example suggests, Griffin rejects any form of experience requirement (*WB* 13–14, 19–20). His reason for doing so is the same as his reason for rejecting any version of a mental-state theory: we desire things other than states of our own experience. But this seems a confusion. On a mental-state theory, veridical and illusory experiences are of equal prudential value as long as they are phenomenologically indistinguishable. Adding an experience requirement to the desire theory has no such implication. No version of a desire theory is a mental-state theory, since the actual occurrence of the desired state of affairs (clause (*b*) above) is a necessary condition for a prudential pay-off. An experience requirement makes awareness of this occurrence a further necessary condition. In doing so it does not, and cannot, convert the theory into a mental-state theory.

Since Griffin rejects an experience requirement, he must find some other means of restricting the range of desires whose satisfaction will count as adding prudential value to our lives. His solution is to identify those desires that 'enter our lives in a way beyond just being our desires' (*WB* 21). One way for desires to 'enter our lives' in this way is for them to become 'the sort of aims or goals or aspirations on which the success of a life turns'. This will probably rule out our desire for a healthy ecosystem in the twenty-third century, but it cannot be the whole story, since we can also be made better off by getting things that we have in no way pursued. 'So we should try saying, to introduce more breadth, that what count are what we aim at and what we would not avoid or be indifferent to getting. What counts for me, therefore, is what enters my life with no doing from me, what I bring into my life, and what I do with my life' (*WB* 22).

Griffin leaves this requirement that a desire 'enter our lives' in the appropriate way pretty vague and undeveloped. At first glance it might seem similar in its implications to the rejected experience requirement. But in fact it is quite different, since it is an admissibility condition for desires, not for their satisfaction. An experience requirement will admit any desire whatever but stipulate that its satisfaction can be prudentially valuable for us only if it (somehow or other) enters our experience. Griffin's condition, by contrast, will admit only those desires that have 'entered our lives' in the requisite way, but will then count the satisfaction of any such desire as making us better off regardless of whether we are even aware of it. Thus, for instance, once I have made a desire into one of the aims of my life, the achievement of that aim will count as prudentially valuable for me even if it occurs posthumously (the Russell case).

In the absence of further explication, it is just unclear when desires 'enter our lives in a way beyond just being our desires'. It certainly looks as though being made into an aim cannot be a necessary condition: my desire that my brother be cured of his debilitating illness may be very much a part of my life (I may think of him every day), even though there is nothing I can do about it. Furthermore, if this desire qualifies, it is still difficult to see how I am made better off by the cure, if I never even know that it has been achieved. In the case of desires that have not achieved the status of aims, Griffin's requirement, as I understand it, is that the desire be for something 'we would not avoid or be indifferent to getting'. But this threatens to admit any desire whatever.[6] Perhaps Griffin's idea is that not all desires are for things we can *get* (i.e. bring into our lives). Sagan's desire may be like that (though he has also made it into an aim); certainly my desire for a healthy ecosystem in the twenty-third century is. But a healthy brother is something that I can bring into my life; it just happens that I do not. In any case, this notion of our being able to get or acquire the object of our desire is itself pretty vague (is it satisfied by my desire that England win the next World Cup? or that Amnesty International succeed in its campaign against torture?). Furthermore, this whole exercise of trying to define the boundaries of admissible desires has a rather *ad hoc* air about it. One wants to find a rationale guiding the exercise, but it seems designed just to avoid the awkward results generated by the desire theory.

Not all of those awkward results stem from the intentionality of desire; some result from its future-directedness. In explicating this feature, the analogy between desire and belief will again be instructive. Suppose I now believe that the sun will shine next Tuesday. My belief has two temporal indices, one for the time at which I hold the belief (now) and the other for the intentional object of the belief (next Tuesday). Where beliefs are concerned, these two indices can be ordered in any way whatever: I can hold beliefs at a particular time about earlier, contemporaneous, or later times.

---

[6] Recall Griffin's general account of desiring something as 'in the right circumstances, going for it, or not avoiding or being indifferent to getting it' (*WB* 14).

Now suppose that I now want the sun to shine next Tuesday. My desire has the same two temporal indices. However, unlike beliefs, the two indices for desires must observe a particular order: I can desire now only that something occur later. Desires are always directed on the future, never on the past or present.[7] (I can, of course, want events or activities that I am presently enjoying to continue; but their continuation is still a future state.) To put it crudely, I can want only what I have not yet got (or what has not yet happened).

Because a desire is always for some future state of affairs, at best it represents our *ex ante* expectation that the state will benefit us. But this expectation may be disappointed by our *ex post* experience of the state. Suppose that I want to see a movie tonight and think that I will enjoy a French sex comedy more than a serious drama. Half an hour into the film I discover that I am just not in the mood for it: though undeniably good of its kind, it is just too frothy and lightweight to satisfy. So I walk out, regretting that I missed the opportunity for something more nourishing.

In this case I have done what I (antecedently) most wanted to do, but I have not benefited from it. The problem is not that the event that satisfied my desire failed to enter into my experience, but that my experience of it turned out to be negative. Things did not go as I expected, and yet I achieved my aim. The problem here is the future-directedness of desire. My desire to see the sex comedy represented my *ex ante* expectation that I would find it more enjoyable. But in this I was mistaken. Since our desires always represent our *ex ante* expectations, there is always room for these expectations to be mistaken. But in that case the satisfaction of our desires does not guarantee that we are better off; only our *ex post* experience will do that.

Since it is the future-directedness of desire that creates this problem, it is tempting to try to put matters right by closing the gap between the way we expect things to go and the way they actually turn out. The obvious recourse here is to the requirement that a desire be adequately informed, or (as Griffin puts it) 'formed by appreciation of the nature of its object'. The effect of this requirement will be to screen out some of our actual desires; only the satisfaction of the subset of informed desires will count as enhancing our well-being. However, it is unclear how this will help in the case of my choice of sex comedy over drama, which was as informed as I could make it. All of the information I collected in advance about both options turned out to be correct; I made no mistakes, except in expecting that I would enjoy the comedy. That mistake resulted from the gap between my *ex ante* expectation and my *ex post*

---

[7] I can, of course, wish that past events had been otherwise. I can also have hopes about such events, if I do not know how things turned out. The first time I read Homer I hoped the Trojans would win; now I wish they had. But wishes of this sort cannot be satisfied, and I am assuming that a desire theory will attach no prudential weight to the fulfilment of hopes about the past.

experience, which exists by virtue of the future-directedness of desire: my preferences about the future always represent my view *now* of how things will go *then*. Because the gap results from the very nature of desire, it cannot be closed merely by requiring that desires be informed.

The gap could be closed by stipulating that a desire does not count as informed—and thus its satisfaction does not count as making us better off—whenever the desired state of affairs turns out upon later experience to be disappointing or unrewarding. However, for a desire theorist to take this step would be tantamount to conceding that what matters, so far as our well-being is concerned, is *our* satisfaction and not merely the satisfaction of our desires—how things turn out for us in the actual experience of them, not what we expect from them in advance. And that would lead to a very different kind of account, one that featured an experience requirement and gave no privileged status to desires.

The difficulties for the desire theory canvassed so far have a common logical form. Desires whose objects prove disappointing in the actual experience of them and desires whose objects never enter our experience at all—these are both cases in which the satisfaction of our desires appears insufficient to make us better off. What they demonstrate is that when a desire is satisfied it is a logically open question whether we are thereby benefited. However, they do not exhaust the problems that the desire theory encounters. If desire-satisfaction is not logically sufficient for well-being, it is not logically necessary either. Once again, the root of the problem lies in the very nature of desire. As we have already noted, because desires are future-directed, at best they represent the anticipation of benefit. But, just as we can be disappointed when we get what we expect or have aimed for, so we can be pleasantly surprised when we get what we do not expect and have not aimed for. Having nursed a long-standing suspicion of the Mediterranean, I am persuaded against my better judgement to holiday there and have a wonderful time. In this case I had no antecedent desire for the state of affairs that, as it turned out, enhanced my well-being.

I conclude that certain logical features of desires—their intentionality and their future-directedness—make them ill-suited to playing a constitutive role in a formal theory about the nature of well-being. If I am right then desires are the wrong place to start in constructing such a theory. Griffin, of course, recognizes the problems caused by the intentionality of desires, since he devotes much energy to the attempt to restrict the breadth of his account. I have suggested that this attempt does not succeed, but I have not tried to show, and could not show if I tried, that no such attempt could succeed. So it remains possible that desires are the right place to start, and there is some other way to screen out the ones that 'spread themselves so widely over the world that their objects extend far outside the bound of what, with any plausibility, one could take as touching one's own well-being'. As for the future-directedness of desires, this feature Griffin simply denies: 'The relevant sort of desire does not have to be held antecedently to its fulfilment (a human can enjoy something, want to have it continue or return, that he never knew he would enjoy, or even knew existed)' (*WB* 315). Griffin acknowledges that this is an 'extended sense of desire'. Now there is no point in quibbling over terminology: in Griffin's extended sense desires need not be future-directed. However, there is an important substantive point hereabouts. The desire theory belongs to a genus, each species of which grounds prudential values in some pro-attitude on the part of the subject.[8] Desires form one species of pro-attitude, identified (I have claimed) by their intentionality and future-directedness. These features distinguish them from another species that includes such attitudes as enjoying something, finding it pleasant or agreeable, experiencing it as satisfying or fulfilling, and so on. In contrast with desires (and beliefs), these attitudes can be directed only on contemporaneous states: I can (occurrently) enjoy only what I already have (or what is already happening). In Griffin's extended sense of desire there is no longer any difference between wanting something and enjoying it—or rather, the latter simply becomes a particular instance of the former. But in that case we erase the distinction between different kinds of pro-attitudes, and different kinds of theory about the nature of prudential value. In particular, we make it more difficult to locate a kind of theory that might occupy the space in between desire theories and mental-state theories.

That this difference—between wanting something and enjoying it—can make a difference for a theory of prudential value is what I now want to show. So let us take stock of where we are. Mental-state accounts are too narrow, because they exclude many states of the world that can be ingredients of our well-being. Desire accounts are too broad, because they include many states of the world that cannot be ingredients of our well-being. We ought, as Griffin suggests, to look in between. We know that the breadth of the desire account can be narrowed by introducing an experience requirement, but we also know that some anchoring in states of the world is necessary to avoid backsliding all the way into a mental-state theory. Enjoyment certainly seems to satisfy the first condition, since I can (occurrently) enjoy—find pleasing or satisfying—only what I am experiencing. As for the second condition—well, we need to develop an enjoyment account a little more to see how it might avoid being merely another form of mental-state theory.

I can do little more here than sketch how such an account might go.[9] But I will begin by suggesting that enjoyment is not quite the attitude we are

[8] I have attempted to characterize the genus more fully in *Welfare, Happiness, and Ethics*, §2.2.
[9] I develop it at greater length in ibid., ch. 6.

seeking here; we will do better to work instead with the more complex notion of happiness. The relevant sense of happiness for our purposes is that in which someone can be (or have been) happy or can have (or have had) a happy life. Being happy in this sense means having a certain kind of positive attitude towards your life, which in its fullest form has both a cognitive and an affective component. The cognitive aspect of happiness consists in a positive evaluation of the conditions of your life, a judgement that, at least on balance, it measures up favourably against your standards or expectations. This evaluation may be global, covering all of the important sectors of your life, or it may focus on one in particular (your work, say, or your family). In either case it represents an affirmation or endorsement of (some or all of) the conditions or circumstances of your life, a judgement that, on balance and taking everything into account, your life is going well for you. The affective side of happiness consists in what we commonly call a sense of well-being: finding your life enriching or rewarding, or feeling satisfied or fulfilled by it.

The notions of enjoyment and happiness (in this sense) are certainly related. However, occurrent enjoyments are too episodic, too tied to experiences of specific activities or conditions, to be identifiable with happiness. It is true that, *ceteris paribus*, having more episodes of enjoyment, and fewer episodes of suffering, in your life will make you happier. But there is no algorithm for computing your level of happiness from the intensity or duration of your particular enjoyments or sufferings. (It was the root mistake of the classical hedonists to believe there could be such an algorithm.) Enjoyment is one standard source or ingredient of happiness, but it is not the only one: success in the pursuit of your aims counts as well. The desire theory went wrong by treating desire-satisfaction not as one important source of well-being but as constituent of its nature. Hedonism, even a more sophisticated version that takes enjoyment and suffering as its central notions (rather than pleasure and pain), likewise confuses an important source of happiness with its nature.

The notions of enjoyment and happiness come closest to converging when the object of the former is one's life as a whole, either at a given time or over an extended stretch. It makes perfectly good sense to ask whether you are currently enjoying your life, or whether you enjoyed some particular part of it. And that is nearly the same thing as asking whether you are, or were, happy at that time. But not quite. For one thing, enjoyment understates the judgemental component of being happy, the sense of your life measuring up well against your prudential standards for it. But it even fails to capture the full range of the affective dimension of happiness, which can extend from bare contentment to deep fulfilment. Enjoyment is simply too mild to cover the more intense regions of this scale. (The opposite is true for suffering, which overstates the blander feelings of discontent or ennui: 'I certainly wouldn't say that I was suffering at that stage of my life; I just wasn't very happy.') Happiness is better understood in terms not of enjoyment but of something like satisfaction or fulfilment. The desire theory, of course, uses these terms in its own way: a desire is satisfied just in case its object comes to exist. However, as we have already seen, there is a logical gap between the fulfilment of any of your desires and your fulfilment, a gap that is fatal to the desire theory. Happiness is a matter not of desire-satisfaction but of personal or life satisfaction.

Suppose that this is right so far: happiness, or life satisfaction, is a positive cognitive/affective response on the part of a subject to (some or all of) the conditions or circumstances of her life. What remains to be decided is what all of this has to do with well-being. The simplest relationship between happiness and well-being would, of course, be identity: the prudential value of your life is just a function of how happy you are. However, there is a serious problem with this view, which was pointed out by Griffin when he considered and rejected the possibility of 'something in between' mental-state and desire accounts:

Suppose that someone is duped into thinking that those close to him are behaving authentically. What enters his experience is the same whether he has the real thing or a successful deceit. But it is only the real thing, he thinks, that makes his life better. According to the enjoyment account, what affects well-being can only be what enters experience, and the trouble is that some of the things that persons value greatly do not. My truly having close and authentic personal relations is not the kind of thing that can enter my experience; all that can enter is what is common to both my truly having such relations and my merely believing that I do. (*WB* 19)

This objection was raised against what I was calling in the 1980s an enjoyment account, and specifically against the role of an experience requirement in that account. I have since moved on from that early version of the sort of theory I want to defend to the current (and, of course, much more sophisticated) version that is formulated instead in terms of happiness. However, Griffin's objection retains its force against any straightforward identification of well-being with happiness.

The important point is that happiness is a response by a subject to her life conditions as she sees them. It is a matter of whether she is finding the perceived conditions of her life satisfying or fulfilling. But what if her perception of important sectors of her life is a misperception? What if she is deceived (by others or by herself) about them? Suppose, for instance, that her happiness depends in part on her confidence in the loyalty and affection of a partner who in fact is merely using her for his own purposes. When she discovers the truth she will, of course, be miserable. But what are we to say of those months or years during which she was deluded? She was certainly happy then, but was her life going well for her?

If we identify well-being with happiness, and if we treat happiness solely as a function of a subject's experience of her life, then the result will be a mental-state theory of welfare. It will not be a version of hedonism, since we will have resisted a reduction of happiness to pleasure or enjoyment. However, it will encounter the same objections as hedonism, since it will still assess a subject's well-being entirely 'from the inside' with no reference to the actual conditions of her life. If the objections to mental-state theories are decisive, as I earlier agreed they are, then this equation of well-being with happiness must be rejected.

For those who think that there is some interesting connection between these two notions, there are two ways to go from here. One is to modify the foregoing account of happiness in such a way as to ensure that it is not a mental-state account. This could be done by adding the condition that a person's positive evaluation of her life will count as (real or true) happiness only if it is based on beliefs about the world that are true (or at least justified). But this seems an implausible, and desperate, gambit. Consider the woman who for months or years has believed in, and relied on, the devotion of a faithless and self-serving partner. Her belief concerning a crucial condition of her life—a state of the world—was false. Whether it was also unjustified depends on the evidence of the deception that was available to her, whether or not she chose to take it on board. But let us assume, for the sake of the example, that there were sufficient cues for her to pick up, had she not been blinded by love. If you ask her during this period whether she is happy, she will say that she is; if you ask her whether her life is going well for her, she will say that it is. If you ask her how she sees the same period after the delusion has been exposed, she will probably say that it now seems to her a cruel hoax and a waste of that part of her life. Clearly she now thinks that her life was not going well then; she has retrospectively re-evaluated her well-being during that period. But will she now deny that she was happy then? To do so would seem a mistake, a rewriting of a piece of her personal history. She may resent the fact that her happiness was bought at the price of an elaborate deception, she may especially resent ever having been happy with such a jerk, but happy she was all the same. Wasn't she?

For better or worse, happiness does seem to be a (complex) mental state, dependent on how we see our lives and not (necessarily) on how they really are. Where our assumptions about the conditions of our lives turn out to be mistaken, therefore, happiness and well-being may part company. If we retain the idea that well-being is in part a matter of happiness, then it must also be in part a matter of something else. But what else? The most uncompromising view would be that we need to add a truth or reality requirement, which would stipulate that happiness counts as well-being only when it is based on a view of the conditions of our lives that is (at least) free from factual error. But this stipulation would be unreasonably puritanical. We do not invariably reassess earlier periods of happiness in this austere manner once we realize the extent to which they depended on false beliefs about states of the world: the intentions of a lover, the integrity of a public figure, the prospects of success at a new enterprise, or whatever. We always have the alternative available of accepting the good times we enjoyed with little or no regret and then moving on with our lives. In my younger days I derived much comfort from the conviction that the course of my life, and of the world as a whole, was being directed by a benevolent deity. When I could no longer sustain this illusion, I did not disavow the earlier comfort I derived from it; it got me through a difficult period of my life. When we reassess our lives in retrospect, and from a superior epistemic vantage point, there is no right answer to the question of what our reaction should be—that is surely up to us. Because a reality requirement stipulates a right answer—any happiness based on illusion can make no intrinsic contribution to our well-being—it must be rejected as presumptuously dogmatic. It seems even more dogmatic from a third-person standpoint: who are we to dictate that the solace someone else finds in a comforting fantasy should count for nothing?

A justification requirement would be weaker than a truth or reality requirement, since it would not discount the meaning brought to our lives by beliefs that, though false as matters turned out, were at least reasonable under the circumstances. Assuming that we can agree on standards of reasonable belief, a justification requirement would have the mild advantage of moving closer to the subject's point of view concerning the conditions of her life, but, in reserving well-being exclusively for the rational, it is not much less arrogant than the stronger demand for truth. Once again it presumes to dictate to individuals how much their deviations from an ideal epistemic standpoint should matter to them. But that is for them to decide.

We can take a somewhat different direction with this issue if we borrow from the desire theory the requirement that a person's endorsement of the conditions of her life be adequately informed. What we are seeking is a theory of welfare that makes the subject's outlook on her life authoritative for determining when that life is going well for her. By connecting well-being with happiness we have interpreted that outlook as her endorsement or affirmation of the conditions of her life. When that endorsement is based on a clear view of those conditions, we have no grounds for questioning or challenging its authority: in this respect, the individual is sovereign over her well-being. But when it is based, wholly or partly, on a misreading of those conditions, then its authority is open to question, since it is unclear whether or not she is endorsing her life as it really is. Where someone is deceived or deluded about her circumstances, in sectors of her life that clearly matter to her, the question is whether the affirmation she professes is genuine or authentic. In order for a subject's endorsement of her life accurately to reflect her own priorities, her own point of view—in order for it to be truly hers—it must be authentic, which in turn requires (at the very least) that it be informed.

At this point an information requirement could be pushed in the direction of either a reality requirement (ideal information) or a justification requirement (reasonable belief given the information available). Since either of these directions would be incompatible with the individual's ultimate sovereignty over her well-being, we must find some other way of determining how well informed a subject must be in order for her level of happiness to determine how well her life is going. The place to start is with a (slightly) different question: 'When is information adequate?' or 'When would more information be relevant?' The obvious answer is: 'whenever it would make a difference to a subject's affective response to her life, given her priorities.' Return to the case of the woman who, for a while, lives in ignorant bliss with a faithless partner. Her endorsement of her life lacks information about his character and intentions. Is this information relevant? It is if her possessing it would undermine that endorsement. There are, therefore, two possibilities, which open up once she has been undeceived. One is that she re-evaluates how well her life was going (not how happy she was) during the period of deception: 'I thought everything was going so well, but now I can see that it was all a farce.' In that case, the discount rate she now imposes on her earlier assessment of her well-being determines how relevant the information was. The other possibility is that she does not care: '*C'est la vie*; at least he was charming and we had a lot of fun.' Here the information turns out to have zero relevance, since that is the status she confers on it.[10]

The problem with reality or justification requirements is that they impose uniform discount rates on everyone alike: happiness has no prudential payoff unless fully informed, or is discounted at a steady rate as it becomes less informed. The relevance of information for a person's well-being is a personal matter to be decided by personal priorities; there is here no authoritative public standard. In the example sketched by Griffin in which he is deceived about the authenticity of his close personal relations, he would clearly regard the actual facts of the matter as highly relevant; if so, then his deluded (uninformed) happiness will have no prudential value for him. The best way to put

---

[10] The same options are available in the extreme case of illusion—namely, Robert Nozick's science-fiction example of an experience machine (*Anarchy, State, and Utopia* (New York: Basic Books, 1974), 42). A subject who recognizes the illusion, in retrospect, may respond by regretting having passed that period of her life floating in a tank or, alternatively, may embrace the experiences that were artificially induced for her ('Too bad it wasn't real, but it was a gas'). The extent to which the illusoriness of the experiences matters for an individual's well-being therefore depends on the extent to which she decides (or would decide) to make it matter. By the same token, plugging into the machine for a stretch of time may be differentially attractive for different folks.

the point generally, I think, is to say that someone's self-assessment, reflecting his actual epistemic standpoint, is defeasible: it is authoritative unless we have some reason to think that it does not reflect that person's own deepest priorities. Where a person's endorsement of his life is factually uninformed, or misinformed, that gives us one reason for doubting its authority (whether it is a sufficient reason depends on whether the endorsement will, or would, survive the acquisition of the missing information).[11]

A happiness theory of prudential value needs much more elaboration before its prospects can be adequately assessed. But it should be clear by now, even on the basis of this very schematic outline, how such a theory might be 'something in between' mental-state and desire theories, avoiding both the solipsism of the former and the disengagement of the latter from our lived experience. In some important respects a happiness theory resembles hedonism, most obviously in its inclusion of an experience requirement: according to the theory, it is a necessary condition of a state of affairs making me better off (directly or intrinsically) that it enter into my experience. It was the absence of an experience requirement that was fatal to the desire theory. However, in an equally important way a happiness theory will side with the desire theory against hedonism. Since it also incorporates an information requirement, it is not merely a mental-state theory. That a state of affairs enter my experience is necessary in order for it to benefit me, but (since the experience may be illusory or deceptive) it is not sufficient.

I cannot conclude this discussion of one of the principal projects of *Well-Being* on a negative note. Obviously, despite Jim Griffin's best efforts, I remain stubbornly unpersuaded of the merits of a desire account of prudential value. (Maybe he is now also unpersuaded, but not because he has switched allegiance to a rival theory.) But one learns most from the best version of any theory, whether in the end one accepts or rejects it. I cannot now calculate how much I learned from working through Part One of Griffin's illuminating and insightful book. It was against the view it articulates that I first began to develop my own alternative account, and the journey I have taken from the earliest and most naïve versions of that account to its present incarnation have been enormously influenced by my exposure to Griffin's ideas, as expressed both on the printed page and in personal conversation. He will wish to assume no responsibility for the errors of my present ways, but I owe him a great debt.

---

[11] There can be a second reason as well—namely, that the values or standards that underlie the person's endorsement are not autonomous. But that is a matter for another occasion (see Sumner, *Welfare, Happiness, and Ethics*, 161–71).

2

Incommensurable Values

John Broome

1. THE IDEA OF INCOMMENSURABILITY

You might join the army or you might become a priest. Which would be
better? Intuitively it seems this question may have no determinate answer; the
values realized by these two careers seem to be so very different that they
cannot be weighed against each other in a precise way. In some circumstances
there will be a determinate answer to the question—for instance, if you do
not believe in God and like guns. But, in more balanced circumstances, it will
not be determinate which is the better option. This phenomenon of indeterminacy is often called the 'incommensurability' of values. It is often thought
to be a central feature of ethical life.

James Griffin has taken up the subject of incommensurability several times
during his career.[1] He is not enthusiastic about its importance, and even casts
some doubt on its existence.[2] He points out, first, that what many philosophers have called 'incommensurability' is not really that at all, or ought not
to be called that. 'Incommensurability' ought to be reserved for cases where
alternatives are 'incomparable', as Griffin puts it, by which he means that they
cannot be put in an order. When a philosopher says the value of free speech
is incommensurable with the pleasure of eating pizza, she means that free

I have received penetrating comments on this paper from Ruth Chang, Ingmar Persson, Franz
Prettenthaler, Jonathan Riley, John Skorupski, and the editors of this volume. The comments are
so penetrating, and the subject so difficult, that I have been able to take account of only a few
of them in this chapter. They have set me a programme for future work.

[1] See his IV, WB ch. V, and I. The latter is Griffin's most recent piece on the subject, and my
main source for the views I attribute to him.

[2] Actually, he only doubts the incommensurability of what he calls 'prudential values'.
He thinks moral values may well be incommensurable (see I). But Griffin's 'moral values' are
more strictly moral rules such as: 'Do not deliberately kill the innocent.' I take value to be syn-
onymous with goodness, and since these rules are not about goodness, I do not count them as
values at all.

speech is immeasurably more valuable than this pleasure. That is to say, free speech and this pleasure *can* be ordered, emphatically. A small amount of free speech is better than any large amount of pizza-pleasure. This is not really incommensurability but extreme commensurability. Griffin mentions other misuses of the term too. If we set the misuses aside, and concentrate on true incommensurability, he thinks it may be hard to find any.

So values are commensurable in Griffin's sense if alternatives can be ordered. It is not the values themselves that can be ordered. Griffin is not interested in ordering enjoyment and understanding—to take two of his examples of values. These values cannot be ordered—neither is better than the other—because they come in various amounts. Wren's enjoyment in designing St Paul's is better than understanding Article iv of Section 3.8 of Regulation 294 issued by DG65 of the European Union, whereas understanding evolution is better than enjoying a pizza. So we cannot order the values of enjoyment and understanding themselves. But we might be able to order events that realize these values, such as designing St Paul's or eating a pizza. Each event realizes one or more values to some degree. If the values are commensurable, that means they can be measured on the same scale. So a degree of one can be compared, as greater or less, with a degree of the other. Consequently the events can be ordered. We often need to compare other things besides events, so for generality I shall say that 'options' can be ordered, without specifying what sort of options. To claim that values are commensurable is to claim that options can be ordered.

Ordered with respect to what? Their goodness. Values are goods of different sorts, which contribute to the goodness of the options that realize them. To say that values are commensurable is to say that options are ordered by their goodness.

Griffin himself sometimes seems not to have recognized clearly enough that it is options rather than values themselves that need to be ordered. As part of his argument against incommensurable values, he mentions that we can and do compare values. 'We can and do compare pain and accomplishment. If the pain is great enough and the accomplishment slight enough, we should not consider this accomplishment worth the pain' (*WB* 80). But this is beside the point. Undoubtedly, *some* amount of pain-avoidance can be compared with *some* amount of accomplishment; indeed there may be no two values such that some amount of one cannot be compared with some amount of the other. Perhaps all values are commensurable in this sense. But we are not interested in comparing values themselves; we need to compare options that realize values. Options realize values to various degrees. A great accomplishment achieved with a little pain is better than painlessly accomplishing nothing. And painlessly accomplishing nothing is better than very painfully accomplishing very little. But if pain and accomplishment are to be thoroughly commensurable, *any* amount of pain-avoidance must be comparable with *any* amount of accomplishment, so that all options that realize pain-avoidance or accomplishment to any degree can be ordered by their goodness.

Still, despite this slip, Griffin does correctly identify the question of commensurability as a question of ordering options. Actually, the ordering of options is a more fundamental and more general matter than commensurability. To ask whether values are commensurable is implicitly to make a presumption about the way individual values combine together to determine the overall goodness of an option. It is to presume that the goodness of an option is determined by the various values it realizes, acting independently of each other. If that is so, and if these independent values are commensurable—so they can be measured on the same scale—then they can be added up to determine the overall goodness of the option. But actually the goodness of an option may not be determined simply by adding up independent values. It may be determined in a complex fashion by the interaction of values with each other and with other features of the option that are not themselves values. If values and other features interact like this, the notion of commensurability is obscure. But the question of ordering remains clear. However complex the determination of goodness, we can ask whether options are ordered by their goodness. This question of ordering is the subject of this chapter, though I shall use the terms 'commensurability' and 'incommensurability' loosely to refer to it.

Actually, I shall be asking two questions. First, are options always ordered by their goodness? Second, if they are not, how important is that fact in ethics? Section 4 aims to answer the first question, and Section 10 returns to it; Sections 5–10 aim to answer the second. But before coming to the two substantive questions, I need to deal with some formal matters in Sections 2 and 3. I have suggested that options might or might not be ordered by their goodness. What, exactly, is the difference?

2. THE STANDARD CONFIGURATION

I find a particular formal device useful for answering this question; I call it a 'standard configuration'.[3] Take the career example again. You have a choice between joining the church and joining the army. In practice there is bound to be a great deal of uncertainty about how each of these careers will progress if you choose it. But for simplicity let us ignore that; imagine each can be

[3] See my 'Is Incommensurability Vagueness?', in Ruth Chang (ed.), *Incommensurability, Comparability and Practical Reason* (Cambridge, Mass.: Harvard University Press, 1997), for more details.

← worse   better →
Possible careers as a priest

Fig. 2.1

← worse   better →
Possible options

Fig. 2.2

accurately predicted. So you have a choice between a particular career as a soldier, which is mapped out in detail, and a particular career as a priest, also mapped out. Now, imagine variations in the church career that make it better or worse. For instance, imagine the community becomes more religious, which makes for a better career, or less religious, which makes for a worse one. Think of a whole sequence of imaginary church careers, each a little bit better than the previous one in the sequence. I shall call this sequence a 'chain'. Next, fill in the spaces in the chain until we have fully continuous variations in goodness as we move along it. For instance, imagine continuous variations in the community's religiousness. Then our chain can be represented as a continuous line, as shown in Fig. 2.1. Each point on the line stands for a particular possible career. Each career on the line is better than every career that lies to its left.

A standard configuration consists of a continuous chain like this, together with a single alternative that I call the 'standard'. In our example, the standard is the career available to you in the army. We hold that constant, while comparing it with all the various careers in the chain. In a standard configuration, the chain must be sufficiently long for the worst options in the chain to be worse than the standard and for the best options to be better than the standard.

The choice of careers is only an example. Standard configurations can be drawn up in other contexts too. Suppose you are choosing between dinner and a film. You can hold the film constant as standard, and form an imaginary chain of dinners that varies continuously from grim to superb. A general chain is shown in Fig. 2.2. As we move from left to right along a chain, two things are essential for my purposes. First, there is improvement all the way: every option is better than every option to its left. Secondly, the improvement is continuous. Joseph Raz thinks this may not always be possible.[4] He suggests some values may not be continuously variable; they can change only in discrete steps. Myself, I can think of no values that are discrete like this. But even

---

[4] J. Raz, *The Morality of Freedom* (Oxford: Clarendon Press, 1986), 326.

if there are some, we can still always change the goodness of an option in a continuous fashion, because options need not realize only one value. We can simply add or subtract amounts of some value that is not discrete. For instance, the service at dinner might be quicker or slower; that is a quality that can certainly vary continuously. I am sure there are at least some continuous values. So I see no difficulty in assuming the chain is continuous.

3. DEFINITIONS

Now we have the standard configuration, let us start to compare the options in the chain with the standard—in the example, the church careers with the army career. At the left of the line there are options that are worse than the standard; they form the 'worse zone', as I shall call it. At the right are options that are better than the standard; they form the 'better zone'. What happens in between? There are three possible cases. There may be more than one option between these zones—between options that are better than the standard and those that are worse. There may be just one. Or there may be none. This third case is genuinely possible, but it is not important for this chapter and I shall say no more about it.[5] So we have two cases to consider.

In the first, where more than one option lies between the worse zone and the better zone, there must be many that do. If there are two options between those zones, any option in the chain that lies in between these two options must also lie between the zones. So there will be an intermediate *zone* of options between the worse and better zones. The cases we need to consider, then, are, first, where there is an intermediate zone and, second, where there is just a single intermediate option.

Take some intermediate option. Suppose it happens to be equally as good as the standard. Then any option better than it (to its right on the line) would be better than the standard, and any option worse than it (to its left) would be worse than the standard. It would therefore be the only intermediate option between those that are better than the standard and those that are worse. So if there is more than one intermediate option—an intermediate *zone*—no option within this zone can be equally as good as the standard.

In this argument, I assumed that, if one option is better or worse than

---

[5] One way it can arise is if one value lexically dominates another. This means that any increase in one value, however small, is better than any increase in the other, however big. Suppose water and whisky are both good, but any increase in the amount of whisky is better than any increase in the amount of water. Suppose the standard is one litre of whisky, and the chain is composed of various amounts of whisky together with one litre of water. Then any option in the chain with less than a litre of whisky is worse than the standard. Any option in the chain with a litre or more of whisky is better than the standard. The chain contains no options in between.

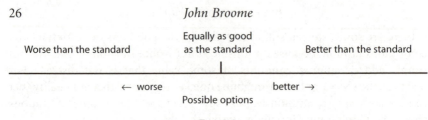

Fig. 2.3

another, and the other is equally as good as a third, then the first is, respectively, better or worse than the third. This is part of the meaning of 'equally as good as'. (It is an extension of transitivity.) It prevents any option in an intermediate zone from being equally as good as the standard.

But if there is only a single intermediate option, nothing of this sort prevents it from being equally as good as the standard. In this case, indeed, I think it must be equally as good as the standard. The slightest improvement or deterioration in this option would make it better or worse than the standard. If a choice is so finely balanced that the slightest change in one of the alternatives can make the difference between its being worse and its being better than the other, surely the alternatives are equally good.

Indeed, I think we may *define* a single intermediate option to be as good as the standard. I propose this as a definition of 'equally as good as': one option A is equally as good as another B if and only if any possible option that is better or worse than A is also, respectively, better or worse than B, and any possible option that is better or worse than B is also, respectively, better or worse than A. (This definition does not state explicitly that A is neither better nor worse than B, because that is implied by the rest.) This is an acceptable definition because it meets the formal condition that 'equally as good as' must satisfy analytically: it must be an *equivalence relation*—it must be transitive, reflexive, and symmetric.

The definition has the effect that, when there is just a single intermediate option, it must be equally as good as the standard (except in some peculiar cases). The picture is, then, as Fig. 2.3. Let us call this 'the equality case'.

Next, let us define one option A to be 'incommensurate' with another B if and only if it is not the case that A is better than B, and not the case that B is better than A, and not the case that A and B are equally good. We have found that, if there is an intermediate zone, all the options in it are incommensurate with the standard. Let us call this the 'incommensurate case'. Its picture is as Fig. 2.4.

To sum up. We have only one primitive relation to deal with: 'better than'. 'Equally as good as' and 'incommensurate with' are defined in terms of that. The difference between them is fixed by the structure of the better-than relation. This relation picks out the zone of options that are better than the

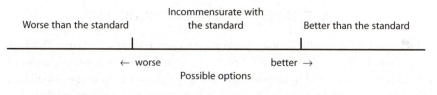

Fig. 2.4

standard and the zone of options that are worse than the standard. If it leaves only one option in a chain intermediate between these zones, this option is equally as good as the standard. If it leaves an intermediate zone, the options in this zone are incommensurate with the standard. The difference between equality and incommensurateness is simply whether there is one intermediate option or many. There is no further, intuitive distinction between the two.[6]

My definition of 'equally as good as' may seem unsatisfactory, because it may seem to deny a significant possibility. When there is only a single intermediate option between the worse and better zones, there may seem to be two possibilities for it: it might be equally as good as the standard or it might not be. When I defined it to be equally as good as the standard, I was denying the second possibility.

However, I do not think this is unsatisfactory; I think it is correct. I see no genuine second possibility. What real difference could there be between a case where this intermediate option is equally as good as the standard and a case where it is not? Presumably, the difference would have to show up in some practical way: it would have to make some difference to your decision-making, if you ever had to make a choice between this option and the standard. Now, it certainly makes a practical difference whether there is a single intermediate option or a whole intermediate zone; I shall explain why in Section 8. But when we are anyway dealing with just a single intermediate option, I see no real difference. Various things would be true if you had to make the choice between the intermediate option and the standard: it is not the case that you ought to choose the intermediate option, nor that you ought to choose the standard; choosing either would not be wrong; it is not determinate which you ought to choose; and so on. But all of these things are true simply because neither alternative is better than the other; none of them indicates a difference between their being equally good and their not being equally good. I shall say more about this in Section 7.

---

[6] Raz (*The Morality of Freedom*, 326) takes the existence of an intermediate zone as a central feature of incommensurability, though not its definition. (I did the same in my 'Choice and Value in Economics', *Oxford Economic Papers*, 30 (1978), 313–33.) My account of incommensurability agrees with Raz's in many ways.

4. IS THERE INCOMMENSURABILITY?

Having set up the definitions, we can turn to substantive questions. The first question I mentioned at the end of Section 1 is: are options necessarily ordered by their goodness? As I have now formalized it, this question has become: does the incommensurate case really exist, or is it only a technical possibility? Let 'commensurabilism' be the view that it does not exist. We can now see that commensurabilism is implausible. It is very stringent because it requires a sharp division between options that are worse than the standard and those that are better. There is at most one intermediate option. But this is implausible in, for instance, the careers example. It is implausible that a tiny change in the conditions of a church career could make all the difference between this career's being worse than soldiering and its being better. This example seems to have an intermediate zone; it seems to fit the incommensurate case.

At first, one might think commensurabilism could be supported by the epistemicist theory of vagueness. Take a vague predicate such as 'red'. Most people believe there are borderline cases between things that are red and things that are not red. Of these borderline cases, we cannot say definitely that they are red, nor that they are not red. But *epistemicists* about vagueness believe there is a sharp boundary between red and not red, despite appearances. All coloured things are either red or not, and for apparently borderline cases we are simply ignorant which they are. Although epistemicism is intuitively unattractive, there are arguments in its favour; epistemicists believe their theory is the only way to avoid certain logical problems that afflict other theories of vagueness.[7] So if epistemicism implied commensurabilism, it would give commensurabilism support.

But epistemicism does not imply commensurabilism. Consider the predicates 'better than soldiering' and 'worse than soldiering'. Epistemicism implies these predicates have sharp borderlines. A tiny improvement in the career of a priest takes us across the borderline from a career that is worse than soldiering to one that is not worse than soldiering, and from one that is not better than soldiering to one that is better than soldiering. In the incommensurate case, epistemicism implies that the borderline between the worse zone and the incommensurate zone is sharp, and so is the borderline between the incommensurate zone and the better zone. But it does not rule out the existence of an incommensurate zone. Only if these borderlines had to coincide would this be ruled out. Epistemicism does not imply they coincide, so it gives no support to commensurabilism.

Given that, I think we may safely reject commensurabilism because of its sheer implausibility. I shall go on to the second of the two questions men-

---

[7] See Timothy Williamson, *Vagueness* (London: Routledge, 1994).

tioned at the end of Section 1: given that commensurabilism is false, and options are not necessarily ordered by their goodness, what importance does that have for ethics? I can now express this question more precisely: how ethically significant is the difference between the equality case and the incommensurate case? Sections 5 and 6 consider two arguments about this that have to do with the form of the betterness relation. Sections 7 to 10 consider the importance of the difference for practical decision-making.

5. ROUGH EQUALITY

Griffin does not support commensurabilism as I have defined it. For example, he would accept there may be a range of careers as a priest that are intermediate between those that are better than soldiering and those that are worse. So he accepts there are incommensurate cases. However, he seems to think they are all, or at least mostly, cases of 'rough equality'. We might call Griffin a 'rough commensurabilist'. Evidently he thinks the difference between equality and incommensurateness is not very important.

What does 'rough equality' mean exactly? Griffin presents an analysis (*WB* 96–8), but we do not need to analyse the concept far in order to see that rough commensurabilism is implausible. So long as 'roughly equal' has something like its ordinary meaning, this must be true: two options that are each roughly equal in goodness to a third cannot differ very much from each other in their goodness. They do not have to be roughly equal in goodness to each other; that would follow if rough equality was a transitive relation, but (as Griffin points out) it is not. Nevertheless, they plainly cannot differ very much in their goodness. So if two priest-careers in the incommensurate zone were each roughly equal to the standard soldier career, they would not differ much in goodness from each other. Griffin is evidently assuming no incommensurate zone can be very wide. But there seems to be no reason why it should not be. We would generally expect the zone to be narrow when we are comparing similar types of thing, and wide when we are comparing very different things. Between joining the Northumberland Rifles and the Fifth Lancers, the zone may be narrow, but between the church and the army it may be very wide. A mediocre career in the church may not be definitely worse than a career in the army, and a successful career in the church may not be definitely better than a career in the army. But a successful career in the church is much better than a mediocre one. It follows that not all careers in the incommensurate zone are roughly equally as good as a career in the army.

To make this argument, I have presumed we have some scale of goodness. It need only be a rough scale, just enough to give sense to such expressions as 'much better', 'do not differ much in their goodness', and so on. The idea of rough equality itself presumes a rough scale, so I have taken one for granted in arguing against it.

Commensurabilism is very implausible because it presumes there is no intermediate zone at all, but at most one intermediate option. Rough commensurabilism is less implausible, but implausible none the less because it presumes the intermediate zone is narrow. If we are to believe it, at least we need from Griffin an argument why this zone should be narrow.

6. VAGUENESS

Griffin does make one point that I think is intended as such an argument. He claims that incommensurability is vagueness (*WB* 96). When two options are incommensurate, we cannot say either is better than the other. This leaves open several possibilities. Griffin's view is that, although we cannot assert 'This one is better', we also cannot deny it, and although we cannot assert 'That one is better', we cannot deny that either.

Take the career example again. Griffin believes the predicates 'better than soldiering' and 'worse than soldiering' are vague. Unlike the epistemicists, he believes this means there is no sharp borderline between priest-careers that are better than soldiering and those that are not, nor between priest-careers that are worse than soldiering and those that are not. More than that, he thinks these borderlines overlap and extend across the whole incommensurate zone. The consequence is that, although we cannot assert of a career within this zone that it is better than soldiering, we cannot deny it either. Also, although we cannot assert it is worse than soldiering, we cannot deny that either. The incommensurate zone is a zone of vagueness.

Joseph Raz disagrees. He thinks that, of a career in the incommensurate zone, we can deny it is better than soldiering and deny it is worse than soldiering too.[8] The issue between these views is a fiddly question of logic. As it happens, I think Griffin is right and Raz wrong, but since the arguments are fiddly I shall not present them here.[9]

The real difference of opinion between Griffin and Raz is not the fiddly one about logic, but that Raz thinks incommensurability is important, and Griffin thinks it is not. They both seem to take it for granted that, if incommensurability was vagueness, it would not be important. That is why they disagree about whether it is indeed vagueness.

[8] Raz, *The Morality of Freedom*, 324.
[9] They are set out in my 'Is Incommensurability Vagueness?'.

But if incommensurability is vagueness, why should that make it unimportant? Raz says it would merely be an instance of the general indeterminacy of our language.[10] That is true; at least, vagueness is a common feature of our concepts. But why should it make it unimportant? If 'better than' is vague, I see no reason why that should not be a significant feature of ethics. Vagueness in general is not unimportant in ethics. The vagueness of 'person' is a very important feature of several ethical problems.

I think Griffin believes that, if the incommensurate zone is a zone of vagueness, then it cannot be very wide, and that would make it unimportant. It would support his contention that options within the zone are roughly equal to the standard in goodness. But vagueness can be very extensive. The Southern Ocean is a vague expanse of water whose boundaries with other oceans are indeterminate to the extent of many hundreds of miles. So the claim that incommensurability is vagueness does not support the claim that it is rough equality.

I think the question of vagueness is a red herring when we are interested in the importance of incommensurability. It does not provide an argument why the incommensurate zone must be narrow, and it does not suggest independently that incommensurability must be unimportant.

The real question about importance is whether incommensurability makes an important difference to practical decision-making. In the next section I shall turn away from the formal questions of vagueness and rough equality to consider decision-making directly. In doing this, I shall assume incommensurate zones exist, and that they need not be small. We have found no reason for doubting either of these assumptions.

7. PRACTICAL DECISION-MAKING

What implications does incommensurability have for how we ought to act? What ought we to do when faced with a choice between two options that are incommensurate in their goodness? To smooth the way for answering this question, let us make the assumption that the goodness of the options is the only consideration relevant to the choice. This is to assume *teleology*; teleology is the view that how one ought to act is determined by the goodness of the available options. Non-teleological theories deny this. For instance, some non-teleological theories hold there are rules of right action—deontic rules— that are not determined entirely by the goodness of the options. To get a clear

---

[10] Raz, *The Morality of Freedom*, 324.

view of the importance of incommensurability, let us set non-teleological theories aside.

Granted teleology, when you are faced with a choice between two options, if one is better than the other, you ought to choose the better one. It would be wrong to choose the other. But if the two options are either incommensurate or equally good, what then? We cannot say that you ought to choose one, nor that you ought to choose the other. Choosing either would not be wrong. It is not determinate which you ought to choose. Reason, as it were, leaves you on your own. You must simply decide without the guidance of reason.

This is mysterious in one way. Rational creatures have to be able to decide without the guidance of reason, and it is mysterious how we can do that. Buridan's ass could not manage it; how can we? It is not simply a matter of choosing which we like, since we may not like either of the options any more than the other. So how do we choose? One might be tempted to use this mystery as an argument against incommensurability. One might argue that reason simply cannot leave us in the lurch like this; there must always be something we ought to do.[11] But if this were a valid argument, it would work just as effectively against equality of goodness as against incommensurability. Since equality of goodness is surely possible, the argument must fail. It leaves us with the mystery of how we choose. But I have no need to solve this mystery, because it applies equally to the incommensurate case and the equality case; it does not distinguish them.

If you are faced with a choice between two options, and they are equally good, it does not matter which you choose. If they are incommensurate, it does matter. People often identify this as the practical importance of the distinction: one type of choice matters and the other does not. But actually this remark is a mere tautology. To say a choice between two options does not matter—literally, and not simply that it does not matter much—is simply to say the options are equally good, and to say it does matter is simply to say they are not equally good.

I conclude that, when we think about an isolated choice between two options, there is nothing in practical decision-making that is different between the incommensurate case and the equality case. To find a difference we need to look further. In Section 3, I distinguished the cases by means of a structural feature of betterness that does not show up in an isolated choice like this. Using the device of the standard configuration, I made the distinction depend on whether there is an intermediate zone or a single intermediate option between options that are better than the standard and those that are worse. So this structural feature is where we should look for a practical

---

[11] Raz develops this argument and responds to it in 'Incommensurability and Agency', in Chang (ed.), *Incommensurability*.

difference between the cases. The difference must depend on there being an intermediate zone rather than a single intermediate option.

8. A PUZZLE

Here indeed there is a significant difference. Decision-making in the incommensurate case, but not the equality case, can lead to a puzzle. Suppose two careers are open to you: a career in the army and a good career as a priest. Suppose they are incommensurate in their goodness. Then choosing either would not be wrong. You have to choose without the guidance of reason, and suppose you choose the army: you commit yourself to the army career, and give up the chance of a good career in the church. In doing so you are doing nothing wrong. But then suppose another opportunity comes up to join the church, this time in much worse conditions. You now face a choice between the army or a much less good career as a priest. Suppose these two, also, are incommensurate. Choosing either would not be wrong. You have to choose without the guidance of reason. Suppose this time you choose the church. Once again you do nothing wrong. But though you have not acted wrongly in either of your choices, the effect of the two together is that you end up with a much worse career in the church than you could have had. Surely rationality should be able to protect you from this sort of bad result; surely there is something irrational in what you have done. Yet apparently neither of your decisions was irrational. This is puzzling.[12]

No such bad result could have emerged had you only been choosing amongst options that are equally good. Suppose you have a choice between *A* and *B*, and the two are equally good. Suppose you choose *B*. Next suppose you have a choice between *B* and *C*, which are also equally good, and you choose *C*. Neither of your choices is contrary to reason. But in this case you are no worse off with *C* than you would have been with *A*. *A* and *C* must be equally good because the relation 'equally as good as' is transitive. On the other hand, the relation 'incommensurate with' is not. So we have identified a practical difficulty that arises in the incommensurate case but not in the equality case. This certainly makes the difference significant.

The puzzle is that rational decision-making leaves you worse off than you could have been. But what is puzzling about that? The same thing can happen in ways that are not puzzling at all. For example, you might rationally make a decision that could be expected to lead to a good result, but by sheer bad luck it might lead to a bad result. The example I described can also be

---

[12] The same point is made by Ruth Chang in 'Incommensurability, Incomparability and Value: A framework', in Chang (ed.), *Incommensurability*.

interpreted in a way that is not puzzling. You might just change your mind between one decision and the next. Having chosen the army, you might decide that that was a mistake, and make the best of a bad job by taking up the only church career that is still available. Then you would not have acted irrationally. Nor is it puzzling that you end up worse off than you could have been.

The puzzle only arises if, when you make the second choice of a poor church career rather than the army, you do not at the same time repudiate your first choice of the army rather than a good church career. If at one single time you are willing to endorse both decisions, then you are certainly in a puzzling condition.

9. BAYESIANISM

Compare a similar puzzle that arises in a different context. Suppose you are at a horse race, knowing absolutely nothing about the horses. You have no information whatsoever about which horse is likely to win; indeed you do not even know the number of entries in the race. You find the bookies offering even odds on Gorgeous to win. Having no reason not to, you place a £10 bet on Gorgeous. In that, you are doing nothing wrong. Next you find even odds are also offered on Screaming Angel to win, and having no reason not to do this either, you place a £10 bet on it. Again, you are doing nothing wrong. Finally, you find even odds offered on Intravenous to win, and you place a £10 bet on Intravenous too, once more doing nothing wrong. By these three bets, you have guaranteed yourself a loss of at least £10. You have accepted what is known as a 'Dutch book' against yourself. This is puzzling, since you have done nothing wrong. (Let us abstract from the fun of the game and assume your only object is to make money.)

Once again, there are ways this can happen that are not at all puzzling. For instance, you might change your mind about the horses' chances as the afternoon progresses. Having bet on one horse, you might decide another is more likely to win and bet on that one, resigning yourself to losing on the first, and hoping to recoup some of your losses. But you are in a puzzling condition if you are willing to endorse your bets on the three horses at the same time.

Here is a Bayesian solution to the puzzle. Your bets are in fact irrational. True, none is individually irrational, because you have no reason not to bet on each of the horses individually. But each bet you place on a horse implies you have a particular degree of belief in that horse's winning. When you bet on Gorgeous at even odds, that implies you believe to some degree more than a half that it will win. You have no reason either to have this belief or not to have it, so it is rational for you to make the bet or not to make it. But you should make it only if in fact you do have this degree of belief in the horse's winning. Similarly, you should bet on Screaming Angel only if you believe to a degree more than a half that Screaming Angel will win, and you should bet on Intravenous only if you believe to a degree more than a half that Intravenous will win. Now, it is irrational to believe to a degree more than a half that Gorgeous will win, and to a degree more than a half that Screaming Angel will win, and to a degree more than a half that Intravenous will win. So your three bets together are irrational.

Let me put this Bayesian argument in better order. Bayesians think, first, that reason imposes particular constraints on the combinations of bets you should make. These are constraints of consistency, and they are laid down in the 'axioms' of Bayesian theory. The grounds for the axioms are that, if you do not stick to them, you will be vulnerable to traps such as Dutch books.

Bayesians next claim that bets imply particular degrees of belief. For instance, betting on a horse at particular odds implies a particular degree of belief in its winning. They then demonstrate mathematically that, if your betting is consistent according to the axioms, it implies a consistent pattern of beliefs. Otherwise it implies an inconsistent pattern. 'Consistent' here means conforming to laws of probability. For instance, your degrees of belief in various horses winning a race must not add up to more than one. This consistency of belief gives further support to the consistency requirements of the axioms: bets that are consistent according to the axioms can be interpreted in terms of consistent beliefs.

The upshot is that, if you are to be rational, you must act according to some probability beliefs or other. This is so whether or not there are rational grounds for having some beliefs rather than others. If there are none—for instance, if you know nothing about the horses—you should still have beliefs. As it is often put, you should have subjective probabilities and act on them. This is so even if there are no objective probabilities, so reason does not determine which subjective probabilities you should have. Reason still determines that you should have some. That is the Bayesian view.

10. REASONS AND INTENTIONS

We might take a similar Bayesian line about the career example. Neither of your decisions—to join the army rather than to take up a good career as a priest, and to take up the less good career as a priest rather than join the army—is irrational on its own, but they are irrational in combination. Your decisions should be consistent with each other in particular ways, because otherwise you may find yourself in traps such as the one that actually caught you. Just as Bayesians interpret betting decisions as implying beliefs, we can interpret your decisions as implying values. Your first choice in the example implies that you value a career in the army at least as highly as a good career in the church. On the other hand, your second choice implies that you value a less good career in the church at least as highly as a career in the army. So these two decisions imply inconsistent values. Consistent decisions will imply a consistent value-system. In this case, the objective facts of goodness do not determine what values you ought to adopt. They do not determine whether you should value an army career higher than a good church career, or a less good church career higher than an army career. So reason does not determine what your subjective values should be. But it does determine that you should have some and act according to them.

This Bayesian line is commensurabilist in a sense. Values may be objectively incommensurable, but subjectively they should not be. Objective values may leave room for subjective choices, but to act consistently you need to settle on subjective values for yourself, and these must have no incommensurability. Moreover, this is a sort of commensurabilism that many people might find credible even if they agree with my claim in Section 4 that commensurabilism is implausible. They might think objective commensurabilism is implausible, but the need for consistency in decisions gives grounds for subjective commensurabilism. Whatever the objective facts, we need to create fully commensurable value-systems for ourselves.

This conclusion would have made a pleasant ending for a chapter in honour of James Griffin. However, I am sorry to say I shall have to end with doubts about it. There is a good objection to the Bayesian line. When you make your decisions in the career example, there is no reason to think you are reflecting your values. You have to decide between one career and another. If there are no grounds for your decision, you have to make it all the same, without grounds. Consequently, the fact that you make it does not show you have grounds.[13] In particular, your decision need not imply a subjective system of values that gives it grounds.

The same objection may be raised against the Bayesian line on probability. You have to choose whether or not to bet on Gorgeous. Since you have no information relevant to its chances of winning, you have no grounds on which to base this decision. You have to decide, so you decide without grounds. The fact that you decide to bet does not show you have grounds for doing so. In particular, it does not show you believe to a degree greater than a half that Gorgeous will win.

Bayesians might not be troubled by this objection. To avoid a Dutch book, you must certainly act *as if* you have a consistent pattern of beliefs. Whether you actually have one or not might not particularly concern a Bayesian. If the

---

[13] This point is made in my 'Choice and Value in Economics', and by Raz in *The Morality of Freedom*, 338–40.

Bayesian favours a behaviourist or functionalist notion of belief, she will think you do indeed have consistent beliefs, because acting consistently is a criterion for having consistent beliefs. But Bayesians are more concerned with the rationality of your behaviour than with the state of your mind, and they may be perfectly content so long as you act as if you have consistent beliefs.

But I am not satisfied by this casual response. Once you have bet on Gorgeous and Screaming Angel, Bayesians think you ought not to bet on Intravenous, unless you have repudiated your previous bets. So they think you have some reason not to bet on Intravenous. But what could that reason be? It can only be that you believe, to a degree more than a half, that Intravenous will not win. Your belief must be substantive enough to generate a reason for you. We may have a notion of belief that entitles us to attribute to you particular beliefs on the basis of your previous bets. But could these beliefs be reason-giving for you? Could your previous bets give you a reason not to bet on Intravenous? I doubt it. You have no information about the horses that could justify you in having particular beliefs and acting on them. Your placing a bet gives you no information either. So how could placing a bet make it the case that you now have a belief, and that this belief gives you reason to act in a particular way? I doubt it could.

Similarly, I doubt that your decision to join the army, in preference to a good church career, necessarily makes it the case that you value the army career more highly than the church career. I recognize that decision-making can sometimes stimulate you to form values, and it may even be a way of forming your values, but I doubt it is necessarily so. You have to act, whether or not you form values that determine how you should act. Consequently, I do not see how your first decision gives you a reason not to make your second one (not to choose a poor church career rather than the army). True, it is common nowadays to think that decisions are themselves reason-giving.[14] For example, if you have decided on some end, that gives you a reason to take an appropriate means to this end. In a similar way, your decision to join the army rather than take a good church career could give you a reason not to take a worse church career rather than join the army. But I think this common opinion is incorrect. If you have no reason to pursue some end, even if you have decided to do so, you have no reason to take some means to this end. I do not believe decisions create reasons.

So I doubt the Bayesian idea. But since it was a solution to a puzzle, I need an alternative. The one I have to offer is only a suggestion, which will have to be worked out properly another time.[15] Take the means–end connection again.

---

[14] For instance, see Edward McClennen, *Rationality and Dynamic Choice* (Cambridge: Cambridge University Press, 1990).

[15] See my 'Are Intentions Reasons?', in Christopher Morris and Arthur Ripstein (eds.), *Preferences, Principles and Practices* (Cambridge: Cambridge University Press, forthcoming).

Deciding on an end gives you no reason to take a means to it, but in a different way it does commit you to taking a means. Deciding on an end is itself deciding to take some means to it. Deciding to go to the cinema is itself deciding to take some means of getting there. To put it another way: intending an end is intending some means to it. So the movement from end to means is mediated not through reasons but through intention. The difference is important. You can intend a means to an end without its being the case that you ought to take a means to this end, and even without your believing you ought to. Moreover, there is absolutely nothing wrong with changing your mind and deciding not to (unless you have already invested some effort). On the other hand, if you had a reason to take the means, there would be something wrong with changing your mind.

Similarly, if you decide to join the army rather than take a good job as a priest, that in itself is plausibly a decision not to take a worse job as a priest rather than join the army. You can change your mind, but not without repudiating your earlier decision. So I suggest that the connection between the two decisions is mediated by intention rather than reason. One intention implies another. The structure of intentions—what intention is implied by what—and the nature of this implication still need to be worked out.[16]

The Bayesian solution implies that subjective values must be commensurable, because it assumes only commensurable values can resolve the puzzle I mentioned. My alternative does not require even subjective values to be commensurable. The puzzle can be resolved by the structure of intentions, rather than by the structure of values. I suggest incommensurability of values is indeed an important phenomenon in ethics, which cannot be dissolved away by the Bayesian method.

[16] See my, *Preferences, Principles and Practices.*

3

Recognition and Reaction

Jonathan Dancy

In this paper I discuss one of the many themes of Jim Griffin's recent *Value Judgement*. This is the claim that we will not be able to make progress in a certain area of moral theory unless we succeed in blurring the distinction between recognition and reaction. My own view, in brief, is that blurring this distinction would not be enough. What we need to do is to transcend it altogether. So I agree with Griffin that the distinction needs philosophical treatment, but think that the sort of treatment it needs is much more radical than the one that he seems to think appropriate.

1

How are we to understand the notion of value? Early in his book Griffin considers two approaches, both of which he finds unsatisfactory. These he calls the taste and the perception models. The taste model takes value to be a function of what is desired; the perception model thinks of the desired as a function of what is desirable. Less formulaically, on the taste model something is valuable if it is something that people want. On the perception model, by contrast, desire aims at the valuable and may miss it; we want something if we recognize it as valuable. This does not mean that to want it is to recognize it as valuable; the recognition is one thing and the desire another. What it means is that the desire is a response or reaction to the recognized value.

This chapter continues themes that I first explored in *Moral Reasons* (Oxford: Blackwell, 1993), §§2.5–2.6, and in 'Why there is really no such thing as the theory of motivation', *Proceedings of the Aristotelian Society*, 95 (1994–5), 1–18. I have been helped by discussions with Al Mele and John Heil, and by audiences at University College, Cork, Georgetown University, the University of Chicago, and the University of Maryland.

According to Griffin, something like this way of thinking has been the cause of a great sea of philosophy, all of which depends on accepting an unnecessarily sharp form of the distinction between recognition and reaction. The sharp distinction causes one to think that the two options above are the only options. This might lead someone to adopt the second, despite its difficulties, merely on the grounds that the first is worse. If there is something wrong with the distinction, as Griffin suggests, any such move would be unsound.

The reason why I am interested in all this is that I think that Griffin is on the right track here, but that his good thought takes him much further than he recognizes.

If the distinction is too sharp, what it needs is a bit of blurring, and that is what Griffin purports to offer. He considers three ways of blurring the distinction. The first stems from the thought that recognition is not entirely free from desire; this blurs things from the recognition end. The second is the claim that desire is subject to rational evaluation; this blurs things from the reaction end. The third is that the active/passive distinction, even if it is sharp itself, cannot be mapped at all sharply onto the recognition/reaction one; this blurs things from the middle. I will take these three thoughts in turn, and what I will be suggesting is that none of them achieves what Griffin hopes for.

The first idea, that recognition is not entirely free from desire, needs elucidation before it can be criticized. What Griffin means by this, it seems, is that to understand (and so to be able to recognize) something as valuable is to grasp certain desirable features that it has—its desirability features. These desirability features owe their status as such to normal human desires or motivation. Another way of putting what I think is the same point is to say that to understand something as valuable is to recognize a practical reason, and practical reasons must mesh with characteristic human motivation. At one point Griffin writes that reasons 'are reasons only because they incorporate a movement of the human will' (*VJ* 35). He gives no further account of this notion of incorporation of the human will. I think, however, that he cannot mean the will of the person who recognizes the reason, but rather the normal or characteristic human will.

What is wrong with this is that as such it does nothing to blur the distinction between recognition and reaction in the place where it needs to be blurred. It does nothing, that is, to show that the two are other than essentially distinct. The ontological status of reasons will not be as extreme, on Griffin's account, as it might have been had reasons been capable of existing out there in the world entirely unrelated to any thoughts about human desire and motivation. But the notions of recognition and desire (reaction) that are being used to make this point are still the same sharply distinguished notions that we started with. What Griffin wants to show is that recognition and reaction are somehow mutually intertwined, in the sort of way that it is sometimes suggested that description and evaluation are mutually intertwined in a thick concept. But though I am very sympathetic to this enterprise, I don't think that he has found a way here of promoting it. He has not shown that recognition requires reaction in one and the same individual.

What about his attempt to blur the distinction from the other end, by making use of the familiar points that Hume was wrong in holding that desires cannot be rationally evaluated, and that one of the things we appeal to in evaluating a desire is whether its object is in fact worth desiring? Griffin argues that a desire for something intrinsically valueless, such as knowing the number of blades of grass in a lawn, does not succeed in turning the valueless into the valuable. But though I am convinced that this is true, it seems to me not to be of any help in the present situation. Griffin's point is surely available to those who hold the recognition/reaction distinction in the sharp form that he is trying to unsettle; it merely evinces a preference for one side of the distinction over the other. For this reason I am unsure that I am right in attributing to Griffin this way of blurring the distinction at all. But if he is not appealing to this idea, I can find in his text no other way of blurring the distinction from the reaction end.

Why can't Griffin just say that desire thinks of itself as a response to the desirable, and as such cannot occur in the absence of (what purports to be) recognition of desirability in the object? The answer is that, even if this were true, it does nothing to blur the distinction between desire (reaction) and recognition. The recognition needs to be in place *before* the reaction is able to swing in; so we have as yet seen no reason to say that the recognition itself *involves* the reaction. There would be nothing in this scenario that looks like the sort of mutual non-disentanglability that Griffin is after. The sharp distinction is still as much in place as it ever was.

This leaves the third and last thought, that the sharp distinction is seen as being held in place by the distinction between active and passive. One thing that this might mean is that recognition is taken as being wholly active, and reaction as wholly passive. We cannot help how we react, but we can help how we judge. It might, however, be taken quite the other way around, as when we say that I can want what I want to want, but I cannot believe what I want to believe; this way round, it is the recognition that is passive, and the reaction that is active. Both of these contrasts are defective, however. In the sort of terms in which they are being run, we should say that both recognition and reaction are partly active and partly passive. Both are passive in the sense that they are responses to the environment, and that our relation to them is not the same as our relation to our actions, where there is something distinctive called choice (deciding-to is quite different from deciding-that); both are active in the sense that they are things that we do, and for which we can be held responsible. Would this sort of mixture of active and passive give Griffin what he wants in the way of a blur? The answer, I am afraid, is no. Even if neither recognition nor reaction were wholly active nor wholly passive, this would do nothing to alter the nature of the choice between the taste model and the perception model that we started with. Both recognition and reaction can be thought of as active in some respects and passive in others, without either essentially involving the other.

Perhaps, however, there is another way of understanding what is meant by the active/passive distinction in this context. We have so far supposed that, though there may be several things that are being got at once by the terminology of active and passive, once disentangled from the other each is perfectly sound. Of course we should be suspicious of the terminology in the first place, since it comes from the grammarians and there is no reason to suppose that categories appropriate for grammar or syntax are also appropriate for philosophy. But such suspicions can be stilled. The dubious thing that may be being got at by the active/passive terminology is the post-Humean idea that desire (passion, reaction) is active, though blind, and belief (reason, recognition) is *inert*. Desire needs the eyes that belief supplies, for two reasons: first, one needs to have certain beliefs in order to have any desire (one cannot want an orange without having some beliefs about what an orange is); second, one needs to have some beliefs about the circumstances in which one is placed if a desire is to lead to this action rather than that. But this thought is all about blindness; it does not tell us the sense in which desire differs from belief in being active. Traditionally, that point was made in semi-hydraulic terms. Belief itself needs the thrust that is desire if it is to affect action, for a belief is just a map of the world, and the existence of such a map could never suffice to explain an action. If desire is a kind of surge or thrust, it is going to be capable of moving a previously inert body, when belief is not. But how much of the active/inert contrast remains when we abandon the hydraulic metaphor? The general idea is that there is an asymmetry in causal role; each state needs the other if there is to be an action, but the contributions of the one are of a different style from those of the other. But can we now say anything about this supposed difference in style?

It seems to me that this contrast between the active and the inert has got itself added to a generally Humean picture without being at all essential to it. Hume himself would have seen no sense in it. First, his account of causation leaves no room for any such contrast in terms of causal efficacy. Second, the genuinely Humean claim that reason is the slave of the passions can get along quite well on its own. What that claim essentially requires is a suitable asymmetry between the roles of reason (belief) and passion (desire) in the explanation and generation of action. And one can establish a perfectly good asymmetry without any appeal to the distinction between the active and the inert. If I think that action requires both passion and reason, and then tell a story under which passion sets the goals towards which reason seeks available means (which passion will again evaluate without itself being evaluable by reason), I already have a nice asymmetry that explains the need for both, each providing something that the other lacks. Thoughts about differences in style of causal efficacy seem redundant here. One can read Hume's remark that reason is the slave of the passions as a claim that in its combination with reason passion is somehow dominant, and so more important in the causal story. But I think that we can reasonably think of reason as subserving passion, in the sense given above, without insisting on a causal asymmetry of that sort.

The sad upshot of all this is that the sharp distinction between recognition and reaction is as unchallenged as ever. What we have is that passion sets goals (ultimate or intermediate), and reason provides a map of the world that tells us how to set about achieving those goals, in ways that we might reject because they would interfere with the pursuit of other goals. But neither of these activities has in any way been permeated by the other, though we have made no appeal to the active/inert distinction to keep them separate.

The old idea that passion sets goals while reason provides a map is the one that is expressed by contemporary theorists in terms of directions of fit. Belief aims to characterize the world, and desire aims to change it. So belief has one direction of fit (it aims to fit the world) and desire has the other (it aims to get the world to fit it), and no single mental state could possibly have both. And this tells us why it is going to be so hard to blur the distinction between recognition and reaction. For as long as desire counts as a reaction, and belief as recognition, it is going to seem inescapable that one of these mental states has one direction of fit and one has the other, and that there is a clear difference between the two. Despite continuing difficulties in getting the notion of a direction of fit into a form with which one can be entirely satisfied, it still seems to me that there is going to be something right about the general idea. And the difference between the two directions is such that it is hard to see how it could be blurred at all effectively.

It is because of this that we feel that we know in advance that any state that appears somehow to have both directions of fit must in fact be a disentanglable compound—that with sufficient ingenuity we will be able to break it up into its component parts, each of which has only one direction of fit. Even signal failure to achieve this for any interesting state will not daunt us in our confidence that somehow or other it must be able to be done. And if so, we have come to see that the project of blurring the distinction between recognition and reaction is bankrupt. This would mean not only that Griffin's own attempts to blur the distinction fail, but also that he fails to address the core of the distinction at all.

There are only two ways that I know of to escape the grip of the notion of a direction of fit. The first, and less radical, is to argue that though action requires both belief and desire, only the belief motivates. The desire, though it is present, is not present as something that motivates, since it is itself the state of being motivated. On this account, belief alone motivates, and it does this by generating a suitable desire in the agent; but the occurrence of the desire is unable even to contribute to the explanation of the fact that the agent is motivated, since it *is* that fact. This picture has in one way transcended the belief/desire distinction, since it awards to belief what has almost universally been held to be the main feature of desire; but in another it has not, since it admits the need for two distinct mental states, each with its own direction of fit, if there is to be an intentional action. The distinctness of the two types of mental state is left in place, but their interrelations have been revamped.

The more radical way of escaping the notion of a direction of fit requires a complete change of focus. So far we have been asking about a distinction between two mental states, and wondering how we could blur this distinction so as to make available philosophical positions that for the moment are hidden from us. We have supposed that the discussion of the nature of value is properly conducted in these terms. Griffin, for example, supposes that the status of something as a reason depends on its relation to characteristic human motivation, and immediately characterizes motivation as desire—i.e. as a mental state or cause of action. But this is to adopt without argument a very significant part of the post-Humean position he is trying to escape, the part that tells us that the right way to understand reasons for action (motivation) is to look at prior mental states that function as causes of action. But there is a completely different way in which we could move. We could allow that anything that is a reason must be capable of being someone's reason for what he did, and would be when he acts in the light of that reason, without our supposing that the right way to express this is to talk about motivation at all. Now this sort of approach is quite compatible with claiming that reasons for action are facts or states of affairs, as when we say that the reason why I should help her is that she is in need (whether this is a fact or a state of affairs I leave undetermined for the moment). And if so we make available to ourselves an account of why we act that is no longer vulnerable to the distinction between two directions of fit. For if a state of affairs or a fact is a reason, it appears in a sense to have both directions of fit. Her need is a way in which the world is, and it is a reason to change it.

We do not escape the distinction between directions of fit entirely here, since we still have to say something about the states of mind that respond to that reason as a reason. But now we seem to me to be in a much better position to say, as Griffin wants to, that recognition and reaction permeate each other in this sort of case. For when I recognize something as a reason for action, I accept it as a feature of the world that calls for change. Motivation is present in that recognition (normally, no doubt—but for the moment such qualifications are, I hope, understood), and this is so in a way that does not challenge the claim of the relevant mental state to be non-compound. Now this is surely the position that Griffin wanted to get to. But to achieve it we have had to make an alarming number of highly contentious claims, and whether Griffin would wish to make those claims or not, it is not clear to me that they are available to him.

The most contentious of all is the idea that beliefs and desires, understood as mental states, are not reasons for action at all. I think of the 'psychologism' that is being denied here as the central core of Humean philosophy of action. We can argue as hard as we like about whether belief needs desire to motivate action, or whether it can do it all on its own, or whether it can only do it by generating a desire that joins it as a reason. But all this argument is conducted within the assumption that the right way to understand action is in terms of the combination of mental states that cause it, and that this sort of understanding is an understanding of the reasons for which we act, since it is the agent's beliefs and desires that render her action rational. And all this will go if we take the route that I recommend. What will render the action rational, on my account, will be what we believe, not our believings; it will be the way the world is, as we see it, not the nature of some mental state.

What might make it hard for Griffin to accept the suggestions that I am making here (other than their obvious falsehood, I suppose) is that he seems committed to understand the nature of a reason in terms of the nature of a mental state that grasps that reason, rather than doing things the other way round. His commitment emerges when he maintains that reasons require a relation to motivation—that is, to desire—and that desire is a form of reaction whose relation to recognition needs to be properly understood. So he hopes to reunderstand that relation by a direct frontal attack on the sharpness of the distinction between the two *relata*, thinking of himself as aiming to improve our categories in the philosophy of mind. My approach, by contrast, would be to concentrate on the nature of a reason in the world, and then to move from that to an understanding (which cannot of course be avoided) of what it is to grasp that reason and act on it. Doing things this way round, I maintain, would make it possible for us genuinely to transcend the distinction between recognition and reaction.

2

I have suggested that if we are really to escape the sharp distinction generated by the notion of a direction of fit, we need to take a new starting point, and to try to understand reasons for action before we turn to examine the nature

of a mental state that is a grasp on such a reason. We should, that is, attempt
first to understand what it is for a consideration to favour one action rather
than another, before we try to construct an account of what it is to act *in the
light of* that reason. In the rest of this chapter I defend this suggestion against
some of the main criticisms to which it is subject.

Here is the first such criticism. I said that reasons can in a sense be thought
of as having both directions of fit, in such a way that a grasp on them combines both recognition and reaction without therefore appearing as a compound state, part of which has one direction of fit and part of which has the
other. But, we might say, isn't it one thing to recognize a consideration, and
another to recognize it as a reason? For surely one person may recognize a
child's need, without taking it as a reason for action, while another who recognizes that need also takes it as practically relevant. Isn't this a clear proof
that we have two mental states, one of which may be present without the
other? In general, the proper response to this is to be wary of treating mental
states as countable in the sort of way that this argument wants. More directly,
there are two ways in which we could seek to solve this problem. One is just
to insist that we do not conceive of practical recognition as a combination of
theoretical recognition *plus* something else (a desire or reaction, presumably).
The fact that we use the word 'recognition' of both of them is no reason to
suppose that one is an element in the other. This is the path of stubbornness.
The other way is to announce that of course it is possible to recognize the
child's need without recognizing it as a reason. But the state we were describing as somehow enjoying both directions of fit was the state of recognizing
the need as a reason—i.e. taking it as relevant to one's choice of action. This
sort of taking is recognitional taking, not because one is recognizing the need
but because one recognizes the need as a reason; one supposes the child's need
to have a relevance that does not depend for its existence on one's recognition
of it. But it is also motivational, since in taking things this way one's will is
affected (normally).

The second criticism starts from where the answer to the first left off. Sometimes one recognizes a feature as a reason, but one's will is not affected at all.
Isn't this enough on its own to show that, when one's will is affected, this is a
further state, over and above the recognitional one? For the one can take place
without the other. My reply to this now standard argument is contained in
the notion of an intrinsically motivating state, which I developed in chapter
2 of *Moral Reasons*,[1] in response to the difficulty for internalism in the theory
of moral motivation that stems from the phenomenon of accidie or listless-
ness. The idea here is to admit the possibility that recognition of a reason
should occur without any effect on the will, but to deny that this possibility

---

[1] (Oxford: Blackwell, 1993).

is enough to require us to carve up the apparently unitary phenomenon of practical recognition into two separable parts. Instead, we say that practical recognition is capable of motivating in its own right, and normally does; but that occasionally things happen that undercut or subvert the normal. An analogous situation occurs in the theory of reasons rather than in that of motivation. What is normally a reason for action may be undercut as such by a feature of a new case, in such a way that here it is no reason at all, even though it is a perfectly good reason elsewhere.

I now move away from problems in the mathematics of mental states to graver difficulties. The first of these is whether we are going to be able to think of the explanation of action as causal, if, as I am recommending, we abandon the view that mental states are reasons. The answer to this question is affected by our decision on a point that I have so far hedged, in speaking of reasons as facts or states of affairs (or features of the situation, indeed). For if reasons are states of affairs, we can conceive of them as potential causes without strain. But if they are facts, to conceive of them as causes we would have to make some sense of the idea that a fact can be a cause; and although we do often speak in such terms, there is a long philosophical tradition of thinking that causes must be events of some sort, in such a way that the event can be a cause when the fact that it occurred cannot. Let us then take the worst-case scenario: reasons are facts, and facts are causally impotent; so reasons are not causes. Could such a view be defensible? Despite the general agreement to the contrary, I think that the answer is still yes.

What about Davidson's master argument[2] that reasons *must* be causes? This argument is that we might have available more than one potential explanation of a particular action—more than one set of things capable of explaining it. In such a case, what makes it the case that one set constitutes the reasons for which we acted rather than another? Davidson's answer to this question is an appeal to causation: one set caused the action and the other did not. Can non-causal accounts of action-explanation do as well?

It is not obvious to me that causal approaches do really have the advantage here that Davidson supposes. His idea is that to characterize the relation between reason and action as causal is to make a move beyond saying that these features were one's reason for action and those were not. I think that we need to distinguish two thoughts here. The first is the idea that there is a philosophical theory of causation to give theoretical depth to the distinction in terms of causes, where there is no competing theory of support by reasons to give philosophical depth to the non-causal alternative. A different way of putting this point is to say that the causal approach sees the relation between reasons and actions as philosophically analysable, while the non-causal one

---

[2] This argument occurs in very abbreviated form in his 'Actions, Reasons, Causes', repr. in *Essays on Action and Events* (Oxford: Clarendon Press, 1980), 3–19, at 9; see also p. 11.

does not. The second thought is that the causal approach does not see the truth that these things were my reasons and those were not as a *bare* truth; for causalists, this truth holds in virtue of another truth, while for non-causalists it does not. The two contrasts are different, because a bare truth might still be analysable. But both contrasts seem to me to be dubious.

As far as the first goes, the appeal to the existence of a philosophical theory of causation is effective in the present context only if that theory is actually able to distinguish an active from an inactive but potential cause, and it is well known that many theories of causation are incapable of drawing that distinction. (Take counterfactual analyses of causation as a notorious case.) In fact, I don't know of one that I do think capable of this feat.

The second contrast, in terms of bareness, is not itself very effective; if causal truths were bare truths, the fact that the causal approach gives us a move before we reach bareness is not, I think, a great theoretical advantage. It is no help here to say that a causal story can always be unpacked, or broken down into micro-elements. For, first, it is not clear that this is true in the present case; secondly, it might be that the notion of causation is itself bare at every stage of the unpacking. I think that the contrast in terms of bareness really requires the other contrast, in terms of theoretical depth. But, as I have said, I think that contrast would be effective only if the theory of causation were in better shape than it is at present.

None of this should be taken to obscure the fact that, in seeking to replace a causal account of the relation between reasons and action with that of acting 'in the light of' the reasons, I have offered no analysis of the 'in the light of' relation at all.

The next difficulty is the charge that explanation of action in terms of reasons is compatible with, and cannot therefore replace, explanation in terms of mental states. If this were true, it would, I think, show that we must have failed in our attempt to transcend the distinction between recognition and reaction. For there will be enormous pressure to show how the two forms of explanation are related, and the distinction between directions of fit that operates in the mental realm will be in danger of being reapplied to the realm of reasons, with the eventual effect that we have failed altogether in our attempt to blur the contrast between recognition and reaction.

There is a reason for thinking that there can be more than one style of explanation of the same event, without either competing with the other. Daniel Dennett has made us used to the idea that the behaviour of a chess-playing computer can be explained in three different ways.[3] So why should not human actions be explained not only by appeal to mental states, but also in a quite different way that appeals to reasons? The beginning of an answer to this is

---

[3] See his 'Intentional Systems', ch. 1 in *Brainstorms* (Montgomery: Bradford Books, 1978).

that it might perhaps be possible if the second way were *quite different* from the first, as it would be if the first were, as we might put it, brutely causal and the second were quite other—rational and normative. But that is not how things are in our case. Explanation by appeal to mental states is not presented as brutely causal, but causal and rational at once, since it is supposed to be a sort of causal explanation that is subject to normative rational constraints. That being so, one might think, it is necessarily incompatible with the coexistence of another style of rational explanation.

One might reply to this that two of Dennett's three styles are rational and normative: the design stance and the intensional stance. Doesn't this show that there can be distinct but non-competing rational/normative explanations in our case?[4] The direct answer to this is that the design stance is not normative in our sense, since it does not generate actions as done because there was more reason to do them than to do any alternative. The design may be a normative object, but the moves explained by appeal to the design are explained by the mere fact of the design, without further appeal to the thought that that move was the best one in the circumstances, or that the design was optimal.

The real point, however, is that the notion of belief is still going to feature in our non-psychologistic account of the explanation of action, since (normally at least) if a reason is to explain an action it must be recognized (believed) by the agent. But this story allots to belief a role quite different from the role that belief (or recognition in general) plays within the psychologistic account of action-explanation that I am trying to reject. One might even say that the crucial difference between the two accounts lies in this matter of how they understand the role of belief. This is the fact that seems to me to render the two forms of explanation incompatible; they require of us opposed understandings of the role of belief in action. This being so, it is impossible for anyone to run both understandings at once.

In an excellent article,[5] Arthur Collins argues that teleological and causal explanations are compatible in biology—and even that, without the support of causal explanations, teleological ones would appear miraculous and have to be abandoned. He then argues that the same is true in the explanation of action. Purposive explanation is teleological, he claims (fairly convincingly), and it is compatible with the existence of psychologistic explanations of the same events in terms of prior mental states. He then goes on to give independent argument that psychologistic explanations are not in fact available. Should I then take Collins to have shown that psychologistic and non-psychologistic explanations are compossible? There are two difficulties with

[4] I owe this objection to Mark Rowlands.
[5] 'Action, Causality and Teleological Explanation', in *Midwest Studies in Philosophy*, 8 (1984), ed. P. A. French, T. E. Uehling, and H. K. Wettstein (Notre Dame, Ind.: University of Notre Dame Press), 344–69.

this for me. First, his claim that actions are explicable teleologically applies only to purposive actions. But it seems to me (and I argue at the end of chapter 2 of *Moral Reasons*) that some actions, and especially some moral actions, are not purposive. The example I gave was of comforting someone who is distraught. I claimed that at least sometimes one does this because that is what is called for by the situation, without taking as one's purpose anything like: one's having done some comforting of the distraught, the distraught person's being comforted (if he does not feel comforted, that does not show that my comforting was a *failure*), one's having done a right action, or whatever. But if this is right, there are some intentional actions that are not explicable teleologically, and that must therefore be explicable in the only other way that Collins countenances—namely, the psychologistic one. But if so, psychologistic explanations must make sense and be occasionally successful, contrary to Collins's final position.

The second difficulty is more profound. This is that Collins's two forms of explanation of action do not both give some role to beliefs. For him, teleological explanation is explanation by appeal to facts—to an outcome; that the boat would thus regain its former course is the explanation of why the helmsman moved the tiller. Causal explanation, by contrast, speaks ordinarily of beliefs and desires. So the situation that Collins envisages is quite different from the one that I am concerned with, where beliefs figure differently in both possible forms of explanation. So even if Collins's two forms of explanation were compossible, that is no reason for thinking that mine are.

There are two different forms of argument to the effect that facts cannot be reasons. The first is the one that Collins is concerned with, where the facts are facts about outcomes; here the pressure comes from the sense that actions can be explained *causally*, when we feel that this rules out the possibility that they should also be explained by appeal to outcomes. The second is the one that concerns me more, that focuses on the possibility of false belief. Collins does not really consider this at all.[6] But we can see the sort of pressure that falsehood brings in, even in Collins's purposive cases. Surely, we will be told, what explains the helmsman's action when he moves the tiller is not that this will lead to a correction of his course, but that he thinks it will. For suppose that

---

[6] At least not in the paper I am here considering. He does consider this point briefly in the last chapter of his *The Nature of Mental Things* (Notre Dame, Ind.: University of Notre Dame Press, 1987), where his response to it is determined by his overall view that beliefs and desires are not to be understood as psychological states, and so *a fortiori* are incapable of functioning as causes in the explanation or generation of action. I am not at the moment willing to subscribe to this very extreme view, though I can see its attractions. I would prefer to stick with the intermediate position that beliefs are indeed psychological states, and that they are necessary for the success of action explanation, but that that form of explanation is not causal and they do not make a causal contribution to it. Collins does consider the role of the case where one's belief is false in his 'The Psychological Reality of Reasons', *Ratio*, 10 (1997), 108–23.

he is wrong in this belief. He will still act, and we will know why; it was because of his belief. If belief is what explains the action in the case of false belief, and if we admit that there must have been a belief present in other cases as well, what can prevent our thinking of belief as what explains action in every case?

This is the last difficulty that I want to consider. The pressure is to accept that there is belief present in every case of intentional action, and therefore to accept that the sort of explanation at issue in every case is a psychologistic one, run in terms of mental states. Here we are no longer concerned with the question whether psychologistic and reasons-based explanations might be compatible. We are dealing instead with an attempt to collapse reasons-based explanations back into psychologistic ones. If belief is admittedly present in every case, what role can it be playing other than that of a mental state, conceived of as a cause?

My answer to this question is that the belief is present as an enabling condition. It enables the reasons to explain the action, without itself being part of that explanation. This kind of situation, where a feature is required for the explanation to go through but is not itself part of the explanation, is one we can see elsewhere. For instance, the reasons that favour an action explain why it was right. But there will often be further features, which are not themselves reasons favouring the action, but which are required for the explanation of the rightness to go through, in the simple sense that, if they were absent, the action would not have been right. For instance, if we think that 'ought' implies 'can', we think that if I cannot do it it is not true that I ought to do it. But my ability to do it need not for that reason be conceived as among the reasons why it is right for me to do it; it is merely a feature in the absence of which the things that make the proposed action right are unable to do so. It is an *enabler*. It enables the things that justify the action to do so, without itself contributing to that justification. We can see the same structure operating in scientific explanation. Here is an example I gave in *Moral Reasons*, which still seems to me to be a good one. If there were no gravity, the balloon would just keep on going upwards; but that is no reason to believe that the balloon's being stationary is partly explained by the operation of gravity. In fact, it is explained by relative densities. More generally, we cannot show that the non-occurrence of event e is part of the explanation E of outcome O just by showing that, if e had occurred, O would not have.

There is a general pressure here that is coming from general thoughts about explanation. This is the idea that a complete explanation should be inclusive. By this we mean that where a purported explanation E of outcome O leaves it possible that the events e^1-e^n specified in E should have occurred without O occurring, we know that E is incomplete. The idea that a perfect explanation should be inclusive in this sense seems to me to be an unreal and unmotivated ideal. But it lies behind the common view that the sorts of explanation we ordinarily offer are enthymematic: that, though they may be adequate for practical purposes, they cannot be truly adequate because they do not *guarantee* the occurrence of the event explained. This requirement that only guaranteeing explanations are complete seems to me to be simply bogus. And, what is more, it is bogus not only in the explanation of action but also in scientific explanation.

If there are non-guaranteeing explanations, of course there must be such things as enabling conditions, or enablers. For a non-guaranteeing explanation is just one that, though as good as an explanation needs to be, is compatible with the non-occurrence of the explanandum O. If O occurs in one place where the explanation goes through perfectly, and not in another, this will be because of some feature or features present (or absent) in the first and absent (or present) in the second. In that case the presence (or absence) of those features must be an enabling condition.

It seems to me, therefore, that there is real room for a non-causal account of action-explanation; the admission that in the absence of relevant belief the action will not occur should not and need not be taken as an admission that psychological states are necessary parts of the explanation of the action; though they are indeed necessary, they function as enabling conditions for the explanation, not as part of the explanation itself.

CONCLUSION

My overall conclusion is that there is a radical alternative to the belief-desire model of action-explanation, one that explains actions in terms of reasons, but understands reasons as features of the world rather than prior psychological states of whatever sort. The belief-desire model, or any psychologistic successor, will find it effectively impossible to get away from the distinction between two directions of fit, and so remain incapable of escaping (or transcending) the distinction between recognition and reaction. Griffin is right to be suspicious of that distinction, but we need to take a much more radical turn than any that he contemplates before we can begin to shake ourselves free of it.

4

Taste and Value

Peter Railton

1

I am visiting a friend in Austria and he has arranged for us to go to a tasting of local wines. Not something for tourists, but something serious—for local restaurateurs, merchants, *aficionados*. I have been enjoying the visit and his company, and I gladly go with him to a large hall where a boisterous tasting is in progress. Warmly encouraged by my host, I begin trying the wines—though, from a misplaced sense of delicacy, I do not spit out the samples. At first the wines taste a little green, but I am no expert, and before long I have found a few that strike me as really delightful. 'These are good,' I say to my host with pleasure. 'I'm glad you like them,' he replies modestly; 'some Austrian wines are not so bad, you know.' But I persist. 'No, I mean they're really good—this one in particular is great. I haven't tasted a wine this good in a long time.'

My host is polite enough to hold his tongue. He knows that I tasted a much better wine just last night—the German wine he served with dinner. He says to himself: 'Well, it's nice that he's enjoying himself. But either he's drunk or he has very mediocre taste in wine.'

The appearance of the word 'taste' introduces me to the theme I'd like to explore here, with the help of James Griffin's important recent book, *Value Judgement: Improving Our Ethical Beliefs*. Griffin begins his discussion of the theory of value with an examination of (what he calls) *prudential value*—the goodness of a life for the person who lives it (*VJ* 19). By way of introducing his own account, he considers and rejects two alternative models of prudential value: the taste model and the perception model. These two models offer complementary priority theses about the relation of reason

I would like to thank Elizabeth Anderson, Stephen Darwall, Allan Gibbard, Ed Green, James Griffin, Roger Noll, Robert Solow, and Hal Varian for helpful discussion.

and desire in our evaluative practice. According to the *taste model*, a prudential good, such as accomplishment, is valuable because we desire it: 'given the
sort of biological and psychological creatures we are, our desires come to fix
on certain objects, which thereby acquire value' (*VJ* 20). According to the
perception model, value is something to be 'discovered . . . quite apart from
my personal desires and inclinations', so that we can be said to come to
desire accomplishment, say, because we recognize it to be valuable (*VJ* 20).
Different as they seem, these two models share an underlying view of understanding and desire as sharply distinct; where they differ is over priority—is
accomplishment good because we desire it, or do we desire it because it is
good (*VJ* 20–1)?

Of course, each thesis becomes a good deal more complicated in the hands
of philosophers. Perception theorists recognize the looseness of the term
'desire' as used in philosophical discussions, and work to distinguish desires
that thrust themselves upon us willy-nilly, such as 'cravings, obsessions, com-
pulsions, post-hypnotic suggestions, addictions, habits' (*VJ* 27), from 'desires
that are part of normal intentional action . . . [and that] aim at the good' (*VJ*
27). Taste theorists, for their part, also recognize the vagaries of desire. Typically, they locate the origin of value not in what we actually happen to desire,
but in what we would desire (or desire to desire) were we informed, vividly
aware, logical, rational (*VJ* 21).[1]

Griffin argues that neither model captures the whole truth about prudential value, since each bears the disfiguring stamp of an overly dichotomous
view, which places reason and understanding to one side, and desire to the
other. The taste model, however, is the one Griffin sees as the more pressing
object of concern:

David Hume, for instance, thought that, despite first appearances, all cases [of value]
really fit under the taste model. Many who disagree with him about moral standards
agree at least about prudential ones. That position seems to me typical of current
thought: reject the taste model for moral standards, but retain it for prudential ones.
The taste model, with that restriction on its scope, is now widespread in philosophy,
and, even without the restriction, dominates the social sciences. (*VJ* 21)

If this is right, and if the taste model is indeed inadequate, then that is cause
for considerable alarm.

Reason and understanding, on Griffin's account of the Humean view, have
only a limited office in the formation of value. They may bring an object of
potential interest into more accurate focus and give us more insight into its
effects upon us, but from that point forward the job of making value falls to
desire: 'once the object is in focus, it will, according to the taste model, owe

---

[1] Of course, taste theorists differ over what these various elements might involve.

its status as a value to its then being desired' (*VJ* 21). Desire, the 'value-maker', is also a 'value-breaker'. According to the interpretation of the taste model Griffin offers, if an aim would *not* be present in my own personal 'final subjective set of improved desires', then it could not be prudentially valuable for me to have or realize in my life. But this seems wrong, for, as he notes: 'If certain desires happen not to be present in [one's] final subjective set of improved desires, perhaps they ought to be' (*VJ* 24). The taste model begins to make it look as if one could secure oneself against the criticism that one's aims are shallow or obsessive simply by *being* sufficiently shallow or obsessive. But surely, Griffin contends,

We ask more searching questions about our aims, and resort to more radical criticism to answer them, than the taste model allows. If I am a fool-like person living for day-to-day pleasures and meet a Socratic sort of person who strikes me as making something of his life, I might start on the [path of] radical reflection. . .   (*VJ* 24)

2

Now we must slow down for a detour. Why cannot the taste theorist point to my encounter with the Socratic as a case of new information (observing a Socratic example) interacting with my underlying motivational tendencies (being 'struck' by this example in a positive way)? Of course, as a fool I have no antecedent desire *identifiable* as a desire to lead a more reflective or more Socratic life. But, if my motivational set contained no potential positive sentiment that could be 'recruited by' the information I gain about the Socratic life, then how could my novel exposure to the Socratic have any tendency to engage me or to induce in me the unease antecedent to second-guessing?

There is an unfortunate tendency in debates over (what is called) the Humean model of action for great weight to be placed on what is, for the Humean, a term of art—'desire'. (I would not claim that Griffin himself is guilty of this.) Humeans divide the explanation of action into (at least) two components, a representational component and a motivational component—namely, belief and desire. Consider the belief side first. Must Humeans think that belief corresponds to the active entertaining of a discrete proposition? Or that belief revision requires a deliberative process going from currently entertained propositions via a conscious inferential route to some newly adopted propositions? This would be, to put it mildly, wild. We could not begin to handle the amount of information we actually do process minute by minute in ordinary experience. Humeans can see belief as a complex phenomenon, at least partly dispositional. Dispositionally, I suspect, is the way you believe that I will end this detour in a few paragraphs and get back to Griffin, and also how you believed that the floor underneath you would not give way as you read the first clause of this sentence.

Now consider the motivational side of action. Must *bona fide* Humeans think that *desiring X* corresponds to the active presence in our psychic life of an identifiable *desire to X* or *desire for Y* (which I believe *X* would promote), where *X* and *Y* are linguistically encoded and the motivational state is itself an object of deliberative awareness? And must the formation of any new desire 'based on' my present desires come about through some self-aware, inferential deliberative process? If the Humeans held these views, they would have to say that pre-linguistic children and animals lack desires, and they would be hard pressed to explain some quite familiar phenomena: the rapid desire revision we seemingly undergo when scanning the entries on a weekend events calendar or the shelves of a supermarket; or the fact that, in the course of a long drive, it can properly be said of me that I have been wanting a break for some time (and beginning to pay closer attention to restaurant billboards) even before the thought of how much I would like to stop has actually crossed my mind.[2] The Humean can allow that underlying, unvoiced, frequently updated desires explain a good deal of our intelligent, voluntary behaviour, as well as helping to account for what we notice, which mental associations we form, or what thoughts pop into our minds. The Humean thus is able to view desire as well as belief as dispositional in character.

The Humean need not believe, moreover, that motivation begins where understanding leaves off, or vice versa. She can hold that certain kinds of motivation require a degree of development of the understanding. A person, but not a sheep, can be intrinsically motivated by considerations of autonomy. An adult, but not a newborn, can be intrinsically motivated by considerations of the welfare of future generations. (In both these cases, I think, the existence of the motivation in question does not depend upon the individual *representing to himself* such motives.) Moreover, the Humean can hold that some kinds of understanding characteristically originate in our motivated responses, and thus may be unavailable or may lack their ordinary role in such cognitive tasks as inference, deliberation, or decision in those individuals incapable of certain motivations. An understanding of the mental states of others adequate to the tasks of predicting and causally attributing their behaviour (or even their view of oneself) might, for example, be virtually unattainable for those with no empathetic capacity (and thus limited ability to simulate).[3]

---

[2] See R. Brandt and J. Kim, 'Wants as Explanations of Actions', *Journal of Philosophy*, 60 (1963), 425–35.

[3] For discussion of the role of various motivation-linked states in cognition, see e.g. the debate between Robert B. Zajonc, 'On the Primacy of Affect', *American Psychologist*, 39 (1984), 117–23, and R. S. Lazarus, 'On the Primacy of Cognition', *American Psychologist*, 39 (1984), 124–9; see also J. E. LeDoux, 'Cognitive–Emotional Interactions in the Brain', *Cognition and Emotion*, 3 (1989), 267–89.

Is there a danger here of trivializing Humeanism? Decidedly. A trivial Humeanism attributes beliefs and desires *ad hoc*, gerrymandering an individual's imputed psyche for each bit of overt behaviour to ensure that no evidence could tell against the theory. Then there would indeed be no explanation, no *model*, worth troubling with. But the Humean typically has lots of things he wants beliefs and desires to do, even when realized dispositionally. We have already mentioned some—to explain which propositions or inferences an individual might accept, to explain what he notices or thinks of, to explain why he responds in one way (while others do not) to a given bit of environmental input—and there are countless others: to account for a surge of adrenalin or the watering of the mouth, to explain differential success at test and task performance, to produce various personal stabilities and instabilities in conduct, and so on.

The functional descriptions for belief and desire are intricate and interwoven. The Humean need not take these functional descriptions as giving us the *concepts* of belief and desire, or their *phenomenology*. He might. But he could properly be said to hold a distinctive, non-trivial *Humean model* if he gives a non-trivial account of (among other things) the *roles* they play—'the typical syndrome of causes and effects'. So belief and desire attribution can be disciplined theoretically without the hobbling assumption that beliefs and desires must somehow be deliberatively present to the mind's eye if they are to be active in the agent at all.

3

The Humean's point about the fool then is this. The fool's underlying motivational states play some role in explaining why the Socratic—of all the people he has encountered recently—suddenly strikes him as 'making something of his life' and perhaps even as someone to emulate.

But could there not be perfect fools—individuals with no motivational capacity that could be engaged on behalf of a more Socratic life? They would be proof against the influence of the Socratic example, for they could observe how the Socratic acts and this would not in the least resonate for them—they just would not get it. We certainly cannot rule out the existence of perfect fools a priori; nor, I suspect, would most of us want to do so a posteriori.

Perhaps Griffin can make his point, then, by shifting his example to one of an enlightenment-proof fool. Thus he considers an obsessive-compulsive, who possesses

a particular irrational desire—say, one planted deep when one was young—[that] might well survive criticism by facts and logic . . . take a man with some crazy aim in life—say, counting blades of grass in various lawns. . . . [We may suppose that] he makes no logical error [and is missing no information]. But it is very unlikely that we can see the fulfilment of this obsessive desire as enhancing his life—apart, that is, from [merely] preventing anxieties . . .   (*VJ* 22)

This singular desire must be thought of here as an *intrinsic* desire. Otherwise, the compulsive's problem might not be an entrenched, bizarre motivational state but rather an entrenched, bizarre belief—he cannot help thinking that counting blades will (say) protect him from harm (if only he could be sure he did not miss one!), or reveal information his neighbours are desperate to hide from him.

Now those of us concerned with this man's well-being will believe—and almost certainly correctly so—that he actually has many desires and interests that are not present to his consciousness and not well satisfied by this compulsive blade counting. So we believe—and, again, almost certainly correctly so—that we do him some good by encouraging him to come away from his counting and go off with us to dinner and a movie. Griffin can grant all that. His point is more subtle: however much the blade-counter himself intrinsically desires to carry through his compulsive behaviour, and however unshakeable that life-dominating desire might be under information and reflection,[4] it still does not make the activity valuable. *This* informed intrinsic desire—or even intrinsic desire to desire—is not a value-maker. But then the taste model has erred: 'A very odd person might care a lot about counting the blades of grass in various lawns, but that does nothing to make it valuable' (*VJ* 28).[5] Nor does Griffin's argument depend upon the mere peculiarity of this preference for blade counting: 'this point does not depend upon his being odd. The same applies to a train-spotter or a piano player. For anyone to see anything as valuable, from any point of view, requires being able to see it as worth wanting' (*VJ* 28). Griffin believes that we, as competent users of the concept 'prudential value', cannot accord intrinsic prudential value to blade counting unless we can see it as worthwhile, worth wanting. And we do not. Moreover, the only evidence we seem to have for saying it is worth wanting is that this person wants it, and we clearly see him as an obsessive-

---

[4] Actual obsessive-compulsive disorder (OCD) is typically experienced by the individual as a plague, an overwhelmingly powerful force in his life that he wishes to be rid of (it is, after all, often ruining his life). Psychologists also distinguish, however, an obsessive-compulsive *personality* disorder (OCPD), which usually has less severe behavioural manifestations, is thus less crippling of everyday life, and usually is viewed by the affected individual as *justified*. For example, the 'obsessively neat' person who insists everything in his apartment must be just so even before leaving for work in the morning, and who thinks that those who do not aspire to this level of organization are slobs.

[5] As before, we must be careful to note (with Griffin) that there may be some good, for anyone, simply in not having his or her desires frustrated (whatever these desires happen to be).

compulsive—his recalcitrant desires have no authority for us on value questions.

Is our unwillingness to accord him authority, and our associated unwillingness to see blade counting as intrinsically valuable, mere prejudice on our part? Why not treat it as a *personal value*—a 'value-for-him'? Now Griffin's point may come into full view. It concerns the tenability of the notion of a personal value in the light of what he believes the *concept* of value to involve—that is, in the light of what it is for anyone to see anything as *valuable*. He writes:

it is doubtful that there are any such things as personal values, in this sense (there are, of course, things that are valuable to only a few people, but that is different). . . . What could make [some activity such as blade counting or] playing the piano well worth wanting is that it would be in some way rewarding: I should enjoy it, or it would be an accomplishment, and so on. But this is to fall back on impersonal values. So long as one defines 'personal values' in terms of what a person wants or cares about, one retains too much of the taste model. (*VJ* 27–8)

It emerges that the taste model fails as a model, according to Griffin, even after we have disentangled this question from the quite different issue whether it is, or even purports to be, a satisfactory analysis of the concept of prudential value. This model claims to tell us where value comes from ('valuable *because* desired' (*VJ* 20)), yet it appears to be *extensionally inadequate* since it will license some things as valuable (blade counting) that we competent users of value concepts can see plainly are not. 'To see anything as prudentially valuable, then, we must see it as an instance of something generally intelligible as valuable and, furthermore, as valuable for any (normal) human. Prudential deliberation ends up, I think, with a list of values' (*VJ* 29).

Griffin had earlier claimed, concerning 'general intelligibility as valuable', that: 'This is a perfectly general requirement on values; it is the basis of the distinction between mere wanting and the sort of wanting that connects with values' (*VJ* 28). The desire to count blades is not 'generally intelligible as valuable' or 'as valuable for any (normal) human'; therefore, we are confident, it will not be on the list of prudential values. (Freedom from frustration and anxiety, by contrast, are bound to be on the list (*VJ* 29–30). That explains why, if the blade-counter is truly incorrigible, we can still see *some* good in letting him go ahead and count. This is instrumental good, arising from the prudential value, other things equal, of satisfying a strong desire.)

I think Griffin is right about the inherent generality of the value concepts. Even our blade-counter, in so far as he deems his activity intrinsically valuable, is claiming a kind of authority and must think there is more to be said for blade counting than 'well, I happen to like it'. I suspect he thinks it an under-appreciated activity, much the way I think (at the tasting) that the Austrian wines are under-appreciated. The point is, we are both wrong, and Griffin gives an explanation of why: our particular likings are not good gauges of normal human likings. Naturally, then, they lack authority.

4

But is this the best explanation? And, when fully spelled out, is it something contrary to the taste model?

Let me take up the second question first. Is the inherent generality of value concepts, or even the connection to that which is valuable to any (normal) human, something at odds with the Humean taste model? One reason for doubting this is the very naturalness of my host's thought at the wine tasting: 'Agreeable as this fellow Railton may be, he lacks taste. Typical American—all enthusiasm and no discrimination.' Hume (a believer in national character—one of his few intellectual vices) would probably concur. I may like the wine enormously, but this does not make a good wine. Hume would be ready to show that I lack authority about matters of wine taste—he would have me tackle the complex identification and discrimination tasks that expert wine-tasters master with ease. I could not reliably tell a Mosel from a Rhine wine, much less tell you which grapes, or year, or slope.

One can fairly say, I think, that the Humean taste model is designed to show how there is, after all, a common subject matter to aesthetic disputes, such as my defence of Austrian wine in the face of contrary opinion. His account of taste links standards of aesthetic (or gustatory) value to general human interests in a way that parallels the conceptual linkage between prudential value and general human interests that Griffin proposes. I say 'parallels' because I doubt Hume takes the linkage to be conceptual in nature (Hume seems more concerned with explanation and adjudication than with conceptual analysis), and because the linkage connects a *standard of value* with human interests, not value itself. But it does seem to me that Griffin need not see himself as arguing against a 'Humean taste model' in his discussion of value and desire; in the large scheme of things, they are very much on the same side. Hume's account of taste can lend support to a claim of the generality of value judgement. Indeed, fully developed, it may even notch the generality up one rank.

So, let us say a bit more about the Humean model of aesthetic taste. We're all familiar with the cliché, 'I don't know much about art, but do I know what I like.' Suppose your friend invokes this phrase, adding, 'And I know I *don't* like de Kooning,' as he recounts to you his rather unfulfilling weekend visit with an enthusiast friend to the new show at the Modern. This cliché is useful, and makes some sense, precisely because it enables the speaker to express enjoyment or disappointment while *declining to make an aesthetic judgement*—in this case, of de Kooning. He did not find it rewarding, but that is not to say he takes that as an indicator of lack of aesthetic merit—he will leave such questions to others, who know more about art. Put another way, he is not claiming authority, not claiming that his failure to resonate with de Kooning is attributable to his good taste. (No doubt the cliché came in handy in smoothing his dealings with his enthusiast friend.) In consequence, he is not trying to recruit us to a negative evaluation of de Kooning or to answer our question directly if we ask: 'I gather you saw the show at the Modern; was it good?'

Move now from aesthetic to gustatory taste, and return to the scene of the Austrian wine tasting. My host is glad to see that I like these modest Austrian wines, but I attempt to insist on something stronger—my liking is not the point, or at any rate not the whole point. Some of these wines are downright good, I claim, and merit greater appreciation. I am no longer speaking with a personal voice, but rather invoking a non-personal notion of goodness in wine. What might be my grounds for such a claim—what challenges might I have to meet if I am successfully to defend it? Because it is not a merely personal claim, I cannot respond to a wine *aficionado* who dismisses the Austrian wine as 'naïve' by saying, 'Well, *I* really like it.' Nor can I answer the *aficionado* by saying that I have a distinctive notion of excellence in wine all my own, and that I do not care a straw for the judgement of even the most refined palates. If this were so, then what I say would be irrelevant to his challenge, and would be largely irrelevant, too, to the question whether anyone else should pay more attention to Austrian wines. The *aficionado* is not disputing whether the wine fits my pet likes or my pet theories of wine excellence. Nor can I say, 'Well, people *like me* like this kind of wine', and leave it at that. If the compass of 'people like me' is narrow and otherwise unimpressive (for example, includes mostly people incapable of making reliable gustatory discriminations), why should anyone else listen to the preferences of such people as a guide to which wines really are good?

What I am claiming to my friend at the tasting is something like: this wine *has what it takes* to be a good wine. I am convinced (for now, at any rate) that, absent prejudice, those who are able to discriminate the features that make for goodness in taste will find them in this wine—they are there to behold. I am convinced of this because I take my own experience of the wine to be at least somewhat sensitive to these features, and not simply a reflection of my suggestibility, or of the grossness of my palate, or of my tipsiness. From a conversational perspective, we can note that I am purporting to say something relevant and informative: though I might not know a great deal about wine, I do take myself to know enough to say, 'This is a *good* wine.'

My judgement is, however, controversial. This sort of variation in judge-ment and resultant dispute over taste is the classic problem Hume sought to address with his taste model. Not for him the easy way out of *de gustibus non disputandum est*—he does not attribute the bulk of observed aesthetic discord to irreducibly different sensibilities and preferences. On the contrary, he believes that there is a very great deal in common among humans in their per-ceptual and cognitive faculties, as well as in their sentiments, which in turn are similarly keyed to experience. He therefore seeks to reconcile the evident diversity of actual judgements with these underlying similarities, and in such a way as to capture some unquestionable facts: some works of art are greater than others; the judgements of some individuals carry much greater author-ity than that of others; and great works can show themselves to be such by meeting 'the test of time' or winning the praise of expert judges. He writes:

Whoever would assert an equality of genius and elegance between Ogilby and Milton, or Bunyan and Addison, would be thought to defend no less an extravagance than if he had maintained a mole-hill to be as high as Tenerife, or a pond as extensive as the ocean. Though there be found such persons, who give the preference to the former authors; no one pays attention to such a taste; and we pronounce without scruple the sentiment of these pretended critics to be absurd and ridiculous.[6]

Like Griffin, Hume links value to 'general human interests'. And, like Griffin, he rejects the idea that personal liking gives the content of judgements of value. Indeed, Hume is seeking a 'standard of taste' to afford a way of adjudi-cating disputes among conflicting sentiments, or 'at least, a decision . . . confirming one sentiment, and condemning another'.[7] Hume contends that commonalities of human perception, cognition, and sentiment provide (what we might call) the *infrastructure* for an aesthetic evaluative practice in which sentiment can be confirmed or condemned on non-arbitrary, non-personal grounds. It can, in a word, possess authority—rather than 'pretended author-ity'—over a common subject matter.[8]

In Hume's account, the highly developed perceptual and discriminatory capacities and highly sensitive responses of experts are of interest to us not because we cravenly defer to snobs, but because they are equipped by their sensitivity, experience, knowledge, lack of conflicts of interest, and so on, to attend much more accurately to 'the beauties' in things that are (we might say) of *human* interest rather than merely local, esoteric, or fashionable concern. Since I am a fairly typical human (I assume), these are part of a world of enjoy-ment open to me. Similarly, the 'test of time' brings to bear a large and dif-ferentiated human population with a wide range of experience, knowledge,

---

[6] David Hume, 'Of the Standard of Taste', repr. in *Of the Standard of Taste and Other Essays, by David Hume*, ed. John W. Lenz (Indianapolis: Bobbs-Merrill, 1965), 7.
[7] Ibid. 6.   [8] Ibid.

sentimental responses, and reasoning capacities. Tastes that endure in this population over time therefore will manifest a kind of impartiality, for there will be a tendency towards the mutual cancellation of various merely local, partisan, or trendy interests. This 'test' thus affords typical humans rich information about what can reliably engage general human capacities to produce enduring enjoyments, and does not merely happen to delight for now because of novelty, peculiarities of context, or limitations of experience and awareness.

Call this sort of feature—a capacity to engage human perceptual and cognitive faculties in such a way as robustly to lead to favourable sentiments and enjoyment—a *match* between our capacities, on the one hand, and objects, performances, and other sources of experience, on the other. The test of time and the consilience of expert opinion are, in effect, highly sensitive means for detecting such matches—enough so as to afford 'at least, a decision . . . confirming one sentiment, and condemning another', that is, a standard of taste. If we ordinary humans accord special authority to expert opinion, or to the test of time, this is because we learn thereby about our own taste, and about the possible delights of art, cuisine, and so on that await us. Such delights are, as Hume points out, more within my voluntary power than many others—we have more choice in the books we read than in the friends we have (or in the health we possess, or in the fortune we enjoy). Moreover (and here I may be putting words in Hume's mouth), I care deeply and sincerely about how my own choices, opinions, and creations—what I write or say, the food I cook, the way I dress or comport myself—will strike others. If Hume is right about human commonality, he is able to explain why we go in so much for aesthetic evaluation—debating movies, giving and taking advice on where to eat or what to do, consulting published guides, ratings, and reviews, gossiping about appearances ('Did you *see* his hair?'), and so on. We have something to learn, and something to contribute that others might want to hear.[9]

So far, I take it, Griffin would not object to seeing prudential value as parallel with aesthetic value. Our prudential evaluative practice is sustainable owing to an infrastructure as well—enduring, common human interests provide us with a common subject matter, and shared evaluation, advice giving and taking, gossip, and so on are rife. Merely subjective likings and dislikings, with 'no reference beyond themselves', and no claim to authority concerning the actual or potential experience of others, are not the coin of the realm. And those with widest experience, and greatest sensitivity and knowledge, possess the greatest authority. Mill's view that the consilience of opinion among those of wide experience best reveals utility—that is, best reveals 'utility in the largest sense, grounded on the permanent interests of a man as

---

[9] For a fuller (albeit still preliminary) discussion, see P. Railton, 'Aesthetic Value, Moral Value, and the Ambitions of Naturalism', in Jerrold Levinson (ed.), *Aesthetics and Ethics: Essays at the Intersection* (Cambridge: Cambridge University Press, 1998).

a progressive being'—is an example.[10] It is the prudential analogue of Hume's standard of taste.

5

Thus far we have been discussing the infrastructure of a shared domain of value, first aesthetic and now prudential. Does this show, as Griffin claims, that 'normal human interests' are built into the *concepts* of aesthetic and prudential value? Regarding the latter, Griffin writes: 'For me to see anything as prudentially valuable, for example, I must see it as enhancing life in a generally intelligible way, in a way that pertains to *human* life, not to any one particular person's life' (*VJ* 27).[11] I suspect, however, that a conceptual linkage of prudential value to '*human* life' or to 'general human interest' (*VJ* 27) is parochial in a way we would reject on reflection, indeed, a way Griffin himself has eloquently argued against.[12] Similarly, I suspect we would misinterpret Hume if we saw as essential to his view a claim that (something like) 'normal human interests' are to be found written into the very concept of aesthetic value. That, too, would be parochial, robbing our aesthetic language of some of its generality and expressive power.

Towards whom would we be showing parochialism? If *normal human* is built into the very notion of prudential value, then we are elbowing aside both the *non-normal human* and the *non-human*. At first, this may seem harmless. When we first think about departures from the normal human, we may think of an *abnormal* human of a kind whose perceptual faculties or characteristic ranges of response are truncated or freakish, and so sufficiently unlike our own that his likes and dislikes, even when they are developed or informed as far as possible within the constraints of his faculties, lack relevance or authority. If someone were able to hear only loud, deep notes, or heard all sounds as if they were vibrations of a tin can, we would not think his prefer-

---

[10] See his essays 'Utilitarianism' and 'On Liberty', repr. in *John Stuart Mill: Utilitarianism and Other Essays*, ed. Mary Warnock (New York: New American Library, 1962), esp. 136, 258–62.

[11] Do I misread Griffin's talk of 'seeing something as *F*' as a way of encoding a claim about the concept *F*? This seems to fit his own inferential uses—such talk plays a crucial role in his claim that, for example: ' "That's cruel" [is] . . . a moral judgement, which I presented it as . . . the notion [concept?] of "cruel", I think, leaves no space for disapproval to be a further, independent stage. To understand "pain" involves regarding it as a disvalue' (*VJ* 80). But Griffin, not me, is the authority on this question. (The question of where there might be 'space' for deliberation will figure prominently in the discussion below.)

[12] In *WB* (see below). The relation between the views expressed about value and desire in *WB* and the views expressed in *VJ* deserves more developed discussion than I am able to give it here.

ences bore on the question of the comparative aesthetic merits of Italian operas.

But consider a different sort of case, involving a *constitutionally different normalcy*.[13] Since Griffin at one point introduces a Martian anthropologist (*VJ* 34), I will assume he would not object strenuously if I introduce a Martian music critic. Martians are constitutionally different from us—quite different frequencies register in their auditory systems and quite different sounds strike them as pleasing or unbearable. They are not without a practice of aesthetic criticism—this particular Martian is, after all, a music critic. Indeed, he is widely deemed (on Mars, that is) the leading music critic. The Martians, like us, have traditions of performance and instrumentation adapted to their sound range and sense of harmony, and associated practices of training, criticizing, and so on.[14]

Let us imagine that I am to greet the visiting Martian music critic and his translator at the spaceport and drive them to my university, for the awarding of an honorary degree. I have carefully put an exquisite recording of Chopin in the CD player of my car's expensive stereo system (were it only so!—as I said, this is fiction). I beam with pride at mankind as the music fills the car, but the Martian critic asks through his translator whether I cannot do something to stop that irritating metallic rattle, since he hears something else—something simple but delightful. This turns out to be the somewhat irregular whines and squeaks of my car's worn v-belts (not fiction), which he finds utterly charming. Aesthetically at home, he half closes his eyes and enjoys a relaxing ride to campus after a strenuous flight.

Clearly disappointed, do I think to myself: 'This Martian may be regarded as the leading music critic on the Red Planet, but he obviously has no taste—the Chopin is beautiful, not annoying, and the v-belt noise is merely ugly. His idiosyncratic personal likings cannot make such a noise aesthetically valuable'? But his likings are *not* idiosyncratic or personal—apart from his greater discernment, he is like almost all Martians. Martians strive to make such sounds, and have a long-standing critical practice founded on highly practised discriminations and delicately attuned sensibilities. Indeed, their

[13] Later we will return to (what might be called) 'constitutional abnormalcy'.

[14] Given the tremendous evolutionary importance of coordination and communication, it should be not much more surprising to find music among Martians than to find bird calls among birds, or rhythmic chanting and hooting among primates. Is it not tendentious for me to speak of a Martian *music*, or Martian *music criticism, harmonies, performances*, etc.? After all, Martian hearing is (we suppose) rather different from our own. Yet I take it that we actually have relatively little trouble saying what it might be like for Martians none the less to have practices that we would be comfortable calling playing or composing music, building and using musical instruments, enjoying or criticizing music, etc. Of course, Martians might have practices we would be hard put to classify as musical or not—just as they might have practices we would be hard put to classify as anthropology or not. But we are supposing here that such imponderables are not present, or are not central, to the case.

hearing range extends well beyond ours. This individual is acclaimed within Martian critical practice. Does he speak with no authority on matters of beauty—his celebrated aesthetic expertise a sham? Shall we call off the degree ceremony?

Not at all. What I really think as we drive along is not: 'This guy wouldn't know beauty if it bit him.' It is something closer to: 'Gosh, the world contains beauties we humans are not attuned to—music that may not be music to our ears.' There is, I would claim, room for this thought within our concepts of 'beauty' and 'music'. My thinking therefore is not: 'This v-belt noise has so-called beauty for Martian ears.' Rather: 'Here's a realm of beauty— of real aesthetic value—that I as a typical human don't seem equipped to tap into.'

But as a typical human I am hungry for new aesthetic experiences. So I will also think: 'All the same, I'm going to listen carefully to that v-belt and also try to gauge any reactions on his part—let's see if I can't begin to catch on.'[15] There would be little difficulty in my speaking of Martians as possessing aesthetic sensibility if I did seem to catch on—that would be like the case of being successfully introduced to a new musical tradition on this planet. But suppose I do not seem to catch on. The best I can do is find some familiar overtones, rhythms, etc., the aesthetic effect of which is only mildly interesting. Moreover, the interesting bits to me are very likely not at all what *he* senses—they do not seem to correlate with whether he seems focused on the sound or looking out of the window or reviewing the contents of a case he is carrying. This particular realm of beauty and delight begins to look closed to me, though I resolve to try again. Such a failure to catch on would sadden me, but not incline me to think him a fraud, or Martian beauty mere (inverted commas) 'beauty'.

Shift now to the case of prudential value. Venusians (we will say) are also constitutionally different from us. For example, they differ in their intrinsic desires. Given our reproductive history, it is unsurprising that normal humans take an intrinsic interest in deep, lasting relations with others—and perhaps especially with mates and offspring (compare Griffin's list of prudential values (*VJ* 29–30)). Venusians, in contrast, have always reproduced amoeba-like, by a kind of whole-body fission. They overcome some of the drawbacks of asexual reproduction by possessing a Lamarckian rather than Darwinian biology of inheritance; the genetic code they pass along to offspring has been updated over the course of their lifetimes. Venusians come into the world much better equipped mentally than most of us leave it. They also photosynthesize. All this is fortunate, since they can barely move and can communicate with one another only with great difficulty. It also means that there is no

---

[15] As a typical human, too, I could not avoid hoping that when he is less exhausted the Martian critic will try Earthling music again. Think what he might be missing!

prolonged period of infancy and dependence among Venusians, and that it would make little real difference to survival whether Venusians took an interest in their offspring. In any event, they do not seem intrinsically desirous of deep, lasting relations with their offspring or with other Venusians, do not prize novel encounters, and are quite content to bask and meditate, striving hard for a kind of ideally complete and coherent consciousness, which is set to an intricate 'mental music'. It is no easy thing for them to succeed at this, and they perform incredible and lengthy feats of concentration and inference to achieve it. To the extent that they achieve it, they derive an intense and complex pleasure. This state, moreover, is the primary precursor to fission, and so an important part of their reproductive life.

Clearly, they do not advance very far in realizing a number of items on Griffin's list of normal human goods, even as they excel at realizing some items not on our list—goods we may lack the imagination to conceive very clearly, or the motivational potential to desire intrinsically, or the wherewithal to realize. Given their difficulties in communication and desire not to be distracted, we would have a hard time gaining much understanding of their lives. But suppose we come to understand them as least as far as this little sketch. Do we conclude that Venusians would be better off if they somehow raised their profile in the realization of normal *human* goods, even at the expense of lowering their profile in the realization of typical Venusian intrinsic concerns ('If they'd just move around and socialize a bit more, or take some real interest in their offspring, they'd be better off.')?

To think this would be to take seriously Griffin's notion of prudential value, the *impersonality* of which is really *human-personality*—it is a matter of the sort of life that is, in a human-typical sense, to *our* taste. But, just as we found it natural (I think) to say in the aesthetic case that there might be music we cannot hear (or, cannot hear *as* music) and beauties we are not equipped to see or appreciate, so does it seem plausible to say that there might be prudential goods we cannot realize, good lives we are not equipped to lead. Although these are not—perhaps even could not be—human goods, it does not follow that they cannot be genuine goods, or cannot afford Venusians genuine reasons to pursue them and Earthlings genuine reasons to assist Venusian pursuits.

If nothing else, they would appear to afford *moral* reasons. Is this not similar in certain respects to our situation here on Earth with regard to non-human animals? Benefits and harms to Venusians—genuine Venusian benefits and harms, not (inverted commas) 'Venusian benefits and harms'—are tied to what matches or fails to match their nature, and yields for them outcomes or experiences of kinds that are for them objects of intrinsic motivation. (We might of course decide that we are poor enough at figuring this out for the appropriate moral relationship to them to be virtually unknowable to us.)

Griffin writes:

It is a requirement of a reason that it have a certain role in human life: that it move one to belief or to action. . . . a putative reason that really did not mesh with motivation would be too remote from human nature to fit intelligibly under the concept of a practical 'reason'. I do not mean that this requirement holds individual by individual. . . . Someone in black despair might recognize some urgently prudential reason, and not care a bit. The requirement is only general: that a practical reason has to mesh with characteristic human motivation. (*VJ* 35)

With much of this I heartily concur, at least in the case of prudential reason. I baulk, though, at the term 'human'. Prudential reasons depend upon the existence of various motivational and cognitive elements in individuals, and upon the nature of those individuals, but not upon normal human motivation as such.

This more generic conception is, I believe, at work in Griffin's own discussion of a Martian anthropologist who belongs to a species constitutionally incapable of feeling pain. Such an anthropologist could, Griffin believes, visit Earth and gain an understanding of 'our disvalue term "pain"' (*VJ* 34).[16] In particular, he could come to see that, 'typically, humans want to avoid it or have it alleviated' (*VJ* 34). Thus: 'The Martian anthropologist will not share our human concerns about pain, but that does not mean that he would not regard our [disvalue] judgements about pain as true, or that he would not see our peculiarly human concerns as concerns' (*VJ* 34). I find this both plausible and congenial.

However, Griffin then continues: 'what seems right—and important—is that all [practical] reasons have to connect . . . with human motivation' (*VJ* 34). Now the Martian anthropologist may conclude that our prudential reasons—and therefore his moral reasons in so far as his conduct affects us— are indeed connected with human motivation. But what of *his* prudential reasons—and therefore *our* moral reasons in so far as our conduct affects Martians?

Moreover, what if our Martian anthropologist were to travel to Venus? Though constitutionally unlike Venusians, might he not understand some of their value judgements as well as he understands our judgements of pain? He might view some Venusian value judgements—for example, concerning a good life—as true, as accurately representing genuine prudential reasons, and therefore as giving him genuine moral reasons. But none of these reasons would be referred to as normal human motivation. And for our part we will say in our own voice, as we look over the anthropologist's shoulder, that he is

---

[16] Although I am uneasy about calling 'pain' a disvalue term, I will accept Griffin's view here for the purposes of argument.

recognizing moral and prudential reasons quite unconnected with peculiarly human motives.

When we reflect on Martian aesthetics or Venusian prudence, we are, I would say, using our familiar concepts of aesthetic and prudential value. They 'have room for' such cases of constitutionally different normalcy. Of course, the ordinary use of these concepts keeps them Earthbound in application—we reflect on our lives as, and among, humans. The question of what matches or fits will typically concern normal human capacities and motivations.[17] It is altogether appropriate, therefore, that Hume refer to normal human capacities and motivations in formulating a standard of taste appropriate for adjudicating *our* disputes.[18] Indeed, if it were not for substantial underlying similarities among humans, we would have considerable difficulty understanding one another at all or evolving a common language, much less acquiring highly articulated, shared practices of aesthetic and moral evaluation.

6

I myself do not know whether to say that this notion of 'matching' belongs to the *concepts* of aesthetic and prudential value, properly so called. Certainly it does not if we identify the concept of *F* as that which every speaker must have in his or her head in order to be a competent speaker of the *F*-vocabulary in our language. But the notion of matching does seem to me to belong to our (shared but usually tacit) understanding of how to think and talk about aesthetic and prudential value.

We acknowledge this in both a forehanded and a backhanded fashion, when we say, as we often do, that aesthetic judgement or a person's own good are *subjective* matters. This way of talking—as well as countless other expressions, such as 'Beauty is in the eye of the beholder' and 'To each his own'—seems to run together two ideas. The first (forehanded) idea is that aesthetic and

---

[17] For some important qualifications, see below.

[18] Could we have a common aesthetic practice with the Martians? That would depend upon how much we could understand of one another's tastes. Do we, therefore, lack a suitably aesthetic subject matter, after all? No, since we can acknowledge that Martians possess real expertise and authority with respect to a whole class of beauties to be found in the world. The aesthetic domain admits incomparabilities. We can see this in an analogy. Paintings need not possess every aesthetic quality in order to be judged beautiful (they are, for example, very dull aurally and usually distasteful gustatorially). Is Vermeer a better painter than Mozart a composer? The infrastructure of aesthetic evaluation need be no more determinate or homogeneous than the practice of aesthetic evaluation itself.

prudential value do not belong to the world of objects independent of how that world is experienced. This idea sits well with the idea of a match, and is not hostile to the existence of a genuine subject matter for aesthetic and prudential judgement, or to the notion of suitably relational criteria of objectivity and correctness. The second (backhanded) idea is expressed when someone who is *questioning* the genuineness of aesthetic and prudential value claims that these are arbitrary matters, fluctuating from person to person in idiosyncratic ways, a reflection of personal taste answering to no objective criteria. This latter view's way of challenging aesthetic and prudential value in effect backhandedly recognizes value's implicit generality. Slogans such as *De gustibus non disputandum est* or 'There's no accounting for taste' are deployed as licences to ignore (except perhaps strategically) any aesthetic judgements just pronounced. 'Well, suit yourself' signals that one has decided that nothing suits everyone, or suits enough people in the relevant community to warrant further aesthetic or prudential discussion in the second person plural.

If aesthetic and prudential value are subjective in the relational sense, is this not yet another way to undermine authority and invite idiosyncrasy and breakdown? How narrow and gerrymandered can the class of subjects be while still providing the requisite infrastructure for a domain of *value*? Ordinarily, it seems, we take the class of subjects to be species-wide, or species-normal, or perhaps at least as wide as a fairly substantial cultural tradition. But cannot we also deploy our value concepts to recognize distinctive value even for *abnormal kinds* of being? Just as there might be beauties accessible to Martians but not us, there might be beauties accessible to humans blessed or cursed with various kinds of abnormal sensory or cognitive capacities. In thinking about such possibilities, the notion of a match does seem to guide us.

Griffin writes: 'Any normal person who is frittering his life away [counting blades of grass, perhaps] has a reason to try to accomplish something with it' (*VJ* 33). That seems right, but he is speaking of normal persons, with normal capacities and motivations to draw upon and develop. Would a severely retarded human among us, whose intrinsic interest in the activity of *counting* is one of the organizing themes of his life, realize no prudential value in so doing? Does he not have a prudential reason to continue, and do we not have a corresponding moral reason to make his endless, repetitive counting possible, perhaps by giving him pleasant, grassy gardens to sit in? But then are we still happy with: 'A very odd person might care a lot about counting the blades of grass in various lawns, but that does nothing to make it valuable' (*VJ* 28)? Evaluation is inherently general, but this is not the same as 'inherently linked to normalcy or species-typicality'. This severely retarded person belongs to that *class of* non-normal humans for whom repetitive counting can be an object of intrinsic concern, and thus potentially a source of prudential value. That may well be generality enough.

Does the generality claim risk losing all content because the classes might be taken to be as finely grained as one likes? Some see the generality of value judgement as flowing from value's *supervenience*.[19] Without deciding that question, we can say that it does appear to be part of our ordinary understanding of supervenience that bare difference in numerical identity (for example) is not sufficient to generate a difference in value. Our evaluative and normative practices support a more substantial notion regarding *which* similarities and differences are, or are not, relevant to value and rightness. We tacitly recognize, as I would put it, that not every arbitrary way in which people differ makes a real difference to the sort of life that would yield for them intrinsically sought-after states, given their capacities and their situations.

It is natural for philosophers to seek a stronger and more intimate grounding of prudential value in our lived, normative, human world than is effected by the Humean taste model. 'Stronger and more intimate' in turn naturally suggests (to philosophers, at any rate) 'conceptual'. But taking prudential value or the good life to be conceptually tied to normal human interests weakens, rather than strengthens, our evaluative language and its claim to objectivity. Our actual evaluative language makes room for a dialogue with normal Martians—or with abnormal humans—in which we understand each other and speak to a common condition and set of concerns. We can put our lives and theirs in a common framework—not only a potentially shared moral perspective, but also a possible common recognition of genuine prudential and aesthetic interests.

The price of being able to use our language to defend our values or explain our reasons non-parochially is to accept that these notions do not reach bottom when they arrive at human normalcy. Remarkably, our human experiences, practices, and interests have led us to create a value language suited for making claims not only human-personally, but universally, non-parochially. That is an objectivity akin to the objectivity our language has achieved in the domain of science, where it has grown from roots in limited

---

[19] Griffin has his own views about supervenience, and they are quite relevant to the present discussion, though space permits only this brief comment on my part. He contests a thesis others have found self-evident—namely, the supervenience of value upon the non-evaluative (sometimes, 'natural') parts of the world (*VJ* 45–8). But we should note that there are two possible supervenience theses: a thesis about value concepts and a thesis about value properties. Value concepts may very well fail to supervene on non-evaluative concepts—this is a way of putting Moore's point in the open-question argument. But this does not mean value properties do not supervene on non-evaluative properties—that anything can possess value without being *made so*, so to speak, by other features of the world. Griffin's doubts about supervenience, I would say, are best construed as concerned with conceptual rather than property supervenience, though he might dispute this.

human experience, practices, and interests, to become capable of sustaining talk about the natural world at large and at small—about particles we will never see, cosmology we will never experience, and laws with content that extends beyond all observed instances.[20] That is the idea, anyhow. Admittedly, these languages of ours, these concepts, are grand. And our practice often fails to live up to them. But, if we have managed not to build specifically human interests into them, then they are not *in principle* parochial or chauvinistic. And if we can manage to look beyond specifically human interests in applying them—the way that, according to Griffin, the Martian anthropologist manages to look beyond specifically Martian interests in applying value terms to us—then they need not be *in practice* parochial or chauvinistic, either.

7

The fact that value judgement speaks in a non-personal voice, even though claims about what is liked or disliked need not, lies behind Hume's own standard of taste as well as behind Griffin's critique of 'the taste model' in modern social science. But has modern social science so lost track of Hume's insights, and reduced the taste model to 'mere liking'? In some corners, social scientists may be as innocent of philosophy as most philosophers are of social science. But not all corners. In particular, social scientists concerned with the assessment of preference are sometimes, in my experience, concerned with—even embarrassed over—the question why, in the end, we should take 'expressed preferences' seriously. As one practitioner of benefit–cost analysis once asked me: 'What do I have to believe in order to do this?'

Here is one thing he might believe, and which fits both Hume on taste and Griffin on preference. Some social scientists, in my experience, believe (perhaps implicitly) something like this.

Let us suppose that we face the task of attempting to measure people's well-being, perhaps in order to study policy consequences or correlations with political activism. If well-being is (on what I have called the Humean taste model) a matter of what matches underlying capacities and sentiments in such a way as to yield intrinsically motivating states of affairs or forms of experi-

---

[20] Certainly, the objectivity in the case of value discourse is objectivity about a fundamentally 'subject-ive' domain—i.e. a domain whose essential constituents are subjects. That is not, however, a principled reason for doubting that the domain is apt for objectivity or opinion- and interest-independent truth. As Griffin notes, 'reality includes, besides rocks and chairs, people. People have minds' (*VJ* 154 n. 6). We could add: reality includes as well other sentient organisms (subjects of experience). This is the ground of well-being in the world. For the distinction between 'subject-ive' and 'subjective', and its relation to questions of objectivity, see P. Railton, 'Subject-ive and objective', *Ratio*, 8 (1995), 259–76.

ence, then we need a lot of evidence.[21] Individuals are far from perfect judges of what, in this sense, 'suits them'. But they are, at least as adults, typically better placed to make such assessments than third parties. Of course, in some areas of life there are third persons who typically are much better placed. Doctors and epidemiologists know more about health effects. Engineers know more about many risks. Economists know more about economic causes and consequences. People in general do not have, and will not come to master, most of this information. So we consult—attribute some authority to—engineers, epidemiologists, and economists when we wish to evaluate the likely risks to health, for example, of various policies or projects. But we also consult—and attribute authority to—those who are most expert on the question of how welcome or unwelcome various health or economic effects would be within the affected populace. That is, we look to the populace itself. To accomplish this empirically, as best we can, we study the choice behaviour ('expressed preferences') of ordinary people. This helps give an idea not only of what matters, but of how much and how widely various things matter.

Certainly some expressed preferences are more credible than others. We all know people whose experience is wider and whose choices seem wiser. But the range of considerations involved in well-being, the complexity of trade-offs in a given life, the diversity of circumstances, the conflicts of interest—all of this tends to make detailed expert judgement no substitute for the expressed preferences of the broad population. (And Griffin is, I think, quite right to urge that those serious about value theory focus on questions of when such expressions are most reliable.) So we arrive at a sort of mixed consumer sovereignty—mixed, that is, with technical expertise and the best available general knowledge of human psychology and of underlying human similarities and differences (knowledge which, among other things, helps us to think about the scope of meaningful interpersonal comparison).

The result is massively imperfect as a way of learning about what will or will not promote well-being. It gives too much weight to mere likings, is distorted by limited information, market imperfections, social inequalities, community pressures, common-sense heuristics and biases—all the ills of the flesh *and* those of the mind. Like political democracy, this has to be the worst

---

[21] We also need to spell out this sort of matching more carefully. For example, if it is *prudential* value we are after, we need to consider intrinsic motivation in so far as this concerns the course or content of the individual's own life (see *VJ* 19). Those concerns need not be entirely experiential or egocentric, but they do need to be tied to a course of life. Mark Overvold has made the most useful suggestions for how to understand this restriction (see 'Self-Interest, Self-Sacrifice, and the Satisfaction of Desires' (University of Michigan Ph.D. dissertation, Ann Arbor: University Microfilms, 1976)). One upshot is to exclude post-mortem states from contributing to a person's well-being. That seems to me right—what happens after I die may affect the meaning of what I have done with my life, or the value my life has for others, but it cannot enlarge or reduce my well-being. Griffin, given his understanding of how accomplishment contributes to the prudential value of a life, would dispute this (*VJ* 54).

system imaginable—except for the alternatives. Social scientists could believe *that.*[22]

8

No one alive today is a more accomplished philosophical investigator of well-being and the theory of value than James Griffin. I would like to think that most of what I have said here will ultimately be agreeable to him. In the great scheme of things, I would like to think, we are on the same side. Indeed, I could have taken as my basic text an important passage from his previous book, *Well-Being*. There he wrote:

if [an objective standard of value] is taken to mean that we can measure changes in a person's well-being just by the amount that he realizes objective values, it must be wrong. . . . In just the way that we can make a fetish of goods—by using them, and not their effect on our lives, as our index of well-being—we can make a fetish of values: even objective universal values matter only by making individual lives better. We have to find some mode of deliberation about values that sees them as they fit into particular lives. The manifestation of these objective values in particular lives is the deepest measure of value.   (*WB* 54–5)

There must, then, be something that stands behind any plausible 'objective list' of prudential value (*VJ* 29–30), and helps us to think about what should be on such a list. This something is, for us in our typical deliberative circumstances, tied to normal features of human motivation. Yet it is not by its nature so tied. Indeed, it is at base no more parochial or particularistic than the idea of a match, or a fit.

---

[22] For some discussion, see various contributions to P. Brett Hammond and Rob Coppock (eds.), *Valuing Health Risks, Costs, and Benefits for Environmental Decision Making* (Washington: National Academy Press, 1990).

5

Objective Human Goods

Andrew Moore

What is well-being? This question is central to two books and many papers James Griffin has published in the last ten years.[1] A key part of his answer is given by the following 'profile of prudential values':

- (*a*) accomplishment
- (*b*) the components of human agency: autonomy, minimum material provision, liberty
- (*c*) understanding
- (*d*) enjoyment
- (*e*) deep personal relations (*WB* 67–8; *VJ* 29–30; WR 159).[2]

Accomplishment is the achievement of something that itself has substantial value. Autonomy is choosing one's own course and making something of one's life according to one's lights. Liberty is the absence of obstacles to action; minimum material provision is 'limbs and senses that work, the minimum material goods to keep body and soul together, freedom from great pain and anxiety' (*WB* 67). Understanding is the responsive grasp of important facts about ourselves and our place in the world. Enjoyment is pleasing, satisfying, or fulfilling experience. Deep personal relations are those 'of love and affection between fairly mature persons' (*VJ* 53).

Having outlined the contents of Griffin's prudential value profile, I turn in Section 1 to a largely expository examination of its structure. In Section 2 I discuss Griffin's distinction between objective and subjective accounts

This paper is dedicated to Jim Griffin with affection, gratitude, and admiration. I also wish to acknowledge with many thanks help from Annette Baier, Kurt Baier, Gillian Brock, Colin Cheyne, Roger Crisp, Paul Griffiths, Brad Hooker, Tim Mulgan, Alan Musgrave, Roy Perrett, Charles Pigden, Christine Swanton, Gwen Taylor, David Ward, Martin Wilkinson, and audiences at Massey University and the University of Otago.

[1] See esp. *WB* and *VJ*. See also ATM, MV, V, HG, and WR.
[2] Disvalues do not appear in Griffin's profile, though he thinks they include ailment, pain, and malfunction (see *VJ* 52–3).

of well-being. I argue that, in general, his account of the prudential values is
subjective, because the values themselves are partly constituted by desire. As
I read him, Griffin also thinks objectivism is mistaken on the question 'What
makes these prudential values valuable?' I argue that he has not yet made a
persuasive case for this view. In Section 3 I examine the contents of Griffin's
prudential-value profile, and argue for the removal of accomplishment,
liberty, and minimum material provision. I conclude with a more tentative
case for rethinking issues of basic prudential value, and for regarding agency
and luck as two key modes of realization for these values.

1

I take Griffin's prudential-value profile to be a summary statement of his views
about which states, relations, and activities are constituents of the well-being
of human individuals. I take his overall aim to be a comprehensive list of the
most general kinds of constituents of well-being, those not subsumable under
any more general prudential value. Call these the *basic* prudential values.[3] The
aim is ambitious, and Griffin does not claim to have finished the job (WR 159;
VJ 66–7, 133–4, 150 n. 19). The life of well-being that is constituted by these
prudential values is analytically distinct from the life valuable to others, or
morally, or aesthetically, or according to a special code, like that of chivalry.
Values or goods of all these other sorts might nevertheless be constituents of
individual well-being (WB 20).[4] Well-being is a matter of prudence, where this
refers to every respect in which life is valuable for the individual whose life it
is. Rough synonyms for 'well-being' include 'utility' (in one sense), 'welfare',
'interests', and 'quality of life' (ATM 48; WB 21; V 297; MV 107). In *Value
Judgement* in particular, Griffin writes more often of 'the good life' and of
'interests' than of 'well-being', but this seems not to mark any change in his
topic.

Griffin's central topic is the life of well-being. Indeed, he argues at one point
for the strong claim that 'prudential assessment has to take whole lives as its
subject' (WB 324 n. 31; see also 54–5). This prudential holism appears,
however, to be inconsistent with Griffin's endorsement of a prudential value
profile. The profile takes valuable parts of life, not whole lives, as its subject.
Deep personal relations and accomplishments can involve decades of activity,
but even they generally do not take a whole lifetime. Minor enjoyment is here

---

[3] For the claim that his profile is of 'irreducibly different' values, see VJ 69, 149 n. 18; MV
101–2.
[4] On perfectionist value, see T. Hurka, *Perfectionism* (New York: Oxford University Press,
1993). For a theory of well-being centred on happiness, see W. Sumner, *Welfare, Happiness, and
Ethics* (Oxford: Clarendon Press, 1996), esp. ch. 6.

today and gone tomorrow, or even more quickly. And so on. It seems that Griffin must drop either his holism or his value profile.

The conflict between Griffin's prudential holism and his value profile is best resolved, in my view, by taking advantage of a distinction between two kinds of prudential assessment. The point of the prudential value profile is to outline all and only the kinds of states, activities, and relations that, *considered on their own*, contribute to life's going well for individuals. One might call these things the 'constituents' of well-being. I take Griffin's view to be that, considered on its own, every instance of a prudential value makes life go that much better for any individual in whose life it is realized, and every such instance would contribute positively to the well-being of anyone in whose life it were to be realized. As he puts it, 'there are prudential values that are valuable in any life' (*WB* 70). If you understand a lot about religious belief or human interdependence, for example, you are that much better off for it. If you do not, you would benefit from its acquisition. These claims stand whether or not the understanding in question generates or would generate further goods or bads. *All-things-considered* prudential assessment, on the other hand, must take whole lives as its subject. It must do so because it must somehow recognize the effect that any given relationship, experience, or activity has throughout one's life. Griffin rejects the strong claim that every instance of a prudential value makes a positive contribution *all things considered* to individual well-being. He notes, for example, that there may be rare persons for whom accomplishment comes or would come at such cost to their own enjoyment, deep personal relations, and other values that for them it is a value simply not worth it overall (*VJ* 30–1; *WB* 33). Whatever is and is not good on its own, the mix and range of prudential values best, all things considered, for an individual depend largely on her or his capacities, talents, and other life circumstances.

Generalizing from Griffin's unfortunate accomplisher cases, it is possible to enjoy a life of well-being without any deep personal relations or accomplishments. Furthermore, any instance of a prudential value, considered on its own, makes a contribution to a good life for the individual in question, but, in general, it will not contribute enough on its own to make life as a whole go well. In short, neither accomplishment nor any other prudential value is necessary or sufficient for a life of well-being.

There are issues of scope concerning Griffin's prudential-value profile. If certain states, activities, and relations contribute to individual well-being wherever they are found, then presumably this is universally so among human beings. In some places, Griffin seems clearly to endorse this view, but in others, his claims concern only individuals in large modern societies.[5]

---

[5] For the endorsements, see *VJ* 59, 64–5, 150 n. 19; *WB* 54, 315 n. 19. For the more restricted claims, see *VJ* 132–4; ATM 51. In this chapter I leave aside issues of prudential value in non-human lives.

One objection to universalism about prudential values is that some values are simply unavailable in certain cultural and historical settings. Suppose, for example, that having a successful legal career or a sophisticated lifestyle is prudentially valuable in itself. Perhaps 'one cannot pursue a legal career except in a society governed by law'.[6] Perhaps the injunction 'be sophisticated' would not even be intelligible to a Neolithic farmer in Upper Syria.[7] And so on. Even if true, however, these unavailability theses do not embarrass universalism about prudential values. It claims that every instance of prudential value contributes to the well-being of every individual in whose life it is realized, and would do so for any individual in whose life it were to be realized. It makes no claims about the availability, even to thought, of any particular prudential value in any specific cultural or historical setting.

Griffin's prudential-value profile is a summary statement of his views about the basic prudential goods. It is his answer to the question, 'Which things are (prudentially) good?' A complete answer would include full details on the nature of enjoyment, accomplishment, and so on. Even then, it would not amount to a complete theory of well-being. In particular, it would lack an account of the good-maker, to answer the question, 'What makes those things (prudentially) good?' The desire theory of well-being is one answer to that question. It claims that their fulfilment of desire is what makes things good, and that the goods themselves are 'states of the world which fulfil desires' (*WB* 7).[8] Its account of the good-maker thus drives its account of the good, in so far as it offers the latter at all. One rival view is that basic prudential goods are given by a profile like Griffin's, and that each good is its own good-maker. This theory's account of the good(s) thus drives its account of the good-maker(s). Other accounts give good(s) and good-maker(s) some independence from each other. The goods might be intellectual rationality, practical rationality, and physical excellence, for example, and the good-maker might be the development of essential human nature.[9] Griffin's account of the prudential good-maker is not in any straightforward way a theory of any of these sorts, though it includes elements of all of them. I examine some of its details shortly.

Given the distinction within theories of well-being between accounts of the good and accounts of the good-maker, distinctions can also be made among

---

[6] J. Raz, *The Morality of Freedom* (Oxford: Clarendon Press, 1986), 310.

[7] C. Taylor, 'Irreducibly Social Goods', in G. Brennan and C. Walsh (eds.), *Rationality, Individualism, and Public Policy* (Canberra Centre for Federal Financial Relations, 1990), 50.

[8] See also DB 135: 'Desire fulfilment seems to me best seen not as a substantive value, but as a formal notion of what it is for something to be prudentially valuable.' Griffin's 'formal notion' is my 'good-maker'. For a simple form of desire theory, see R. Taylor, *Good and Evil* (Buffalo, NY: Prometheus Press, 1984).

[9] See Hurka, *Perfectionism*.

accounts of the good. Griffin has a pluralistic account of the basic prudential goods. Monism is the obvious rival view. Some hedonists argue, for example, that pleasure is the only basic prudential good. Existentialists might reply that freedom is the only basic good. And so on. A less obvious rival for pluralism of Griffin's kind is radical or particularist pluralism, which claims that there are innumerably many basic prudential values, discernible only in the particulars of individual lives.[10] Simple forms of the desire theory seem to be radically pluralistic about the good.

2

I have so far been concerned to set out what I take to be the main structural features of Griffin's account of the prudential goods. Is his profile objective or subjective? Is this even the right place in the theory of well-being to raise the issue? To answer these questions, we need first to look at the objective/subjective distinction itself. Here is Griffin's formulation: 'By "subjective", I mean an account that makes well-being depend upon an individual's own desires, and by "objective" one that makes well-being independent of desires' (*WB* 32).[11] This distinction is exclusive, since no account can make well-being both dependent on and independent of desires. It is not exhaustive, however, because Griffin qualifies 'subjective' with 'individual's own desires', and he does not similarly qualify 'objective'.[12] This could be tidied up, but I shall leave it as it is, and instead say more about objectivity.

I shall understand independence from desires to include independence from the individual's own desires, and from everyone else's too: those of the ideal individual or observer, God, the theorist of well-being, normal human beings, and so on. I take it also to be independence from all actual, counterfactual, informed, and uninformed desires. 'Desire' should itself be construed broadly, to include all preferences, wants, and any other intentional and motivational states that can be fulfilled, where this consists in the desired thing's existing or being the case.

Griffin is sceptical about the objective/subjective distinction: 'the distinction between objective and subjective . . . does not mark an especially crucial distinction. It would be better if these terms (at least in this sense) were put into retirement. But if they are not, if the question "Subjective or objective?"

---

[10] There are analogies between these various pluralisms about prudential standards, and various deontological pluralisms about moral standards. On the latter, see *VJ* 108–9.

[11] See also V 302; *VJ* 35.

[12] Griffin (*VJ* 35) does add the qualification to both 'objective' and 'subjective'.

is pressed, then the answer has to be "Both"' (*WB* 33).[13] The answer cannot be 'Both', since the distinction is exclusive, but perhaps Griffin just means that one part of the best theory of well-being is objectivist and another is subjectivist. Should these terms instead be put into retirement? I think not. Even Griffin's own nuanced conception of well-being can be usefully analysed using them.

If Griffin's objective/subjective distinction is applied to his account of the prudential goods, the results are generally subjectivist. The reason is that most items on his profile are partly constituted by individual desire. Enjoyment is one example (*WB* 18–19). Understanding is another, for Griffin takes this to be partly constituted by agent motivation. Accomplishment typically includes a desire to pull off the valuable achievement in question. Some, perhaps all, deep personal relations necessarily involve a desire for the good of the other person. What makes all these values desire dependent and therefore subjective is the fact that they are partly constituted by desire. The components of agency are more tricky. Kantian conceptions sharply distinguish autonomy from any matter of desire. Higher-order desire accounts, by way of contrast, are straightforwardly subjectivist.[14] Griffin does not say enough about autonomy for his view on this to be placed clearly in either camp. Liberty and minimum material provision, on the other hand, seem not to be constituted by agent desire, so they appear not to be subjective goods.

Griffin's distinction can also be applied to accounts of the prudential good-maker. Desire theories, for example, make the subjectivist claim that their fulfilment of desire or preference makes things good. Objectivists about the good-maker might reply that accomplishment, deep personal relations, and so on develop desire-independent human nature, and that this makes them good. They might alternatively claim that desire-independent reason requires one to pursue the prudential goods, and also makes them goods.[15] Need theories too are sometimes regarded as objectivist accounts. Typically, however, they claim that a need is important just in case one is seriously harmed if it is not met. Since serious harm is itself a matter of individual good (or bad), these need accounts depend upon, and cannot be the basis of, any account of well-being.[16]

---

[13] See also *VJ* 35–6. Griffin adapts his objective/subjective distinction from T. Scanlon, 'Preference and Urgency', *Journal of Philosophy*, 72 (1975), 656–8, who now also has doubts about it. See Scanlon, 'Value, Desire, and Quality of Life', in M. Nussbaum and A. Sen (eds.), *The Quality of Life* (Oxford: Clarendon Press, 1993), esp. 188–9.

[14] Griffin (*VJ* 146–7 n. 3) discusses Kantian conceptions of autonomy. An excellent collection on the nature and value of autonomy is J. Christman (ed.), *The Inner Citadel: Essays on Individual Autonomy* (New York: Oxford University Press, 1989).

[15] On this 'Kantian' view, see *VJ* 59.

[16] On this feature of need accounts, see *WB* 329 n. 24; D. Wiggins, 'Claims of Need', in his *Needs, Values, Truth* (2nd edn., Oxford: Basil Blackwell, 1991), 7 n. 10.

The claim that certain states, activities, and relations are prudentially good in virtue of their own nature or desirability properties is also generally regarded as objectivist. But there is a problem here. If goods have desire-dependent natures, and if these natures make them good, then their good-makers also are desire dependent. For example, if desire is in the nature of enjoyment, and if enjoyment's own nature makes it good, then enjoyment's good-maker too is desire-dependent. Subjectivism about goods plus goods as good-makers thus give birth to subjectivism about good-makers. Rather than go down this track, I suggest we revise Griffin's account of objectivity. Instead of making objectivity simply a matter of desire independence, let us say that an account is objective if and only if it claims that what makes things good is independent of whether they are or would be *objects* of any desire.[17] On this account, even if goods are subjective and their own desirability features make them good, it does not immediately follow that their good-makers too are subjective. That further result follows only if desirability features owe their status as good-makers to their being objects of desire.

This brings us to Griffin's complex account of the good-maker: 'Values are ... what one would want if one properly appreciated the object of desire .... To recognize the nature of the relevant object is to see it under some desirability characterization, such as "accomplishment" or "enjoyment"' (*VJ* 35–6).[18] Griffin appears here initially to endorse the subjectivist view that values are made so by being objects of informed, and perhaps counterfactual, individual desires. 'Informed' turns out, however, to involve 'desirability characterizations', and these pick out 'desirability features'. Desire seems at this point to drop out of the good-making picture, in favour of the view that things are made good by their own desirability features, and that desire re-enters only when we grasp these features, and grasp that those things have them. Griffin himself makes this point more clearly than I can:

What makes us desire the things we desire, when informed, is something about them— *their* features or properties. ... If what really matter are certain sorts of reasons for action, to be found outside desires in qualities of their objects, why not explain well-being directly in terms of them? It does not seem that it is fulfilled desire that is the basis of well-being, but certain of its objects.   (*WB* 17)

I find this line of thought compelling. Griffin does not. It will be easier for me to examine why not if I first have to hand a more detailed account of one specific prudential value. My choice, and it is frequently Griffin's too, is accomplishment.

---

[17] Griffin himself relies on this narrower account of objectivity at least some of the time. See e.g. *WB* 32, and especially his contrast between objective accounts and those that claim things are 'valuable because desired'. I owe this point to Roger Crisp.

[18] Related passages include *VJ* 23–5, 32–6, 41–2, 47–8, 151–2 n. 10; *WB* 12–13.

Griffin sketches as follows the reasoning one might go through to characterize and properly appreciate the prudential value of accomplishment. Suppose you are a happy-go-lucky person, occupied largely with day-to-day pleasures. You are struck by the life of a Socratic type, which seems worthwhile in a way yours is not. It has weight, point, and substance. The Socratic individual achieves something that itself has substantial value. It is not a matter of bare achievement, for one can be a compulsive and widely admired achiever who always sets and realizes goals, yet accomplishes nothing. Nor can accomplishment be secured through such remarkable deeds as goldfish swallowing, walking on one's hands from Oxford to London, flag-pole sitting, or grass-blade counting, even to Guinness book of records standard. These activities might generate amusement, but they lack weight, point, and substance. Here, and in more serious pursuits too, success in the struggle can be enjoyable. But enjoyment is one prudential value, and accomplishment is another. Accomplishment is also distinct from a sense of accomplishment, and from knowledge that one has accomplished. Nor is it the development and exercise of skills. Again, then, what is it? Griffin's answer comes primarily through examples. One might lead a rich and rewarding personal life, or make a work of the art of life, lead a saintly life, save Venice from destruction, discover a safe and effective new disease treatment (even one quickly superseded), write poetry that expresses deep understanding, make a contribution to nuclear disarmament, or give a child a good start in life.[19]

Why *not* say that accomplishments such as those I have just sketched are prudentially valuable simply in virtue of the kinds of activities they are, and not at all because they are or would in certain circumstances be objects of desire? Here is part of Griffin's answer:

Any normal person who is frittering his life away has a reason to accomplish something with it. The more ambitious sort of prudential deliberation that I sketched earlier is what he would have to go through to recognize it as a reason. It neither appeals to some pre-existing member of his personal motivational set, nor is entirely free from desires either: the understanding that is needed is a grasp of certain desirability features, and they owe their status as such to normal human desires. Understanding and motivation cannot here be very sharply separated.   (*VJ* 33)[20]

Griffin seems here to endorse the claim that their own desirability features make accomplishments and other prudentially good things good. The obstacle for objectivists is his further claim that these desirability features owe

[19] For various parts of this accomplishment narrative, see *VJ* 19–20, 56; *WB* 29–30, 64–5; *V* 297–8, 302; ATM 59–61, 63.

[20] See also *VJ* 35–6, 55–6; *V* 302. J. Dancy (Chapter 3, this volume) argues that Griffin's rejection of the distinction between recognition and reaction is actually not radical enough.

their status as such to normal human desires. His rationale is that prudential understanding cannot be sharply separated from motivation. Here is a further statement of both the claim and its rationale: 'Now motivation is internal to something's being a general human interest. That follows from the earlier rejection of any sharp split in these cases between recognition and reaction' (*VJ* 73).

Let us make the internalist assumption that, in Griffin's senses of 'separated' and 'split', prudential understanding and motivation cannot be separated and prudential recognition and reaction cannot be split. It seems to me that, from this assumption on its own, nothing follows about any role for desire in making something a desirability feature, nor about any place for motivation in making something a general human interest. Prudential internalism is compatible with prudential objectivism. It is true that, on Griffin's account, understanding is itself a prudential value, and prudential understanding is one of its varieties (*VJ* 70–1). Understanding prudential values such as accomplishment is consequently one of the things that contributes directly to life's going well. Since motivation is internal to prudential understanding, and reaction is internal to prudential recognition, prudential understanding is to this extent a subjective good. It does not yet follow, however, that desire or motivation plays any good-making role for (prudential) understanding. *A fortiori*, it does not follow that motivation or desire plays any good-making role for anything else, such as accomplishment, that might be an *object* of prudential understanding. In short, from the claim that prudential understanding has a desire-dependent nature, one cannot infer that any of its objects has a desire-dependent good-maker.

Recall Griffin's statement of the objectivist challenge: 'What makes us desire the things we desire, when informed, is something about them— *their* features or properties. But why bother then with informed desire . . . ? It does not seem that it is fulfilled desire that is the basis of well-being, but certain of its objects' (*WB* 17). The objectivist does not claim here that being informed about certain things, rather than desiring them, is the basis of well-being. That claim does presuppose a sharp distinction between recognition and reaction, but it is beside the point. The objectivist claims instead that the *objects* of informed desire and prudential understanding are the basis of well-being. Griffin appears not to join the argument on the objector's ground, and consequently does not satisfactorily answer the objectivist challenge.

I conclude that Griffin's 'recognition–reaction' argument is not persuasive against objectivism about the prudential good-maker. In particular, his internalism about prudential understanding is consistent with and does not count against objectivism. If this is correct, Griffin needs at least one additional premiss to get him from prudential internalism to non-objectivism about the good-maker. One possibility arises from the rejection of a second kind of objectivism.

Griffin distinguishes objectivism as desire independence from objectivism as thought independence. As he puts it: ' "Objective" is also used to mean, roughly, "exists independently of human thought, feeling, knowledge, response . . ." ' (*VJ* 35; see also 7, 60, 141 n. 9). His own view seems to be that prudential values are non-objective in this second sense. He argues, for example, that 'persons generally have to be able to see a prudential value as something to go for if it is to be a prudential value at all' (*WB* 32).[21] The conjunction of this second kind of non-objectivism with internalism about prudential understanding generates the following argument: Prudential values are not objective, in the sense of thought independent. The kind of thought on which they depend is prudential understanding. Prudential understanding necessarily involves motivation. Therefore prudential values themselves depend on motivation. Consequently, they are also not objective, in the sense of being desire independent.

As far as I know, Griffin nowhere explicitly makes the 'objectivity argument' I have just sketched. I shall, therefore, comment on it only briefly. First, even if it goes through, it gives us only a very modest desire dependence in the good-maker. The dependence is only upon a desire that persons in general have to be *able* to have, and the desire in question enters at all only because of its internal connection to acts of value cognition. Secondly, questions arise about the scope of Griffin's claim that persons generally have to be able to see a prudential value as something to go for if it is to be a prudential value at all. If an analogous claim is true for ethics generally, and if analogous claims are true for all judgements,[22] we have here no distinctive desire dependence of prudential goods or good-makers.

The objectivity argument raises large issues. I cannot here adequately deal with them, nor am I sure that Griffin even endorses the argument from which they arise. I shall consequently pursue these matters no further now.

I have argued that, with the possible exception of the objectivity argument, Griffin's main case against prudential objectivism is in fact compatible with that position. In particular, Griffin's arguments are compatible with the objectivist claim that goods are made so by features or properties of theirs that are independent of whether they are or would in certain circumstances be objects of desire. I conclude that Griffin has not yet mounted a persuasive case against objectivism about prudential values.

---

[21] See also *VJ* 20, 27–9, 35–6, 149 nn. 15–17; ATM 51–2. Also relevant is *VJ* 64: 'Accomplishment is a prudential value only because we regard a life without it as wasted.'

[22] Griffin (*VJ* 64–5) considers but sets aside generalizations of these sorts.

3

My earlier discussion of prudential goods focused on the structure of Griffin's prudential-value profile. In the light of the important good-making role he assigns to desirability features, it is time now to assess the contents of his profile. Recall the main details: accomplishment; the components of agency (autonomy, minimum material provision, liberty); understanding; enjoyment; and deep personal relations. Are these all basic prudential values?

Consider first the components of human agency. Griffin sometimes presents autonomy as a basic prudential value (see e.g. *VJ* 52), so I assume that he intends liberty and minimum material provision to have this status too. If there is any basic prudential value here, however, I think it is autonomy alone. If I were merely at liberty, with no obstacles to my actions, and yet no further good came of this, I think I would be no better off for it. If autonomy requires a plurality of worthwhile options, one might sometimes need liberty to keep them open. The mere thought that one is at liberty to do various things can itself be enjoyable. And so on. These are all reductions of the prudential value of liberty to that of other values, however, and they look promising. Now consider minimum material provision. This consists in 'limbs and senses that work, the minimum material goods to keep body and soul together, freedom from great pain and anxiety' (*WB* 67). Freedom from pain and anxiety are absences of certain kinds of ill-being, rather than positive prudential values. If bare togetherness of body and soul is all one has, furthermore, one has little or nothing of well-being; and minimum material goods are only necessaries for this bare togetherness. Finally, limbs and senses that work generally do assist the pursuit of well-being, but it seems to me that their benefit comes only through autonomy, understanding, and the like. In short, with the exception of autonomy, it seems fetishistic to attribute basic prudential value status to the components of human agency.

Deep personal relations, understanding, and accomplishment all figure on Griffin's profile of basic prudential values. I shall consider them together. Accomplishment is the achievement of something that itself has substantial value. Deep personal relations too seem to have substantial value, however, for they contribute directly to making one's life go well (*VJ* 69–70). It consequently seems that securing and sustaining them is a kind of (joint) accomplishment, among however many parties these relations link. Griffin thinks the asymmetrical personal relation of giving a child a good start in life is an accomplishment, so why not also these more symmetrical personal relations? This reductionist strategy can also be applied to understanding, by treating it as the accomplishment of sustained valuable states of comprehension or insight. Reduction to accomplishment in fact seems feasible wherever substantial value is achieved by an agent. This includes autonomy and enjoyable activity, as well as deep personal relations and understanding. One simply sets the threshold for an achievement to be good enough to count as accomplishment wherever one has set the threshold for it to be good enough to count as a token of its own basic value type. In other words, an achievement has *substantial* value whenever it has enough value, considered on its own, to add to the well-being of any individual who realizes it.

I suspect Griffin would reply to the reductionist position I have sketched that accomplishment belongs only among major life-structuring activities, those which give life weight, point, and substance.[23] It has no home among minor contributors to well-being. Griffin does think that understanding and accomplishment overlap at certain points, such as in Charles Darwin's huge advances in the life sciences (*VJ* 26–7; see also 46–7, 70–1; V 317). But perhaps he thinks it at best inflationary to regard (say) the acquisition of a modest new piece of prudential understanding as an accomplishment.

Griffin must overcome several problems if he is to keep accomplishment just for life's weight and point. First, his prudential value profile leaves a large gap between non-accomplishments, such as goldfish swallowing and flagpole sitting, and accomplishments, such as poetry that expresses deep understanding, major research breakthroughs, and giving children good starts in life. He does not specify the thresholds good enough for accomplishment, and it is no easy task for him to do so. He needs a separate threshold for each basic prudential value that is achievable in substantial amounts.[24] Secondly, Griffin's account will generate anomalies over goods not otherwise on his prudential-value profile, when these are achieved to a standard just short of accomplishment. I have in mind artistic or moral or environmental sub-accomplishments. Griffin's approach seems to commit him to the view that any prudential value these sub-accomplishments have is fully reducible in terms of enjoyment, autonomy, and the like. This misses something prudentially important. If the achievement of substantial value of these sorts itself makes a substantial prudential contribution, then achievement of less-than-substantial value also makes a direct prudential contribution, even if a less-than-substantial one. Thirdly, saving accomplishment for life's weight and point at best generates theoretical untidiness in Griffin's profile of basic prudential values. He must claim, I think, that deep personal relations, under-

---

[23] Accomplishments need not structure large amounts of life's *time*. The compositions of Mozart's last year did not take him long. For men, a world record 100 metre sprint takes less than ten seconds. And so on. Accomplishments instead structure large amounts of life's *value*.

[24] Poetry that expresses deep mistakes, or partial understanding of middle-weight matters? Adults who give a child a reasonable but not excellent start? Modest research contributions to the team that discovers the new wonder drug? And so on.

standing, and so on below the threshold for accomplishment are instances of those basic prudential values, but not instances of accomplishment; that accomplishment itself is a distinct prudential value; and that understanding, autonomy, and so on above the threshold are either instances of accomplishment and not instances of their own basic value kinds, or instances of both basic value kinds.

Accomplishment is the achievement of substantial value. Could it be the only basic prudential value? Suppose 'substantial value' is construed in the very broad way I proposed above, and that accomplishment is consequently rebaptized as 'achievement'. This broader value does seem able to accommodate all constituents of well-being that are attributable to the agency of the individual in question. Whether or not this is the whole of well-being depends largely on whether there are prudential goods attributable to fortune, rather than to the agency of the individual concerned. That depends in turn on, amongst other things, whether in the end there is any distinction between agency and luck.

On the face of it, there *are* goods of individual fortune. They come to us not just when we are on the receiving end of pleasure machines and the like,[25] but also near the heart of clear cases of achievement. Suppose, for example, that I have just completed the first proof of a theorem *T*, which I believe has little significance outside my branch of pure mathematics. If some years later it turns out that I have formulated a powerful and perspicuous new description of black holes, then that good fortune arguably affects the nature and prudential value of my achievement. Fortune cannot move things too far from agent intention, of course, or we lose touch with what the agent genuinely achieved. It can nevertheless play some legitimate prudential role (*VJ* 54).[26] To take another example, it seems clear that luck arising from illness, accident, social circumstance, and so on frequently makes the difference between successful and failed attempts to give a child a good start in life.

If achievement is not the only basic prudential value, then might good fortune and achievement nevertheless be the only two? Roughly speaking, good fortune is fortune that bestows goods on people, often independently of their achievements, in deep personal relations, understanding, enjoyment, and so on. It is the good that happens to one. Achievement is the good that one does.

One problem for the view that achievement and good fortune are the

[25] See J. Smart and B. Williams, *Utilitarianism: For and Against* (Cambridge: Cambridge University Press, 1973), 19; R. Nozick, *Anarchy, State, and Utopia* (Oxford: Basil Blackwell, 1974), 42–5.

[26] Griffin (*WB* 23) offers the example of Bertrand Russell, who thought success in reducing the probability of nuclear war might keep his life from futility. Here, too, luck played a leading role.

only basic prudential values is that strands of both seem to be ever-present, threaded tightly through one another. Even with goods of fortune, one's own agency can play a role; even in clear cases of achievement, luck can loom large. Both are realized on nearly every occasion of individual benefit. A second and more important objection to the inclusion of achievement and good fortune on any profile of basic prudential values is that these are really ways in which values are realized. They are not themselves values, basic or otherwise. They are modes of realization of values.

On Griffin's account, accomplishment is the achievement of substantial value. I have argued that 'accomplishment' should be turned into 'achievement'. Whether or not this is done, it should, I think, also be removed from Griffin's prudential value profile. Along with good fortune, it should instead be recognized separately as a mode of realization of value. Or rather, since dis-value too is realized in individual lives, the modes should be specified neu-trally as agency and luck. I have also argued that all components of human agency except autonomy should be removed from Griffin's profile. If all these recommendations were implemented, we would have agency and luck as modes of value, and autonomy, understanding, enjoyment, and deep personal relations as basic prudential values. Problems would remain. In particular, it seems that prudentially important aesthetic, moral, and other accomplish-ments would disappear along with their parent value.

Two main responses suggest themselves. Neither can be pursued in any detail here. One is to reassert the claims of accomplishment to basic prudential-value status, and to try to clear the obstacles in the path of this move. A more revisionary response is to rethink the basic values, perhaps starting with broad categories such as intellectual value, agency value, experi-ential value, relationship value, aesthetic value, environmental value, and moral value. One might then move to more specific candidates for basic value status. An account of basic disvalues would also be needed. Prudential value would just be value of some basic sort realized in individual lives through agency, or luck, or a mix of both. It would consequently not itself be theoret-ically basic. Only individually realizable values could be constituents of human well-being. The best general theory of value might even turn out to include things that no individual can realize. For example, certain sorts of environmental value might have this character.

4

I have argued in this chapter for the viability and importance in the theory of well-being of a distinction between goods and good-makers. In my view, the best way forward for accounts of human good is along these twin tracks, following James Griffin for much of the journey. I have also argued that Griffin's distinction between objective and subjective accounts can illuminate our travels on both tracks.

6

Does the Evaluative Supervene on the Natural?

Michael Smith

One of the few claims accepted by nearly everyone writing about the nature of value is that the evaluative features of things supervene on their natural features. Take any two persons, actions, characters, or states of affairs that are identical in all of their naturalistic features: every naturalistic feature that is a feature of the one is a feature of the other, and vice versa. These two persons, actions, characters, or states of affairs must be identical in evaluative respects as well. There can be no evaluative difference without a naturalistic difference. So, at any rate, it is said.

Those who flout the supervenience requirement when they make evaluative judgements are supposed thereby to reveal themselves to be incompetent in their use of evaluative terms. The supervenience of the evaluative on the natural thus purports to operate as a conceptual constraint on evaluative judgement. This too is accepted by nearly everyone writing about the nature of value. Given that supervenience operates as a conceptual constraint on evaluative judgement, it follows that the right way of thinking about an evaluative theory, at least in its most abstract form, is as a mapping of natural features onto evaluative features. An evaluative theory, in its most abstract form, is thus simply a long list of supervenience conditionals, conditionals such as 'If objects have natural features N then they have evaluative features E', 'If objects have natural features N^* then they have evaluative features E^*', and so on.

Not everyone is convinced that the evaluative does supervene on the natural, however. In recent work James Griffin has expressed his misgivings in the following terms. 'Supervenience is often regarded as an indisputable fact

Thanks to Roger Crisp, Richard Holton, Brad Hooker, and Frank Jackson for very helpful comments on a draft of this chapter.

about value that we must come to terms with. I doubt, though, that values are supervenient. I put it inconclusively because I think that, for reasons I shall come to, it is not easy to say' (v. 316).[1] Griffin then goes on to provide a number of reasons for thinking that the supervenience of the evaluative on the natural demands, at the very least, serious rethinking, if not outright rejection.

Griffin's attack on the claim that the evaluative supervenes on the natural comes as a welcome prompt. As with many theses put forward as candidate conceptual truths in philosophy, and subsequently accepted as such by philosophers quite generally, it is not until someone asks 'Why?' that we begin to think more carefully about what, exactly, the thesis we profess to accept really amounts to. When we ask ourselves what the thesis is, and why we believe it, we all too often discover how inadequate the answers we come up with really are. The candidate conceptual truth is just an empty form of words with no clear content. So we discover all too often. But, I will argue, it is not what we discover when we ask what it means to say that the evaluative supervenes on the natural.

The chapter is in seven main sections. In the first three sections I characterize the natural features upon which evaluative features are supposed to supervene. In the fourth section I consider, and reject, a further restriction on the class of natural features, a restriction proposed by Griffin. In the fifth section I consider, and argue against, Griffin's suggestion that a commitment to the supervenience of the evaluative on the natural requires commitment to a bogus fact/value gap. In the sixth section I provide an argument for the claim that the evaluative supervenes on the natural. And then in the seventh and final main section I explain what I take myself to have shown and what I take myself not to have shown. In a brief conclusion I summarize the main points made in the chapter.

1. A TRIVIALIZING DEFINITION OF 'NATURAL'

We are told that the evaluative features of things supervene on their natural features. But what makes something a natural feature? Without an adequate answer to this question the supervenience thesis will not even get off the ground.

It might be thought that we can afford to be relaxed about this. Perhaps we should just say that the natural features of things are those that we would all

---

[1] The same arguments appear in *VJ*, ch. III.

ordinarily agree they have as part of our everyday commerce with them: the painfulness of the feeling I have in my neck, the telling of an embarrassing joke about someone behind his back, the writing of certain words, and so on and so forth. They are, if you like, the features that we commonsensically ascribe to persons, acts, states of affairs, and the like. But, given the role that the concept of the natural has to play in a statement of the supervenience thesis, it seems to me that we need something much more constrained than this. The problem is that, if our conception of the natural is too relaxed, then the claim that the evaluative features of things supervene on their natural features is in danger of utter trivialization.

Suppose, for example, we are very relaxed. Because 'is good' functions grammatically as a predicate, it follows that we can move back and forth between saying 'Bloggs leads a good life', on the one hand, and 'The life Bloggs leads has the property of being good', on the other. Though utterly pleonastic, it thus looks as though we commonsensically ascribe the feature of being good to lives.[2] But then, if to be a natural feature is to be a property that we commonsensically ascribe to objects, it seems that being good turns out to be a natural feature in its own right. It is a natural feature simply in virtue of the fact that 'is good' functions grammatically as a predicate. The claim that there can be no difference between the value of two objects if they have the same natural properties then turns out to be utterly trivial, because the difference in value *itself* amounts to a difference in natural features.

Given that this completely trivial doctrine is not what is intended by the claim that the evaluative supervenes on the natural, it follows that we need to come up with a more circumscribed conception of the natural. While talk of evaluative features may be utterly pleonastic, talk of natural features cannot be: not, at any rate, if we wish to formulate a non-trivial supervenience thesis.

2. A BETTER DEFINITION OF 'NATURAL'

We began with the idea that the natural features of things are those that we would all ordinarily agree they have as part of our everyday commerce with them. This idea can be developed in a more circumscribed way if we insist, commonsensically I think, that the features of objects that we would all ordinarily agree they have as part of our everyday commerce with them are

[2] Steve Schiffer talks about pleonastic properties in his *Remnants of Meaning* (Cambridge, Mass.: MIT Press, 1987), 51.

those to which we need to appeal in *causally explaining* our commerce with them.

In essence this is what G. E. Moore had in mind when he suggested that the natural features of objects are those that are the subject matter of the natural sciences.[3] Or, rather, it is what Moore had in mind provided we have a very liberal conception of what it is for something to be a natural science, a conception according to which, as Griffin usefully puts it, 'a natural science is any systematic set of empirical regularities' (V 306). Thus, according to Moore's suggestion, as his suggestion is developed by Griffin, natural properties are best thought of as those properties of objects—including those ordinary, everyday, properties that we ascribe to macroscopic objects—that figure in statements of empirical regularities.

Note how commonsensical this suggestion really is. The painfulness of the feeling I have in my neck, the telling of an embarrassing joke about someone behind his back, the writing of certain words, and so on, all these turn out to be natural features, just as we said they were initially. They are all natural features because they are all properties that figure in empirical regularities. The pain causally explains my going to the doctor. The telling of the embarrassing joke about someone behind his back causally explains the subsequent shock that he experiences when he hears about it. The writing of certain words causally explains the acquisition of someone else's belief as regards the content of those words when he reads them. And so we could go on. Moore's suggestion, as developed by Griffin, thus delivers up as natural features a set of features that is easily recognizable as the ordinary, everyday, features of objects with which we have commerce.

We are now in a position to state a non-trivial supervenience thesis. Any two objects that are alike in those of their features that figure in empirical regularities—that is, any two objects that are such that every property that figures in an empirical regularity that is a property of the one is a property of the other, and vice versa—must be alike in their evaluative features as well. Unfortunately, however, the thesis so stated also presupposes something that some might think is false. It presupposes, after all, that properties that do not figure in empirical regularities make no difference at all to value. But, once it is admitted that properties that do figure in empirical regularities can make a difference to value, it might be thought that we have to admit that properties

---

[3] G. E. Moore, *Principia Ethica* (Cambridge: Cambridge University Press, 1903), 40–1. It is noteworthy that David Wiggins, who seems to accept Moore's account of the distinction between the natural and the non-natural, goes on to claim that non-natural properties *can* figure in causal explanations: see his 'Postscript', in *Needs, Values, Truth* (Oxford: Blackwell, 1987), 355. Is this a real disagreement between Wiggins and me? I do not think so. Rather I suspect that Wiggins's claim reflects a conservative conception of what it is for something to be a natural science, coupled with a liberal conception of the properties that can figure in causal explanations.

that do not figure in empirical regularities, but that at least could have figured in such a regularity, can make a difference to value as well. Let me illustrate this point with an example.[4]

Imagine that in the actual world we believe property P to be the most beautiful feature we have ever seen. Of course, since we have managed to form a belief about P, it follows that P does figure in some sort of empirical regularity in the actual world. But now imagine that P is also instantiated in a possible world in which it does not figure in any empirical regularity. What should we say about P in that possible world? It seems at least conceivable—at least on the line of objection that I am presently considering—that we should say that the most beautiful feature we have ever seen is instantiated in the imagined possible world. If what made P beautiful was not the fact that it figured in any empirical regularity, but rather just its intrinsic nature, then the fact that it does not figure in an empirical regularity in that world seems to be neither here nor there.

If this is correct, however, then we have a potential counter-example to the supervenience thesis just stated. Imagine a pair of objects that are identical in all of the properties they have that figure in empirical regularities. In addition, however, imagine that one of these objects also has P and that the other lacks P, where P is a property that figures in no empirical regularity at all. If the situation is as described above, then we must surely suppose that these two objects will differ in their value, notwithstanding the fact that they are identical in all of those of their features that figure in empirical regularities. They will differ in their value because one of them—the one with P—will have a feature that is the most beautiful we have ever seen (though presumably we will not see it, if it figures in no empirical regularity) and the other—the one without P—will not.

Can we modify the definition of a natural property suggested by Moore and developed by Griffin so as to avoid this objection? It seems to me that we can. We can retreat to the view that what is crucial to the idea of a natural property is not the fact that natural properties *do in fact* figure in an empirical regularity—whether or not P figures in an empirical regularity is, after all, an extrinsic fact about it, a matter of whether or not it happens to be instantiated in a regular pattern throughout space and time—but rather the fact that it *could* figure in an empirical regularity. P may not figure in an empirical regularity in fact, but it should count as a natural property anyway, in the terms required by the supervenience thesis, because it would if it were instantiated in a possible world in which it was part of a regular pattern. A natural property, let us say, is thus any property that could figure in an empirical regularity; or, as I shall put it from here on, any property that is *such as to* figure in an empirical regularity.

---

[4] See Mark van Roojen, 'Moral Functionalism and Moral Reductionism', *Philosophical Quarterly*, 46 (1996), 77–81.

Armed with this amended account of what it is to be a natural property, the modified supervenience thesis can be stated in the following terms. Any two objects that are identical in those of their features that are such as to figure in empirical regularities—that is, any two objects that are such that every property that is such as to figure in an empirical regularity that is a property of the one is a property of the other, and vice versa—must be identical in their evaluative features as well. The modified supervenience thesis differs from the thesis stated earlier in that it assigns no special significance to the properties that do in fact figure in empirical regularities. What is important, from the point of view of value, is whether objects are alike in those of their properties that are such as to figure in empirical regularities: that is, those of their properties that do or could figure in such regularities.

The supervenience thesis so stated is still non-trivial provided it is a non-trivial fact about evaluative features, if it is a fact about them at all, that they are such as to figure in empirical regularities. And this assumption in turn seems to be very plausible. Certainly the fact that evaluative features are such as to figure in empirical regularities does not follow trivially from the superficial grammar of evaluative language. If we think that evaluative features are such as to figure in empirical regularities, then, it seems, that would have to be something we come to believe as a consequence of some non-trivial argument, an argument that proceeds by allowing us to identify evaluative features with features whose status as natural features is established independently.[5]

This is just as it should be. The supervenience thesis itself should not rule out the possibility of a non-trivial argument for the claim that evaluative features are natural features. Evaluative naturalism is a possible position on the metaethical landscape, after all. All supervenience requires is that, if evaluative naturalism is true, then it needs to be shown to be true by some such non-trivial argument. Evaluative naturalism cannot follow trivially from the definition of 'naturalism'. It seems that this is indeed the case if we define natural features as those that are such as to figure in empirical regularities.[6]

---

[5] For an account of just how non-trivial the argument would have to be, see Section 5. There I discuss whether the supervenience thesis has any bearing on the debate between evaluative realists and irrealists, and the debate between those realists who are evaluative naturalists and those realists who are non-naturalists. My claim is that the supervenience of the evaluative on the natural is consistent with all these views. For the purposes of understanding the supervenience thesis, talk of evaluative features is utterly pleonastic.

[6] Is the category of the natural vague, when it is so characterized? Griffin thinks it is (V 306). Let us suppose we agree. It is important to realize that it need not follow from this that it is vague whether or not evaluative features supervene on natural features. Suppose that evaluative features do supervene on certain features whose status as natural is vague. It will be vague whether evaluative features supervene on natural features only if the features whose status as natural is vague do not themselves supervene on features whose status as natural is determinate. See also n. 10 below.

3. A FURTHER RESTRICTION ON THE CLASS OF NATURAL PROPERTIES

There remain some ambiguities in the supervenience thesis, ambiguities that need to be removed before we go any further. In removing these ambiguities we will see the need further to restrict the class of the natural upon which the evaluative can plausibly be said to supervene.

The supervenience thesis has us doing pair-wise comparisons of objects with the same natural features. But are we allowed to consider any pair of objects, without regard to the possible worlds in which those objects happen to exist, or are we restricted to comparing pairs of objects where both objects exist in the same possible world? In other words, does the supervenience thesis purport to tell us that objects with the same natural properties, even objects in different possible worlds from each other, have the same value? Or does it tell us that, within a single possible world, pairs of objects with the same natural properties cannot differ in value? The latter allows that an object with those same natural properties in another possible world may have a different value. The former precludes this. The latter is an *intra-world* supervenience claim. The former is an *inter-world* claim.

The only plausible answer—the answer I assumed in my previous remarks about beauty—is that the supervenience thesis is an inter-world claim, not merely an intra-world claim. To suppose otherwise is to suppose that the mere fact that an object happens to exist in *this* particular possible world as opposed to *that* particular possible world can somehow make a difference to its value, independently of the features it has in those worlds that could be possessed by objects in other possible worlds. This, after all, would seem to be the only reason available to explain why, on the intra-world claim, objects with the same natural features in different possible worlds can differ in value. But this seems incoherent on the face of it.

The reason is that particularity itself is entirely arbitrary, from the evaluative point of view. The fact that my life is Michael Smith's life, say, cannot be what makes mine a good life or a bad life, because it could make such a difference only if being Michael Smith's life was somehow a special feature of a life, a feature that is special in a way that being Joe Bloggs's life or John Doe's life is not. But the fact that a life is Michael Smith's life seems to be of no consequence or significance in and of itself. Of course, the fact that my life has other features—the fact that it is a life with a certain amount of pleasure and pain in it, a life in which there have been certain successes and failures, and so on—could be such as to make my life something special. The features that make my life something special might even uniquely pick my life out in actuality. But it is consistent with this that the fact that the life that has these features in actuality is Michael Smith's life is evaluatively irrelevant. Someone else's life in another possible world could have precisely these features.[7]

It therefore seems to me that a ban on particularity is a further constraint that needs to be placed on the ordinary, everyday, features that count as natural features, in the sense required by the supervenience thesis. Value cannot supervene on facts about particularity, so, in the sense of 'natural' required by the supervenience thesis, no natural features can be defined in terms of particulars.[8] But, if this is right, then it follows immediately that the fact that an object happens to exist in *this particular possible world*, as opposed to *that particular possible world*, must also be irrelevant to the value of that object. In other words, if an object is good or bad then it must be so in virtue of its possession of features that could be possessed by objects in other possible worlds. It follows that the supervenience of the evaluative on the natural is an inter-world supervenience claim, not merely an intra-world claim.[9]

There is another related ambiguity in the supervenience thesis as well. As we are now understanding the supervenience of the evaluative on the natural, it has us doing pair-wise comparisons of all possible objects, even objects that exist in different possible worlds from each other. For each of these pairs it purports to tell us that they cannot differ in their evaluative properties if they are exactly alike in their natural properties, where natural properties are

[7] The modern champion of this constraint is, of course, R. M. Hare. See his discussions of universalizability in *The Language of Morals* (Oxford: Clarendon Press, 1952), and, in more recent times, in *Moral Thinking* (Oxford: Clarendon Press, 1981).

[8] Note that the ban on particularity is indeed a *further* ban. It does not follow straight from the fact that natural features are those that are such as to figure in empirical regularities. There is, after all, an empirical regularity connecting persistently and belligerently asking Joe Bloggs questions with giving Joe Bloggs a headache. Persistently and belligerently asking questions of Joe Bloggs, as opposed to John Doe, is the feature of acts we need to appeal to if our aim is causally to explain giving Joe Bloggs, as opposed to John Doe, a headache.

[9] In *Spreading the Word* (Oxford: Clarendon Press, 1984), Simon Blackburn seems to suggest that the supervenience of the moral on the natural is an intra-world supervenience claim (p. 184). In fact, Blackburn would not disagree with the point just made in the text, however. Blackburn's point is that those who fail to apply 'good' to objects with the naturalistic features that in fact make them good need betray no failure of competence in their use of evaluative concepts. There is, then, a possible world in which someone without conceptual confusion applies 'good' to objects with natural properties that do not make them good. But, he says, people would betray a failure of competence if they both claimed that objects with certain naturalistic features were good, and yet failed to go on to apply 'good' to all possible objects with all and only the same naturalistic features. Blackburn's point about conceptual competence is thus evidently consistent with—indeed, it presupposes—the point just made in the text, which is that it is a conceptual truth that, if objects with certain naturalistic features are good in the actual world, then all possible objects with all and only those same naturalistic features are likewise good. For an irrealist account of what it is to accept a supervenience conditional, see the discussion in Section 5 below.

those that are such as to figure in empirical regularities, and that, further, are not defined in terms of particulars. (From here on I take this last qualification as read.) But when we talk of those of an object's properties that are such as to figure in empirical regularities, we might have in mind two quite different things.

On the one hand, without regard to the possible world in which the object we are considering happens to exist, we might have in mind those of its properties that are such as to figure in empirical regularities in a particular possible world: the particular properties that happen to be such as to figure in empirical regularities in actuality, say. If we think of an object's natural properties in this way, then what the supervenience thesis tells us is that the only properties that can make a difference to an object's value, in any possible world, are those that happen to be such as to figure in empirical regularities in actuality. Two objects in any possible world that are exactly alike in respect of these properties—those that happen to be such as to figure in empirical regularities in the actual world, say—are alike in their evaluative properties no matter what other properties they possess. Other properties—properties that these objects have that are such as to figure in empirical regularities in the possible world in which these objects exist, for example, but not in actuality—are irrelevant to the value of those objects.

On the other hand, when we talk about those of an object's properties that are such as to figure in empirical regularities, we might have in mind all of those properties, whatever they might happen to be, that are such as to figure in empirical regularities in the possible world in which the object we are considering happens to exist. If we were to understand what an object's natural properties are in this way, then the supervenience thesis would tell us that any two objects that are exactly alike in respect of the properties they possess, where these properties are chosen from among those that are such as to figure in empirical regularities in the possible worlds in which they happen to exist, must be alike in respect of value. On this way of thinking, the properties that are such as to figure in empirical regularities in the actual world are not a privileged set with regard to value. Any properties that are such as to figure in empirical regularities in any possible world can potentially make a difference to the value of an object in that possible world.

Once we spell out this ambiguity in the notion of a natural property, it is, I think, plain that the only plausible way to interpret the supervenience thesis is as the claim that objects that are alike in all of their natural properties in the second of the two ways just described, not the first, must be alike in respect of their value. To think otherwise is once again to suppose that the mere fact that properties happen to be such as to figure in empirical regularities in a particular possible world—the actual world, say—is somehow important from the point of view of value. But the fact that properties happen to be such as to figure in empirical regularities in a particular possible world seems once again to be an evaluatively irrelevant fact about them. To suppose that they can alone contribute to value is once again to suppose that particularity can make a difference to value.

It is important to note that this is not to deny that we might eventually come to the conclusion that the only properties that can contribute to the value of an object are properties that happen to figure in empirical regularities in, say, the actual world. For example, in the course of constructing a theory of prudential value, we might convince ourselves that certain properties that figure in empirical regularities in the actual world—pleasure and pain, say—are the only *possible* sources of intrinsic value of a life. For this reason we might go on to conclude that the value of any possible life supervenes on facts about properties that happen to figure in empirical regularities in the actual world: any two possible lives that are identical in terms of certain properties that happen to figure in empirical regularities in the actual world—specifically, pleasure and pain—are identical in value.

The important point about this way of coming to the conclusion that certain properties that happen to figure in empirical regularities in the actual world are especially significant from the point of view of value, however, is that what makes them especially significant is not the fact that they happen to figure in empirical regularities in the actual world, but rather the fact that they emerge as significant in the most plausible theory of prudential value. The latter fact, unlike the former, is an evaluatively significant fact about a property *par excellence*. Prior to constructing a theory of prudential value, then, we should leave it as an open question whether there are sources of intrinsic value that are not present in the actual world, but that are present only in other possible worlds in virtue of the empirical regularities in which those properties are such as to figure in those worlds. That is, we should leave it an open question whether we are cut off from all sorts of sources of intrinsic value in our lives by the fact that the properties that happen to be such as to figure in empirical regularities in the actual world are only some among the many possible such properties. The supervenience thesis itself must, therefore, be interpreted in the second of the two ways described, not the first.

Let me sum up the argument so far.

I have tried to spell out the claim that the evaluative supervenes on the natural in a non-trivial way. In essence this has required me to spell out what a natural property is in such a way that it is a non-trivial fact about evaluative features that they are natural properties, if indeed evaluative features are natural properties (indeed, if evaluative features are features at all, in anything other than a pleonastic sense). My suggestion has been that natural properties are all and only those properties that are such as to figure in empirical regularities, with the further proviso that, in characterizing these properties, we mention no particulars. Given this account of what natural properties are, we should understand the claim that the evaluative supervenes on the natural in terms of the following inter-world supervenience claim.

Consider any pair of objects in any two possible worlds. If every non-particular property that is such as to figure in an empirical regularity in the possible world in which the first object exists, and that happens to be a property of the first object, both is a property that is such as to figure in an empirical regularity in the possible world in which the other object exists, and happens to be a property of that other object, and vice versa (that is, if every non-particular property that is such as to figure in an empirical regularity in the possible world in which the second object exists, and happens to be a property of the second object, both is a property that is such as to figure in an empirical regularity in the possible world in which the first object exists, and happens to be a property of the first object), then, if the first object has a certain evaluative feature, so does the second, and vice versa (that is, if the second object has a certain evaluative feature, so does the first).

My aim in the sections that follow is further to clarify and defend the claim that the evaluative supervenes on the natural in this sense. Though, as we will see in the next section, stronger supervenience claims might be true, these stronger supervenience claims are not plausibly thought to be conceptual truths. The supervenience thesis just stated is the strongest that can plausibly be suggested to be a conceptual truth. So, at any rate, I want to argue.

4. DO WE NEED TO ADD A FURTHER RESTRICTION ON THE CLASS OF NATURAL PROPERTIES?

Griffin thinks that the supervenience thesis I have just described needs to be further constrained in order to be interesting. But he thinks that further constraining the thesis is problematic because, once we add the further constraint that is required, the supervenience thesis looks false.

The further constraint Griffin thinks the supervenience thesis requires is outlined in the following passage.

It is part of the definition of supervenience, as it stands, that the properties supervened upon are specified according to kind, and are of a different kind from the supervening properties. And the specification makes the relation non-tautological: the properties supervened upon are not defined as 'any properties, regardless of type, relevant to something's having the supervening property' (e.g. in the present case, relevant to being valuable), but as being of one independently specified kind (e.g. in the present case, natural properties). But I think that something yet stronger is intended. We do not, in the present case, mean any natural property at all, but only ones that appear in explanatory regularities at the natural level, and those explanatory regularities mention kinds of spatial and temporal relations but do not mention such particulars as, say, occurring today and in Parks Road, Oxford. But I think that we have to go somewhat further and add a relevance requirement. . . . What we are interested in is whether values supervene not on any natural properties, but some subclass of the natural, a subclass relevant to something's being valuable. Though it is not easy to specify the subclass, I think we should accept the relevance limitation that it represents. Most moral philosophers do.   (V 314–15)

The constraint is thus to be a further constraint on the class of natural properties. The natural properties on which the evaluative supervenes are a 'subclass of the natural': those 'relevant to something's being valuable'.

Griffin's reason for thinking that a relevance limitation of this sort is required in order to make the supervenience thesis interesting is explained in a later passage.

Can we supply difference in prudential value without any difference in relevant natural properties? I think that the answer is unclear. If we could mention any natural property to establish a difference, then we could always, though uninterestingly, come up with one. Smith's poetry is a genuine accomplishment; Jones's poetry, just as long, varied, innovative, and so on, is not. But Smith and Jones must at least have written in different-coloured ink or in different places. But these differences will not do; we need properties that are 'relevant' in the sense explained earlier.   (V 317)

The reason we need to add a relevance limitation is thus supposed to be that, without it, the claim that the evaluative supervenes on the natural is uninteresting. It is uninteresting because we can always 'though uninterestingly' come up with a naturalistic difference between any two objects whose value we wish to compare.

But once we add the relevance limitation Griffin thinks that the claim that the evaluative supervenes on the natural looks like it might well be false. The passage just quoted continues as follows: 'can we supply difference in prudential value without any difference in relevant natural properties? I think that the answer is unclear . . . It is the relevance limitation in particular that seems to me to introduce a measure of doubt. A lot that is natural is not relevant, and a lot that is relevant is not natural' (V 317). Griffin thus concludes that the supervenience of the evaluative on the natural suffers from a fatal flaw. With the relevance limitation on natural properties the supervenience thesis seems to be false. But without it it is uninteresting. The defender of the supervenience thesis should therefore choose their poison.

Quite a lot needs be said in response to this argument.

Griffin claims that the supervenience thesis looks to be false once we add the relevance limitation. His reason for thinking this is that, as he puts it, 'a lot that is natural is not relevant, and a lot that is relevant is not natural' (V 317). The way his argument develops, it is plain what he means. Once we add the relevance limitation to the properties on which evaluative features supervene, we open the door to the possibility that other *evaluative* features are relevant. But, while this last idea might have some independent plausibility— I discuss the idea at some length in Section 7 below—I do not see how Griffin thinks it can be embraced by someone who accepts his official definition of what it is for a property to be relevant. According to his official definition, the relevant properties are a *subclass of the natural*. But it follows immediately from this that *only* natural properties can be relevant. Nothing can be a member of a subclass of the natural, after all, that is not a member of the class of the natural.[10]

Next consider Griffin's suggestion that the supervenience thesis without the relevance limitation is uninteresting. His reason for thinking this is that we can always supply a naturalistic difference between two objects that we think differ in value, and that we must therefore think differ in naturalistic features, if the supervenience thesis is correct. Suppose, as in the example he considers, we are comparing the poetry that Smith writes with the poetry that Jones writes, and we think that Smith's is superior. 'Smith and Jones must at least have written in different coloured ink or in different places' (V 317). But why does Griffin think that the supervenience thesis puts any constraint at all on our relative assessments of the value of the poetry that Smith writes and the poetry that Jones writes?

Remember that the supervenience thesis without the relevance limitation that I have characterized above is an *inter-world* supervenience claim. It tells us that two objects with exactly the same naturalistic features, even objects in different possible worlds, must be exactly alike in terms of their evaluative features. It is, therefore, consistent with this inter-world supervenience thesis that no other object in the actual world has exactly the same naturalistic features as the poetry that Smith writes in the actual world. So perhaps Griffin is right that Smith's and Jones's poetry will not have the same naturalistic features. But it does not follow from this that the inter-world supervenience thesis is thereby made uninteresting.

[10] It might be thought that Griffin's real concern at this point is, as he puts it elsewhere, 'the fuzziness of the notion of the natural' (V 310). But, if he is concerned with vagueness, then he did not need to add a relevance limitation in order to bring that concern out. Even without a relevance limitation we can see that, if the evaluative supervenes on a class of properties whose status as natural is vague, then it will be vague whether, in virtue of supervening on those properties, the evaluative meets the supervenience condition. But remember what I said in n. 6 above.

What would make the inter-world supervenience uninteresting is if there were no *possible* object with exactly the same natural features as the poetry that Smith writes. But, given just a principle of plenitude about possibilia, we know that there most certainly is a possible world in which there is poetry written by someone else, not Smith, with exactly the same naturalistic features as the poetry that Smith writes. And what the inter-world supervenience thesis that I have characterized above tells us is that, if Smith's poetry has a certain value, then so does this other person's poetry in this other possible world. Griffin's claim that without a relevance limitation the supervenience thesis becomes uninteresting thus seems to me to lapse.

But not only does Griffin's reason for adding a relevance limitation lapse; it seems to me that he was quite wrong to suggest that we should even consider adding a relevance limitation in the first place. The supervenience thesis that we are trying to state is supposed to be a conceptual truth. The question we must, therefore, ask in deciding whether or not to add a relevance limitation is thus not whether most moral philosophers would accept a supervenience thesis with a relevance limitation, but rather whether such a supervenience thesis would be a plausible candidate for a conceptual truth. For that to be so we would have to be able to defend the particular relevance limitation we came up with as a conceptual truth. But any particular relevance limitation we might come up with would surely be a substantive evaluative truth, one that reflects our commitment to one particular evaluative theory rather than another.[11] And, worse still, there are substantive views about the nature of value, views that it seems to me we should not rule out as based on *conceptual* confusion, according to which no relevance limitation at all is defensible. What I have in mind are the views defended by particularists.[12]

According to particularists about value, the very best we can do when we try to construct an evaluative theory is to supply an endless list of supervenience conditionals: a mapping of every possible total way objects could be naturalistically onto evaluative features. This is because, according to

---

[11] One of the questions Griffin is concerned to answer is how we are to distinguish one kind of value from another (V 310–11 n. 14). How, for example, do we distinguish prudential values from moral values? Do we not need a relevance limitation in order to do this? The answer to this question is much the same as I have just said in the text. The difference between the moral and the prudential is extremely vague, and that vagueness in part reflects the fact that there is no conceptual barrier to people holding different substantive moral and prudential theories from each other, theories that draw the border between the moral and the prudential at different places. It therefore seems to me to be best if we do not distinguish prudential values from moral values at the most abstract conceptual level, but rather allow that distinction to get fixed by the substance of the theories that people happen to hold. For an example of just how vague we might have to be in order to distinguish the moral from the non-moral, see my own characterization of the difference between moral reasons and non-moral reasons in chapter 6 of *The Moral Problem* (Oxford: Blackwell, 1994).

[12] See e.g. Jonathan Dancy, 'Ethical Particularism and Morally Relevant Properties', *Mind*, 92 (1983), 367–85, and also his *Moral Reasons* (Oxford: Blackwell, 1993), chs. 4, 5, 6.

particularists, the evaluative difference any particular naturalistic feature makes depends on the other naturalistic features it occurs in combination with: any naturalistic feature could make an evaluative difference to the value of an object if it was in suitable combination with other natural features.

But, if particularists about value are right, then it follows immediately that no relevance limitation is defensible. After all, a relevance limitation purports to tell us that some naturalistic features are irrelevant to an object's value, whereas particularists tell us that every naturalistic feature is relevant in some context or other. They therefore hold that facts about the value of a life, say, really are sensitive to *every single* naturalistic feature that that life possesses, features that might well go back to the Big Bang. Nothing short of the endless list of inter-world supervenience conditionals of the sort characterized above, supervenience conditionals with endlessly complex naturalistic antecedents detailing every single naturalistic feature a life possesses, will therefore be guaranteed to provide the correct mapping of naturalistic features of lives onto facts about the value of lives. So particularists claim, at any rate.

What Griffin's suggestion that we add a relevance limitation to the supervenience thesis thus seems to me to reflect is his implicit commitment to generalism about value. According to generalists, if we were to state the endless list of inter-world supervenience conditionals linking every possible way a life could be naturalistically with the value of the life so characterized, then a higher-order pattern would be discernible. This pattern could itself be stated in the form of a shorter list of inter-world supervenience conditionals, conditionals that provide a mapping from some subset of a life's natural features onto its evaluative features. For example, at the other extreme from particularism, a generalist might hold that a single pattern is discernible, a pattern according to which, say, the value of a life is always and only sensitive to facts about the pleasure and pain in that life. Notwithstanding all of the other naturalistic differences between lives, pleasure and pain might be the only relevant naturalistic features when it comes to value. So a generalist—a generalist who is in effect a monist rather than a pluralist—might say.

As it happens, my inclination is to agree with Griffin that generalism about value is more plausible than particularism. Most moral philosophers would agree. That is why they would accept a supervenience conditional with a relevance limitation. Generalism seems to be more plausible than particularism, because, as I see it, we do in fact seem to be able to discern higher-order patterns in the endless list of inter-world supervenience conditionals that we have reason to believe are true. But the crucial point for present purposes is that I do not think that generalism is any sort of conceptual truth about value, and nor, it seems to me, do most moral philosophers. Rather, if it is a truth at all, it is a truth we discover by attempting, and succeeding, in the task of discerning such higher-order patterns: that is, by attempting and succeeding in the task of constructing monistic, or at least not radically pluralistic, evaluative theories. It therefore seems to me that it would be quite wrong to add a relevance limitation to the inter-world supervenience thesis that I have characterized. Such a limitation would simply undermine the thesis's claim to operate as a *conceptual* constraint on evaluative judgement.

5. THE SUPERVENIENCE THESIS AND THE FACT/VALUE GAP

Another of Griffin's misgivings about the claim that the evaluative supervenes on the natural is that it presupposes a bogus fact/value gap.

How valuable a thing is *must* depend upon what it is like. If there is a difference in supervening property, how could it *not* show up in a difference in base properties? But this is where the dubiousness of the separation of fact and value . . . matters. To regard some properties as 'base' suggests that *they* are where it all happens and that valuing is something entirely different—a human response, say, or a rather mysterious epiphenomenon. To contrast a thing's 'value' with 'what it is like' suggests that values have no hand in what it is like. Then, of course, our strong pro-supervenience intuition is easily explainable: things are valuable because, and only because, of what goes on in the (natural) world. But this picture begs the central question: what are the boundaries of the *world* or *reality* or *fact*? Once one has reason to doubt that those boundaries simply coincide with those of the natural world, and once one sees how much goes into a value concept besides the natural (indeed, how relatively unimportant the natural component is compared to the rest), then our pro-supervenience intuition starts to weaken.   (V 316–17)

But does the supervenience thesis I have described make any presuppositions at all about the boundaries of the world or reality or fact? I do not think so. As far as I can see, the supervenience thesis is consistent both with realism about evaluative features, and with irrealism, and it is also consistent both with the idea that the world is naturalistic, and with the idea that the world has non-naturalistic features.

Consider a supervenience conditional of the form 'Objects with natural features N have evaluative features E' that someone might accept. One possibility is that acceptance of this supervenience conditional amounts to a disposition to express approval—or disapproval or whatever else the judgement that something is E might be supposed to express—towards objects with N. Irrealists who give this interpretation of what it is to accept the supervenience conditional do indeed believe in a fact/value gap of the sort that Griffin rejects. They believe that the world contains all and only natural features, and that there is no place in the world for evaluative features. But another possibility is that acceptance of the conditional amounts to a belief that objects with one property, N, have another property, E. Realists who give this interpretation of what it is to accept the supervenience conditional hold that evaluative features are part and parcel of the world, and so of reality. They therefore hold that there are evaluative facts. It thus seems to me quite wrong for Griffin to suggest that a commitment to supervenience itself requires us to contrast 'a thing's "value" with "what it is like"', and so 'suggests that values have no hand in what it is like'. Acceptance of the supervenience conditional is consistent with both realism and irrealism.

Is it possible, though, for a realist who is committed to the supervenience thesis to deny that 'the boundaries of the *world* . . . simply coincide with those of the natural world'? Or does a commitment to the supervenience thesis require the realist to suppose that, since there are evaluative properties, so it follows that these properties are really just natural properties? Griffin might suggest that this is the presupposition he wants us to question, the presupposition of *naturalism*. But it seems to me that a realist's commitment to the supervenience of the evaluative on the natural simply does not all by itself require her to identify evaluative properties with natural properties. Evaluative naturalism only follows given an additional premiss. As it happens, the additional premiss required does seem to me to be very plausible. But it is an additional premiss all the same, one that some reject. For this reason it also seems to me wrong to suppose that a commitment to the supervenience of the evaluative on the natural, together with realism, entails evaluative naturalism. In order to see that this is so, let me spell out the various steps in the argument from realism about evaluative features, together with a commitment to the supervenience of evaluative on the natural, to evaluative naturalism.

Suppose we have a long list of all the conditionals that map every possible way things could be naturalistically onto evaluative features. We could then in principle collect together all of the different ways things are naturalistically that map onto one particular evaluative feature—all of the different ways of living a life, naturalistically characterized, that map onto that life's being good, for example—and then disjoin them, and then rewrite the whole statement as a biconditional linking that disjunctive set of natural features with that particular evaluative feature. In this way a claim like 'Lives have natural features N or N^* or N^{**} or . . . or N^{***} if and only if those lives are good' can be seen to be entailed by the long list of supervenience conditionals of the form 'If lives have natural feature N then they are good.' But, if this is right, then, in the light of the metaphysical principle banning necessary connections between distinct existences, it follows that a life's being good simply is its having naturalistic features N or N^* or N^{**} or . . . or N^{***}. The properties must be one and the same, because there is no possible world in which an object has the one property but fails to have the other, and vice versa. They cannot be distinct.

In this way realism, together with supervenience, can lead to evaluative naturalism. But, as should now be plain, an additional premiss is indeed required for this argument to go through. The additional premiss is the metaphysical principle banning necessary connections between distinct existences. Without this metaphysical principle, the argument for evaluative naturalism is a *non-sequitur*. The realist who rejects this principle is therefore free to embrace an enriched conception of reality as comprising both natural features, on the one hand, and metaphysically distinct but necessarily connected evaluative features, on the other, evaluative features that play no causal role. In this way someone committed to both evaluative realism and the supervenience of the evaluative on the natural can deny that 'the boundaries of the *world* . . . simply coincide with those of the natural world'. They can be non-naturalists.

6. SUPERVENIENCE AS THE DENIAL THAT EVALUATIVE CLAIMS CAN BE BARELY TRUE

My task thus far has been to clarify what it means to say that the evaluative supervenes on the natural. Though I have not yet explicitly said why we should believe this claim to be true, I do hope that what I have said thus far makes it at least look plausible. The time has come, however, to give a more positive argument.

The claim that the evaluative supervenes on the natural divides into two parts. The first part is the claim that the evaluative is *supervenient*; the second part is a claim about what the evaluative supervenes on—namely, the *natural*. Let me consider these two parts in turn. As regards the first part, the relevant fact seems to me to be that it is simply incoherent to suppose that evaluative claims could be *barely* true. Evaluative claims must always be *made true* by other claims. Because evaluative claims are always made true by other claims, it follows that, in possible worlds that agree in the truth of all of the same claims that make evaluative claims true, the same evaluative claims will be true. This is all it means to say that the evaluative is supervenient.

Note that the fact that evaluative claims cannot be barely true is reflected in ordinary evaluative practice. Suppose I say that a particular life is good, but then look totally flummoxed when asked to provide the features of the life that make it good. Perhaps I say, 'You clearly don't understand. It isn't made good by *other* features. *It's just good!*' If I am using 'good' as an evaluative term, then I would plainly violate the rules that govern the use of the word 'good'. When I say of a life that it is good, using 'good' as an evaluative term, I thereby incur an obligation to say why my ascription of goodness to that life is appropriate in the light of the features that the life possesses. If the life is good, these are the features of the life that make it good.

This is not to deny that I might have all sorts of difficulties in saying which features of a life I judge to be good make it good. But, if I use 'good' as an evaluative term, the pressure I would feel under to overcome these difficulties, and so to provide an account of the properties that make it good, is sufficient to prove the point. Having made the claim that a life is good, I am under conceptual pressure to admit that it is made good by other properties it possesses, and so to provide an account of such properties if needs be. In this way, ordinary practice bears out the fact that claims about the goodness of a life cannot be barely true. Ordinary practice bears out the fact that the evaluative is supervenient.

When Griffin discusses the way in which we justify evaluative claims, he in effect concedes that we always incur an obligation to say what it is about an object that has a certain value that makes it true that it has that value. However, in his view, we might simply cite other evaluative features. What he denies is thus not the claim that the evaluative is supervenient. Rather he denies the claim that what the evaluative is supervenient on is the natural. Here is a representative passage.

If I am a Fool-like person living for day-to-day pleasures and meet a Socratic sort who strikes me as making something of his life, I might start on [a process of] radical reflection . . . Does accomplishing something with one's life make it prudentially better? What is accomplishment? I should then be embarked on the search for the definition of the possible value. I should have to use value-rich vocabulary to focus on it: accomplishment is roughly the achievement of the sort of value that gives life weight and point. But, then, having isolated it, I should have to decide whether the apparent value is really a value, or, rather, since the search for a definition already brings in value rich language, these two processes—definition of the putative value and decision about its value—go hand in hand.   (V 302)

Griffin's idea in this passage seems to be that the Fool-like person can succeed in justifying to himself the claim that the Socratic sort's life is good by citing the fact that the life she leads is a life of accomplishment. But, given that accomplishment itself is defined in value-rich terms, it follows that the Fool-like person succeeds in saying what makes the Socratic sort's life good only by mentioning another evaluative feature of her life. Admittedly, it is a more specific evaluative feature than the feature of being good. But it is still an evaluative feature for all that.

It thus appears that, though Griffin agrees that evaluative claims are never barely true, and though he agrees that it follows from this that evaluative claims are always made true by other claims, the other claims that he thinks make evaluative claims true are themselves further, more specific, evaluative claims. Evaluative features are, therefore, supervenient in the following sense: more general evaluative features supervene on more specific evaluative features. In this way he leaves himself free to deny that the features evaluative features supervene on are natural features. But, while this might initially seem plausible, I think it looks decidedly less plausible once we subject it to closer examination.

Let us agree that accomplishment is defined in value-rich terms, and let us also agree that the Fool-like person can justify the claim that the Socratic sort's life is good by citing the fact, if it is a fact, that her life is a life of accomplishment. The problem is that, since the claim that the Socratic sort's life is a life of accomplishment is an evaluative claim, it follows that it cannot plausibly be supposed to be barely true either—true but not in virtue of anything. The claim that her life is a life of accomplishment thus stands in need of something to make it true, but so far the Fool-like person has not told us what that thing is. True enough, *if* the Socratic sort's life is a life of accomplishment, then it is a good life. But *is it* a life of accomplishment? What is it about the Socratic sort's life that makes that claim true? The Fool-like person clearly does not understand what it is to make an evaluative claim if he simply says, 'You don't understand. The Socratic sort's life isn't made a life of accomplishment by *other* features it possesses. *It's just a life of accomplishment!*'

At this point Griffin will presumably agree but then insist that the Fool-like person can say that what makes it true that the Socratic sort accomplishes something with her life is the truth of *yet other* evaluative claims about her life. Perhaps she lives a life in which she gives *good* philosophical arguments; and so on. My reply will then be the same. True enough, *if* the Socratic sort lives a life in which she gives good philosophical arguments, and so on, then she accomplishes something with her life. But *is it* a life in which she does these things? Since these are evaluative claims about her life, they cannot be barely true either. So what makes them true?

Griffin might say that the Fool-like person can say that what makes the claim that the Socratic sort lives a life in which she gives good philosophical arguments, and so on, is the truth of yet other evaluative claims about her life. Perhaps she lives a life in which she writes articles that display her understanding . . . At this point, however, as Griffin himself notes, it is not clear that we have not broken through a crucial barrier. A characterization of a life such as this—a life in which articles are written that display understanding—seems as though it might itself be a characterization of a life in terms of naturalistic features (V 318). After all, understanding does seem to be something that fairly straightforwardly figures in empirical regularities. (It is because she understands various complex philosophical issues that the Socratic sort is in demand to give lectures.) But, if this is wrong, and understanding is not a naturalistic feature, then my reply will be the same as before.[13] True enough, *if* . . .

If this line of questioning is followed to its logical conclusion, then it seems to me simply irresistible to suppose that the Fool-like person will eventually have to admit that something in the sphere of the natural is what makes true the evaluative claims he makes about the Socratic sort's life. In this particular case, for example, if he has not already appealed to a natural feature in saying that the Socratic sort writes articles that display her understanding, then he will eventually have to appeal to such features in any case, because what makes it true that the Socratic sort lives a life in which she writes articles that display her understanding is evidently the fact that she writes the particular words that she writes in those articles. (Likewise, what makes it true that the Socratic sort understands various complex philosophical issues is the fact that she is disposed to think and say the particular things she is disposed to think and say about them.)

Once this is agreed, however, the crucial point has been established. What makes the Socratic sort's life good is the fact that she lives a life in which she does things like writing the particular words that she writes. The evaluative claim about the Socratic sort's life is made true by a claim about the natural features of her life after all. Evaluative features therefore supervene on natural features, not merely on more specific evaluative features. The halfway house Griffin wants to occupy cannot be occupied.

In fact, much the same conclusion can be reached from another direction. Focus on a different example, not on the value of a life, but on the value of an act. People do things that add value to their lives, and they do things that diminish the value of their lives. But it is a truth of action theory that, though agents do all sorts of wonderful things, and all sorts of awful things, they are able to do these things only in so far as there are things that they can *just do*, movements they can make with their bodies (or, in the case of mental acts, thoughts they can have, or whatever) that have the effects that are wonderful or awful in the various ways that they are. What makes it true that they do wonderful or awful things is thus the fact that they make movements with their bodies (or think the thoughts they think, or whatever). But the fact that they make movements with their bodies (or think the thoughts they think) is the paradigm of a feature of their lives that is such as to figure in an empirical regularity.[14]

Viewed from this perspective, the idea that more general evaluative features supervene on more specific evaluative features, but not on natural features,

[13] Here we recall the discussion in nn. 6 and 10 above of the idea that the class of natural properties is vague.

[14] For a discussion of the point in action theory, see Donald Davidson, 'Agency', repr. in his *Essays on Actions and Events* (Oxford: Clarendon Press, 1980).

looks as if it requires the assumption that there is something that someone can just do, a basic act he can perform, that constitutes, all by itself, the making-true-of-an-evaluative-claim. But I cannot see how to make sense of the idea. It is as though we are to suppose that we could set ourselves to act, and believe ourselves to be (say) writing an article that displays our understanding (assuming for the moment that this is not a characterization of an act in terms of natural features), but yet suppose that whether or not we do anything with our fingers on a keyboard (or our hand on a pen, or whatever), or have thoughts with particular contents when we do, is completely irrelevant to that act that we are performing. Writing an article that displays our understanding is (we are supposed to think) something we can *just do*, not something we have to do by doing something else.

But it is just obviously false that anyone can do any such thing. Someone who does not put his fingers on a keyboard (or his hand on a pen, or whatever) will never write anything at all. Moreover, once he puts his fingers on the keyboard, it is absolutely crucial what he does with them: crucial which thoughts he has. This is because the keys he hits with his fingers fix the facts about which letters appear on the page; and the facts about which letters appear on the page, together with the facts about the ways in which those letters are used more broadly in the community, fix the facts about the meaning of what is on the page; and the meaning of what is on the page fixes whether he has managed to display any understanding at all. The evaluative features of acts must, therefore, supervene on natural features. They must supervene on natural features because all acts are, at bottom, bodily movements with certain characteristic causes—desires, beliefs, thoughts—bodily movements that in turn cause effects in a naturalistic world. These are one and all natural features *par excellence*.[15]

7. METAPHYSICS VERSUS EPISTEMOLOGY

Let me make it plain what I do and do not take myself to have shown.

I do take myself to have shown that Griffin is wrong to suppose that, even though the evaluative features of things do supervene, they supervene only on other more specific evaluative features of those things. If the life of the Socratic sort of person is good, then so is the life of any other person, in any other

---

[15] In Frank Jackson's terms the point can be put this way. We must suppose that the evaluative supervenes on the natural because we know, in advance, that we never need to appeal to evaluative features in order to discriminate between possibilities: natural features suffice for that purpose. Jackson makes the point in chapter 5 of his *From Metaphysics to Ethics: A Defence of Conceptual Analysis* (Oxford: Clarendon Press, 1998).

possible world, whose life is an exact duplicate in every naturalistic respect of the Socratic sort's life. This is because evaluative claims cannot be barely true, but have to be made true by facts about naturalistic features.

What I have not shown, however, is that we could ever give a compelling argument for the truth of any particular supervenience conditional—any particular claim about which naturalistic features of a life are such that any life with those features is a good life—without appealing to all sorts of other evaluative features. In fact, I suspect that we would need to appeal not just to other evaluative features, but probably to other supervenience conditionals as well. This is because the task of justifying a particular supervenience conditional and the task of (partially) constructing an evaluative theory are one and the same task. But constructing an evaluative theory is a reflective equilibrium process, a matter of bringing our various evaluative commitments into a harmonious relationship with each other. There is, therefore, no process of giving such a justification that somehow isolates the supervenience conditional being justified from others, and so from evaluative claims more generally.

Sometimes it seems to me that Griffin's real reason for rejecting the idea that the evaluative supervenes on the natural is his appreciation of this fact. It is as though he asks, 'If in order to justify a particular supervenience conditional linking a natural feature with an evaluative feature we have to appeal to various ancillary evaluative commitments we have, then how can we seriously suppose that the presence of that natural feature is sufficient, *all by itself*, for the presence of that evaluative feature?' But, of course, that is precisely what appeal to our various ancillary evaluative commitments justifies us in believing. Consider an analogy.

In order to justify my belief that, if it rains tomorrow, then the football match will be cancelled, I may have to appeal to the source of my belief. Let us suppose I was told that this is what will happen by someone who is trustworthy, and that reflection on this fact is enough for me to feel justified in holding the belief. But just as in this case there is no temptation at all to suppose that rain tomorrow must not really be sufficient, all by itself, for the cancellation of the football match—that really what is required is *both* rain tomorrow *and* the trustworthiness of my informant (as though the officials in charge of the football match could care less about my informant!)—so the fact that we have to appeal to various ancillary evaluative claims in justifying a particular supervenience conditional should not tempt us to suppose that the natural features mentioned in the antecedent of that conditional are not really sufficient for the evaluative features mentioned in the consequent. They are sufficient. It is just that, if we are to believe this to be so, then we have to have other evaluative beliefs as well.

The crucial point thus seems to be that we need to distinguish sharply between, on the one hand, the reasons we might have for believing that evaluative features supervene on natural features, and, on the other hand, the reasons we might have for believing that some particular supervenience conditional linking natural features with evaluative features is true. I have been talking exclusively about the former, not at all about the latter. My argument has been that the reasons we have for believing that the evaluative supervenes on the natural are conceptual. But much of what Griffin has to say in opposition to the claim that the evaluative supervenes on the natural makes me think that he is really more interested in the latter, and not so much in the former. Whereas his interests seem to be more broadly epistemological, mine have been more narrowly metaphysical.

8. CONCLUSION

There are many different interpretations we could give to the claim that the evaluative supervenes on the natural. I have argued for a particular interpretation, an interpretation according to which all of those non-particular features objects have that are such as to figure in empirical regularities are supposed to be sufficient for whatever evaluative features they have. All possible objects with the same such features must have the same value.

We have seen that commitment to a supervenience claim of this kind is consistent with both particularism and generalism about value; that it is neutral with regard to the debate between evaluative realists and irrealists; and that, among evaluative realists, it is neutral as regards the debate between evaluative naturalists and non-naturalists. Moreover, we have seen that the reason we have for believing that the evaluative does indeed supervene on the natural in this way is that it is a conceptual truth that evaluative claims cannot be barely true. They must be made true by other claims, and what they must be made true by are claims about naturalistic features.

I said at the outset that one of the few claims accepted by nearly everyone writing about the nature of value is that the evaluative features of things supervene on their natural features. Notwithstanding Griffin's misgivings, it seems to me that we have seen good reason to believe that this is true.

7

Griffin's Pessimism

Roger Crisp

1. VARIETIES OF PESSIMISM

How far can philosophy improve our ethical beliefs? And what attitude should a philosopher take to those we already have? Henry Sidgwick's view was that, though 'Common Sense' constrains philosophical conclusions, the philosopher's 'function is to tell men what they ought to think, rather than what they do think: he is expected to transcend Common Sense in his premises, and he is allowed a certain divergence from Common Sense in his conclusions'. Further, telling people what they ought to think about ethics will involve supplying them with 'real ethical axioms' (*ME* 373). But Sidgwick's conclusion was that, though philosophy can provide such axioms, they are ultimately inconsistent. Of the first edition of *The Methods of Ethics* he said: 'Now it is written. I have adhered to the plan I laid out for myself; its first word was to be "Ethics", its last word "Failure".'[1]

Sidgwick's pessimism consisted in his conclusion that there is an irreconcilable dualism in practical reason between rational egoism and utilitarian duty.[2] James Griffin's view of the limits of philosophy is yet more pessimistic, since on his view we cannot begin to approach even the level of system Sidgwick finds in ethics. Philosophy has taken us to the wrong place, 'a spare landscape in which . . . ethics . . . will not grow' (*VJ* 136). In this chapter I wish to compare Sidgwick's approach to ethics with that of Griffin, as expressed in his significant book, *Value Judgement*. Sidgwick's ethics is not quite as ambitious as some have claimed, but it is markedly more so than Griffin's. This in itself

For comments on a previous draft I am grateful to Robert Audi, Robert Frazier, Brad Hooker, and Mark Nelson.

[1] Quoted by F. H. Hayward; see B. Schultz (ed.), *Essays on Sidgwick* (Cambridge: Cambridge University Press, 1992), 4.

[2] See J. L. Mackie, 'Sidgwick's Pessimism', *Philosophical Quarterly*, 26 (1976), 317–27.

suggests the aptness of a comparison, for the two philosophers have much in common in their epistemologies. Griffin's arguments against system in ethics are subtle and powerful, but I shall conclude that, because the debate about the merits of system remains open, there is still room for systematic ethical programmes. I shall suggest also that Griffin, interestingly enough, provides a plausible route out of Sidgwick's own pessimism, but that there is a further reason for pessimism about philosophical ethics that neither Sidgwick nor Griffin makes much of.

2. FOUNDATIONALISM AND SYSTEM

As I say, there is epistemological common ground between Sidgwick and Griffin. And, since it is ground very securely held, there is a further motivation for examining the different edifices constructed by each upon it. First, though neither is a pure foundationalist, both advocate what might be called 'elements' of foundationalism in their moral epistemologies. According to Sidgwick, 'there are certain absolute practical principles, the truth of which, when they are explicitly stated, is manifest' (*ME* 379). These include a formal principle of universalization, as well as the conflicting principles that one should seek one's own good on the whole and that one is morally bound to view another's good as on a par with one's own (*ME* 379–83). These practical principles are 'self-evident', in the sense that they require no external support (*ME* 383). This is the main claim underlying Sidgwick's intuitionism, but it is important to note his insistence that intuitive principles should be not held as mere dogmas, but accepted on the basis of impartial reflection, and that reflection on an apparently self-evident intuition may well lead to its being rejected (*ME* 211, 339).[3] That is what happens to the morality of common sense as a result of Sidgwick's examination of it (*ME*, bk. 3, ch. 11).

Like Sidgwick, Griffin believes that much of philosophical ethics develops out of reflection within common-sense morality (*VJ* 1).[4] He suggests that there are some 'beliefs of high reliability', by which he means beliefs whose credibility does not depend on their being inferred from other beliefs (*VJ* 13).[5]

---

[3] See R. Audi, 'Intuitionism, Pluralism, and the Foundations of Ethics', in W. Sinnott-Armstrong and M. Timmons (eds.), *Moral Knowledge?* (New York: Oxford University Press, 1996), 101–36, at 107–8, 131.

[4] For a good example of such reflection, see *VJ* 24–5.

[5] We must assume that 'beliefs of high reliability' is a technical term for Griffin, referring only to non-inferential beliefs, since he almost certainly accepts that some inferential beliefs are highly reliable.

And, as the complexity of Griffin's own arguments suggests, any such beliefs can be relied upon only after serious reflection.[6] They are, then, straightforwardly analogous to Sidgwick's intuitionist foundations for ethics. They include the prudential beliefs that pain is bad and understanding and accomplishment good, and the moral beliefs that cruelty is wrong, that we should show respect for others, and that the fact that you are in pain can give me a reason to act (*VJ* 13, 52, 125).

What would Sidgwick himself make of these beliefs? He would accept that pain is bad and that your pain can plausibly be said to give me a reason to act. But he would deny Griffin's objective account of prudential value, and dismiss the cruelty principle as part of common-sense morality (*ME* 400–1). The important content of these beliefs, however, could probably be restated in a way that both philosophers would accept.

It might be said that Sidgwick's own intuitive principles are more 'abstract' than Griffin's beliefs of high reliability. That seems true enough of the formal principle of universalizability. But it is not clear what is meant by the suggestion that the egoistic and utilitarian principles are more abstract. Both, after all, can be seen as resting on a substantive view of well-being, and thus to be as 'thick' as any of Griffin's foundational beliefs. The real difference between Griffin and Sidgwick here lies in their attitude to system. Sidgwick believed that philosophy aimed at the complete systematization of human knowledge, including that gained by the sciences.[7] The aim of moral philosophy he states on the very first page of *The Methods*: 'The student of Ethics seeks to attain systematic and precise general knowledge of what ought to be.' The search for system drives Sidgwick throughout, and its ultimate unavailability is what licenses his pessimistic conclusion. Griffin, however, sees a less ambitious role for ethics. We need ethical beliefs so as to decide how to live, he suggests, but this need not 'take us far down the road to either explanation or system' (*VJ* 15). Consider, for example, moral institutions, such as property, which have developed piecemeal to solve cooperation or coordination problems (*VJ* 93–4). Once these problems are solved, little system is required.

Griffin's claim, Sidgwick might argue, runs together the practical and the intellectual roles of philosophy. Philosophy aims at understanding, even when

---

[6] Griffin is sometimes pessimistic about the possibility of a criterion for distinguishing sound from unsound judgements (see *VJ* 142 n. 26). But at other times he implies that philosophy *may* have the resources to achieve such a distinction (see e.g. *VJ* 66–7). An implication of the pessimistic view might be thought to be nihilism, and that is far from Griffin's conclusion. I discuss this matter further in the text below.

[7] H. Sidgwick, *Philosophy, its Scope and Relations* (London: Macmillan, 1902); see J. Schneewind, *Sidgwick's Ethics and Victorian Moral Philosophy* (Oxford: Clarendon Press, 1977), 52–5.

the world is working perfectly well. If the common-sense principles on which our moral institutions rest are incomplete, unclear, or conflicting, the demand on a philosopher is to seek to clarify, to explain, and to systematize, in the hope that better principles may emerge. Griffin does not see philosophy, however, as entirely a practical art, and does not rule out from the start the possibility that some credible system may be identified. But, he says, 'we have no reason to assume that it will' (*VJ* 16). This modesty, we can agree, should characterize any impartial philosopher. The question is what the attitude of the philosopher should be if system does not emerge. According to Sidgwick, this result would be a failure of philosophy, and the philosopher's task would be to continue to seek for system. Griffin, however, on the basis of a substantive enquiry into the circumstances of human agency and an examination of previous philosophical attempts at systematization, concludes that the systematizing aim of philosophy is vain. It is to those arguments, and in particular their implications for a Sidgwickian view, that I shall turn shortly. At this stage, all I hope to have demonstrated are the foundationalist elements in the thought of both Sidgwick and Griffin, and their different attitudes to the failure of system.[8]

3. COHERENCE

Minimal foundationalism in ethics I take to be the view that the ultimate justification for an ethical belief can consist in the credibility or plausibility of that belief itself, and not necessarily on any inference from or coherence with other beliefs. Pure foundationalism is then the view that, for ultimate moral beliefs, this is the only kind of justification available. Pure foundationalism in ethics is to be rejected, since it fails to acknowledge the support beliefs can derive from one another. But neither Sidgwick nor Griffin is a pure

---

[8] Both Sidgwick and Griffin see system as consisting in precisely stateable principles that can guide action fully. It might be thought that Griffin, in his attitude to system, is lining up, against systematizers such as Sidgwick, with Aristotle-influenced Rossian pluralist intuitionists (see e.g. J. Dancy, 'An Ethic of Prima Facie Duties', in P. Singer (ed.), *A Companion to Ethics* (Oxford: Blackwell, 1991), 219–29). But such pluralists do not have to adopt such a pessimistic view of ethical system that they advocate giving up on it as an ideal to be aimed for. Aristotle himself, after all, did not. Consider his attempt to define our different obligations to those close to us: 'The comparison is easier when they are of the same class, and more of a job when they are different; and yet we should not for that reason shrink from the task, but define things as best we can' (*NE* 1165[a]33–5, my translation). That there are practical limits on moral philosophy ought to be accepted by all philosophers, including systematizers such as Sidgwick. For presumably even he would have thought that, if act utilitarianism could be justified as the single principle of practical reason, there would still be (and indeed always would be) a great deal of systematic philosophical work to be done in characterizing the nature of utility and the effects of various actions upon it.

foundationalist, since both allow elements of coherentism into their moral epistemologies.

Sidgwick saw himself as combining rationalistic intuitionism with the empiricist method of 'Discursive Verification', that is, 'contemplating the belief that appears intuitively certain along with other beliefs which may possibly be found to conflict with it'.[9] Sidgwick goes on to advocate a third type of verification, influenced by Aristotelian dialectic—namely, 'Social Verification'. This requires one to examine one's conclusions in the light of the views of other thinkers, whether contemporary or past. Sidgwick argued that a close examination of common-sense morality showed both that the utilitarian principle, itself implicit within common-sense morality, could provide common-sense morality with a systematic foundation, and that the fact that common sense itself implies the need for the utilitarian principle to play this role itself adds to the proof of utilitarianism (*ME* 383–4, 422). Further, he suggests, his conclusions are in line with those of previous thinkers such as Clarke and Kant (*ME* 384–6).

Griffin also shows concern for the views of Kant, as well as other past and present moral philosophers, though he tends to argue against them rather than line himself up with them. He does see a role for convergence, though it must be a convergence that itself cannot be explained away as the result of, say, social conditioning or some other process independent of credibility itself (*VJ* 18, 58–9, 64). Nor, in principle, does he deny that sound ethical beliefs can provide a resource for criticizing other ethical beliefs (*VJ* 16). No belief is immune, since we cannot resist holism, 'the thesis that justification comes only from a whole set of beliefs' (*VJ* 12).[10]

Minimal coherentism in ethics is the view that the justification for an ethical belief can consist in the coherence of that belief with certain other beliefs.[11] Pure coherentism is then the claim that this is the only kind of justification available. Pure coherentism is even less plausible than pure foundationalism, as the so-called regress argument shows.[12] If the credibility of belief *a* comes entirely from its coherence with belief *b*, and that of *b* from its coherence with *c*, and so on, but there is no reason to accept any of these beliefs *in themselves*, then justification becomes impossible to explain. But

---

[9] H. Sidgwick, *Lectures on the Philosophy of Kant and other Philosophical Lectures and Essays*, London: Macmillan, 1905, p. 462; cited in Schneewind, *Sidgwick's Ethics*, 59.

[10] Holism here is a very general theory of which both (pure) coherentism and (pure) foundationalism are examples. The point Griffin is stressing here, and to which I am drawing attention, is that the final plausibility of any theory of justication can be assessed only in the light of its account of the justification of our whole set of beliefs, not any subset.

[11] Different versions of coherentism will, of course, give different accounts of just which beliefs or sets of beliefs these other beliefs are.

[12] The argument derives from Sextus Empiricus. See W. Sinnott-Armstrong, 'Moral Skepticism and Justification', in Sinnott-Armstrong and Timmons (eds.), *Moral Knowledge?*, 9–14. See *VJ* 10.

this is not a problem with non-pure coherentism. Let us assume that *a* is non-inferentially plausible upon reflection, and that this provides some justification for accepting it. If *a* coheres with beliefs *b–d*, does that count further in its favour? The answer depends on the kind of coherence at stake, and the content of the beliefs in question. Pure logical consistency of *a* with the further beliefs adds nothing in itself, independently of the credibility of those further beliefs. But if *b* is independently credible, and *a* can (plausibly) *explain b*, this adds to the credibility of both *a* and *b*.[13] Imagine, for example, that *a* is the belief that suffering is bad and to be avoided, and *b* the belief that that child should not be torturing the cat. The general principle here is that explanatory coherence adds to the credibility of a set of beliefs, and hence to the credibility of members of that set. (These beliefs need not be those of a single person, thus leaving room for Sidgwick's method of social verification.)

Combining foundationalist and coherentist elements into a single moral epistemology avoids excluding for no good reason what seem to be promising sources of justification. Both Sidgwick and Griffin, though prepared to privilege certain beliefs because of their intrinsic plausibility upon reflection, will not allow these beliefs to be insulated from others. What seems attractive about their pluralist epistemologies is their readiness to test beliefs in whatever ways seem likely to lead to, or away from, their credibility.

I have been suggesting that there is epistemological common ground between Sidgwick and Griffin. There are, nevertheless, hints in Griffin's writings of a general retreat from a conception of moral philosophy as normative or justificatory. There is, he claims, no domain of 'the moral', just the domain of 'the social' (*VJ* 119; cf. 116–17). And there is no hard-and-fast line to be drawn between morality and the rules of etiquette (*VJ* 126). If Griffin here has in mind what we might call 'lived morality', that set of institutions and practices which we refer to as the morality of a society, then he is right. But, from the perspective of philosophical justification, most philosophers will want to place morality and etiquette in quite different categories. There are no ultimate 'reasons of etiquette'. Any reason for participating in some practice of etiquette will be of some independent kind—such as the moral principle that one should avoid causing pointless offence to others at no cost to oneself. These hints in Griffin are of a kind of ethical nihilism: all there are are ungrounded ethical practices; there is no justification for or against them. And they may explain why he is prepared to countenance the mere existence of the rules of some practice as providing a justification for adherence to them (see below). But the general tenor of his book, I think, is not nihilist, so much as modest. In that sense, there is a domain of the moral, but it is not occupied by the kind of moral principles advocated in modern (and indeed much

---

[13] We will, of course, require here some account of what makes for a plausible explanation.

ancient) moral philosophy. Nor is it only philosophers who engage in practices of justification, or who are especially privileged in such practices (*VJ* 131).

4. IMPARTIALITY AND THE GOOD LIFE

The difference of attitude towards system taken by Sidgwick and Griffin emerges within substantive philosophical enquiry itself. So it is to that enquiry as engaged in by Griffin in particular that I shall now turn. One question we can ask of systematic moral philosophy, Griffin suggests, is what kind of agents human beings would have to be to live the kinds of life demanded of them by particular moral theories (*VJ* 18). Any such theory is under the constraint of a 'requirement of psychological realism' (*VJ* 84). 'Action-guiding principles must fit human capacities, or they become strange in a damaging way: namely, pointless' (*VJ* 164).[14] After a detailed enquiry into these issues, Griffin concludes that modern ethics tends to ignore the nature and circumstances of human agency. Sidgwick's version of utilitarianism—act utilitarianism—is one of the most ambitious systematic moral theories in the history of philosophy. If it can withstand Griffin's criticisms, then it is likely that the other theories Griffin attacks, such as deontology and virtue ethics, will at least stand a good chance of doing the same. So let me now turn to Griffin's anti-act-utilitarian arguments.

One of the most immediately striking features of act utilitarianism is its stringent conception of impartiality. According to this view, 'the good of any one individual [e.g. the agent or someone close to them] is of no more importance . . . than the good of any other' (*ME* 382). This version of impartiality has long been subjected to the criticism that it ignores the special weight agents attach to their own well-being, and that of others close to them. Griffin offers his own version of this critique:

> On the prudential theory that I am proposing, one should become deeply partial. That partiality is, I think, bound to be in some tension with the moral point of view . . . Somehow, these two parts of ethics, the demands of others and the goal of individual flourishing, must be rendered, if not entirely harmonious, at least combinable in one normative point of view, and in one personality. (*VJ* 86)

Act utilitarianism's impartiality rests on a denial of any intrinsic importance to the fact of the separateness of persons. Other things being equal, my pain gives me only as strong a reason to act as your pain gives me a reason to act. Egoists, of course, offer exactly the opposite position: the fact that your

---

[14] Cf. S. Scheffler, *Human Morality* (New York: Oxford University Press, 1992), ch. 7.

pain is not mine means that I have no direct reason to alleviate it. Whatever the flaws in egoism, utilitarianism does seem blind to one of the most salient features of our lives, as Griffin points out: 'anything approaching a full account of pain-based reasons for action will indeed give weight to the "my" or "your"; egoism is in that respect right; it is only that the relevant weight seems to me to tip the balance away from complete impartiality rather than toward egoism' (*VJ* 75).

I believe that Griffin is here pointing to a genuine deficiency in act utilitarianism as it is usually stated. The separateness of persons does indeed ground reasons in tension with pure impartiality. But that, it seems, does not prevent act utilitarians from offering their view not as a theory of practical reason, period, but as a theory of morality.[15] This leaves all the options open regarding the differential weight to be attached to the agent's own interests or the interests of those close to him. Sidgwick recognized the plausibility of egoism, but made no attempt to reconcile egoism and impartiality. Here, Griffin makes an advance on Sidgwick, suggesting a 'halfway house' between egoism and impartiality (*VJ* 77; see also 29). Sidgwick failed to allow for the possibility that reasons can be plural and yet in particular cases outweigh one another. For example, consider a case in which 'the benefit to you . . . is great, and the cost to me negligible (I just have to dial 999)' (*VJ* 73).

As Griffin notes, the distinction between prudence and morality should not be pushed too far (*VJ* 76–9). The act utilitarian can, however, accept the gist of Griffin's remarks here. Morality penetrates prudence, in the sense that living a life good for oneself will require one to recognize the value of others. Certain prudential values, such as accomplishment or deep personal relations, themselves involve the promotion of the value of others' lives. And there is penetration the other way too. Much of morality is concerned with the promotion of well-being. And morality also requires us to have strong dispositions not to be cruel (something a multi-level utilitarian would be quite happy to accept). These dispositions require some degree of respect for one's own importance, since without it shame would be unable to gain a foothold in one's moral consciousness. Utilitarianism, then, can incorporate many of Griffin's insights about agency, its essential point being that, whatever conceptions of human well-being and agency we have, our only ultimate *justifying* reasons are impartially to promote well-being overall. The flaw we have identified in most versions of act utilitarianism is the failure to give weight to the separateness of persons at the level of justifying reasons. And that flaw can be remedied by restating utilitarianism as a theory of morality rather than of practical reason.

[15] I provide some defence for such a view in 'The Dualism of Practical Reason', *Proceedings of the Aristotelian Society*, 96 (1996), 53–73.

5. THE LIMITS OF THE WILL AND THE LIMITS OF NORMS

The utilitarian can, then, accept most if not all of Griffin's illuminating discussion of the 'limits of the will'(*VJ* 87–92, 96). Given our evolutionary and cultural heritage, complete impartiality is certainly an absurd goal for us to aim at either in our own lives or in the moral education of our children. 'Ought' implies 'can'. But, Griffin asks, what kind of 'can't' might defeat an 'ought'? His answer is that the most relevant sense is, 'can't by someone in ordinary circumstances with suitable, settled dispositions in a sustainable social order', and he claims that, 'we must largely live as, anyway, we were going to live' (*VJ* 90–1).[16]

Here Griffin is somewhat pessimistic about the empirical matter of what level of sacrifice human beings are capable of. I suspect that many act utilitarians would be less pessimistic, claiming, for example, that none of us *has* 'to be prepared to raise children' (*VJ* 90–1). Any psychologically stable human being can refrain from reproduction on the ground, for example, that the emotional, financial, and material resources used on a child in our culture would be better employed elsewhere, in alleviating poverty or preserving the environment. But, as I suggested, a utilitarian can accept any view of human nature and the circumstances of human agency, even psychological egoism (the claim here would be that, though we are motivated by concern for ourselves, what grounds or justifies any action is its promotion of the overall good). A utilitarian can even accept that the limits of the will are, even in individual cases, entirely unclear. If that were so, what morality required would be entirely unclear too. But that would be not a flaw in the theory of utilitarianism, but a tragic aspect of the human condition.

There seems little reason, however, to accept this pessimistic position. In his discussion of the limits of knowledge, Griffin asks the question, 'To what extent can I deny myself and my family in order to help the world's starving?' (*VJ* 96). His answer—obviously correct—is that we are largely ignorant about this, and about how much good various development charities achieve, and so on. But vagueness does not justify a lack of concern. It is important to recognize at this point that indeterminacy does not imply a lack of guidance.

---

[16] The notion of 'suitability' here requires some further clarification. I take it that dispositions are suitable if they are such as are necessary for ethical practices to exist in a society. An act utilitarian might wish to know at this point why ethics might not require some particular individual to be much more impartial, even if it is the case that for ethical practices in his or her society to exist requires that other people be partial. Griffin's response will be that this kind of impartiality is for almost everyone going to be impossible (see *VJ* 90, and my discussion in the text below).

Whether you should give 24 per cent or 25 per cent may be unclear, given the limits of our knowledge. But utilitarianism's requirement is perfectly clear: 'you should give as much as you can.' How much you are capable of is something that you may find out by experiment, and there is surely a fact of the matter about your capabilities, even if you are ignorant of it (there is some possible world (or set of possible worlds in each of which you give equal amounts), in which you give more than in any other possible world). As Griffin suggests, we have to choose a policy and adhere to it. What should that policy be? Justifications are comparative. Giving 2 per cent of my income to Oxfam is better than giving nothing. But giving 10 per cent is even better, and 25 per cent is yet better. At this point—depending of course on one's salary, commitments, and so on—the claim that I have reached my psychological limit at least begins to sound plausible. But, the utilitarian will point out, this is much more than most of us give, so the check on utilitarian moral radicalism placed by the limits of knowledge of our motivational capacities is largely academic.

Griffin has a further argument, however, to deploy against the utilitarian at this point. On the utilitarian picture, what lies behind all our practices and actions is the ultimate justificatory norm: 'maximize utility'. But, Griffin suggests, there is no room for such a norm in our conceptual economy: 'Moral norms are shaped for us, with all our limitations. There are no moral norms outside the boundary set by our capacities' (*VJ* 100; see also 105–7). A useless norm is not a norm, and, because we cannot be sure which act, strategy or life will maximize utility, then the utilitarian norm has no application.

There are two responses available here to a utilitarian systematizer. The first is *ad hominem*, that Griffin's stringency here regarding norms would leave us with very few if any norms at all. Consider the norm he often discusses, 'Limit the damage' (see e.g. *VJ* 99). This norm is said to imply that I would be justified in diverting a runaway trolley from a track on which it will kill five people to a track on which it will kill only one. But in any such real situation I cannot be sure that the norm really does require me to divert the trolley. Maybe the five people are terminally ill, and will die within hours anyway. Perhaps the one is a brilliant surgeon, who has dedicated his life to relieving severe suffering in hundreds of patients that no one else is capable of preventing. Any application of a norm is always something of a gamble.

Secondly, the utilitarian can draw the distinction between criterion and decision-procedure, to argue that, even if utilitarianism is entirely inapplicable, it can still be correct.[17] No heavy commitment to moral realism or to any particular theory of truth is required here, only the assumption that we can have reasons to act on particular occasions of which we are unaware.

[17] See R. E. Bales, 'Act Utilitarianism: Account of Right-Making Characteristics or Decision-Making Procedure?, *American Philosophical Quarterly*, 8 (1971), 257–65.

Anyone who thinks I have a reason not to drink a deadly poison that I take to be wine can accept this position.

Griffin, however, claims that 'any criterion for a human practice cannot become too remote from them without losing its standing as a criterion' (*VJ* 105). And, he goes on, the utilitarian criterion just is too remote. This position is clearly linked to that concerning the practical role of moral philosophy discussed above. There, I suggested that Sidgwick was right to think that philosophy has a purely intellectual as well as a practical aspect. There could, in other words, be a truth about our reasons for action that was normative, in the sense that it concerned ultimate reasons for action, but did not feature in non-philosophical life.

But, whatever the merits of this position, how remote is remote? How often is utilitarian thought 'squeezed out'? In one sense, the utilitarian can suggest, never. For any justification must ultimately refer to the advancement of well-being, and, if that reference is unavailable, then so is the justification. Nor need one think that such reference will be rare. Griffin agrees that much of lived morality is concerned to promote human well-being (see e.g. *VJ* 57, 68, 126). Restrictions on harming or killing others, principles of justice, contractual institutions, virtues such as honesty and kindness, prudence even—all, as Sidgwick demonstrates so well, can be given a solid utilitarian rationale. Further, as Hare's development of a two-level utilitarian theory has brought out, utilitarianism can often work well in deciding between conflicts at the level of common-sense principle.[18]

The question the utilitarian will try to answer, when offered any picture of agency and society, according to Griffin, is: 'What set of rules and dispositions will most promote interests, given agents of such-and-such a nature and a society that works thus-and-so?' (*VJ* 106). As he suggests, this calculation is beyond us. But, the utilitarian can reply, our question is not this, but rather: 'What improvements can we make—*in the light of the utilitarian principle*—to the set of rules and dispositions that guide our lives at present?'. And here calculation is not beyond us.[19] Consider the following important areas of moral life: our lack of concern for the distant poor and for future generations; our willingness to inflict severe suffering on non-human animals for no good reason; and our adherence to outdated principles of the sanctity-of-life in medicine, resulting in much avoidable suffering.[20] In all of these areas, and many more, utilitarianism is clear in its requirement that, individually and collectively, we change our practices drastically. It is not remote.

[18] R. M. Hare, *Moral Thinking* (Oxford: Clarendon Press, 1981), ch. 2.

[19] It is likely to be along similar lines to Griffin's discussion of euthanasia in *VJ* 130.

[20] Note that all of these areas can be seen to concern the diminution of suffering. Utilitarian principles concerning the morality of killing and saving life in themselves do indeed seem to me to be underdetermined (see *VJ* 107), largely because of our ignorance concerning the optimum population level. But strong side-effect arguments are anyway available.

6. MORAL JUSTIFICATION AND THE DEMANDS OF SOCIAL LIFE

Having discussed in the important seventh chapter of *Value Judgement* the limits placed on the ambitions of moral theory by prudential value and the will, Griffin moves onto 'the demands of social life' (*VJ* 93–5). In his previous work, Griffin has brought out especially clearly the problems inherent in individualistic, act-by-act moral decision-making (see e.g. *WB* 195–206). Here in *Value Judgement* he applies some of his conclusions to the question of the relation between lived morality and moral theory. Many moral institutions are already in place in our society: promising, property, obligations of parents to children. Like Sidgwick, Griffin believes that moral philosophers should accept the existence of these institutions, and not develop utopias from scratch. Rather they must ask questions such as what in our institutions requires alteration. Griffin, however, is happier philosophically to remain at the level of these institutions than is Sidgwick. Since the obligations that partially constitute them are responsible for most of the significant goods in our lives, 'unless we have reason to think that these social institutions are seriously defective, we have good reason to accept these obligations' (*VJ* 95).

The utilitarian might ask why, if we have reason to think that these institutions are only mildly defective, we do not have good reason to decline to accept the defective obligations. Griffin might well accept this point. Consider our institution of property. It is not perfect, but, if we were to change it at the margins to allow for, for example, a decent minimum social provision for all, then on Griffin's view we would have to stick by the institution *in the knowledge* that we have no reason for thinking this present institution better than some alternative: 'What will then lie behind the claim that we ought to do this or that will not (that is, not entirely) be the general good, but that this is the way our society happens to work' (*VJ* 96; see also 95, 99, 159).

A reason for any action *a* is always a reason for performing *a* rather than some other action *b*. This is because of the link between reasons and justification. In the court of justification, the agent is being asked to provide a satisfactory rationale for performing some action *rather than* some other action (or doing nothing).[21] Let us assume that *a* is consonant with our present institution of property (improved as far as possible). Griffin's suggestion is that my justification for performing *a* can at least partly be that this is our present institution. This does not sound like a plausible justification. Often, of course, there will be a justification for performing *a* rather than *b*: *a*, for example, is what is expected by others, and performing it will not disappoint their expectations; there are advantages to be gained from coopera-

---

[21] There may of course be ties.

tion, and the fact that nearly everyone else is working with the present institution gives me a reason to do so as well; there would probably be costs in any individual shift on my part, or any attempt to change a group of others to accept an alternative institution. But all of these justifications themselves depend on the fact that *a* promotes value more effectively than *b*, for the contingent reason that it is consonant with an existing institution. The mere existence of an institution speaks neither in favour of nor against acting in accordance with it.

7. AGENCY AND COMMON SENSE

Reflection on common-sense morality has led many moral philosophers to accept at the philosophical level certain distinctions that seem implicit within that morality. Utilitarianism tends to deny many of these distinctions, and this, Griffin suggests, poses another agency-related problem for the theory:

The source of the moral prohibitions we have been considering is located, not exclusively but in no small measure, in the nature of agents. A consequence of this is that we are right to attach moral weight to certain common-sense distinctions—for instance, between *acting* and *omitting, doing* and *letting happen,* duties *not to harm* and duties *to aid.* We live by, and can only live by, the moral norms and relations that I have been speaking of, and they embody a form of these distinctions. But the source of the distinction lies, I suspect, in the nature of agents, not in the nature of the two kinds of behaviour—acting and omitting, doing and letting happen, and so on. (*VJ* 119–20)

This sounds like another move from 'is' to 'ought'. Let us take the distinction between killing and letting die. There is no doubt that all of us, at the level of lived morality, tend in most cases to view killing entirely differently from letting die. This way of looking at things may be unavoidable. But, the utilitarian can suggest, if it is, that does not count against the utilitarian theory itself, since that is a theory about justification which can be bolted on to any account of human agency, as we saw above. But is there anyway reason to think it *entirely* unavoidable? I think not. Many of those influenced by the writings on world poverty of, for example, Peter Singer would probably accept that they have come to see letting die as, morally speaking, much more like killing than they had previously thought.

Further, reflection upon the history of our moral norms might suggest that there is room for further *rapprochement*. Our norms concerning killing obviously emerged in societies much smaller than our own. It was a necessary condition of these societies' existence that individuals who could gain from killing others refrain from doing so. On the other hand, the society could probably continue to flourish if certain of its members were left to die in extreme situations, partly because the situations would be rare and partly because one fewer person would not cause any fundamental problem for the society as a whole.

This story probably captures the essence of the truth about why we view killing and letting die so differently. But the question is whether reason can sanction this difference of view. The utilitarian, of course, will say that it cannot, that there is no moral difference to be found here 'in the nature of two kinds of behaviour'. As yet, non-utilitarian moral philosophers have made little if any progress in grounding any fundamental moral distinction between killing and letting die, and the implication of utilitarianism in this case is clear enough: we should seek to amend our practices, primarily in the direction of taking letting die far more seriously than we do at present, but also, particularly in medicine, of not attributing any special intrinsic importance to killing.

It is here, at the interface of theory and real life, that pessimism about philosophy seems most justified. The limits of the will are constraints not just on the content of the norms grounded in ambitious impartial philosophical theory, but on the effectiveness of such theory to move those who accept it. I have suggested that it need not be the case that we *must* 'largely live as, anyway, we were going to live' (*VJ* 91). But even after systematic philosophy has done its best, we probably shall, pretty much.

Academic philosophy is unlike, say, politics, in which it is becoming daily more true that medium matters more than message. Any hope philosophy has of influencing people for the better depends on its plausibility. I have suggested in this chapter that some of Griffin's arguments against system in ethics are unsuccessful. But systematizers in ethics must not be immodest, since a credible ethics for human beings must be based on a plausible account of their nature, and in particular their capacities as agents. It is here that systematic ethics has much to learn from Griffin. The good life is to some extent independent of morality, our wills are limited, many social norms are in place, and our knowledge and predictive powers are circumscribed. A judicious systematizer in ethics must face up to these and similar facts, and in seeking to understand them will find no better source of illumination than Griffin's writings.

8

Impartiality, Predictability, and Indirect Consequentialism

Brad Hooker

James Griffin's *Well-Being: Its Meaning, Measurement, and Moral Importance* was a model of sophisticated and reasonable consequentialism. His more recent *Value Judgement: Improving Our Ethical Beliefs* includes a rejection of consequentialism. So Griffin is an apostate. What makes apostates so threatening and interesting is that they know well—from the inside, as it were—what they are rejecting. In this chapter I examine the charge prosecuted by the later Griffin against indirect consequentialism. The question I will be asking is whether anything recognizable as indirect consequentialism can survive Griffin's charge.

1. WHAT EXACTLY IS INDIRECT CONSEQUENTIALISM?

Consequentialism is a species of moral theory, of which utilitarianism is a subspecies. A consequentialist theory assesses acts either by their own actual or expected consequences, or by the actual or expected consequences of motivations, dispositions, rules. Utilitarianism assigns non-instrumental value to only one kind of consequence—effects on overall well-being. Non-utilitarian consequentialist theories assign non-instrumental value to consequences other than well-being, though of course they also typically care about well-being too. But for the rest of this paper I shall follow Griffin in taking the most plausible form of consequentialism to assign non-instrumental value to well-being and fairness (*VJ* 165).

I am grateful to Roger Crisp, Keith Horton, and the Press's anonymous reviewer for helpful comments on an earlier draft of this paper.

Direct consequentialism is usually construed as holding that an act's moral permissibility depends on a comparison of that act's actual or expected consequences with the consequences of alternative acts open to the agent. Maximizing direct consequentialism judges an act to be permissible if and only if its consequences would be at least as good as the consequences of any other act open to the agent.

Indirect consequentialism judges an act permissible if and only if it accords with the motivations, dispositions, rules, and kind of conscience that are favoured by a consequentialist assessment. But how does this assessment go? Different indirect consequentialists give different answers. And the difference between the answers makes some versions of indirect consequentialism more plausible than others. This will be the focus of some of my later remarks.

Sometimes the distinction between direct and indirect consequentialism is framed differently. I have identified the distinction as one about the criterion of permissible action. Bernard Williams, who introduced the terminology, wrote:

The term *direct* I use—putting it . . . very roughly—to mean that the consequential value which is the concern of morality is attached directly to particular actions, rather than to rules or practices under which decisions are taken without further reference to consequences; the latter sort of view is *indirect* consequentialism. The distinction, or one very like it, is often labelled, as it is by Smart, as a distinction between *act*-utilitarianism and *rule*-utilitarianism. . . . in the present matter, the term 'rule-utilitarianism' is less than useful, particularly because I am concerned with the indirect value of various sorts of things besides rules, such as dispositions.[1]

Williams's introduction of new terminology seems to me unfortunate. Though he was correct that the indirect value of things other than rules matters, rule-consequentialists should hardly be thought to have ignored such things. Take the particular case of dispositions. Acceptance of a rule, at least the kind of acceptance that rule-consequentialists have in mind, centrally involves people's having certain dispositions.[2] So, in thinking about rules, rule-consequentialists *are* thinking about dispositions. True, there are dispositions that do not involve anything as conscious as accepting a rule. But consequentialists should focus on dispositions that can be shaped by moral

[1] Bernard Williams, 'Critique of Utilitarianism', in J. J. C. Smart and Bernard Williams, *Utilitarianism: For and Against* (Cambridge: Cambridge University Press, 1973), 81. This and other passages from Williams I quote refer to utilitarianism rather than consequentialism. The difference does not matter for the purposes of my chapter.

[2] Richard Brandt, 'Some Merits of One Form of Rule-Utilitarianism', *University of Colorado Studies in Philosophy* (1967), 39–65, (repr. in Brandt, *Morality, Utilitarianism, and Rights* (New York: Cambridge University Press, 1992), 111–36), §8; *A Theory of the Good and the Right* (Oxford: Clarendon Press, 1979), 164–76; and *Facts, Values, and Morality* (New York: Cambridge University Press, 1996), 67, 69, 145, 156, 201, 266–8, 289.

considerations, and at least typically these will be dispositions that can go hand in hand with acceptance of a rule.

To say that a disposition should be shaped by moral considerations does not mean that the *original cause* of the disposition must lie in attention to moral considerations. The origin of some of our dispositions is socio-biological. But, as our reasoning capacities develop, we learn that moral considerations call for the reinforcement of some of these dispositions, for the refinement or even suppression of others, and for the development of some dispositions not already programmed into us by biology or fostered in us by social forces.

Furthermore, to say that a disposition should be shaped by moral considerations does not mean agents must be thinking about such considerations while acting. Moral considerations require people to pay special attention to the needs of their own children. This does not mean they will be thinking about morality while they are attending to their children's needs. Better that they act out of spontaneous affection. Still, when spontaneous affection wanes, a feeling of duty should be ready to step in and motivate action.

Having made these points about the relation of dispositions to rules, I now return to the distinction between direct and indirect consequentialism. What makes indirect consequentialism different from direct consequentialism is *not* that indirect consequentialism is interested in the indirect value of dispositions and direct consequentialism is not. Direct consequentialists can be interested in the value of dispositions. But direct consequentialists think the value of dispositions does not determine the rightness of action, and indirect consequentialists think the value of dispositions does determine the rightness of action. As Williams wrote,

Direct utilitarianism regards that act as right which has the best consequences. So indirect utilitarianism may be expected to deny this, and to hold that some acts are right even though they are not utility-maximising—for instance, because they are done in accordance with a rule which is utilitarianly valuable. . . . Thus if we ask the indirect utilitarian 'What does the rightness of acts consist in?' we shall get an answer with which the direct utilitarian will to a certain extent disagree; and conversely.[3]

So, when Sidgwick wrote, 'we must carefully distinguish between the recognition of goodness in dispositions, and the recognition of rightness in conduct' (*ME* 428), he was in effect throwing his hand in with the direct consequentialists. Indirect consequentialists disagree with Sidgwick because they hold the rightness of an act depends on the goodness of the dispositions that would allow that act.

[3] Williams, 'Critique of Utilitarianism', 121.

2. GRIFFIN'S OBJECTIONS TO DIRECT CONSEQUENTIALISM

We can better understand Griffin's objections to indirect consequentialism if we first understand his objections to direct consequentialism. Griffin's view of direct consequentialism is reminiscent of Williams's. Williams moved from a claim about direct consequentialism as a theory about the criterion of moral rightness to a claim about direct consequentialism as a doctrine about how we should decide what to do:

There is no distinctive place for *direct* utilitarianism unless it is, within fairly narrow limits, a doctrine about how one should decide what to do. This is because its distinctive doctrine is about what acts are right, and, especially for utilitarians, the only distinctive interest or point of the question what acts are right, relates to the situation of deciding to do them.[4]

The implication is that direct consequentialism has got to be a decision procedure as well as a criterion of rightness.[5]

However, in the twenty-five years since the publication of the passage from Williams that I have just quoted, a quite different view has taken hold. This is the idea that there is a form of consequentialism that insists (*a*) the consequences of an act determine its rightness but (*b*) the agent should typically *not* be deciding what to do by thinking about those consequences. But, like Williams, Griffin now thinks consequentialism cannot *plausibly* take such a form:

Although criterion and decision procedure can indeed diverge, they may not, I think, get far apart from one another. Our decision procedures will, of course, be restricted by our capacities, but any criterion for a human practice cannot become too remote from them without losing its standing as a criterion.   (*VJ* 105)

Why must the criterion of moral rightness not diverge too far from our decision procedures? The answer, I think, is that such divergence undermines the importance of rightness. If you obtain the best information available,

<hr/>

[4] Williams, 'Critique of Utilitarianism', 128.
[5] The distinction between a decision procedure and a criterion of rightness is implicit in Mill's *Utilitarianism* (1861), ch. II; *ME* 405–6, 413, 428, 489–90; and G. E. Moore, *Principia Ethica* (Cambridge: Cambridge University Press, 1903), 162–4. For explicit contemporary discussions, see R. Eugene Bales, 'Act-Utilitarianism: Account of Right-making Characteristics or Decision-Making Procedure?' *American Philosophical Quarterly*, 8 (1971), 257–65; Peter Railton, 'Alienation, Consequentialism, and the Demands of Morality', *Philosophy and Public Affairs*, 13 (1984), 174–31, at 140–6, 152–3; Derek Parfit, *Reasons and Persons* (Oxford: Clarendon Press, 1984), 24–9; David Brink, *Moral Realism and the Foundations of Ethics* (New York: Cambridge University Press, 1989), 216, 256–61; and Roger Crisp, *Mill on Utilitarianism* (London: Routledge, 1997), ch. 5. For the moment, I omit references to Griffin's own discussion of the distinction, because I shall be coming back to his discussion.

follow the right decision procedure, and then act in accordance with the decision reached by that decision procedure, you cannot rightly be blamed for your action. But, if the criterion distinguishing right from wrong is something completely different from the procedure you are supposed to use when making moral decisions, then wrongness has wandered off from blameworthiness. There seems little reason to care whether acts are wrong if wrong action is not something for which you would blame yourself and others.[6] So, to retain its importance, wrongness must stay fairly close to blameworthiness. And to stay close to blameworthiness, it must have a potential role in our decision procedures. (What role? If 'wrong' plays a role in our moral decision procedure, it will override other moral considerations. After all, what could be more morally important in the moral evaluation of acts than whether they are wrong?)

So let us take direct consequentialism to be a view not only about right and wrong action but also about moral decision-making. But now direct consequentialism is open to the familiar objection that it is not a *good* decision procedure (*WB* 195–206). As a decision procedure, it would require the agent to decide on the act with the greatest expected value. The expected value of an act is calculated by multiplying the probability of each possible outcome times the value of that outcome, and then summing the products. If a consequentialist theory requires us to calculate the expected values of each option before each decision, then (even if we are not caught in an infinite regress of calculating the expected value of further calculations) we will spend too much time and energy gathering information and calculating. There is a lot more to life than doing cost–benefit analysis.

Furthermore, direct consequentialism makes unacceptable demands on the will. As a decision procedure, direct consequentialism would require us to make every decision by choosing the act with the best consequences impartially considered, no matter what the inconvenience or harm to our friends, our family, ourselves. Direct consequentialism seems thus to require a relentless and constant impartiality in our day-to-day thinking. But, Griffin insists, such a demand is psychologically unrealistic.

No one has argued so carefully for this thesis. Griffin starts by being a realist about human nature. 'The enormous problem is how we move human agents, who are genetically programmed to be highly selfish and whose natural concern for others is limited and fragile, to act better' (*VJ* 75). The task must

---

[6] But perhaps we could think of direct consequentialism as a theory about what you have *most reason* to do, rather than as a theory connecting to blameworthiness. For some suggestions in this vein, see *ME*, esp. 382, where Sidgwick takes rational benevolence to be an account of what one has reason to do, and 490, where he contemplates the possibility that utilitarianism would itself condemn an attempt to make it into the public moral code. See also Roger Crisp, 'The Dualism of Practical Reason', *Proceedings of the Aristotelian Society*, 96 (1996), 53–73, esp. 56–7.

not be underestimated. To get people 'to see themselves and others . . . in such a way that they will be more prepared than they are naturally to give others their due . . . usually takes a lifetime of training, and success is always in doubt' (*VJ* 76). While, of course, some kinds of altruism are natural, even these militate against complete impartiality:

there is genetic bonding to a few others. Many species, humans among them, are capable of great self-sacrifice, especially to protect offspring. But how can we expect beings like that, profoundly self-interested and of very limited altruism, to be capable of complete impartiality, counting everybody for one and none for more than one? (*VJ* 87)

And it is not just natural feelings that pull so recalcitrantly towards partiality. Careful reflection on the nature of our good does so as well. Griffin argues that among the central components of the good life are accomplishment and deep personal relations (*WB*, chs. 2, 4; *VJ*, ch. 2). Accomplishment and deep personal relations involve 'long-term, life-structuring' aims and focus:

To have deep attachments to particular persons is to acquire motives that shape much of one's life and carry on through most of it. To accomplish something with one's life requires dedication to particular activities that typically narrow and absorb one's attention. Many prudential values involve commitments—to particular persons, institutions, causes, and careers. One cannot live a prudentially good life, one cannot fully flourish, without becoming in large measure partial. That partiality becomes part of one; it is not something one can psychologically enter into and exit from at will. (*VJ* 85)[7]

So personal good has as components accomplishment and deep personal relations, and these components require partiality.

This partiality precludes one's always aiming to do what maximizes the impartial good:

An obvious doubt about a direct form of utilitarianism is whether persons can have the commitment to their family, their pursuits, and their community that they must have for private and public life to go well, yet be able to drop these commitments whenever utility calculation beckons. . . . Some commitments do not leave us able, occasion by occasion, having reviewed all actions . . . to choose the best; some will not leave us with time to notice chances for doing more good; others, especially to other persons, will not leave us able to take such chances even if we see them. (*VJ* 104)

But suppose you made maximizing the impartial good your overriding personal goal. In that case, you would achieve a personal accomplishment by maximizing impartial good. Griffin rightly notes, however, that this accom-

[7] See also *WB* 196, 198, 199.

plishment is but one personal good, and it would probably come at the expense of others, such as deep personal relations and enjoyment (*VJ* 86).

Why are deep personal relations incompatible with constant impartiality? It is just an empirical fact that human beings cannot have for very many others the strength of personal affection and concern involved in deep personal relations.[8] Likewise, I believe Griffin thinks it an empirical fact that a life focused exclusively on increasing the impartial good will contain less enjoyment than one involving a wider variety of projects. In any event, a life of constant impartiality would not be one beneficial to the agent. And, once agents see this, trying to train them to be constantly impartial will be all the more quixotic (*VJ* 88).

Yet could not some inspiring ideal transport people to saintly impartiality? Griffin writes:

> If I thought I was created by God, that my bodily life was an illusory passage to eternal bliss, that my flourishing consisted in the extinction of my own ego, and if I had the psychological support of a community of believers living the same sort of life, then I could probably make sacrifices I cannot now make. I might also hope for some sort of transformation of my will through divine grace. But I do not, nor do many religious believers, think that. (*VJ* 89)

Nor should we be too influenced by the fact that people are capable of making huge sacrifices in the pitch of excitement. That people are capable of making huge sacrifices in the pitch of excitement does not show that they can be trained to make large sacrifices for the impartial good on a day-in, day-out basis (*VJ* 88–90).

But suppose it were possible to get everyone to be utterly and constantly impartial, by suppressing everyone's concern for and commitments to particular others. Would this be desirable? Griffin takes it that the answer is 'No': 'A world in which everyone's life were as good as possible would be a world in which people were full of commitments. The impartial ideal, then, would be a world populated by agents incapable of promoting the impartial ideal' (*VJ* 86).

In short, then, direct consequentialism should be understood as a moral doctrine not only about what distinguishes right and wrong but also about how agents should make moral decisions. But, as a decision procedure, direct consequentialism requires calculative and affective resources human agents do not have. If there is to be a plausible form of consequentialism, it must be an indirect form.

---

[8] Hence Griffin writes, 'One can raise one's capacity for complete impartiality and generalized love of humanity only by reducing one's commitments to particular persons and projects' (*VJ* 77). See also Parfit, *Reasons and Persons*, 27–8, 30, 32–5.

3. INDIRECT CONSEQUENTIALISM AND THE WILL

Griffin suggests indirect consequentialism is reasonable about the will. Indirect consequentialism does not require the relentless, constant, day-to-day, 'first-order' impartiality that direct consequentialism requires.[9] Rather, indirect consequentialism holds that our moral decision-making should be governed by, among other things, duties to give special weight to the interests of those with whom we have especially strong connections, such as friends and family.

Indirect consequentialism will not merely allow partiality, but require it (within limits). Other things being roughly equal, in your reasoning about what to do with our own resources (time, energy, material goods) you should favour your own parent, or spouse, or child, or friend over those who do not have any special relationship with you. If you could give your painkiller either to your own child or to a stranger suffering the same amount or even a little more, you should give it to your child.

Sometimes other things are not even roughly equal. You may have already promised the painkiller to the stranger. Moreover, often professional roles demand absolute impartiality—for example, a nurse deciding to whom to give the only remaining medicine. This sort of role-based obligation to ignore personal relationships arises from the fact that the agent in that role is allocating resources (money, services, whatever) that do not belong to that agent.[10] Nevertheless, with respect to your own resources and absent special circumstances, your reasoning about what to do should give greater weight to the welfare of those who stand in special relationships to you.

The indirect consequentialist reasons for requiring such partiality are twofold. First, there is again the point that having deep personal relations with others is an important component of the agent's good, and partiality towards them is part of these deep personal relations. Secondly, virtually everyone needs the special concern of some others. Indeed, people need assurance that their welfare will *consistently* get special weight in someone else's practical deliberation. And we cannot depend on affection to secure this attention and deliberative priority every time they are appropriate. Affection is not reliable enough, being so easy to forget or ignore when anger, jealousy, or disap-

---

[9] The terms 'first-order' and 'second-order' impartiality come from Brian Barry, *Justice as Impartiality* (Oxford: Clarendon Press, 1995), chs. 8, 9. But the distinction these terms mark is hardly new. Sidgwick wrote, 'Bentham's dictum [every man to count for one, nobody for more than one] must be understood merely as making the conception of the ultimate end precise—laying down that one person's happiness is to be counted for as much as another's (supposed equal in degree)—not as directly prescribing the *rules of conduct* by which this end will be best attained'(*ME* 432, emphasis added).

[10] This point is made in John Cottingham, 'The Ethical Credentials of Partiality', *Proceedings of the Aristotelian Society*, 98 (1998), 1–21, at 11.

pointment intrudes. Moral requirements of loyalty are thus needed for the common enough occasions when affection is not up to the job.[11] In other words, special moral obligations towards family and friends can then be justified on the ground that internalization of these obligations gives people some assurance that some others will consistently take a special interest in them. Such assurance answers a powerful psychological need.

So indirect consequentialism endorses partiality towards family and friends when one is deciding how to use one's own time, energy, money, and so on. Is Griffin thus right that indirect consequentialism does not make unreasonable demands on the will? As already noted, partiality is not something one can drop at will. But does this mean equal concern for all others is never possible? If even indirect consequentialism demands impartial concern at some point, and such impartiality is impossible, then indirect consequentialism is clearly in trouble.

Griffin writes that the central question for indirect consequentialists 'would be something along these lines: What set of rules and dispositions would, over society at large and in the long run, most promote well-being, fairness, and equality, and how are these competing goods to be weighed against one another?' (*VJ* 165–6).[12] Apart from certain qualifications that I will come back to in a moment, this does seem the indirect consequentialists' central question. Now, does this question—i.e. does indirect consequentialist thinking— require impossible impartiality?

I am not suggesting that Griffin thinks indirect consequentialist thinking does require impossible impartiality. But I can see how someone might be tempted to think it does. Partiality naturally and rightly runs so deep in our motivational structure that we often cannot set it aside when we see that we could choose an act benefiting strangers rather than another act that would bring lesser benefits to those towards whom we are partial. Why is not what is true of choice among *acts* also true of choice among *sets of rules*? Why think we can set partiality aside when choosing among sets of rules and dispositions? Why think that, when we are deciding upon rules, we will *ever* have enough concern for those outside the circle of family and friends to sacrifice the interests of those inside the circle?

Well, consider this example. Many people endorse greater burdens (such as higher taxes) for their own families and friends, for the sake of benefits

---

[11] Richard Brandt wrote, 'Michael Stocker seems to think that interiorizing the aversions (etc.) of an optimal morality is incompatible with the existence of motives like love, friendship, affection, and community. I fail to see why. The moral motives here will operate as a "back-up" system when direct affections fail' (Brandt, 'Morality and its Critics', *American Philosophical Quarterly*, 26 (1989), 89–100, at n. 22, repr. in Brandt, *Morality, Utilitarianism, and Rights*). See also *ME* 435.

[12] In the rest of this chapter I will ignore the question about weighing well-being, fairness, and equality against one another. I have addressed this question in my 'Rule-Consequentialism, Incoherence, Fairness', *Proceedings of the Aristotelian Society*, 95 (1995), 19–35, §4.

(redistribution) to needy strangers. Not all of the people supporting higher taxes on themselves for the sake of redistribution care more about needy strangers than they do about their own families and friends. If they did care more about the strangers, then presumably they would make far more regular sacrifices for the needy. They would more often give to worthwhile charities when they see that such contributions would do needy strangers more good than would expenditure on themselves or their family or friends.

Many people who endorse higher taxes on their own families and friends for the sake of redistribution to needy strangers take this stand because they care about impartial justification. To be more specific, they think morality requires them to support impartially justified rules, and they think impartially justified rules include ones mandating redistributive taxation. They also think that impartially justified rules do not go so far as to require giving to strangers whenever this would benefit them more than would expenditure on self, family, or friends. If I am right that there are people with this psychology, then they illustrate that the sort of impartiality needed by indirect consequential-ists is possible.[13]

This concern with impartial justification can seem far less generous and admirable than a more direct concern for the well-being of strangers. But what we need is some motivation strong enough to override love for friends and family and self. And the question we should ask is which of the following it is more realistic to expect and require: (*a*) a direct concern for the well-being of strangers that is strong enough to overcome love for friends, family, and self, or (*b*) a concern for endorsing and following impartially justified rules that is strong enough to overcome love for friends, family, and self. I think it more realistic to expect and require (*b*). True, charities often seem to think they can raise more money by appealing to people's sympathy than to their sense of duty. But I still think sympathy for strangers the less enduring coun-terpoise to concern for one's own friends, family, and self.

4. INDIRECT CONSEQUENTIALISM AND PREDICTABILITY

I turn now to Griffin's reason for rejecting indirect consequentialism. He maintains that indirect consequentialism is unreasonable about rationality. He thinks we cannot do the calculations, even to a reliable degree of prob-ability, which would be necessary to decide which rules, feelings, dispositions are *best*.

Consider Griffin's own proposals. He suggests that, when we try to refine

[13] This connects with my discussion in 'Rule-Consequentialism, Incoherence, Fairness', esp. §3. See also Brian Barry's discussion, cited above.

our crude, vague moral notions such as benevolence and justice, we have to think like legislators who worry about the long-term consequences of changes in our practices and institutions. 'Moral legislators' will, of course, have to pay attention to basic facts about what humans need, and pay attention to the affective and cognitive limitations of human agents. Moral legislators will also have to consider knock-on effects, such as the extent to which one change might undermine other norms.

What he contends we cannot do is calculate to a sufficient degree of reliability which set of rules and dispositions would, if they were to prevail in society, produce the most good in the long run (*VJ* 106–7, 165–6). Or rather, his contention is that we cannot do the calculation often enough to keep indirect consequentialism from being squeezed out of the centre of moral life:

> We may know enough to identify fairly obviously inadequate rules and dispositions, but there will be many left that we cannot rank. And it is in the wide band that they would constitute that many of the hard choices in morality—choices, say, about the particular form that respect for life should take—would have to be made. (*VJ* 107)

Is Griffin here attacking the best version of indirect consequentialism? One version claims that an act is wrong if and only if it is forbidden by the code of rules whose social prevalence would *actually* produce the best consequences. On this version of indirect consequentialism, in order to know what acts are wrong, we would have to know which rules actually would produce the best consequences. If Griffin is right that we often do not know which rules actually would have the best consequences, then we cannot know which acts are wrong on this version of indirect consequentialism. This does seem to undermine this version.

A different version of indirect consequentialism is framed in terms of *reasonable expectations* about the consequences of the internalization of rules. On this version, an act is wrong if and only if it is forbidden by the code of rules whose social prevalence could reasonably be expected to produce the best consequences. Since Griffin thinks we regularly cannot confidently predict which rules would be best, this version of indirect consequentialism is also in trouble.

At this point I think indirect consequentialists need to make their theory even more modest. First, they need to admit that, as far as we can tell, more than one alternative code of rules may seem to us at least as good as the best other codes we can identify. Indirect consequentialists can then propose that, of these codes with unsurpassed expected value, the one closest to conventional morality determines which kinds of act are wrong.[14]

---

[14] Cf. *ME* 467–71, 473–6, 480–4; Richard Brandt, *A Theory of the Good and the Right*, 290; 'Fairness to Indirect Optimific Theories in Ethics', *Ethics*, 98 (1988), 341–60, repr. in Brandt, *Morality, Utilitarianism, and Rights*, 137–57, at 147, 154; and *Facts, Values, and Morality*, 143–4; *WB* 206, 302.

A number of possible objections to this proposal present themselves. Suppose that, when we are considering which set of rules to advocate, the best alternatives we can identify seem equally close to conventional morality. This case illustrates that the test I have advocated will not necessarily always determine exactly which set of rules to choose. But how serious a problem is this? How often will we be presented with two or more alternative possible codes with not only just as much expected value as one another but also the very same proximity to conventional morality? I do not know.

Another possible objection to my proposal is that it permits indirect consequentialism to let us down just where we need help. For if indirect consequentialism tells us that, as between codes as good as any other as far as we can tell, we should choose the one closest to conventional morality, then indirect consequentialism takes onboard some of the problems with conventional morality. One such problem is that there are 'hard cases', cases for which conventional morality provides no determinate answer. So, to the extent to which indirect consequentialism follows conventional morality, indirect consequentialism will also lack a determinate answer.

In reply, I concede that indirect consequentialism will sometimes be no more determinate than conventional morality. But in other cases indirect consequentialism is clearly better, in that it provides reasonable grounds for criticizing conventional morality when different norms would produce more well-being or fairness. Is indirect consequentialism also sometimes worse than conventional morality? I have argued elsewhere that it is not.[15] If I am correct, then indirect consequentialism is never worse and sometimes better than conventional morality. Thus, even if (as in the cases where indirect consequentialism mirrors the indeterminateness of conventional morality) indirect consequentialism is *sometimes* no better than conventional morality, indirect consequentialism can still be clearly better overall.

Yet another possible objection to my proposal is that any role for conventional morality is too conservative. The suitably modest form of indirect consequentialism here under discussion holds that, if we *can* identify an alternative to the conventional code that we can confidently predict would have better consequences, then we should move to it. And if we *cannot* identify an alternative we can confidently predict would produce better consequences, then sticking with what we have and know can hardly seem unreasonable.

In any case, Griffin himself cannot complain against this form of indirect consequentialism that it is too conservative, for he gives tradition a large role in determining what is right. Where we cannot predict to a reliable degree of probability what the consequences of various codes would be, he holds that tradition and extant convention should be our guide: 'If we are wise, we shall

---

[15] See my 'Compromising with Convention', *American Philosophical Quarterly*, 31 (1994), 311–17.

then recognize our limits and settle for living within, while also reforming, the society that seems generally satisfactory that we have inherited' (*VJ* 96; see also 119–21).

Griffin's complaint is rather that for indirect consequentialism to rely to this extent on tradition and convention marginalizes indirect consequentialist thought (*VJ* 108, 165–6). He writes that indirect consequentialism, in relying to this extent on tradition and convention, can no longer plausibly claim to be the overall form of moral rationality.

I cannot see that this is the conclusion to reach. If reasonably expecting that changes to traditional and/or conventional rules and norms would result in better overall consequences is the sole ground we have for revising traditional and/or conventional rules and norms, and if we think we should stick with traditional and/or conventional rules only when we cannot confidently identify which changes to them would result in better overall consequences, then indirect consequentialist endorsement for moral change provides the necessary and sufficient conditions for moral change.[16] To admit this is to admit that indirect consequentialism is our basic morality.

And when Griffin discusses changes to existing moral practices, his reasoning looks consequentialist. For example, his approach to the question whether euthanasia is permissible plays off a concern with maintaining a general respect for life against a concern to 'limit the damage'—to wit, to prevent avoidable suffering (*VJ* 120–1).[17] This seems to me just what a rule-consequentialist would worry about: Would the immensely valuable *general* taboo on killing the innocent be undermined by allowing active euthanasia under tight restrictions?

Admittedly, his discussion of euthanasia is introduced as an example of how utility can provide a lever for criticism of inherited moral beliefs and practices. He mentions other possible sources for criticism: reflection on rights, reflection on the nature of society, and reflection on the nature of agents. I will argue now that none of these precludes indirect consequentialism.

First consider rights. Suppose we follow Griffin in thinking autonomy an important component of well-being. Suppose we also follow him in thinking rights are grounded mainly in the protection of autonomy. This puts us in a position to see rights as having a fundamentally consequentialist, indeed welfarist, grounding. Hardly something inimical to indirect consequentialism.

What of the other sources he mentions? Of course indirect consequentialists will focus on facts about human nature and the workings of society, as Griffin acknowledges (*VJ* 106). He goes from acknowledging this to saying

---

[16] This is true even if we can only rarely predict with confidence that changes to moral rules will improve things overall.

[17] Note the similarities to my 'Rule-Utilitarianism and Euthanasia', in Hugh LaFollette (ed.), *Ethics in Practice* (Oxford: Blackwell, 1997), 42–52.

that indirect consequentialism 'cannot admit that our ignorance justifies the sort of reliance on tradition that I have defended' (*VJ* 109). But I have argued that indirect consequentialism can and should stick with inherited practices where we cannot confidently predict that a change will have better overall consequences. So we have still to find something that is in Griffin's view a legitimate source for revision of existing moral belief and practice and yet is not consistent with a suitably modest indirect consequentialism.

9

The Improvisatory Drama of
Decision-Making

Amélie Oksenberg Rorty

> No action without interaction;
> no interaction without drama.
> no drama without both habit and happenstance
> no philosophy without melodrama

It is no news that the movement from decision to action and from action to outcome are contingent and accident-prone.[1] But we tend to set aside the fact that—for good or ill—intentions and decisions are themselves affected by tangential and accidental contingencies. I want to explore the dynamics of the process of shared or collective decision-making in which participants find themselves improvising dramatic roles and advancing positions that often do not represent their primary aims or views.[2] But, despite the powerful role of chance and accident in decision-making, despite its apparent arbitrariness, there is an Aesopian moral, a surprising set of norms that can, in principle, govern the process.

For their counsel and conversation, I am grateful to Seyla Ben Habib, Myles Burnyeat, Rudiger Bittner, Catherine Elgin, Moshe Halbertal, Shirley Kaufman, Genevieve Lloyd, Clifford Orwin, Ruth Nevo, Jay Rorty, Josef Stern, and Eleanore Stump. A version of this essay was delivered at the World Congress of Philosophy, August 1998 and at DAI in Heidelberg, July 1999. The Van Leer Foundation and the Hartman Institute, both in Jerusalem, generously provided hospitality for reflection and writing.

[1] The distinction between contingent and accidental events is germane to the evaluation of decisions. Talented and foresighted decision-makers weigh the probability of relevant but hypothetical contingent factors in the course of their deliberations. See Michael Bratman, *Intention, Plans and Practical Reason* (Cambridge, Mass.: Harvard University Press, 1987). But, unlike contingencies, accidents, happenstance, and chance are not open to the same kind of calculation. In the very nature of the case, they are unlikely to be foreseeable by even the most astute decision-makers. See Aristotle, *Physics*, 2. 3–6; Machiavelli, *The Prince*, ch. 25.

[2] Although decision-makers may represent groups—Labor and Likud in Israel, the Congress Party and the BJP in India, factions within any political party—I shall, for the sake of convenience, refer to players and participants in the singular.

By way of surveying the territory, we will begin with a case study, an example of the ordinary dramas of decision-making. That story should, I hope, be sufficiently vivid and familiar to convince you that This is How Things Are. We will then turn to a summary of what our story reveals about (what we rather grandly call) practical deliberation. Our story brings us to the centre of James Griffin's work, his account of human thriving, and his analysis of the criteria for evaluating competing ethical theories (see especially *WB* and *VJ*). We'll address these issues by presenting a brief review of several contemporary rational reconstructions of the norms of deliberation; and end with another Aesopian observation about the role of philosophy as critic and legislator of criteria for the evaluation of ethical systems.

1

Our story is meant to represent a wide array of ordinary and familiar types of decision-making, but any resemblance to specific persons—living, dead, or imaginary—is purely coincidental.

Consider a fictional Prime Minister (call him 'Clint') of a self-styled constitutional democracy (call it 'Luna') that is formally structured by a checks-and-balances separation of powers among its executive, legislative, and judicial branches. Although the military of Luna is under the direct command of the PM as the head of the executive branch, the legislature controls the military budget. In principle, a declaration of war must be approved by the legislative branch, but in fact the executive can mandate limited military action under special circumstances.

Let's suppose that Lunar decision-makers agree on at least three principles that should govern policy directives: (1) Luna is—and must remain—the dominant political, economic, and military world power. (2) While Luna does not have a mandate to intervene in the internal affairs of other nations, it has undertaken some (undefined) responsibility to preserve international peace and to protect human rights. (Let's ignore the Lunar motivations for undertaking such a role.) When this commitment seems to conflict with (what is presumed to be) Luna's national interest, the timing, focus, and strategies for its exercising its presumptively humanitarian obligations should—at the very least—be compatible with general perceptions of Luna's national interest. (3) Luna is protective of its military personnel: because it is reluctant to engage its force without a reasonable assurance assured of attaining a well-defined objective, with minimal cost in lives, it prefers to act at a distance—for example, with missiles rather than with ground forces.

Suppose there is a serious crisis in a neighbouring state—a famine, civil war, persistent and organized terrorism—a crisis that does not directly involve Luna, but that could eventually affect its interests. Suppose decision-makers find themselves individually and collectively uncertain and conflicted about the policy priorities that Luna should adopt in such circumstances.

What happens is this. Without consultation or collusion, the various branches of the government adopt a division of rhetorical labour: Clint makes belligerent and threatening speeches to confirm Lunar global dominance. The majority of influential legislators, stressing the priority of Luna's internal financial needs and interests, take a non-interventionist stand; pressing for a carefully defined objective, the military urges caution. In short, they each play different roles in a drama whose outcome will be affected by a vast array of contingencies, many of them accidental, unforeseeable, and largely beyond their control: the support of allies, an assassination, a terrified soldier shooting into a crowd, the reactions of an uninformed dictator, a terrorist attack. And this is just within Luna: the ambitions of other nation states (call them 'Mars' and 'Venus') also affect Lunar deliberations; and, of course, their decisions are equally dynamic, dialectical, and accident-prone. Moreover, decision-makers on all sides may misunderstand one another's priorities and conventions; they may be misinformed about one another's political structures, constraints, and struggles.

The role that each participant plays in the drama of the decision-making process depends only in part on his own preferences and judgement.[3] The momentum or timing of a situation may move him to accept a role—a position—in the expectation that it will be blocked by that of other actors. Because each player counts on the others to represent counterbalancing and counterpoint policies, he may advance and defend a view that is stronger than one he would actually countenance.[4] Indeed he may depend on the other actors in their drama to check and block the policy he proposes. He—and his countering players—may all agree that it is strategically important to express the entire and potentially conflicting range of Luna's general aims.

Sometimes the casting of policy roles may occur fortuitously, by sheer happenstance, rather than by serious differences in the participants' own

---

[3] In speaking of aims and preferences, I include moral principles, ideals, and values as well as wants and desires. Of course these may conflict with one another in complex ways, but I shall set aside the presumed distinctions between individual/cultural preferences and moral ideals. For arguments against the special status of the moral domain, see my 'The Many Faces of Morality', *Midwest Studies in Philosophy*, 20 (1996), 67–82.

[4] See Alasdair MacIntyre, 'How Virtues Become Vices', in H. T. Engelhardt and S. F. Spicker (eds.), *Evaluation and Explanation in the Biomedical Sciences* (The Hague: Mouton, 1982), 97–111; A. O. Rorty, 'From Exasperating Virtues to Civic Virtues', *American Philosophical Quarterly*, 33 (1996), 303–14.

priorities and judgements. Had a set of tangential circumstances—circumstances irrelevant to the matter at issue—been slightly different, the legislators might well have taken the belligerent stance, leaving the Prime Minister to urge conciliation. He might, for instance, have been the only person empowered to resolve a critical labour strike whose outcome could affect the international crisis. The dynamic momentum of the decision-makers' interaction—embedding as it does a wide range of extraneous factors (accidents of timing, other overriding preoccupations, the rhetorical powers of the participants)—leads to a decision that may not represent the preferences of any of the participants, acting individually or collectively. Needless to say, the final decision may not be in Luna's best interests, either in its own terms or objectively considered. But it may also, by happenstance, serve the participants better than any of them, acting individually, collectively, or in their roles, could have imagined. Happenstance is impartial; and (what seems to be) today's beneficial happenstance may come to seem like tomorrow's disaster. (And contrariwise.)

The drama of the division of roles appears in ordinary collective decision-making. It can also occur in the very process of articulating the most general aims of an association or group.[5] It occurs in department meetings and corporate board rooms, in families and town councils, in labour unions and law firms. It can also occur within an individual in the dynamic tensions among his diverse interests and general aims.

Even the most sober, rigorous and least dramatic philosophic and scientific discussions—where neither decisions nor actions appear to be in the offing—can take this dynamic, improvisatory, dialectical . . . and accidental form. Philosophers and scientists develop positions that they might not have taken but for the counterpoint of others in the field.[6] That counterpoint often represents a host of accidental, as well as intellectually germane features. The charm, wit, and rhetorical power of a philosopher, the lineage and power of his patrons and teachers, often affect the hearing and discussion his position receives. Like decisions, philosophic positions are dramatically and substantively affected by minute social and political factors as trivial as those of many current intellectual fashions.

---

[5] See *The Federalist Papers*, Thucydides' reports of the Athenian debates (*The History of the Peloponnesian War*), and David Wiggins, 'Deliberation and Practical Reason', *Proceedings of the Aristotelian Society*, NS 76 (1975–6), 29–51. Decisions about means and about ends are interwoven: the choice of means subtly affects—and sometimes even constitutes—the ends they are meant to serve; and, of course, every specification of an end constrains the range of means appropriate to its fulfilment.

[6] See Mikhail Bakhtin, *The Dialogic Imagination*, trans. C. Emerson and M. Holquist (Austin, Texas: University of Texas Press, 1981), and his *Speech Genres*, ed. C. Emerson and M. Holquist (Austin, Texas: University of Texas Press, 1981); Wolfgang Iser, *Languages of the Unsayable* (New York: Columbia, 1989); and my 'From Exasperating Virtues to Civic Virtues'.

Think of the way in which a discussion, a real conversation, a common investigation rather than a comforting ritual or an exchange of monologues, takes place.[7] In a real conversation the participants do not know, ahead of time, what they will say, or even sometimes what they think. To be sure, there are constraints: interlocutors want (among many other things) to arrive at what is true, and they are guided by what they presently believe is true. But at any moment in the discussion there are an indefinite number of relevant, consecutive true things they could say and think. Since every conversation carries the weight of many other projects besides that of conveying or discovering what is true, the segue of conversation also serves other ends (wooing, showing off, competing). Our views and attitudes are affected by the minutiae of interactions: puzzlement or indignation on an interlocutor's face, reactive irony or admiration, the elation of common pursuit, or fear of an impending economic catastrophe. Of course the dynamics of such interactions vary with the context and participants: but they follow patterns of minute interactions. Relentless optimism can be infectious, or it can elicit sceptical reactions; frivolity can produce general merriment, or it can provoke stern gravity. Even when we act in solitude or in character, from deeply entrenched traits, decisions often emerge from an inner dialogue with familiar and usually idealized figures, many of whom have influenced the complex configuration of our habits. Some elicit our (very own) boldness, others elicit our (very own) caution. The more subtly partners in a conversation understand each other—the more they are familiar with one another's gestures, facial expressions, and reactions—the more condensed and improvisatory their conversation is likely to be. Like improvisatory jazz musicians, they sometimes lapse into a familiar habitual riff for a little rest, finding something in that riff that will lead them in a new direction. The improvisatory swerve can be set by random beats on a drum . . . or the sound of a beeper phone or a policeman's siren. Many of our basic decisions also take this improvisatory dramatic form: designing a curriculum or a playground, choosing a restaurant or planning a meal, selecting a Supreme Court justice, hanging paintings for an exhibition.

Decision-making is, in its fine-grained details, improvisatory and collaborative.[8] While collaborative decision-makers sometimes reach a consensus, they can also emerge with quite different opinions or decisions. Even at their best, individuals are rarely inclined to ask themselves searchingly critical questions; they are rarely well equipped to consider important, remote, and

[7] See my 'Virtues and their Vicissitudes', in *Mind in Action* (Boston: Beacon Press, 1988), 314–29.

[8] See Jonathan Adler, 'Moral Development and the Personal Point of View', in Eva Kittay and Diane Meyers (eds.), *Women and Moral Theory* (Totowa, NJ: Rowman & Allenheld, 1986); Annette Baier, *The Commons of the Mind* (Chicago, Ill.: Open Court, 1997), and my 'Witnessing Philosophers', *Philosophy and Literature*, 22 (1998), 309–27.

undesirable consequences. It is especially difficult for decision-makers to give due weight to the antagonistically polemical contributions in collaborative decision-making: they are often impelled to become further entrenched, insistent on their views.[9] Participants may have focused on aspects of issues that they believe to be neglected by their colleagues. Because they attempt to complement or supplement what they perceive as lacunae in their opponents' views, their argumentative rhetoric tends to become stronger and more exclusionary. Each side brackets the claims of the other in a sweeping *ceteris paribus* clause. What appear to be deep polemical disagreements sometimes arise out of the accident-prone dynamics of dialectical role playing. Ironically, even discussions that end by moving participants farther apart are nevertheless collaborative: the articulation of each view is affected by those of others in the drama.

In asking, 'How should we choose between ethical theories?', Griffin wants to evaluate and arbitrate just these sorts of disagreements, as they have been expressed by competing moral theories. Besides discussing consequentialist, deontological, and virtue theories, he might readily extend his investigation to the disagreements between cosmopolitanism, ethical particularism, and ethical pluralism. But, despite the breadth of its scope, his project appears within, rather than above the fray of dialectical disagreement. 'No thought without interaction; no interaction without drama; no drama without happenstance' also describes the activities of contemporary normative philosophic discussion of the ethics of deliberation and decision-making.

2

The Aesopian moral of our story does not, alas, have an elegant and pithy formulation.

First, the process of decision-making is dynamically improvisatory: each 'moment' or 'stage' in the specification of a decision or conclusion opens new alternatives and sets new problems. Decision-makers are rarely able to foresee

---

[9] Consider the sobering fictional and historical examples of the ways that dynamic interactions between strong antagonists can move them to express—and destroy—their characters: Sophocles' Antigone and Creon, Thucydides' account of some of the debates over Athenian policies during the Peloponnesian Wars, *Lear*, and the late novels of Thomas Hardy. Each protagonist impels the other to an ever-more antagonistic—and self-destructive—decision. For discussions of the compatibility of accident and inevitability in such dramas, see Bernard Williams, *Shame and Necessity* (Berkeley and Los Angeles: University of California Press, 1993); Bakhtin, *The Dialogic Imagination*. For a metaphysical theory that attempts to explain these phenomena, see Spinoza, *Ethics*, bks. III–V; A. O. Rorty, 'The Two Faces of Spinoza', *Review of Metaphysics*, 41 (1987), 299–316.

the directions in which their original projects may be dramatically reframed—their aims and options redefined—in the process of specifying their intentions. Secondly, decision-making is dialectically interactive: it is affected—and sometimes dramatically transformed—by the attitudes and responses of other engaged participants. Thirdly, participants in decision-making are often cast in roles that may not reflect their own initial priorities. The dynamics of their interaction sometimes propels them to take positions that are far more extreme than they had originally intended. Fourthly, the formation of intentions, decisions, and conclusions—and the further habits they engender—are as profoundly affected by chance and contingency as are their outcomes. Fifthly, however responsive decision-makers may be to the accidents of dialectical interaction, they develop entrenched habits of thought, perception, imagination. Many of these cognitive habits are themselves developed fortuitously, accidentally; many are evaluated as virtues and vices.[10] Decision-makers face a tension between strongly entrenched functional habits and equally functional context-and-accident responsive improvisation. Without habits, we lack both intellectual and practical skills; and without improvisation, we may misplace or misdirect those skills. Because the balance between them is constantly shifting, it is difficult to achieve steady equilibrium.

3

What has all this socio-political psychology to do with normative ethics? After all, this volume is a tribute to James Griffin's contributions to ethical theory, to his account of the norms of human thriving, and to his project of evaluating competing moral theories. As it presently stands, our emphasis on the accidental and fortuitous moments in the process of decision-making might suggest that decision-making is arbitrary, without firm or reliable normative control. I want now to turn to how our account—it is hardly more than a story—complements Griffin's proposals about the evaluation of ethical theories: our story has a surprising moral turn.

But first we need to let Griffin speak for himself. He asks, 'How, and how much, can we hope to refine our ethical standards? . . . How are we to decide the relative merits of the competing normative traditions—utilitarianism, deontology, virtue ethics, and so on . . .' (*VJ*, pp. vii–viii). Griffin writes from the headlands of recent ethical theory. Although he says he prefers to avoid methodological issues, to 'start where anyone would be willing to start' (*VJ* 2), his approach is unashamedly metaethical.[11] With a generous spirit and high

---

[10] See Linda Zagzebski, *Virtues of the Mind* (Cambridge: Cambridge University Press, 1996).
[11] Is there anyone who is 'anyone'?

hopes, he intends to bring the benefits of philosophic reflection to normative ethics. The 'we' in his leading question—the 'we' who are invited to evaluate criteria for choosing among substantive ethical systems—are individual agents, serious about their ethical theories because they are serious about their moral activity. But what matters about having the right standards is that we should reliably and systematically act upon them. Having the right standards is not solely a matter of having the right ethical theory: those standards are primarily expressed and articulated, specified in habits of thought and action. And that essentially includes a person's characteristic responses to accidental and unforeseen events. Does a person tend to panic (flee? fight? become detached or indifferent?) when the unpredicted or unpredictable happens? Are there norms governing responses to genuinely accidental contingencies? And how are those norms substantively internalized? How are they reliably instantiated?

Aristotle makes the point powerfully and succinctly: 'In matters of action, the end is not to study and attain knowledge of what is to be done, but rather to do it. Surely knowing about excellence or virtue is not enough: we must try to possess and use it, or find some other way in which we may become good. . . . To change by argument what has long been ingrained in a character is impossible or, at least, not easy' (*NE* 1179^{a}35–1179^{b}19). 'It is difficult to obtain the right training for virtue unless one has been brought up under the right laws' (*NE* 1179^{b}32–3). Of course Griffin does not think that the success of his project would be sufficient to issue in moral improvement. Refining our ethical standards and moral judgements may be a step towards improving our actions and characters; but Griffin's project remains incomplete until we know how the best philosophic reflection issues in moral improvement. Unfortunately, it seems such improvements are rarely achieved by even the most insightful individuals, working on their own. Rather, moral improvement seems largely to take place by changes in the social institutions that form civic life, the mentality, desires, and habits of an entire culture. And again, unfortunately, these changes are rarely themselves brought about by the aftermath of philosophic reflection.

The critical evaluation of ethical standards takes place in the context of a field of action; it begins with a set of assumed—and often conflicted—ideals and values.[12] Even the most refined and corrected evaluations are unlikely to improve even the most earnest agents without the additional support and reform of the kinds of social, political, and economic arrangements that allow

---

[12] See Isaiah Berlin, *Four Essays on Liberty* (Oxford: Oxford University Press, 1958); Michael Walzer, 'The Problem of Dirty Hands', *Philosophy and Public Affairs*, 2 (1973), 160–80; Charles Taylor, 'The Diversity of Goods', in A. Sen and B. Williams (eds.), *Utilitarianism and Beyond* (Cambridge: Cambridge University Press, 1982), 129–44; Stuart Hampshire, *Morality and Conflict* (Cambridge, Mass.: Harvard University Press, 1983).

for genuinely collaborative decision-making.[13] Unless the social and political conditions that sustain the substance of moral activity are in place, unless the conditions that direct and check standard-issue human foibles are assured, even those with the best ethical standards—whatever they may be—are likely to express their morality largely in shame, guilt, and contrition. Without well-formed habits, they are even unlikely to be able to make constructive amends. They may even become dulled to the pains of shame. Again Aristotle makes the point succinctly and powerfully. The virtues involve acquiring the right habits concerning pleasures and pains, habits that are acquired in early childhood. And, as he has it, the habits of virtue—and, by implication, those of vice and *akrasia*—are at least in part formed by political customs and institutions.[14] What Griffin calls 'value commitment' is expressed in intellectual and character habits, acquired in childhood. 'We ought to have been brought up,' Aristotle says, 'in a particular way from our very youth . . . so as both to delight in and to be pained by the things that we ought; this is the right education . . . [For] moral excellence is concerned with pleasures and pains; [and a person's character is revealed by] the [delight] and pleasures or pains he takes in his actions' (*NE* 1104^{b}3–16). And, notably: 'It is the role of the political philosopher to study pleasure and pain. For he is the master-craftsman of the end to which we look when we call one particular thing bad and another good in the unqualified sense' (*NE* 1152^{b}1–3).[15] Aristotle's emphasis on the political and cultural basis of the formation of habits applies to habits of decision-making, including those implicit in the evaluation of our ethical theories.

Presumably Griffin's investigation is, in the end, meant to guide public policy-makers—those whose decisions form the institutions that affect the mentality of public life—rather than self-reforming individuals. The question, 'How should we choose between utilitarian, Kantian, or Aristotelian ethical positions?', is directed to those whose policies form the institutions that form ethical character. 'We inherit our ethical standards' (*VJ* 1), Griffin remarks, but he brackets the influence of context and history on the formation and evaluation of ethical standards, and concentrates instead on a fundamentally non-historical, contextless normative philosophical question: 'How are we to refine our standards?' It is surprising that someone so alert to the interdependence of normative ethics and metaethics should attempt a philosophical study that moves towards—and then shies away from—an account of politically formed, culturally based psychology. Griffin acknowledges that

---

[13] See Avishai Margalit, *The Decent Society* (Cambridge, Mass.: Harvard University Press, 1996).

[14] See Myles Burnyeat, 'Culture and Society in Plato's Republic', *The Tanner Lectures* (Salt Lake City, Utah: Utah University Press, 1999); and my 'The Political Sources of the Emotions: Greed and Anger', *Philosophical Studies*, 89 (1998), 143–59.

[15] See Myles Burnyeat, 'Aristotle on Learning to be Good', in A. O. Rorty (ed.), *Essays on Aristotle's Ethics* (Berkeley and Los Angeles: University of California Press, 1980), 69–92.

social institutions are 'obligation-generating and rights-bestowing' (*VJ* 95); 'ethics must', he says, 'take account of group actions' (*VJ* 93). But, besides remarking that they are among the considerations that guide our choices and refine our standards, he says little about how they affect us, for good and ill.

4

Our story raises a difficult, even frightening question: how do decisive actions emerge from this dramatic process, fraught as they are with wild accidents and sheer happenstance? After all, dramatists and novelists notoriously have difficulty bringing their work to a plausible closure. Literature provides a set of conventions to solve that problem: a *deus ex machina*, a marriage or death, a family reconciliation, or the return of the rightful heir. Even in the most finished of novels, the reader's imagination—following what it knows of life—continues to ask: 'And what then?' If novelists have difficulty with closure, consider the plight of us poor decision-makers, especially when the philosophic voice within insistently charges. 'Never mind all that psychological and sociological gossip. Stick with normative questions: "How *should* decisions emerge? What *should* hail the end of a philosophical dispute?" ' These are the questions that preoccupy Griffin in his attempts to formulate criteria for well-being, criteria for evaluating well-formed ethical judgements. But his reflective discussions fall within, rather than outside our story. His position emerges within a dynamically interactive field. The aims and intentions (as well as 'the moves or strategies') of the theories he discusses were developed, and remain within, an improvisatory philosophic drama, expressed in the arguments and counter-arguments of conferences, books, and journal articles. The basic issues and categories of the critical evaluation of ethical theories (deontology, consequentialism, virtue theory) are—for better or worse—continuously dialectically redefined; they even sometimes become obsolete. Despite its rigorous internal logic, despite its determination to severe critical evaluation, philosophic drama abounds in accidents.

Still, whatever their status, normative questions about decision-making remain: they confront individual agents, policy-makers and ethical theorists. Of course, any sophisticated normative theory of decision-making recognizes that ordinary decisions are made under conditions of uncertainty and indeterminacy. Our story makes the formulation of norms for sound decision-making even more difficult than the (already formidable) problems of ordinary ignorance and confusion. It adds the sober reminder that, besides changing their aims, decision-makers also sometimes revise the norms for proper decision-making and even the criteria for an appropriate time frame

for evaluating sound decisions. Enlarging the scope of these normative problems to include the psychological and social dimensions of decision-making
allows us to supplement Griffin's purified evaluative reflections. It also adds
a sobering explanation of the remarkable fact that even our best rationally
self-critical, far-reaching deliberations so often issue in tragedy.

The most perspicuous way of addressing these problems is to sketch some
current theories of decision-making, to note some of their shortcomings,
and to show how their sophisticated reformulation embeds elements of our
account.[16] Certainly, expanding standard theories in these directions may
seem as useful and friendly as adding complicated ellipses to save a theory
whose initial attraction was its simplicity. When that happens, we find
ourselves in yet another domain of decisive disagreement about the proper
tasks and aims of theories of decision-making. What are normative theories
of decision-making supposed to do for us, and we for them? (More about
that later.)

(i) The real politik model

Whoever has the most power—however it be directed, defined, or measured,
whatever its aims may be—determines policy decisions. The powerful may act
coercively; they may do it by limiting options in such a way as to make theirs
seem the most acceptable. An astute winner typically provides incentives to
elicit long-term cooperation from dissenters.

But what is power and who has it? Is not the very definition under contention? 'Power comes out of the barrel of a gun.' Who has the financial power
to supply armaments? And who has the power to convince the industrialists
to develop electronic communication technology rather than nuclear
weaponry? Who has the rhetorical and imaginative power to form the mentality of decision-makers?[17] Polemical arguments about the definition and
criteria of power are themselves subject to the model of decision-making we
have sketched.

(ii) The first person instrumentalist model

According to the naïve version of this model, decision-makers have relatively
specific preferences; it is rational for them to opt for the alternative they
believe most likely to achieve satisfaction within a predetermined time frame,

[16] These rough sketches of some familiar theories of decision-making border on caricatures:
they are obviously neither exhaustive nor mutually exclusive. I introduce them to show that their
full development moves them to include our story.

[17] See my 'Power and Powers', in Thomas Wartenberg, *Rethinking Power* (Philadelphia: Temple
University, 1992), 1–13, and 'Imagination and Power', in *Mind in Action* (Boston: Beacon, 1988),
330–47.

bearing in mind the least costly side effects of the most readily available option.

The sophisticated self-corrective version of the instrumentalist model acknowledges that in determining their preferences and calculating the probability of satisfactory outcomes, decision-makers recognize that the process of decision-making is enhanced by collaborative deliberation; and that the dynamics of such deliberation may lead them to change their initial preferences and options quite dramatically.

Sophisticated versions of the instrumentalist model of rational choice are typically developed under the protection of a *ceteris paribus* clause. An idealized rational decision-maker has transparency of information, including a sound understanding of his own psychology (his affections and volatile instability, his (in)capacity to remain steady under stress, the extent to which his desire for harmonious cooperation is capable of overriding his dialectical aggression, etc.). In principle, rational deciders are assumed to be able to control, utilize, or co-opt their various traits, their physical and psychological constitutions, temperament, fantasies, and so on. When that is not readily feasible, idealized sophisticated decision-makers are at least able to factor their psychology among other constraints that govern their decisions, and opt for the alternative that maximizes preference satisfaction under conditions of uncertainty and indeterminacy.

As the instrumentalist model becomes more sophisticated, it adds ellipsis after ellipsis: it becomes more complex, plastic, and flexible than was promised by its original formulation. Seeing the necessity and the utility of a responsive sensitivity to his interactions with others, the rational instrumentalist recognizes the likelihood of dramatic changes in his original preferences; he not only attempts to foresee contingencies, but attempts to develop the second-order skills involved in being able to adapt to unforseeable accidents.[18]

(iii) The negotiation or 'Let's make a deal' model

Like the naïve version of the instrumental model, the naïve version of the negotiation model presupposes that the participants initially begin with a relatively fixed set of aims, staking out an area of maximal and minimal conditions of satisfaction. In the worst cases, the participants do not know their partners' priorities, habits of thought, attitudes to risk, level of trust. Even

[18] (In another context) Stephen White pointed out to me that such decisions—deciding to emigrate, to attend a conference, to have a child, to embark on a course of study—could in principle be analysed as a sequence of discrete moments. To be sure, the improvisatory character of such decisions can be *analytically* subdivided as a sequence of discrete micro-decisions, but they rarely take that psychological form. In any case, an analysis of this kind would not reveal the structure or direction of the process in its entirety, taken as a dramatic whole, with a beginning, middle and end.

when they are aware of one another's bargaining range, they may be naïve or ignorant of the conventions and strategies that govern one another's modes of negotiation. They may fail to perceive good will or fail to see the sources and depths of ill will; they may be unaware of the events, constraints, and contingencies that affect one another's negotiating practices and positions: for instance, the threat of a famine or civil uprising, the protocols of secrecy or publicity that govern public policy, the idiosyncrasies of individual negotiators. Had the negotiating partners been aware of one another's constraints— concerns that (to each from his own perspective) might seem irrational or irrelevant—they might have been able to enlarge or modify their positions. In the absence of ideal conditions, the naïve negotiation model follows the instrumentalist model in counselling approximation: maximize the satisfaction of initial preferences.

The sophisticated version of the negotiation model allows a wider range of adaptability. The very process of negotiating may revise the partners' aims and attitudes by providing a clearer insight into one another's working priorities and premisses. At best, they may be able to substitute collaborative for competitive solutions, removing themselves from the presumption of zero-sum constraints. Rather than each negotiator attempting to approximate his original ideal solution—that of maximizing the satisfaction his initial preferences—he may be able to cooperate in devising a solution that enlarges or changes his conception of a satisfactory solution.[19] By incorporating an account of mutually adaptable dynamic and dialectical adjustment, the sophisticated version of the negotiation model moves towards our story.

(iv) The deliberative and constructivist models

The naïve version of the deliberative model is an extension of the sophisticated negotiation model. Participants present what they take to be the best policy or action, recognizing it as partially vague or indeterminate. Each offers (what he takes to be) the best reasons for adopting a specific version of his preferred options, taking into account his values and principles. Quite independently of whether the partners treat each other as equals, decision-making is considered to be public and collaborative, allowing public deliberation about the merits of each position. Alternatives are continuously refined to accommodate new considerations. Ideally a consensus is formed: a solution emerges, one that accommodates the needs and concerns of the minority, allowing them—perhaps for reasons of their own—to cooperate as best they can, even if that only means agreeing not to obstruct the decision.

[19] See Avishai Margalit's critique of the 'approximate the ideal' model, in his 'Ideals and Second-Bests', in Seymore Fox (ed.), *Philosophy for Education* (Jerusalem: van Leer Institute Press, 1983), 77–90, and his *The Decent Society*, 283–4.

The naïve version of the deliberative model typically assumes that decision-makers share a relatively fixed 'starting point'—a set of general values, aims, principles, or commitments. Within contestable limits, these 'starting points' are recognized to be vague and indeterminate, open to distinctive inter-pretations, that permit them to be implemented in a range of different ways. Rational agents evaluate alternative ways of specifying and satisfying those preferences and select the policies that, all things considered (including their moral commitments as well as existing social and economic constraints), seem best to realize them. They allow that the criteria for satisfaction—significantly including the time frame within which it is to be measured—may themselves be subject to further deliberation.

Sophisticated or constructivist versions of the deliberative model recognize that the presumptive 'starting points' of deliberative decisions may themselves become the subject of deliberation. Normative standards of evaluation—a set of principles or values—could emerge as a late discovery, or even as a late compromise decision.[20] The constructivist model is latitudinarian about including unexpected considerations as relevant. In the course of the discus-sion, a participant may discover that what he had initially only hypothetically treated as tangential notional consideration becomes dominantly relevant to his decision. By sheer accident, what was, for all participants, initially considered to be only marginally relevant can become the central aim.

Decision-makers are purportedly guided by an ideal of *all things considered.* That phrase is, of course, rhetorically inflated: *all* considerations in a decisive deliberation about building a dam on the Yangzee might include a specula-tive calculation of the effects of El Niño on the mean annual rainfall in Brasilia. What is required is 'weighing factors that may reasonably be argued to be relevant'. Constructivists acknowledge that quite unexpected—and indeed accidental—considerations may become relevant to deliberation.

When pressed, the *real politik,* negotiation, and deliberative models acknowledge that each moment or stage of decision-making opens new and unexpected options; each new option brings new problems; each new problem brings new considerations whose relevance must be weighed. The con-structivist model reveals what was latently present in the other models: that dialectically sensitive decision-making acknowledges the possible relevance of tangential, accidental, and ironic contingencies. In sum: the extent to which current models of decision-making become more descriptively sophisti-

---

[20] See Christine Korsgaard, *Creating the Kingdom of Ends* (New York: Cambridge University Press, 1996); Jurgen Habermas, *Moral Consciousness and Communicative Action* (Cambridge, Mass.: MIT Press, 1990); Seyla BenHabib (ed.), *Democracy and Difference* (Princeton: Princeton University Press, 1996); Amy Gutmann and Dennis Thompson, *Democracy and Disagreement* (Cambridge, Mass.: Harvard University Press, 1996).

cated—the extent to which they add ellipses to accommodate the dramatic dynamics of decision-making—marks the extent to which they move to incorporate the elements of our account.

5

But we have not yet satisfied the philosopher within, the Griffin-minded philosopher who says: all this is very well as a description of the gory mess of decision-making. How—normatively speaking—should rational decision-making proceed? After all, the instrumental, negotiation, and deliberative models present norms and criteria for rational decision-making. Philosophic responsibility requires adjudicating or reconciling competing criteria for moral decisions.

As so often in discussions of this kind, we find ourselves enmeshed in the very kind of process we are trying to understand. We have come to a basic philosophical disagreement about the criteria for a sound and sensible model of decision-making. How much of the conditions of our social psychology—our being role cast in dynamic, interactive dramas—should an ideal model of rational decision-making take into account? What, exactly, does the best account of rational, or just, decisions *describe*? For whom—for what sorts of people, with what sorts of psychological and intellectual equipment, in what sorts of situations—does a rationally reconstructed model serve as an ideal to be emulated or approximated? Griffin's discussion of competing ethical theories embeds a theory about what we want—what we should want—from ethical theories. As before, we might ask: what should they do for us, and we for them?[21]

Griffin's answer might be: a comprehensive ethical theory should provide an ideal to which we should attempt to approximate; it outlines the lineaments and requirements of human well-being, the directions of our striving and improvement. Griffin says he begins 'where anyone would be willing to start'. Initially he means that he starts where any reflective philosopher would be willing to start. But, as his analysis develops, it seems that the philosophic starting point should also be that of any human being engaged in making ethical choices. But what is the psychology of an agent capable of striving to follow the best ethical theory? Given our psychology—our dramatic dialectical accident-prone interdependence—are we best served by earnestly attempting to approximate that idealized model for decision-making? If—as I have suggested—we are not well served by models that counsel idealized rational

---

[21] See Samuel Scheffler, *Human Morality* (Oxford: Oxford University Press, 1992); Bernard Williams, *Ethics and the Limits of Philosophy* (Cambridge, Mass.: Harvard University Press, 1985).

decision-makers to approximate their initial preferences, are we left without any reasonable norms or directions for sound decision-making? Does our story mean that there are no better or worse ethical decisions, no criteria for evaluating ethical theories?

Norms remain; but they have neither the form of a confident calculation, nor a set of guidelines for deliberative evaluation, with fixed ends or set rules of procedure. To turn our problem around: you may have wondered whether our characterization—our account of the accident-prone dramas of decision-making—is itself subject to the story it has sketched. I believe it is. Although ours is primarily a descriptive account, it involves a normative view—developed as a decision—about the kind of phenomena that should be incorporated, should be acknowledged within a sound theory of decision-making. Like other descriptions and decisions, it has been developed in dialectical response to others in the field; its details will be further specified in different ways, depending on the sheer accident of those who enter the discussion. That is how things are.

You might think that all this is nothing more than armchair sociology, mere speculation about the psychological susceptibilities of intellectuals and politicians. You might think that serious philosophy requires a reflective assessment of the arguments of competing positions. For those who see philosophy as a strongly normative enterprise, I fear that the promise—or threat—of our Aesopean ending may be embarrassingly deflationary. Honesty recommends that we drop our Olympian pretensions and admit ourselves to be role cast in the dramas of philosophic discussions, recognizing that our most considered reflective views and decisions embed the chance and accidental imprints of our colleagues' role-enacting participation. This retreat to modesty goes much further than the familiar admission of fallibility. It counsels against a generalized, contextless, ahistorical meta-theoretical attempt to formulate criteria or norms for evaluating ethical theories. It recommends not only that each participant decision-making philosopher present the best, weightiest arguments and considerations for her position, but that she also openly acknowledges their limitations, their lacunae. She may not always be able to locate her perspectival, dialectical role, but she can at least indicate her uncertainties and hesitations.

10

Anna Karenina and Moral Philosophy

Jonathan Glover

It is obvious that *Anna Karenina* is not in the ordinary sense a work of philosophy.[1] It is a novel, a story about a group of particular people. Admittedly some of the characters 'philosophize' in a popular sense, expressing opinions on life, death, love, morality, and religion. But the book does not have the apparatus of a real piece of philosophy: arguments, analysis of concepts, rebuttals of opposing points of view. Yet virtually anyone who reads it must come away with the sense that it is not just a book about those particular people, and that its subject matter includes some of the central philosophical questions. (Not quite everyone: when it came out, the reviewer for the *Odessa Courier* wrote: 'Food, drink, hunting, balls, horse races and love, love, love in the most naked sense of the word, without psychological ramifications or moral interest of any sort—that is what the novel is about from start to finish . . . I challenge the reader to show me one page, nay! one half-page, that contains an idea, or rather the shadow of an idea.')

Some of us come away from the book with the sense that there is at least as much to learn from Tolstoy about how we should live as can be learnt from Aristotle or from Kant. If this is right, philosophy will be poorer if philosophers stay in their professional compartment and ignore Tolstoy and other novelists. But there is a difficulty in the project of bringing these two kinds of writing in contact with each other, a difficulty that haunts my attempt here to link Tolstoy with moral philosophy. It is hardly a mere accident that

---

I have learnt much, both from Jim Griffin's writings and from his friendship. I like to think these Tolstoyan reflections (first presented to Martha Nussbaum's class at Brown University) have an affinity with two themes in *Value Judgement*. One is Jim Griffin's denial of 'the sufficiency of the moral': his insistence in locating morality in wider human concerns. The other is his view that philosophers writing on ethics should take much more notice of what people are like. It is disconcerting how many moral philosophers, in their writings and in person, exude human obliviousness. Jim is their antipodes.

[1] All quotations are taken from the penguin edition: *Anna Karenina*, trans. Rosemary Edmonds (Harmondsworth: Penguin, 1954).

Tolstoy wrote *Anna Karenina* as a novel, or that Kant wrote the *Ground-work of the Metaphysic of Morals* not as a novel. We may fairly confidently hope that no one will try to rewrite the *Groundwork* as a novel. But there is a bit more danger of philosophers trying to extract some set of philosophical propositions from *Anna Karenina*, and in the process squeezing the life out of it.

The danger can be glimpsed when an academic philosopher makes a brief appearance in the novel, in conversation with Levin's half-brother, Koznyshev. Levin listens to them,

but every time they got close to what seemed to him the most important point, they promptly beat a hasty retreat and plunged back into the sea of subtle distinctions, reservations, quotations, allusions, and references to authorities; and he had difficulty in understanding what they were talking about.

Levin asked them a question, which Koznyshev said they were not in a position to answer, a view backed up by the philosopher:

'We have not the necessary data,' confirmed the professor and went back to his argument. 'No,' he said, 'I maintain that if, as Pripasov directly asserts, sensation is based directly on impressions, then we are bound to distinguish sharply between these two conceptions.' Levin listened no longer, but sat waiting for the professor to go.

One danger is of being heavy-handed. I once heard of a mathematics teacher who would sketch out the solution of a problem, but not work it out in detail, saying, 'the rest is heavy'. There is a risk of this heaviness, taking some economical Tolstoyan gesture and going on about 'what Tolstoy is trying to say'. There is also a danger of being crudely reductive, squeezing the complexity of the people and events of the novel into some Procrustean set of philosophical categories.

These dangers are real, and I am not sure I can altogether escape them. There are reasons that may make them worth risking. One reason comes from the feeling that in Tolstoy's novels, perhaps especially in *Anna Karenina*, there are ways of seeing people and their lives that philosophy is poorer for neglecting.

Maynard Keynes wrote about the influence of G. E. Moore and *Principia Ethica*. He said of Moore that 'he had one foot on the threshold of the new heaven, but the other foot in Sidgwick and the Benthamite calculus and the general rules of correct behaviour'. Keynes and his circle at Cambridge believed in the new heaven of cultivating relationships and states of mind, and ignored the utilitarian part:

We accepted Moore's religion, so to speak, and discarded his morals. Indeed, in our opinion, one of the greatest advantages of his religion was that it made morals unnecessary—meaning by 'religion' one's attitude towards oneself and the ultimate and by 'morals' one's attitude towards the outside world and the intermediate.

In something like this sense of 'religion', many of us who are atheists have a religion as well as a morality: a set of things we hold to be of great personal importance, but which we probably would not expect to be able to defend by argument, and which we would not suppose other people have any kind of duty to promote. This has links with the way we care a great deal about a few people close to us, without thinking that they have any stronger moral claims—for instance, on scarce medical resources—than people we do not know. Some people have living in the country and watching animals as their religion, for others the religion is friendship, or music, or children, or mountaineering. Since first reading *Anna Karenina*, I have been partly Tolstoyan by religion, while having a much more prosaic morality.

But perhaps this distinction between morality and religion may become a bit battered if exposed to much critical scrutiny. And there is also the worry that calling some beliefs or values 'religion' is just a way of leaving them, like many people's theistic beliefs, in a state of unexamined darkness and confusion. So it may be good for me to try to spell out what can be learnt from *Anna Karenina*, but of course my hope is that it will be worthwhile for others too. There is also something puzzling. I find myself disagreeing with some of Tolstoy's main views, while at the same time feeling that underneath them is something both important and right. But, if the views are rejected, what is it that commands assent? If whatever it is has the importance I think it has, it seems worth risking being heavy or reductive in making the attempt to get clear about it. But I know that I run the risk that there is some Levin in the audience, listening no longer, and waiting for me to go.

1. MORALITY AND THE EMOTIONS

(i) *How we should listen to far more than we can analyse*

Tolstoy thinks we should listen to our own emotional responses, even to quite vague pangs of unease at the edge of our attention. When Kitty was thinking of a possible future life with Vronsky, she had a dazzling vision of happiness, but at the same time 'something uneasy clouded her thoughts of Vronsky, though he was all a well-bred man-of-the-world could be, as if there were a false note—not in him, he was very simple and nice, but in herself'. Or there can be an obscure sense that something is significant in a way hard to pin down. Anna, enthusing about Vronsky after their meeting on the train, remembered him giving away two hundred roubles for the widow of the guard who had been crushed: 'But she did not mention the two hundred roubles. For some reason she did not like thinking about them. She felt that there had been something in the incident to do with her personally, that should not have been.'

This false note struck by Vronsky in both Kitty and Anna is a clue, which they mistakenly ignored because it was unwelcome or hard to explain. The tacit knowledge that cannot be spelled out because it is based on subliminal cues is something Tolstoy is surely right to respect. Good doctors sometimes say that they themselves, with their own reactions to people, can be their most sensitive diagnostic instrument.

Obviously there are dangers in the too easy reliance on an intuitive feel for people: where beliefs about people do not have to be backed up by reasons, any old prejudice can have free play. There is a need to be alert to differences between feelings whose reliability is supported by other evidence and those which often have to be revised when there is more information. But when intuitive impressions are under some broad empirical control, to discard them is to lose important clues about people.

Tolstoy goes further than this, and treats some intuitive impressions as the voice of conscience, or as a moral compass. When Vronsky visits Anna during the period of their affair before the break-up of Anna's marriage, he was often troubled by the presence of her son, Seriozha:

The child's presence invariably called up in Vronsky that strange feeling of inexplicable revulsion which he had experienced of late. The child's presence called up both in Vronsky and in Anna a feeling akin to that of a sailor who can see by the compass that the direction in which he is swiftly sailing is wide of the proper course, but is powerless to stop. Every moment takes him farther and farther astray, and to admit to himself that he is off his course is the same as admitting final disaster.

This child, with his innocent outlook upon life, was the compass which showed them the degree to which they had departed from what they knew but did not want to know.

Here Tolstoy suggests that Vronsky's feeling of revulsion is a sign of his having gone astray from 'the proper course'. But there are questions to be asked about this. Are we meant to see *any* feeling of revulsion as a 'moral intuition' that we are off course? This seems much too crude: Tolstoy surely does not think that the revulsion a medical student may have to overcome in order to do dissection is a moral warning of this kind. It must be a particular kind of revulsion, but what are its distinctive features?

Some 'moral-sense' theories suggest that awareness that something is wrong involves an introspectively distinct kind of unpleasant feeling, perhaps marked off from others in the way one kind of bad smell can be distinguished from another. But proponents have had little to say about the special feature we are supposed to notice. Appeal to indescribable inner qualities does not seem promising. A natural alternative appeals to context. If some moral intuitions are rooted in feelings of revulsion, they are distinguished by the reasons for them and by the beliefs that accompany them. This seems to fit Tolstoy's account. The feeling is not cited alone, but together with the claim that the moral compass was 'the child, with his innocent outlook on life'. The feeling should be taken seriously, because it is based on the contrast between the innocence of Seriozha's outlook and the far from innocent outlook inseparable from Vronsky's own behaviour.

There are often problems in identifying the reasons for a feeling of revulsion. For instance, in Vronsky's case, he might suspect that the feeling was based more on guilt about the harm he was doing Seriozha in breaking up his parents' marriage, rather than on any contrast between Seriozha's innocence and his own lack of it. But, if Tolstoy's account is simply taken to be correct, it is worth noting that the emotional response is not a completely independent moral guide. It is to be taken seriously because of the reason for it, and that reason itself appeals to a moral belief that Vronsky's conduct is incompatible with an 'innocent' outlook. There are times when we should listen to our emotions, but more general moral beliefs guide us about when those times are.

But Tolstoy does not make the authority of feelings depend on their moral quality being recognized. When Oblonsky first approaches Karenin to suggest that he should give Anna a divorce, he starts by stammering:

'Yes, I would like . . . I must . . . Yes, I wanted to talk to you,' said Oblonsky, surprised at his own unaccustomed timidity. The feeling was so unexpected and strange that Oblonsky did not believe it was the voice of conscience telling him that what he was about to do was wrong. He made an effort and conquered the timidity that had come over him.

Tolstoy believes that breaking up a marriage is morally wrong, and perhaps this is why he thinks that Oblonsky's feeling of timidity was the voice of conscience. But, without this moral view prior to the feeling, such an interpretation is not the only possible one. Anyone might feel timid about intruding enough to suggest to someone that he should give his wife a divorce, particularly in a society where it was such a rarity. I disagree with Tolstoy's view that Oblonsky's suggestion was morally wrong, but can imagine feeling timid about making it if placed in Oblonsky's position, and I would not take this as showing the suggestion to be morally wrong. Tolstoy would no doubt see this as being deaf to the voice of conscience. But there is the problem of how we are to recognize the voice of conscience. There is also the suspicion that Tolstoy's thinking here is circular: the timidity is the voice of conscience because it fits with his moral beliefs, which are in turn validated by his conscience.

Tolstoy's religious beliefs give him a possible way out of this circularity. It is also worth mentioning that most of us have a circularity problem of this kind. Our moral beliefs and intuitive responses are usually in some kind of mutual support, the state of affairs that John Rawls has perhaps optimistically

called 'reflective equilibrium'. In thinking about whether some feeling of reluctance is a sign of some serious moral objection or *merely* timidity, all we
can do is think carefully about it, and this thinking is inevitably guided by
more general moral beliefs we already hold. So the 'circularity' objection is
not devastating against Tolstoy, but it does bring out that there is room for
disagreement over what counts as the voice of conscience.

(ii) *The opposition to 'Kantian' morality*

Tolstoy's belief in listening to the emotions is linked to his continuing opposition to moralities of cold dutifulness. Anna's tragedy can be traced back to
Karenin's decision to marry her, taken out of duty rather than love. His
feelings had been that 'there were as many arguments for the step as against
it, and no overwhelming consideration to outweigh his invariable rule of
abstaining when in doubt'. But he was persuaded by Anna's aunt that he had
already compromised her and so had a duty to propose marriage. The stiff
coldness of the marriage that resulted made it unsurprising that, when
Karenin knew of the affair with Vronsky, his main demand was that the pro-
prieties should be observed. Anna expresses a natural human revulsion against
all this:

'He's in the right!' She muttered. 'Of course, he's always in the right; he's a Christian,
he's magnanimous! Yes, the mean, odious creature! And no one understands it except
me, and no one ever will; and I can't explain it. People say he's so religious, so high-
principled, so upright, so clever; but they don't see what I've seen. They don't know
how for eight years he has crushed my life, crushed everything that was living in me—
he has never once thought that I'm a live woman in need of love.'

This high-principled coldness is a disaster for Karenin himself as well as for
Anna. Without love, his life has only the satisfactions of careerism. He escapes
its emptiness only by immersing himself in bureaucratic detail. The first time
he feels deep happiness is when Anna seems likely to die in childbirth, and he
acts out of generous feelings: 'He was not thinking that the Christian law
which he had been trying to follow all his life enjoined on him to forgive and
love his enemies; yet a glad feeling of love and forgiveness for his enemies filled
his heart.' The message is that, by comparison with impulses of warmth and
generosity, the duties and rules of conventional morality are nothing. Or they
can be worse than nothing, as in the cruel ostracism at the opera of Anna after
her social disgrace.

A similar point about conventional or rule-based morality comes out in the
case of Vronsky. His code of principles was narrow but clear. 'This code cate-
gorically ordained that gambling debts must be paid, the tailor need not be;
that one must not lie to a man but might to a woman; that one must never

cheat anyone but may a husband; that one must never pardon an insult but may insult others oneself, and so on.' It was a code that made him think of Karenin mainly in terms of a possible challenge to a duel. Its limitations started to appear even to Vronsky himself when Anna told him she was pregnant: 'He felt that this fact and what she expected of him called for something not fully defined in his code of principles.'

As with Karenin, Vronsky's mistake is to live by some conventionally determined set of duties. In a way, what is set against this outlook is the whole novel, in which an astonishing range of people are seen in their complexity, and from the inside. (This is part of what gives the impression that Tolstoy's view is like that of God. And perhaps it was partly this range of understanding and sympathy that led Gorky to write of him: 'Great—in some curious sense wide, indefinable by words—there is something in him which made me desire to cry aloud to everyone: "Look what a wonderful man is living on the earth." For he is, so to say, universally and above all a man, a man of mankind.') This view of people and their variety from inside brings out the inadequacy of the duties people such as Karenin and Vronsky live by. These simple moral rules are insufficiently subtle and flexible, too Procrustean to accommodate the needs and the emotional complexity of people.

2. ANNA

(i) How far Anna could help it

Tolstoy disapproves of Anna's affair with Vronsky and of her choice to leave Karenin and Seriozha for him. But he writes of the affair with a great deal of sympathy and understanding, and also with an awareness of how difficult it would have been for her to have chosen to stay with Karenin. Given the strength of her love for Vronsky and her feelings of being stifled in her marriage, it would have at least been very difficult for her to have made what Tolstoy thought was the right choice. There is the question of whether that choice went beyond the very difficult and was for Anna impossible. Was she drawn to Vronsky by an 'irresistible impulse', as a lenient Tolstoyan moralist might suggest, or was it an impulse she merely *did not* resist, as a severe Tolstoyan moralist might say? We all know how difficult this boundary is to draw in the real world, and the problems this creates for psychiatric witnesses in legal cases.

Because in many cases there seems to be no very sharp boundary, people have some free play for their inclinations towards severity or lenience. Some (mainly the more severe moralists) are drawn towards a Kantian emphasis on the scope of the will, stressing the extent to which we can decide whether or not to yield to a desire, and the way we can shape the desires we have. On this view, self-creation is a real possibility, and the role of good or bad luck in the kind of people we are is minimized. Others (mainly the more lenient moralists) place much more emphasis on the psychological difficulties that circumscribe any project of self-creation. They stress what Bernard Williams has called 'constitutive luck': we are lucky or unlucky not only in the circumstances of our lives, but also in the kind of nature we have, and which we can usually change only to a very limited degree.

Tolstoy does not deny the possibility of self-creation, but his emphasis is in general on the difficulties that set limits to it. He means us to sympathize with Levin's thoughts about his brother:

Levin felt that in his soul, in the innermost depths of his soul, his brother Nikolai, in spite of his dissolute life, was no worse than the people who despised him. It was not his fault that he had been born with a tempestuous nature and a kink in his mind. He had always wished to do right.

Because of his strong sense of the recalcitrance of people's natures (as well as of the role of unpredictable outside circumstances), Tolstoy is sceptical about the idea of drawing up a 'life plan' and then living by it. Levin's own life is a story of repeated decisions in favour of radical self-transformation while he stays recognizably unchanged throughout the book. There is a moment when this conflict surfaces in his mind:

A candle was brought in and gradually lit up the study, revealing the familiar details: the antlers, the book-shelves, the stove with its ventilator which had long wanted repairing, his father's sofa, the big table on which lay an open book, a broken ash-tray, a manuscript-book full of his handwriting. As he saw all this, he began to doubt for a moment the possibility of arranging the new life he had been dreaming of during the drive. All these traces of his old life seemed to clutch him and say: 'No, you're not going to get away from us; you're not going to be different. You're going to be the same as you always have been—with your doubts, your perpetual dissatisfaction with yourself and vain attempts to amend, your failures and everlasting expectation of a happiness you won't get and which isn't possible for you.'

This was what the things said, but another, inner voice was telling him not to submit to the past, telling him a man can make what he will of himself. And listening to this voice he went to the corner where his two heavy dumb-bells lay and started to do exercises with them, trying to restore his confident mood.

The better we know Levin, the more we are inclined to believe the stove with the broken ventilator and the things on the table. The more optimistic inner voice is unconvincing, and it is unlikely that he will keep up the exercises with the dumb-bells tomorrow.

Although Levin is striking in his frequent attempts to change himself, he is not portrayed as more extreme than others in his lack of psychological malleability. The version of nineteenth-century Russian rural life that forms the Tolstoyan background is one long series of attempted reforms of agriculture, which fail because people will not change in the required ways. The Soviet leaders who saw Tolstoy as closer to them, and as more 'progressive' than Dostoyevsky, may have underrated his conservatism: his sense (so relevant to the Soviet project) that the stubborn cussedness of people will usually defeat the neat and tidy plan. Political transformation and self-creation run up against much the same obstacles.

With Anna too, Tolstoy has a vivid sense of how hard it would have been for her to have been different. Whichever way she decides, she feels buffeted by circumstances and at the mercy of her own weakness. When she thought she would not break with Karenin, she

felt that the position she enjoyed in society, which had seemed of so little consequence that morning, was precious to her after all, and that she would not have the strength to exchange it for the shameful one of a woman who has deserted husband and child to join her lover; that, however much she might struggle, she could not be stronger than herself.

And, as she moves in the other direction, she feels the destruction of her marriage by her love for Vronsky as something inevitable. Thinking about how others, and particularly Seriozha, may later judge her, she says to herself, 'Can it be that they won't forgive me, won't understand how none of it could be helped?' And, much later, the same line of thought surfaces when Dolly visits her and Vronsky, and she asks Dolly whether Kitty hates and despises her. Dolly says she does not, but that there are some things one does not forgive. Anna replies, 'I know. But I was not to blame. And who is to blame? What does being to blame mean? Could things have been otherwise? Tell me what you think? Could it possibly have happened that you didn't become the wife of Stiva?'

These thoughts about not being able to be stronger than herself, about how none of it could be helped, and about the obscurity of blame and of the idea that things could have been different are Anna's own, and Tolstoy does not explicitly endorse them. (Though Vronsky is described as 'involuntarily submitting to the weakness of Anna'.) As often in real life, it is unclear whether the thought that none of it could be helped is partly self-deceiving or whether it is simply true. I do not know whether there is a right answer to the question of which view Tolstoy took. There is a tension between his inclination towards moral criticism of Anna and the convincing portrayal of the strength of the pressures on her. At the very least we cannot dismiss her thoughts about not being able to help it as *mere* self-deception.

Towards the end, there are immense pressures on Anna. The humiliations of social ostracism, and perhaps even the loss of Seriozha, might have been bearable if the relationship with Vronsky had been going well. But, as that too disintegrates into quarrelling and bitterness, Anna is left utterly without support in life. (In one of the last quarrels she says, 'When I feel as I do now, that you are hostile—yes, hostile to me—if you only knew what that means for me! If you knew how near disaster I am at such moments . . .') When she self-destructively insists on courting insults by going to the opera, this is immediately after the visit to Seriozha. It is hard to see her as fully responsible for what she does in such a manic state.

And it is hard not to see the pressures on Anna that build up before her suicide as overwhelming. The disastrous failure of the relationship with Vronsky leaves her nowhere to turn. The (perhaps remote) possibility of the relationship reviving if they can marry is blocked off by Karenin's refusal of a divorce. (The fact that this pressure results from something accidental—Karenin refusing because he has fallen under the influence of the loathsome countess and accepts the virtually random advice of her charlatan clairvoyant—is both Tolstoyan and true to life. The same goes for the horribly convincing muddle of crossed messages between Anna and Vronsky just before her suicide.) Her entrapment produces the nightmare psychological state (in which things are seen in a distorting light but with great vividness) of her final ride to the station. It is hard to expect balanced decisions of anyone in such a state.

Tolstoy leaves us with a difficult question. If we are inclined to think Anna could not help her suicide, but are inclined to think that she was responsible for some of her earlier actions, there is the question of where to draw the line between what could and what could not be helped. As she slides down towards final disaster, there seems no single clear point where what before was only hard to resist becomes irresistible. In that way, Tolstoy faithfully reproduces the blurred moral boundaries of real life, rather than the artificially sharp ones of legal and moral theory.

(ii) The Morality of Anna's Choice

Tolstoy's attitude towards Anna has elements of both sympathy and disapproval. He gives a very sympathetic picture of the pressures that made it either very hard or perhaps impossible for Anna to reject Vronsky and save her marriage. But he is also at least inclined to the view that, to whatever extent it could be helped, Anna's choice was morally wrong.

Tolstoy's first intentions seem to have been mixed. His wife, in a letter to her sister in 1870, wrote, 'Yesterday evening he told me that the type had occurred to him of a woman, married and in high society, who had lost her footing. He said his problem would be to present that woman not as guilty, but as merely pathetic . . .'. But early drafts of the book suggest the intention to write something much more crudely moralistic against adultery. In those drafts (which I have not read, but which are described in the biographies of Tolstoy by Henri Troyat and by A. N. Wilson) the wrongness of Anna's conduct was emphasized, while Karenin was portrayed as warm, sensitive, and kind, and Vronsky was 'firm, kind-hearted and sincere'. In the first notes on her, Anna's moral failings went with an unprepossessing appearance: 'She is unattractive, with a narrow, low forehead, short, turned-up nose—rather large. If it were any bigger, she would be deformed . . . But, in spite of her homely face, there was something in the kindly smile of her red lips that made her likeable.' And in an early draft one chapter describing her has the title 'The Devil'.

Tolstoy said to friends, 'Do you know, I often sit down to write some specific thing, and suddenly I find myself on a wider road, the work begins to spread out in front of me. That was the way it was with *Anna Karenina*.' From the sound of the earlier versions, we can be glad Tolstoy found himself on a wider road. The final version is certainly not crudely moralistic. But, without the crudity, the moral condemnation of Anna's choice to break up her marriage and family remains, although interwoven with understanding of the pressures on her. He said to Sofya, his wife, 'If a book is to be any good, you have to love the central idea it expresses. In *Anna Karenina* I love the idea of the family . . .'. And on the title-page the book has the chilling epigraph, 'Vengeance is mine, and I will repay'.

While he was writing *Anna Karenina*, Tolstoy was having his portrait painted by Ivan Kramskoy, who was in turn having his portrait sketched as the painter Mihailov in the novel. Kramskoy wrote up some of their conversations. On a walk, Kramskoy asked how Tolstoy's novel was. Tolstoy said, 'I don't know. One thing's certain. Anna's going to die. Vengeance will be wreaked on her. She wanted to rethink life in her own way.' Kramskoy asked, 'How should one think?', to which Tolstoy replied, 'One must try to live by the faith which one has sucked in with one's mother's milk and without arrogance of the mind.'

Although the novel grew out of being the simple moral tale in which 'the Devil' got her just deserts, the more sympathetic and complex final version does still have the intended moral message in praise of the family and in support of the religious view of marriage and its indissolubility.

This message is one about which I have mixed feelings. The feelings of sympathy are for Tolstoy's praise of the family. It is almost embarrassing now to speak in praise of the family, an institution so loudly supported by politicians eager for it to replace state support for the disadvantaged, and by religious campaigners against abortion and against homosexuals. And feminists and gay rights campaigners have real points to make about the limitations of the traditional family. But, for all this, there are psychological needs, both of children and adults, to which the family (at least after it has been mellowed by attitudes of equality) is well adapted. Perhaps there are no generalizations here that fit everybody. But many adults flourish more in the security and stability of a long-term partnership than with a series of shifting partners. And, when life throws up major problems, it is almost impossible to overrate the advantages of having put down deep roots together. It hardly needs saying that children too benefit from a sense of permanence and from the security it brings, and that for them parental divorce can be a disaster.

But even here absolute rules are too easy. (Anyway, too easy to endorse, if often too hard to live with.) In Anna's case, there is no doubt that the break-up was a disaster for Seriozha. This makes it hard to be certain that Anna was right to leave Karenin. But there are reasons for being less certain that she was wrong than Tolstoy seems to have been. There is the false original basis of the marriage. And there is the nightmare it has turned into for Anna. At one point she says about Karenin, 'I have heard it said that women love men even for their vices, but I hate him for his virtues. Do you understand—the sight of him has a physical effect on me? It puts me beside myself. I can't, I can't live with him.' In the context of the relationship as described, this is totally believable. And the idea that—even when there is a child—divorce is in all circumstances wrong seems too confident and too harsh in a case like Anna's.

Here, perhaps for religious reasons, Tolstoy's normal willingness to be guided by human responsiveness rather than by the rules to some extent deserts him.

Tolstoy's own view emphasized the wrongness of breaking a marriage. But, to those of us who do not share his absolutism on this issue, Anna's deepest mistake was her blindness to what Vronsky was like. The feelings of disquiet he sometimes aroused should have been listened to, and his moral code was shallow and conventional.

The shallowness extended far beyond his moral code. Part of his interest in Anna was his enjoyment of the stir the relationship created and the glamour this gave him. When Anna tells him that she has told Karenin, his response is inadequate, and his thoughts mainly about a duel with Karenin:

If on hearing this news he were to say to her firmly, passionately, without a moment's hesitation: 'Throw up everything and come with me!' she would give up her son and go away with him. But the news had not produced the effect she had expected in him: he only looked as though he were resenting some affront.

Compared to Anna's suicide, Vronsky's earlier attempted suicide seems theatrical. When they are in Italy together, Vronsky is not so much a painter as someone playing at being one, and when the contrast with Mihailov brings out his own lack of talent, he does not face this squarely but in a self-deceiving way just lets his painting career fade away. The life in the country together is more play-acting: the pretentiously furnished house and the playing of the role of the big benefactor of the hospital all seem to be filling a big hole in Vronsky's life.

His life lacks a centre: the love for Anna was never either the overwhelming passion of Anna for him nor the deep straightforward love of Levin for Kitty, but always tinged with consciousness of image. And his life does not have the other kind of centre: something he is really serious about in the way Levin is serious about Kitty, or their child, or about his estate and his work, or about the questions he asks about his life. Tolstoy's belief in seriousness is one of the main links between the part of the book that is about Anna and Vronsky and the part that is about Levin. Vronsky is not right for Anna because he lacks the seriousness that she has. This seriousness is above all exemplified by Levin. This seriousness is one of Tolstoy's deepest values, and it is the central thing I was responding to when I said my religion was partly Tolstoyan.

3. TOLSTOY'S VIEW OF SERIOUSNESS

Tolstoy always gives the same sort of picture of people living in ways that are shallow, or not serious. They are meeting people to advance their career. Or they are saying things that they hope will seem respectable or clever or fashionable. Or they are painting because they care not about painting but about being painters. Or they are paying polite calls and talking about nothing. What all this has in common is what Bertrand Russell, in a letter to Colette Malleson, called 'worldliness'. He wrote that he was 'against worldliness, which consists of doing everything for the sake of something else, like marrying for money instead of love. The essence of life is doing things for their own sakes.'

When Levin is thinking of what it is that Koznyshev lacks, he notices 'not a lack of kindly honesty and noble desires and tastes, but a lack of the vital force, of what is called heart, of the impulse which drives a man to choose one out of all the innumerable paths of life and to care for that one only'. There is no insistence that anyone serious must choose the same path. (Perhaps all shallow lives are alike, but a serious life is serious in its own way?) Anna's love is serious, Levin's questioning is serious, and the peasants mowing the hay (in Tolstoy's perhaps romanticized picture of them) are serious. They care about different things and do different things. Part of what they have in common is that they care about things that are not trivial.

Another part of their seriousness is that they notice things, in a way the person who does everything for the sake of something else does not. John Donne said in a sermon:

We are all conceived in close prison, and then all our life is but a going out to the place of execution, to death. Was any man seen to sleep in the cart between Newgate and Tyburn? Between prison and place of execution does any man sleep? But we sleep all the way. From the womb to the grave, we are never thoroughly awake.

The dark picture of all our life as but a going-out to the place of execution is more like Dostoyevsky than Tolstoy. But going through life thoroughly awake is something Tolstoy cares about, and Anna and Levin are awake as they go through life as Vronsky and Karenin are not.

Another aspect of seriousness comes out in the way people talk to each other. It is a matter of breaking through the barriers of inhibition and convention that keep conversation at the level of politeness and small talk rather than about the thoughts and feelings that matter more. The clearest case of failure to break through these inhibitions is in the scene where Koznyshev and Varenka go collecting mushrooms together. Everyone round them thinks they will decide to get married. Koznyshev goes off gathering mushrooms in another part of the birch wood for a few moments final reflection. He comes back having decided to propose marriage, and they walk a few steps alone:

It would have been easier for them to say what they wanted to say after a silence than after talking about mushrooms. But against her will, and as if by accident, Varenka said:

'So you did not find any? But of course there are always fewer in the middle of the wood.' Koznyshev sighed and made no answer. He was vexed that she had spoken about the mushrooms. He wanted to bring her back to her first remark about her childhood; but after a pause of some length, as though against his own will, he made an observation in reply to her last words. 'I've only heard that the white edible fun-guses are found chiefly at the edge of the wood, though I can't tell a white boletus when I see one.'

More time passed with both of them knowing this was the vital moment. Koznyshev

repeated to himself the words in which he had intended to put his offer, but instead of those words some perverse reflection caused him to ask:

'What is the difference between a white boletus and a birch mushroom?'

Varenka's lips trembled with agitation as she replied:

'There is hardly any difference in the top part, but the stalks are different.'

And as soon as these words were out of her mouth, both he and she understood that it was over, that what was to have been said would not be said . . .

This passage admits of more than one interpretation. One is the 'Freudian' one, that the verbal stumbling was motivated by an unconscious desire not to marry. And perhaps Koznyshev's need for final reflection is some indication that his love was less than whole-hearted. But it also seems possible that, if they had not been defeated by politeness and inhibition, but had broken through to the deepest level of each other, they would have found they both wanted each other. I believe that many people know from the inside this kind of failure to break through the barriers of inhibition and convention. Tolstoy does not respond to it with moral condemnation, and writes of it with marvellous understanding and sympathy. But he still sees it as a failure of seriousness: something sad, which in this case Koznyshev and Varenka perhaps pay for heavily.

There is a contrast with Anna, who, whatever moral criticisms Tolstoy makes of her, does not lack seriousness. When Dolly arrives to visit her and Vronsky, the first conversation turns to Anna's position, but Dolly tries to shy away from this:

'However, we can talk about that later. What are all those buildings?' she asked, wanting to change the subject, and pointing to some red and green roofs that could be seen through a quickset hedgerow of acacia and lilac. 'It looks quite a little town.'

But Anna did not answer her.

'No, no, tell me how you look at my position? What do you think of it, tell me?' she asked.

By pushing through the polite small talk, Anna's seriousness was rewarded by eliciting Dolly's deepest response, which was so warm that Anna replied, 'All your sins, if you had any, would be forgiven you for this visit and what you have just said.'

Seriousness may explain something I have often found puzzling in discussions between people on different sides of disagreements about values. It is something I have noticed sometimes when arguing, for instance, about abortion, a topic notorious for the hostility and vehemence it generates. I am broadly sympathetic to the case for seeing abortion as something that should be available to women if they choose it. I often discuss the issue with people who take the opposite view that even early abortion is murder. My view tells me that they are helping to maintain the unjustifiable coercion of women into having unwanted children, and creating massive unnecessary misery in doing so. Their view tells them that I am advocating treating babies as things, and contributing to a climate in which there is the mass murder of innocent and defenceless human beings on an unprecedented scale. But often I value the discussion and respect the things said by my pro-life opponent. And my impression is that often they have a similar view. At least, they talk to me in a much more friendly way than I would talk to some Nazi who was advocating mass murder. And this is not peculiar to the abortion debate: it can happen in discussions of religion and politics too.

Part of the explanation may be that, on these matters, we are aware that our own views may not be right. There could be reasons that would make us change our minds. But also the explanation has to do with our response to people openly expressing their beliefs about things they have thought about and that matter to them. The combination of seriousness and openness is impressive in a way that transcends disagreement.

These comments on seriousness leave a lot of loose ends. One obvious question (to which I am not sure of the answer) is how far seriousness as I have tried to describe it is a unitary value, and how far it would be better to treat it as a cluster of different values. But I hope there is enough unity to make it worth talking about.

If it *is* worth talking about, not much of that talk seems to take place in moral philosophy. There seems to be a gap in philosophy between highly abstract discussions of rights or happiness or justice at one end of the subject, and very detailed 'applied-ethics' discussions of medical dilemmas or of nuclear deterrence. There is not a lot at about the level of Aristotle's discussion of friendship, or Pascal's of diversion, where there is engagement in some detail with questions about the kinds of life that are most worth living. Perhaps here is where we have most to learn from novels.

Finally, in the context of philosophy, we can go back for a moment to people disagreeing with each other. There is a passage about some thoughts of Levin on this:

Levin had often noticed in discussions between the most intelligent people that after enormous efforts, and endless logical subtleties and talk, the disputants finally became aware that what they had been at such pains to prove to one another had long ago, from the beginning of the argument, been known to both, but that they liked different things, and would not define what they liked for fear of its being attacked. He had often had the experience of suddenly in the middle of a discussion grasping what it was the other liked and at once liking it too, and immediately found himself agreeing, and then all arguments fell away useless. Sometimes the reverse happened: he at last expressed what he liked himself, which he had been arguing to defend and, chancing to express it well and genuinely, had found the person he was disputing with suddenly agree.

This is a marvellous picture of how an argument, perhaps about philosophy, could go. Somehow it does not seem to be quite what is going on in the *Journal of Philosophy* or in *Mind*. But perhaps it is an ideal we could keep at least at the back of our minds. The last part of the passage, about coming to like what the other person likes, may be a bit optimistic. Because we are different, we will *not* always come to like the same things, though we may do so sometimes. But the idea of coming to grasp what the other person likes could come to be seen as an important part of philosophy, perhaps even as important as 'endless logical subtleties and talk'.

11

Cognitivism in Political Philosophy

S. L. Hurley

1. INTRODUCTION

This chapter provides a bird's-eye view of a cognitivist approach to political philosophy, by illustrating its application to three topics: justice, democracy, and punishment. The arguments are merely sketched rather than given in detail, to give an overall picture of the approach.[1]

Cognitivism in political philosophy is not a doctrine or thesis, but a category. Cognitivist accounts are cast primarily in terms of truth and knowledge rather than choice or preference. There are quite different ways of falling under this broad characterization, as we'll see. But some unity can be given to a broadly cognitive approach by two key ideas.

A constraint on political cognitivism is that it gives some basis for responding to certain worries. These worries prompt political liberals such as Rawls to deny that the search for truth can provide a shared basis for a conception of justice in a pluralistic democratic society.[2] On this view, a pluralistic

For helpful comments and criticism I am indebted to Brian Barry, John Charvet, G. A. Cohen, Roger Crisp, Raymond Geuss, Brad Hooker, Christine Korsgaard, Christopher Kutz, Luis Martin, Derek Parfit, Joseph Raz, Andrew Reeve, Tim Scanlon, Paul Seabright, Stephen Shute, Quentin Skinner, Larry Temkin, Andrew Williams, Chris Woodard, and members of audiences on various occasions when I have presented this material.

[1] In some cases the detailed arguments can be found in Hurley (1989 or 1993).

[2] His concern is especially with metaphysical and moral truth. Rawls writes that his conception of justice as fairness 'presents itself not as a conception of justice that is true, but one that can serve as a basis of informed and willing political agreement between citizens viewed as free and equal persons'. Given the existence of 'conflicting and incommensurable conceptions of the good', a fundamental feature of modern culture that social theory must recognize, we secure this agreement by trying, 'so far as we can, to avoid disputed philosophical, as well as disputed moral and religious, questions. We do this not because these questions are unimportant or regarded with indifference, but because we think them too important and recognize that there is no way to resolve them politically. . . . Philosophy as the search for truth about an independent metaphysical and moral order cannot, I believe, provide a workable and shared basis for a political

democratic state that avoids the authoritarian use of state power should be neutral about the conflicting and incommensurable conceptions of the good held by its citizens. Now Rawls is not a sceptic about ethical truth. But he still sees the absence of commitment to ethical ideals, even liberal ideals like autonomy, as essential to liberalism as a political doctrine. There is no practicable answer for political purposes to the question of the true good, since public agreement on this cannot be obtained in a non-authoritarian, pluralistic, democratic society.[3]

How can these concerns be met within a cognitivist approach? This is where two key ideas come into play. One is that we can often know that certain biasing influences tend to undermine knowledge, even when we make no politically controversial assumptions about the truth. Moreover, we do not need to know what precise relationship between truth and belief makes for knowledge in order to know that certain factors tend to defeat knowledge. For example, even if we do not think that the notion of beliefs tracking the truth is all epistemology needs, we may recognize that knowledge can be defeated by influences on belief that could not possibly vary counterfactually with the truth, such as desires to believe certain things. Given lack of public agreement and the difficulty of identifying positive expertise, political cognitivism considers how we can nevertheless seek knowledge of the answers to political questions, by at least avoiding the biasing influences that make knowledge impossible. Note that authoritarian power is itself a biasing influence; those who hold it tend to surround themselves with people who tell them what they want to hear.

A second key idea is more positive: we must develop and use effectively certain capacities of citizens. The cognitive capacities of individuals are valuable both in their own right and in the social search for knowledge of what should be done. We can recognize that general cultivation of the cognitive, deliberative and ethical capacities of citizens is necessary for certain demo-

conception of justice in a democratic society. . . . 'A conception of the person in a political view . . . need not involve . . . questions of philosophical psychology or a metaphysical doctrine of the nature of the self. No political view that depends on these deep and unresolved matters can serve as a public conception of justice in a constitutional democratic state.' In such a state, under modern conditions, conflicting and incommensurable conceptions of the good are bound to exist; this fundamental social fact must be recognized by any viable political conception of justice that avoids reliance on authoritarian use of state power. The absence of commitment to moral ideals, even liberal ideals such as autonomy, he regards as essential to liberalism as a political doctrine; there is no practicable answer for political purposes to the question of the true good, since public agreement cannot be obtained. Rawls (1985: 230–1, 245, 249). See also Rawls (1993) on why the idea of moral truth is not a suitable basis of public justification (e.g. 129, and the chapter entitled 'The Idea of Public Reason').

[3] Of course, people may disagree about the acceptability of Rawls's theory of justice: for example, about the normative significance of the Original Position, or about the significance for justice of those features of persons Rawls considers morally arbitrary. They may also disagree about what constitutes a biasing influence. At some level, almost any substantive theory will be open to disagreement.

cratic procedures to avoid bias, even if we do not know the truth about the questions those procedures address.

James Griffin has made a persuasive case for the need to identify beliefs of special reliability in practical and ethical reasoning. I share with him the view that such beliefs include the core value beliefs that provide conditions of intelligibility. But I am less sceptical than he about the possibility that procedures and institutions can be designed, even in the absence of *ex ante* knowledge of the further truths at issue, which tend to lead to reliable beliefs. He writes: 'to say that we should interest ourselves only in judgements formed in the absence of conditions likely to corrupt judgment begs the important questions. If we knew which conditions did that, and also knew we were avoiding them, we should indeed be able to isolate a class of especially reliable judgments' (*VJ* 142–3). But conditions likely to corrupt judgement can be hard to recognize; self-interest is a master of disguises.

However, these difficulties are greatest in the personal sphere, when cognitive labour cannot easily be divided. When faced by a difficult personal decision, we cannot appeal to institutions that delegate the decision to the least biased decision-makers, or take a crash course in the virtues we need to make the decision well. But, in the public sphere, a political distribution of cognitive labour has a distinctive contribution to make. Political institutions and procedures can be designed and adjusted to avoid overall bias and foster capacities in the long term, while minimizing controversial political presuppositions. These two principles give a cognitive twist to the concerns that motivate political neutrality without actually being committed to neutrality. So they are well suited to play a key role in perfectionist versions of liberalism. They at once make cognitivism politically palatable in non-authoritarian pluralist societies and give politics the potential to be of cognitive value.

These two key ideas will be illustrated by brief sketches of how they can be developed in the three areas mentioned. Both ideas will be illustrated in relation to democracy,[4] bias-avoidance in relation to justice, and the fostering of capacities in relation to punishment. Note that in Section 2 we discuss the just distribution *of goods*, while in Section 3 we discuss the democratic distribution *of cognitive labour*.

2. JUSTICE

Theorizing about distributive justice often seems to be guided implicitly by the assumption that a basic aim of egalitarianism is to neutralize the effects

[4] These two key ideas are importantly related to the views of J. S. Mill (1958: 27–8).

on distribution of brute luck, understood as factors for which we are not responsible. (Here we will use 'luck' as short for 'brute luck'; to neutralize luck in this sense is to track responsibility.) This assumption has been made explicit and clarified in important recent work by Cohen (1989, 1992) and by Roemer (1985, 1986, 1987, 1993, 1996, 1998). Luck in this context is usually understood to include luck in the kind of person you are, such as genetic luck, which supposedly gives rise to what Rawls (1971) calls 'morally arbitrary' natural and social differences between people. The aim to neutralize the influence of such factors on distribution can be seen as having an implicit methodological role in Rawls's theory, in providing the normative significance of choices made in the Original Position. This is the case, despite Rawls's official aim to avoid making issues of desert and responsibility prior to issues of justice. In Cohen's and Roemer's work, the role of luck neutralization or responsibility tracking is more explicit and less methodological, that of a basic substantive aim of justice.

It may be natural to assume that rejection of the aim to neutralize luck has anti-egalitarian consequences. For example, while arguing against Rawlsian egalitarianism, Nozick (1974: 225) implies that you do not have to deserve to *be* everything that you are in order to deserve the results of what you *do*. By contrast, the view taken here is that rejection of the luck-neutralizing aim in its familiar methodological or substantive roles can strengthen rather than weaken egalitarianism. The negative reasons for this suggestion must be passed over here (see Hurley 1993, 1995). Some hints: our concepts of responsibility and luck are not determinate enough to do the work needed by some luck-neutralizing accounts of justice. When someone is not responsible for what he has got, there may simply be no answer to what he is responsible for instead. Moreover, the aim to neutralize the *effects* of luck is tied to the suspect principle that in order to be responsible for something you have to be responsible for its *causes*. This principle makes responsibility impossible, because no one can be responsible for the causes of everything, all the way back. But the supposition that no one is responsible for anything provides no support for the claim that everyone does deserve the same thing.

There are also positive reasons for departing from a luck-neutralizing view: perhaps surprisingly, a stronger case for egalitarianism can be made by assuming a different fundamental aim, which displaces responsibility from centre stage in theories of distributive justice in favour of knowledge. Egalitarianism should give a central role not to the aim to neutralize *luck*, but instead to the aim to neutralize *bias*. We can admit that there is an important general connection between justice and responsibility. But this connection can play a background role, the role of setting certain parameters for incentive seeking. By contrast, in contemporary theories of justice this connection has tended to play central roles, whether methodological or substantive, whether explicitly or implicitly (Cohen 1989).

Biases are influences that distort the relationship of our beliefs about what should be done to any truths there may be about what should be done. It is antecedently unlikely that biased beliefs will constitute knowledge—unlikely, that is, independently of any view about the truth or falsity of the beliefs in question. Biases are cognitive distortions: they distort the relationship of belief to truth in a way that prevents belief from attaining the status of knowledge. For example, a personal desire to believe that something is true is a biasing influence on belief. If you believe something because you want to believe it, then, even if your belief just happens to be true, it is not knowledge. Someone whose beliefs on a topic just happen to be true in this way does not have beliefs that are reliably true under relevant counterfactual suppositions. That his own beliefs on this topic are not reliable may mean that they are not a reliable general source of input to deliberation about the truth. Many but not all desires distort the formation of beliefs and thus are biasing influences, and so does certain information that bears on how such desires can be met.

Bias is issue-relative. The same factor can be a biasing influence with regard to certain issues, but not others; love of your spouse, for example, can make for more accurate insights about his character. When a factor is biasing for one issue but not another and both are in the public domain, weighing and balancing are needed. Perhaps a degree of patriotism motivates citizens to the cognitive efforts democracy requires, for example, but too much may distort beliefs about the relationship of your own country to others.

We should distinguish two strands of thought about justice, which are often run together. In Rawls's theory, for example, there is a Kantian, luck-neutralizing strand. This plays a central methodological role within his theory. It is implicitly expressed by his concern to eliminate arbitrary natural and social contingencies from the Original Position, and his remark that the Original Position can be thought of as the point of view from which noumenal selves see the world (Rawls 1971: 255). But there is also a distinguishable, arguably cognitivist strand, which can be understood in terms of a concern to neutralize bias.

The latter, cognitivist strand can take us further towards an egalitarian account of distributive justice when detached from the former, in part because it then does not inherit the problems about responsibility. Aiming at *knowledge* provides a reason to adopt a perspective of *ignorance* in thinking about how goods should be distributed: because ignorance of ourselves would rule out many biasing influences, such as those deriving from self-interest.

Egalitarianism can be supported from such a perspective in a way that does not depend on the luck-neutralizing aim.[5]

Consider a generalization of the Rawlsian framework for thinking about distributive justice. We describe some normatively significant, fictional point of view from which principles of distribution are to be derived, under certain constraints. From such a constrained perspective, we consider the question: 'What should be done about distribution?' We do not assume that the answer is necessarily to be motivated by self-interest operating within the given constraints. The general idea is that, if we specify the right, normatively significant constraints on such a point of view, principles of distribution derived from it will be fair, will be principles of justice.[6] But this could be either because, as in Rawls, the procedure determines what *count* as fair principles, or because we think it is *likely* that principles resulting from such a procedure will yield justice—or at least more likely that they will do so than that principles arrived at in other ways will. We can call such a point of view a *perspective of justice*. This is a generalization of Rawls's idea of the Original Position for two reasons. First, because it does not assume that an exercise of constrained self-interest must occupy this perspective. Secondly, because it does allow that the perspective may be a 'device' in aid of the discovery of just principles rather than a way of determining what count as just principles (cf. Scanlon 1982: 122).

We can now further distinguish two ways of setting up the perspective of justice. One, often appealed to by utilitarians, involves assuming you have an equal chance of being anyone in society. That assumption, among others, acts as a constraint on the reasoning to principles of justice. This is the *equal-chance characterization* of the perspective of justice. It assumes there are known probabilities or risks. The other way of setting up the perspective of justice is Rawls's way: to assume instead a different constraint, namely, that you are radically ignorant of who and what you are. This is the *ignorance characterization* of the perspective of justice. It does not assume that risks are known, but merely assumes ignorance or uncertainty.

These assumptions are distinct so long as you do not adopt the principle that lack of information concerning different possible outcomes justifies assigning them equal probability. Some orthodox decision theorists favour this principle, but Rawls explicitly resists it. And experimental subjects tend

---

[5] The claim is not that the bias-neutralizing aim identifies a distinctively egalitarian motivation. Rather, it is employed quite generally within a cognitive approach to political theory and its consequences for various areas are considered. The claim is that, when applied to issues of distributive justice in the way described, the bias-neutralizing aim supports egalitarianism better than the luck-neutralizing aim does.

[6] This claim is not here defended. It has sufficient currency to merit discussion even in the absence of defence. Issues about its justification are, of course, also of interest, but are not the topic here.

to reject the inference from ignorance to equal probability implicitly, by reacting differently to situations involving uncertainty as opposed to known equal probabilities (an example follows). That is, most people are far more averse to situations of uncertainty, where risks are unknown, than they are to running known risks. And there is now a flourishing school of non-expected utility theorists who do not dismiss this tendency as irrational.[7]

An example may help to see the difference between risk aversion and uncertainty aversion. As an empirical matter, most people are risk averse when they know the probabilities involved. This means that, if you offer people the chance to play a game in which they have an objective 50 per cent chance of winning $100, most will pay less than the game's actuarial value of $50, though gamblers will pay more. Consider a game where someone wins $100 if she guesses correctly the colour of a ball drawn from an urn containing fifty red and fifty black balls. It is worth something to play this game; how much? A typical answer, expressing a degree of risk aversion, might be $30. But if you change the game so that there are 100 balls, red or black, but their proportions are unknown, you are now dealing with uncertainty rather than risk. And typical offers drop dramatically, to around $5 (Raiffa 1961). This difference reflects the difference between risk aversion and uncertainty aversion. They are logically independent; a gambler who likes to take known risks could still be averse to acting without knowledge of risks, under uncertainty.

The distinction between the equal-chance and ignorance characterizations of the perspective of justice can be related to several other distinctions: to the distinction between risk aversion and uncertainty aversion, and to the distinction between the luck-neutralizing aim and the bias-neutralizing aim. On the one hand, we have a set of ideas involving risk and luck: the aim to neutralize luck, the assumption that I might have an equal chance of being anyone, and the idea of risk aversion. On the other hand, we have a set of cognitive ideas involving ignorance and knowledge: the aim to neutralize bias, the assumption that I am ignorant of who I am, and the idea of aversion to uncertainty. Consider how various permutations of these ideas might work in derivations of principles of distribution from a perspective of justice.

First, how does the ignorance versus equal-chance issue interact with the risk-aversion versus uncertainty-aversion issue? While as a matter of fact most people are risk averse, Rawls does not want to assume, in the course of reasoning for his principles of justice, that the parties to his Original Position are risk averse. This is because he holds that different attitudes to risk should be

---

[7] See Bacharach and Hurley (1991: Introduction, sections 2, 3, and *passim*), for a view of the debate; see also, e.g., McClennen (1990); Gardenfors and Sahlin (1982); Hurley (1989: ch. 4 and 368–82).

respected as part of people's differing conceptions of the good, which are veiled in the Original Position. And if risks are unknown in the Original Position, risk aversion cannot get a grip anyway; only aversion to uncertainty is relevant.

By contrast, there are very general conceptual reasons to assume that, other things being equal, intentional agents prefer information to lack of information, so are at least weakly averse to uncertainty. Consider the alternative: to accept uncertainty, other things being equal, would be to decide how to act without taking account of available information and reasons. That would be hard to reconcile with the minimal cognitive rationality and capacities we require of intentional agents. So we can justify on conceptual grounds adding an assumption of weak uncertainty aversion to the ignorance characterization, even if we cannot justify adding an assumption of risk aversion to the equal-chance characterization. We will return to this matter.

Secondly, how does the ignorance versus equal-chance issue interact with the bias-neutralizing versus luck-neutralizing issue? Should the hypothetical position from which principles of justice are chosen be understood in terms of ignorance of who we are or rather of equal chances of being anyone? Rawls, of course, favours the ignorance assumption. But what do the aims to neutralize luck or bias have to say on this question?

The aim to neutralize bias *supports* the idea of deciding about principles of justice in a position of ignorance of your own advantages and disadvantages and your probabilities of gain or loss from various options. Knowledge of these matters might well be biasing, whatever the truth about justice. For example, how much truth is there in the view that offering large incentives to the most talented is necessary to get them to produce in a way that benefits everyone (see Cohen 1992)? We do not need to know the answer to this hard question in order to recognize that my beliefs about this may be biased by knowledge of whether I am talented or not, and my corresponding desires to believe one thing or another. You can be biased because you are talented and want very much to believe the talented need large incentives to produce in a way that benefits the less talented, while I am also biased because I am not talented and want very much to believe the talented do not need large incentives to benefit the less talented. Anyone is more likely to reach the right answer if she can abstract from these biasing influences.

The aim to neutralize bias also argues *against* the idea of deciding about justice on the basis of calculations of your chances of gain. But this holds even if these calculations derive from an assumption that everyone has equal chances. Biases can distort beliefs even if they apply equally to everyone.

To elaborate this point: the aim here is to remove information that would allow potentially biasing desires to affect deliberation about what should be done. In this sense, desires relating to your own chances of gain can be just as biasing as desires relating to your own certainty of gain. But this point is not affected by everyone's chances of gain being the same. The kind of bias in question is cognitive: a distortion of the ideal relationship between truth and belief, introduced by certain desires. It is only derivatively bias in the sense of partiality, or differential orientation to or concern for one person as opposed to another. Bias in the cognitive sense may obtain when your beliefs are influenced by desires that operate via calculations of your chances of gain, even if everyone's chances of gain are the same so that impartiality obtains. Cognitive bias is distinct from partiality: the equal-chance characterization can admit bias, expressed in calculations of your chances of gain, even though it excludes partiality. For these reasons the bias-neutralizing aim does not lend itself to conceptions of the perspective of justice as yielding expressions of constrained self-interest, to the extent the constraints in question still admit cognitive distortion. In this respect the position taken here has an affinity with Scanlon's criticisms of the reading of contractualism in terms of rational self-interest operating behind a veil of ignorance.[8]

[8] Cf. Scanlon's (1982: 122–5) remarks about the difference between appealing to the idea of rational self-interested choice under special conditions and appealing to the idea of what no one could reasonably reject, given that they are seeking a basis for general agreement.

Scanlon comments on the moves, first, from the idea of impartiality to the ignorance characterization of a perspective of justice, and, secondly, from the ignorance characterization to the equal-chance characterization (121). While Rawls criticizes the second move, familiar from arguments for utilitarianism, Scanlon focuses on the first move, from impartiality to ignorance (p. 124). He distinguishes a valid version of this first move from a problematic one. If I would have reason to accept a principle no matter which social position I were to occupy, 'then my knowledge that I have reason to do so need not depend on my knowledge of my particular position, tastes, preferences, etc.' (121). This is a valid train of thought, but it does not lead to the different notion of rational self-interested choice under special conditions. Asking what I could agree to in ignorance of my true position is a 'corrective device' for 'considering more accurately the question of what *everyone* could reasonably agree to', and does not reduce to the quite different idea of what would be chosen by a single self-interested person ignorant of his true position (122). If the first move is read in this latter, problematic way, then a mistake has already been made, before we even move from the ignorance to equal-chance characterization. We should think of the interests in question as 'simply those of the members of the society to whom the principles of justice are to apply' (compare the remarks in the text about people's interests engaging the Pareto preference directly), and Rawls's 'reduction of the problem to the case of a single person's self-interested choice should arouse our suspicion' (124). (Cf. Scanlon's criticisms of the first move with Sandel's (1982: 122–32) remarks about 'what really goes on behind the veil of ignorance' and on the way a 'voluntarist interpretation of the original position gives way to a cognitive one'.)

The burden of Scanlon's criticism falls not on the assumption of a veil of ignorance, of which he admits there is a valid version, but on the reduction to the point of view of a single rational individual behind that veil. In this respect the view taken here is related to Scanlon's: it exploits the veil of ignorance as a corrective device, but without assuming an exercise of constrained self-interest. The argument here goes further by pointing out the way in which uncertainty aversion can operate, even if we do not revert to the constrained self-interest picture. The influence of attitudes to uncertainty on decision is not tied to evaluations in terms of self-interest, any more than the pointfulness of the Veil of Ignorance is.

There are further reasons, related to the bias-neutralizing aim, that also favour an ignorance characterization of the perspective of justice over an equal-chance characterization. A fundamental question here is this. Should we model our attitudes to the distribution of resources across persons, all of whom are or will be actual, on our attitudes to the distribution of resources across possible states of affairs, not all of which will be actual? (Cf. Scanlon 1982: 127.) This is what we do when we base an answer to the question of which actual people should get what on the supposition that I have an equal chance of being anyone. The analogy provides a decision theoretic device for reducing interpersonal problems to individual decision problems given risk. But the formal parallel between a life being mine and a possibility being actual is disturbing in the context of thought about justice. For example, we want to say something like: 'So what if the chances of it being *my* handicap are small? It's still *somebody's* real handicap; the relevance of some actual person's actual handicap to considerations of justice just doesn't depend on the chances that it might have been mine.' To the extent attitudes to uncertainty do not reduce to attitudes to risk, the ignorance characterization fares better than the equal-chance characterization in this respect. Imposing ignorance allows the deliberative decision-maker to focus on the human reality of the handicap or other relevant circumstance, by avoiding the bias that goes with knowing that she herself is safe—*or probably safe.*

How does the aim to neutralize luck bear on the ignorance versus equal-chance issue? We can apply the luck-neutralizing aim to luck in the kind of person you are, or constitutive luck. Consider the idea of a natural lottery of constitutions, or sets of essential properties, the outcome of which is morally arbitrary. Suppose that in such a lottery you have an equal chance of being anyone. This assumption can be regarded as giving a very literal reading to the aim to neutralize constitutive luck. That is, making a decision in the *ex ante* position where there are equal chances of various possible constitutions might seem a way to neutralize such luck.

But this literal reading is in danger of incoherence: who or what is the 'I' who has an equal chance of various different sets of essential properties? We should not want to be committed to making sense of such constitutionless selves. So the luck-neutralizing aim does not support the equal-chance characterization, at least not in this way.

Does the luck-neutralizing aim instead support the ignorance assumption? Whether it does or not, we do not need it. The bias-neutralizing aim can support the ignorance assumption without help from the luck-neutralizing aim. Notice that the reasons why the bias-neutralizing aim supports the ignorance assumption are quite independent of the luck-neutralizing aim and worries about the moral arbitrariness of natural advantages or disadvantages, and they carry no implications about constitutionless selves. Here the negative reasons we passed over for avoiding a luck-neutralizing account are also relevant: since we do not need the luck-neutralizing aim to support the ignorance over the equal-chance characterization, we might as well avoid the problems about responsibility that aim generates.

The net result is that the aim to neutralize bias supports the idea of deciding on principles of justice from a hypothetical position of ignorance rather than one of equal chance. To get this far with Rawls we do not need the aim to neutralize luck, with all its attendant problems.

However, we admitted that there is an important general connection between justice and responsibility. We can now get a glimpse of how this can be given a background, parameter-setting role, rather than a central role. How equally resources are distributed by a maximin principle depends critically on what assumptions we make about incentive-seeking (Cohen 1992). If the most productive seek little or no incentives for being highly productive, maximin will yield a very egalitarian outcome. But, if the most productive seek large incentives, maximin may, under further assumptions, allow very substantial inequalities for the sake of raising the level of the worst off a rather small amount.

What assumptions about incentive seeking should we make? Natural and sociological forces may set a range of possible incentive-seeking behaviours that are realistically feasible in modern conditions. But it is reasonable to assume that, within that range, social and ethical norms influence levels of incentive seeking. In particular, norms concerning how responsible people are for the results of what they do will have an important influence on the levels of incentives that are needed to avoid demoralization and economic apathy.

Both the truth about responsibility and popular intuition about responsibility lie between extremes. It is neither true that people are responsible for almost everything they do nor that they are responsible for almost nothing they do. Incentive-seeking behaviour is sometimes and to some extent expressive of a natural and widespread sense of moderate responsibility for what someone does, as a result of his abilities. But this natural sense of responsibility does not license unrestricted incentive seeking. To merit praise and reward for your activities is not to merit any reward you can extract, however exorbitant. The natural sense of responsibility is vague, but carries with it an unavoidable sense of proportion; it is not the view that you deserve anything you can get away with. But equally it is not the erroneous view that no one is responsible for anything he does as a result of his abilities because no one is responsible all the way back for the causes of those abilities.

It is a good thing for everyone that this latter, erroneous view is not widely held, for several reasons. By making responsibility seem impossible, this view would undercut the critically important well-being that derives from our sense of responsibility (Strawson 1986: 87). Moreover—and this is the important point for egalitarians—it would undermine this well-being unselectively, across all socio-economic classes. A view that undercuts the sense of responsibility is a blunt instrument. Its use for egalitarian purposes is handicapped by its universally negative consequences for the well-being that flows from our sense of responsibility.

These vague truths about responsibility set the parameters of incentive-seeking behaviour within the range of feasibility: an assumption of moderate incentive seeking should be made, corresponding to the vague, moderate popular sense of responsibility. Individuals do need some significant portion of their product as incentive to produce, given this norm of responsibility. But they do not require that almost the whole of their extra product be returned to them. We should not look for more determinacy here than the vague truths about responsibility admit of. Nor do we need to, so long as we keep responsibility in this background, parameter-setting role in relation to a general assumption of moderate incentive seeking. We do not need to decide in particular cases what goods someone *does* deserve, when he is not responsible for what he *actually* has. By avoiding such decisions we avoid occasions for bias to outstrip truth.

Notice that, despite any methodological role luck neutralizing may be given in justifying the Original Position and the assumption of ignorance, these general background issues about responsibility and incentive remain. Until responsibility has played its parameter-setting role in relation to incentive seeking, the implications of a maximin principle for distributive justice are indeterminate. The real work done by responsibility is here in the background. But this background work does not require that the luck-neutralizing aim motivate the perspective of justice. The bias-neutralizing aim does a better job in that central methodological role.

Where do we go from here? Rawls wishes to derive a maximin principle of distributive justice from the Original Position, which requires inequalities in primary goods to benefit the worst-off groups in society. So, for example, inequalities resulting from incentives to produce given to the most talented would be permitted only if they benefited the worst off. Now one way to derive a maximin principle from a perspective of justice would be to ignore the distinction between ignorance and equal chance and to assume risk aversion. In the absence of risk aversion, an equal-chance assumption will not generate egalitarian principles. Moreover, we would have to assume extreme risk aversion to get a maximin principle for resources from an equal-chance assumption. Otherwise, reasoning from the equal-chance assumption, I might be tempted to trade risk-avoidance off against my chances of great wealth by allowing further inequalities.

But this is not Rawls's way. He does distinguish ignorance and equal chance. Risk aversion would get no grip under the ignorance characterization, since risks are unknown (and risk aversion is logically independent of uncertainty aversion). In any case, Rawls gives good reasons not to assume risk aversion, as we have seen. People's attitudes to risk vary, as well as their tastes and conceptions of the good. Their different attitudes to risk should be respected; no particular attitude to risk should be enshrined in the Original Position. But how can the rabbit of maximin be pulled out of the hat of ignorance under these conditions?

We cannot discuss Rawls's attempt to do so here. But not all have been persuaded by it. We will try a different way, using an assumption of aversion to uncertainty instead of an assumption of risk aversion. We need only weak, not extreme, aversion to uncertainty in order to derive egalitarian principles of distributive justice from a position of ignorance—though how weak determines how egalitarian.

Is this not just as bad as assuming risk aversion? No: the same objections do not apply. This is not because uncertainty aversion is more marked and widespread than risk aversion, as an empirical matter, though that is true. As we have seen, there is a very general conceptual reason to assume that, other things being equal, intentional agents prefer information to its absence. Our conception of minimally rational intentional agents requires them to be weakly averse to uncertainty, even if in order to avoid bias we put such agents in a hypothetical position of ignorance to choose principles of justice. This combination of uncertainty and aversion to uncertainty yields egalitarian results. And it does so in a way that does not give a motivating role to the aim to neutralize luck or to worries about the moral arbitrariness of natural advantages or disadvantages.

A little uncertainty aversion goes a long way in generating egalitarian results. If you start with equal chance, you need extreme risk aversion to get a degree of egalitarianism that you can get instead from ignorance plus weak risk aversion. If ignorance of your identity and traits is not translatable into known chances of gain or loss, it is not *possible* to trade off avoidance of uncertainty against your chances of gain. Thus such trade-offs are ruled out without assuming extreme uncertainty aversion. Recall that it was for a closely related reason that the bias-neutralizing aim favoured the ignorance assumption over the equal-chance assumption. Part of the point of imposing ignorance, according to the bias-neutralizing aim, is that it gives no scope to calculations of your chances of gain. But by the same token, neither does it give scope to trade-offs of chances of gain against aversion to either risk or uncertainty. So ignorance combines with even weak uncertainty aversion to preclude the influence of desires that relate to your own chances of gain.

However, the ignorance assumption does allow certain desires to operate. First, an aversion to uncertainty may be regarded as equivalent to a desire for information about the way things actually are or will be. Unlike desires relating to your own chances of gain in particular, this desire cannot in general be regarded as biasing in the sense of cognitive distortion. Secondly, we need to depend on some general assumptions about basic goods, in something like the way that Rawls depends on the notion of primary goods. Basic goods may include the realization of capacities and the sense of responsibility. Consider then what we can call the 'Pareto preference': an impersonal and general desire that people be better off in terms of these basic goods rather than worse off, other things being equal. This simply makes operational our necessary assumption of some basic goods, so does not introduce bias: if it did introduce bias, then those goods would be the wrong ones to assume. So uncertainty aversion and the Pareto preference are compatible with the bias-neutralizing aim in a way that concern for your own chances of gain is not. Moreover, uncertainty aversion can be assumed even though we do not assume self-interested motivation.

Consider then a perspective of justice characterized by the ignorance assumption, by weak uncertainty aversion, and by the Pareto preference relative to the assumed basic goods. In this situation, a maximin principle can be seen as the closest you can reasonably come to avoiding uncertainty over fundamental goods. We can reach this conclusion in several steps, by exploiting the connection between uncertainty and the distribution of goods.[9]

First, even if you have no information about your position, distributing a known fixed quantity of goods equally avoids uncertainty over those goods. You can easily calculate what everyone actually gets; there is no uncertainty about people's absolute or relative positions.

Secondly, if the quantity of goods for distribution is not known or fixed, it is no longer possible to avoid uncertainty about absolute positions. But distributing goods equally at least avoids uncertainty about relative positions.

Thirdly, we now remember that uncertainty avoidance is weak, not extreme. Consider setting against it not any known chances of gain for yourself, but rather increases in basic goods for some unknown members of society, so long as the level of the worst off is kept as high as it can be. Moving from equality to maximin admits uncertainty about relative as well as absolute positions, in

---

[9] It may be objected that, once we reject the idea of an exercise of constrained self-interest, there is no reason to stop short of full-fledged impartial-spectator theory. The argument here is indeed aiming to occupy a middle ground between these options. The role given to the Pareto preference is consistent with the perspective of an impartial spectator. But we can nevertheless use the decision-theoretic connection between uncertainty and distribution to structure the argument to maximin, in the way suggested. This connection can hold, even though self-interest is not the relevant motivation. Here I am indebted to objections made by Derek Parfit.

order to satisfy the Pareto preference. But this is compatible with an assumption of only weak uncertainty aversion. You are not here trading off uncertainty avoidance for an increase in your own chances of gain. Rather, you are trading it for increases in some unknown persons' level of basic goods, increases that leave no one worse off. You judge that their improvement outweighs the additional, relative, uncertainty. This is not because you calculate that you have some chance of being them. Their improvement engages the Pareto preference directly. (Again, cf. Scanlon 1982.)

There is a further question as to exactly where the compromise between uncertainty avoidance and Pareto improvements should be struck. Should weak Pareto improvements be permitted, which benefit some and make no one worse off, including of course the worst off? If so, uncertainty about who will benefit is admitted. This will result if we keep the assumption of uncertainty aversion very weak, so that uncertainty should be avoided only other things being equal. Or should only strong Pareto improvements be permitted, which make everyone better off—again, including the worst off? If so, at least we know everyone will benefit. A stronger assumption of uncertainty aversion will move us in this direction, but it does not need to be extreme. The first view would admit more relative uncertainty for the sake of Pareto improvement than the second view would. But neither will permit inequalities that involve anyone's being worse off than they would be if we stopped with the unknown total amount distributed equally at step two.

Notice the way the ignorance constraint and the aversion to uncertainty work together. It is only in the context set by the ignorance constraint that aversion to uncertainty drives us towards equality. But aversion to uncertainty itself supports the ignorance constraint, just because the constraint rules out biasing influences, cognitive distortions. So ignorance can serve knowledge. Given the ignorance constraint, we would still (other things being equal) like to avoid as much uncertainty about actual distributions of goods as possible, and, by keeping everyone equal at an unknown absolute level, we do. If we allow some people to rise above this level but do not know who they are, we sacrifice some knowledge about relative levels. In particular, we do not know which people will be above this level or even the chances that particular people will be above this level. But it is precisely this knowledge about who would benefit that the ignorance constraint has denied us, in the interests of avoiding cognitive distortion. The trade-off we make at step three between uncertainty avoidance and Pareto improvement is in harmony with the underlying aim of bias-neutralization. Ignorance of the identity of those persons who will be above the floor of stage two is precisely the kind of ignorance that avoids cognitive distortions, such as those of self-interest, or envy, that would be introduced if we considered the chances that we would be among those persons.

On the cognitivist view, the normative significance of the perspective of justice characterized by ignorance rather than equal chance is found in the aim to avoid the biasing influences that inevitably go with information, even probabilistic information, about who you are and what you are like, your talents and handicaps. And weak aversion to uncertainty can be justified as part of the minimal cognitive rationality required for intentional agency. By giving a cognitive slant to the perspective of justice, and dissociating it from the luck-neutralizing aim and related ideas, we can reclaim egalitarian results. In this way we can take a lead as egalitarians from Rawls even if we do not share his Kantian, luck-neutralizing sympathies. And this way of developing political cognitivism has not at any point implied authoritarian power or threatened the pluralist and democratic character of liberal society.

3. DEMOCRACY

Let us now move on to a somewhat briefer sketch of a cognitivist approach to democracy. Consider two prevalent assumptions about liberal democracy. *First*, people should vote on the basis of their preferences rather than their beliefs about what should be done. Knowledge about what should be done is not the aim of democracy. The aim is rather to satisfy preferences, which of course requires a way of resolving conflicts between them. This non-cognitivist assumption dominates social-choice theory, which is concerned with how to aggregate individual preference orderings. *Secondly*, the justification of political decisions and procedures should be neutral with respect to the conflicting conceptions of the good held by different citizens, and should not derive from the aim to learn the truth about how such conflicts should be resolved.

These two assumptions contrast with a conception of liberal democracy as deliberative and developmental, such as that found in J. S. Mill (1958), which can be regarded as a form of liberal perfectionism. On one version of such a view, democratic procedures and institutions should meet two conditions.

First, they should embody a *distribution of cognitive labour* (or, in this section, *distribution* for short). This assigns issues to decision-makers or procedures, such as to individuals in their private capacities, to referendums, to the judiciary, to ministers, to the legislature, and so on. Moreover, it aims to do so in a way that *avoids* subjecting the overall decision-making exercise to *biasing influences*, influences that make it antecedently unlikely that the exercise will yield knowledge. As we have already seen, biasing influences can often be identified even when the truth at issue is not prejudged: consider vested interests, self-deception, wishful thinking, prejudice, propaganda, common inferential error, and so on. Even though positive expertise may be difficult to identify without prejudging issues, the distribution can still seek to avoid bias.

Secondly, democratic procedures and institutions should foster and develop the capacities of citizens for practical knowledge, in particular the capacities for public and private deliberation and for the formation of unbiased belief. The cognitive capacities of individuals should be fostered as well as the cognitive capacities of the socially distributed system of cognitive labour. The quality of public deliberative exercises may depend on the capacities of citizens for autonomous deliberation in the face of conflicting goods, and on the education and opportunities for exercise these capacities need in order to be developed and realized. A cognitive conception of democracy gives a critically important role to the education of citizens and makes considerable demands on them, as voters or in whatever capacity they contribute to the democratic decision-making process. It recognizes the cognitive capacities of individuals as valuable in their own right, as well as in respect of their contribution to socially distributed cognition.

The first of these two principles focuses on cognitive capacities at the collective level, and the second focuses on cognitive capacities at the individual level. We should avoid over-simple assumptions about the relations between these levels.

For example, the first of these two principles must be interpreted so as to respect some important features of social distributions of cognitive labour, some of which are related to features of distributed information processing more generally. A group can perform certain overall cognitive functions even though there is no representation of that overall function or central plan anywhere in the system. Distributed cognition may be more adaptable than centralized cognition, both to external change and to the cognitive failures of individuals who are components of the system ('graceful degradation'). Perhaps the most important feature for present purposes is that groups can have cognitive properties that differ significantly from those of the individuals in the groups. Certain forms of collective decision-making may accentuate individual cognitive properties both in the good and the bad direction (as in Condorcet's Jury Theorem). But the cognitive capacities of different groups depend on the social organization of distributed cognition as well as on the cognitive properties of individuals. For example, one way of organizing individuals who display a cognitive failing (such as confirmation bias) may inherit this failing from them, while another may not (Condorcet 1785; Hutchins 1995: chs. 4, 5, and esp. 178, 199, 224, 226–7, 348, etc.; Hutchins describes a neural network simulation of some of these features of socially distributed cognition).

Suppose we wish to find a political distribution of cognitive labour that, among other things, avoids biasing influences on the cognitive performance of the group. We cannot assume that the only way to do this is to avoid dependence on any individual components that are subject to biasing influences. Some organizations of individuals may inherit bias from individuals while others may not. However, we do need to study the relationship between biasing influences on individuals, various forms of cognitive organization, and the cognitive properties of the group. So we do need to identify biasing influences on individuals, in order to consider whether cognitive labour should be distributed in a way that avoids depending on biased components at all, or whether they can rather be organized in such a way as to neutralize bias at the level of the system as a whole. Pitting one bias against another within a socially distributed cognitive exercise may sometimes be an effective way to unbias the overall exercise: consider the adversarial legal system as a possible example. The moral is: we need information about the biasing influences on individuals to design an unbiased distribution of cognitive labour, even though we cannot assume that distributed cognition necessarily inherits bias from individual participants.

Subject to these clarifications, our two principles tell us to find a distribution of cognitive labour that *avoids bias overall* and that *fosters the capacities of citizens*. These two principles can, for example, guide institutional respect for freedom of speech. Disagreement, open debate, and argument are of cognitive value, both in revealing error and flushing out truth, and in forming the autonomous deliberative capacities of citizens. However, protection so motivated might well not extend to forms of expression that systematically damage rather than foster such capacities, as arguably certain types of pornography may (see Fiss 1996). Reasonable adversarial procedures and assignments of procedural rights should be guided by consideration of the cognitive value of such procedures. Pressure groups and lobbyists should not be given a role inconsistent with that value. The variety of opinions and reasoned disagreement in society provide scope for the operation of a distribution of cognitive labour. Such disagreement should be exploited by a thorough distribution of authority that avoids the general potential for bias inherent in concentrations of power *per se*, as well as the more particular sources of bias stemming from particular interests.

A cognitive theory of democracy does not claim that all non-authoritarian distributions that foster the autonomous deliberative capacities of individual citizens will be of overall cognitive value. Or even that they are likely to be. Rather, the claim is the other way around. Distributions that are of overall cognitive value will be non-authoritarian, so more adaptable and less likely than centralized authoritarian arrangements to lead to disastrously wrong answers. By fostering the autonomous deliberative capacities of individuals, a non-authoritarian distribution of cognitive labour can protect the conditions in which the search for right answers at all levels can continue. So authoritarian regimes that neglect development can be ruled out on cognitive grounds. But it is a further question what non-authoritarian distribution is best in a particular context. There are many possible non-authoritarian distributions of cognitive labour. Certain assignments of issues to decision-makers and institutions will fit a certain society's characteristics, and others will not.

Democratic procedures should be a means to knowledge of truths about what should be done. However, their relationship to values and reasons for action is not wholly instrumental and evidential. We can see this by considering the way in which democratic procedures contribute to realizing one important value—namely, the value of individual autonomy. Participation in democratic deliberation is not wholly separate from the development and exercise of individual autonomy, but partly constitutive of it. The importance of this point becomes clearer when we hold in focus the *intra*personal as well as *inter*personal plurality of goods. We should not conceive of social conflict and deliberation as concerning primarily conflicts between persons, each of whom has a unified, comprehensive doctrine of the good.[10] In modern pluralistic societies, very few persons have any such thing; eclecticism is the norm, even in religion. Rather, pluralism reflects conflicts among values that are widely shared. So the conflicts that need resolution cut within people as much as between them, and the intrapersonal plurality of goods provides the basis for exercises of autonomy. In this sense autonomy is a higher-order value: it presupposes and operates on other values. For example, I may be a member of a socialist trade union and of a highly competitive and meritocratic orchestra, and so need to form a view about the relationship between the potentially conflicting values these affiliations express. For these reasons, an individual's deliberation about the conflicts she faces and public deliberation about social conflicts are intertwined. Democratic procedures for public deliberation contribute to realizing individuals' capacities and the value of individual autonomy. None of this requires that autonomy be of overriding value. It may itself conflict internally or with other important values.

We can apply some of these considerations by reinterpreting social-choice results in terms of belief rather than preference. Social-choice theory concerns how the conflicting preference orderings of alternatives by individuals can be reasonably aggregated into a social ordering. It turns out, surprisingly, that no

---

[10] Cf. the contrast drawn by Rawls (1993: 134–5) in terms of 'comprehensive doctrines each with its own conception of the good'; cf. also 'The Idea of an Overlapping Consensus' in that volume.

possible process of aggregation can meet certain combinations of conditions on reasonable aggregation. For example, Arrow's impossibility theorem tells us that no process of aggregation will guarantee that social rankings meeting certain conditions are not cyclical. These conditions collectively rule out all possible methods of aggregating individual preference orderings into social orderings (Sen 1970).

Such results take on a new and significant role in designing a democratic distribution of cognitive labour. The attractiveness of some of these conditions depends largely on the non-cognitivist framework usually presupposed in contemporary social-choice theory. That is, the conditions are conceived to apply to preference orderings rather than beliefs. So the task of aggregation, the reasonableness of which is at issue, is conceived to be a non-cognitive one. By contrast, a cognitive view of democracy as involving the aggregation of beliefs provides a principled epistemic basis for rejecting or restricting some of the conditions. So the corresponding negative results about democracy do not follow, given this cognitive reinterpretation. On this view, what is needed is a method of mapping individual or component beliefs onto collective belief; collective belief is some function of component beliefs. What conditions are appropriate to impose on this function?

Consider, for example, one of the conditions required for Arrow's result, the *Independence of Irrelevant Alternatives*. This ensures that social preference over pairs of alternatives depends only on individual preferences over the same alternatives. So it forbids social preference between any alternatives x and y to vary counterfactually with anything except the preferences of individuals as between x and y. In effect, it says that the impact of individual preferences on social choice between x and y depends only on the *ordering* between x and y given by those preferences, not on how *strong* the preferences are, or on their *motivation or genesis*, on whether they are *well informed or arbitrary*, or on any other information about them.

Why might it be reasonable to forbid all such further information to have an influence on social choice? If you suppose that there are no truths at issue, and the task at hand is a strictly non-cognitive task of preference aggregation, then it might seem that the use of any further information is *ultra vires* and question begging, in implying some objective standard or measure for preferences. Whether it is justified to impose the Independence condition on preference aggregation is controversial, even on a *non-cognitive* view of social choice, because of its role in ruling out interpersonal comparisons of strength of preference. But the point here is that a *cognitive* conception of democratic aggregation provides independent epistemic reason to reject this condition.

If democracy seeks knowledge of what should be done on the basis of the beliefs of citizens in various roles, then it needs some method of aggregating those beliefs. *A method of aggregating beliefs, or function from individual to collective belief, amounts to a method of distributing cognitive labour.* The conditions reasonable to impose on any such method will be conditions that avoid subjecting the distributed cognitive process overall to biasing influences without, as far as possible, prejudging the truths at issue. We should not assume that the overall cognitive process will necessarily inherit the biases of individuals or other components, as we have seen. Given certain biasing influences on individuals, some distributions of cognitive labour may inherit bias, while others may not. Nevertheless, the method of distribution needs information about biasing influences, and about the relations between component and system biases, or individual and collective biases, in order to distribute cognitive labour in a way that avoids bias overall. So the method of aggregating beliefs/distributing cognitive labour should be sensitive not just to the content of beliefs about the alternatives at issue, but also to external information about the reliability of beliefs from certain sources about certain kinds of issue in certain circumstances. This kind of information is needed to assign issues to subdomains of decision-makers in a way that avoids bias overall. If democratic procedures are to have cognitive value, institutions should be designed to arrive at beliefs that are, as far as possible for a particular society, unbiased, well informed, and well considered, not arbitrary. Some persons or group of persons or institution or level or branch of government may be a reliable source of such beliefs for certain circumstances and types of issue, and others for others. A method of aggregating beliefs that places equal reliance on all possible opinions irrespective of their sensitivity to the truth cannot include institutional arrangements that function to distribute cognitive labour in accordance with the distinctions of reliability that fit particular societies and circumstances.

In this light, the Independence condition is a non-starter. Consider how it would constrain a method for distributing cognitive labour. The cognitive analogue of the Independence condition applies to the beliefs of voters and other social decision-makers instead of their preferences. Take a set of the beliefs of all relevant decision-makers. These beliefs will have given contents about whether x or y should be done. The cognitive analogue of the Independence condition would require that beliefs with these contents have a fixed effect on the social view as between x and y, regardless of any further information about the influences operating on such beliefs. This rules out evaluation of the counterfactual reliability of beliefs from different decision-makers on different types of issue. Some sources may be reliable on some types of issue but open to biasing influences on other types of issue. A method of distributing cognitive labour needs that very information to assign issues to decision-makers, procedures, institutions, and so on, in a way that avoids biasing influences overall. This is true even though the method of distribution does not prejudge the truths at issue. As we have seen, some distributions of cognitive labour may work better than others, for given individual or component cognitive properties. So a method of distribution should be sensitive to these properties. Information about, among other things, the biasing influences on individuals or other components of the distributed cognitive system is needed to distribute labour effectively. But the Independence condition applied to a method of aggregating belief/distributing cognitive labour would deny us this information. The counterfactual sensitivity involved in evaluating bias violates Independence. So Independence cannot be a reasonable condition to impose on the cognitive task of aggregating beliefs with the aim of achieving knowledge. Given a cognitive conception of democracy, the Independence condition would amount to an unreasonable handicap.[11]

The basic idea here is that the counterfactual structure given to social-choice theory by various social-choice conditions can be evaluated by reference to the conflicting demands of counterfactual reliability made by knowledge. One of the best-known results in social-choice theory has been used to illustrate how social-choice conditions can be reinterpreted and evaluated in cognitive terms. But related points can be made for other social-choice results and conditions.

4. PUNISHMENT

Let us now turn to the topic of punishment. Here is a brief sketch of how three strands of thought might be woven together into a cognitivist approach to punishment. The suggestion is not that this kind of view should stand alone in justifying punishment. We already have good reasons to think we need a complex overall theory of punishment. But a cognitivist view may well form an essential part of such a complex theory. The three strands of thought are, first, the broadly Aristotelian idea of practical knowledge; secondly, the long-term character-forming influences of punishment emphasized by Scandinavian theorists such as Andenaes and Ross; and, thirdly, the communitarian idea that certain non-neutral social conditions are needed to sustain

---

[11] It may be objected that divisions of epistemic labour that do not give each individual's opinion an equal influence on the result are for that reason undemocratic. On this view, individual rights over certain private issues, judicial review, even federal systems that give regions equal influence but not individuals, would be regarded as undemocratic. Hurley (1989: ch. 15) argues that this objection presumes an over-simple conception of democracy, which cannot account for the respects in which certain divisions of epistemic labour are more democratic than others, any more than it can account for the respects in which certain ways of drawing boundaries are more democratic than others. See also Hurley (1999).

and realize essential capacities of citizens. The idea of bias avoidance emphasized earlier will not be used here, but the other key cognitivist idea, that of
fostering capacities for knowledge, will be.

The first strand is a broadly Aristotelian idea of practical knowledge. This
notion involves an ideal of the rationality of emotional responses. It rejects a
presumed dualism or conflict between reason and emotion and allows that
emotions themselves may be subject to cognitive standards. How should I feel
about something? The way a good person, a person of practical wisdom,
would feel. The practical knowledge that enables someone's feelings to be sensitive to the real nature of the situation, rather than being distorted or inap-
propriate, is acquired through practical experience and training. Practical
education is a matter of practice, habituation, being properly brought up in
a morally civilized community. Alluding to recent moves in cognitive science
that have allied themselves with Aristotle, we could say that practical education is a matter of having your neural networks trained up by interactions
with ethical practices in your environment so that you acquire ethical perceptual capacities and skills (Churchland 1995: 148–50). Among the results
should be feelings of aversion to evil and feelings of shame, where these reflect
the true nature of the situation and are appropriate.[12]

The second strand is an important correction to a gap in many English-language discussions of punishment. This can be found in the work of Scandinavian theorists such as the criminologist Johannes Andenaes and the jurist
Alf Ross. Andenaes distinguishes the long-term character-forming influences
of the practice of punishment from the shallower influence of deterrence as it
is usually conceived. He also emphasizes that, even if long-term formative
influences of punishment are strong and important, certain factors will make
it difficult to acquire evidence for this. Ross rejects the standard contrast
between retributive and deterrence theories of punishment and stresses that
the general preventative effect of punishment depends primarily on the way
the shame and infamy attached to punishment influence and form feelings and
attitudes in society at large. (See Andenaes 1974; Ross 1975, e.g. 89–90.)

Many philosophers have tended to see the influence of punishment in
preventing certain evils along the lines of what we can call *shallow deterrence*.
The word 'deterrence' suggests an influence that holds a great deal about the
potential criminal and his society constant: you take the potential criminal's
personality structure and desires, as well as prevalent social norms, as
exogenously given, and you simply alter the pay-offs that attach to certain

---

[12] Worth considering in this context are Nussbaum's suggestions about the role of praise and
blame in Aristotle's account of the natural animal basis for the development of moral character, and the contrasts she draws with a more Kantian view of responsibility. See Nussbaum (1986:
282–7).

actions by adding penalties to crimes. These penalties may be thought of as the price of the crime. They may be external sanctions, either legal or social, or internal sanctions. But even the internal versions are often thought of as the pricks of conscience, mere internal analogues of the unpleasant external consequences of crime: as if the internalized penalty structure were wrapped around a core character and system of beliefs and desires that are still held constant.

The idea of shallow deterrence, whether it operates externally or internally, can be contrasted with the idea of influences that reach right into the constitution of the self, which alter the very character and personality factors that deterrence takes as exogenously given and by reference to which it calculates its penalties. These would be formative influences on people's characters, values, and systems of beliefs and desires, as they grow up and beyond, in part via the ethical and social norms prevalent in society. But criminal law and the legal practice of punishment might well contribute to such long-term formative influences, and through them have general preventative effects on crime. If so, the theory of punishment should not regard personality, character, and the capacities of citizens for practical knowledge, as exogenously determined; such factors are endogenous to the theory of punishment.[13]

Andenaes notes that most people would not commit certain crimes, regardless of the threat of punishment. But he goes on to ask how long this would remain true if criminal sanctions were abolished. Might they be among the influences that form people's characters, in ways that society cannot afford to dispense with? Such influence would not be impossible to overcome. If the law is simply out of touch with social norms, it will be disrespected, as in Prohibition. Nevertheless, the law is a real influence: Andenaes gives the example of mandatory prison sentences in Norway for driving under the influence of alcohol, and their influence on the development of social mores there. He also describes the way punishment neutralizes the demoralizing consequences of witnessing crime: frustration at seeing the criminal get away with it with impunity, at seeing the bad example reinforced, the tendency to ask why I should restrain myself when others are not, the chain-reaction effects of crime, and so on. Bad examples, which might otherwise be imitated, are made less attractive. Much of the influence of punishment may be unconscious, at the level of absorption of taboos throughout childhood and beyond. This may operate in conjunction with mere deterrence: when someone is deterred by the threat of punishment, there may be a kind of psychological dissonance

---

[13] Shallow deterrence is normally assumed to be in question when the preventative effects of punishment are assessed in utilitarian terms. But, if a system of punishment has deep, long-term influences on social norms and on the formation of characters and desires of persons growing up in society, then these influences may in principle be equally subject to utilitarian calculation.

left, which is resolved by derogation of the action: he did not really want to do it anyway, it was nasty. In this way punishment can prompt unconscious internalization of norms. Also, people have a tendency not to focus on, to blur over, the negative aspects of something they want to do, including criminal acts. Apprehension and the threat of punishment can have an eye-opening effect: Andenaes gives the example of a shop-lifter who has been deceiving himself about his own activity, rationalizing it to himself, not facing up to it. When caught, he suddenly sees clearly what he has been doing and feels terribly ashamed, and his friends are ashamed for him also, and reinforced in their determination never to get themselves in a similar mess. In this way the legal penalty triggers social sanctions. On balance, Andenaes regards the direct short-term moral educational influence of the criminal law to be fairly weak. But he regards its indirect long-term effects in reinforcing inhibitions and influencing character formation as important. He regards criminal law as one of the fundamental socializing influences, which operates not just through fear, but influences human thought and behaviour in varied and subtle ways that permeate society.

Although punishment may in this way have a general preventative influence on criminal behaviour, it will most likely be a very long-term influence, often indirect, with feedback: criminal law and punishment may influence ethical norms and character formation, while ethical norms also influence criminal law. Such long-term influences are extremely difficult to isolate from other influences, especially since they operate through social norms. Even if we assume for the sake of argument that the formative thesis is true, we should expect difficulties in finding evidence for it that meets rigorous scientific standards, for various reasons cited by Andenaes. Our experience of the effects of the criminal law tends to be of people who were not deterred—namely, of criminals, not of people who were deterred. Not only is the true extent of unreported crime of certain kinds unknown, but, much more fundamentally, we do not know how many people have been prevented from committing crimes who would have committed them otherwise. It is difficult to gauge the effects of altering punishments, because it is difficult to establish proper controls. Comparing different geographical areas with different penalties requires us to know whether differences in criminality are due to other social differences; but areas with very similar social conditions and sharply different penal systems may be hard to find.[14] Comparisons across time in one society face

---

[14] Are side-by-side states in the United States with different sentencing policies good counterexamples, if, despite these differences, people pay little attention to state boundaries in going about their business? State boundaries might be largely ignored in many aspects of ordinary life for reasons that have little to do with the criminal law, yet these aspects of ordinary life may create occasions for crime. What is the difference between two distinct systems with different sentencing policies, which might provide a controlled experiment, and one inclusive system with what is in effect a sentencing policy with a random element?

similar problems: penal changes are usually gradual, and are accompanied by other social changes, so how can you isolate factors to be clear about what causes the final result? If the long-term influences of punishment on criminal behaviour take a generation, or several, to operate, in this time many other compounding influences may operate also.[15]

But paucity of evidence for the thesis that punishment *does* have long-term formative influence in preventing crime does not mean that there is evidence for the contrary thesis, that it has *little* such influence. That would be just as hard to come by. We can understand why direct evidence may be hard to get either way here. So we need to ask ourselves what is reasonable to assume as a default position and where the burden of proof should be. This point is obvious, yet its implications are often ignored when the lack of evidence for a disputed proposition is adduced.

The Scandinavian formative view of punishment can be compared to Hampton's (1984) moral-education theory of punishment, which focuses on the education of the individual punished rather than on general social influences. It can also be compared with Feinberg's (1970) expressive view of punishment, which focuses on the immediate expressive function of punishment rather than on the long-term consequences of such expression. But there is not space here to pursue these comparisons.

Finally, we come to the third line of thought. Communitarians have emphasized that capacities essential to sustain respect for justice and political legitimacy require certain social and cultural conditions. This in itself seems relatively uncontroversial. This category of capacities should include the autonomous deliberative capacity emphasized in the discussion of democracy, as well as the capacity for practical knowledge with its emotional aspects. What are more controversial are the further communitarian claims, first, that institutions governed by liberal neutrality will be incapable of supporting the social conditions necessary to sustain respect for justice and legitimacy, and, secondly, that what are needed are a politics of the common good and state support for a shared form of life (Taylor 1985; Kymlicka 1990: 216).

Now it is possible to doubt that liberal neutrality is sufficient to sustain respect for justice and legitimacy without agreeing that what is needed is the fostering and protecting by the state of certain shared ways of life. Liberal perfectionism can be seen as accepting the first of these claims but not the second. Even in the absence of allegiance to neutrality, we may worry that the idea of favouring certain ways of life in the context of contemporary pluralistic societies may lend itself to revival of the white male club, or of similar hierarchical or exclusionary forms of life: that the commonality would be accomplished

[15] Many of the points of the preceding two paragraphs paraphrase Andenaes (1974: chs. 1, 2, 4, 5). Cf. Lacey (1988: 28, 182–3, etc.).

by exclusion of those who are different. However, this is not the only alternative to liberal neutrality. The social conditions for the capacities essential to sustaining justice may depart from neutrality without going all the way to state support for a shared way of life.

Consider the capacity for practical knowledge and for rational and cognitively appropriate emotional responses, including an aversion to evil and a sense of shame where it is appropriate. There are some things, after all, that almost all societies have agreed are evil and shameful, even if they have tolerated them, some things that punishment should not be regarded as simply the price of. Respect for reasonable pluralism should not dilute our recognition of violent crimes and the destruction and suffering they produce as evils. There are some truths we are entitled to prejudge, which we can expect legislatures to respect. The socio-legal practice of punishment may have a long-term influence on the formation of citizens' characters, both as they grow up and beyond into adulthood, so that they see such evils as shameful and so that a basic aversion to the evils of violent crime is an essential part of their personalities. Indeed, we might find communitarian language about the social constitution of the self appropriate in thinking about such influences. There are many differences between the family and political contexts. But punishment in both contexts may be integral to the existence of a properly brought up citizenry, with realized capacities for practical knowledge. If so, the practice of legal punishment may be among the social conditions for the development of capacities essential to sustaining respect for justice. That is, the formative thesis may provide a way of arguing for the communitarian claim.

The Scandinavian formative thesis and the communitarian claim have just been applied to the capacity for practical knowledge and for cognitively appropriate emotions. But is the cognitive aspect of this application doing any work in a justification of punishment?[16] Could not parallel points be dissociated from a cognitive view of the capacities that need cultivating? So long as useful desires and emotions are cultivated, why does it matter if they reflect knowledge or cognitive standards?

This question in effect suggests that we can hold onto the distinction between mere shallow deterrence and long-term formative influences, even if the latter apply to desires and emotions only, and not to ethical perceptions and beliefs. But this is implausible. If we are holding much about an agent's character and world-view constant, as in shallow deterrence, we can isolate certain desires and tinker just with them through penalties and incentives. But, when our aim is to guide the formation of stable, integrated ethical characters in the long term through social practices, perceptions and beliefs do not

---

[16] Here I am indebted to Raymond Geuss.

fractionate from desires and emotions. It is implausible to suppose we could effectively guide the formation of ethical desires and emotions only, in a way that is neutral with respect to ethical perceptions and beliefs. Ethical character formation is an ambition that involves unity and harmony between cognitive and conative aspects of character, rather than merely non-cognitive conditioning. Perceptions of why certain things are wrong should be integral to and in equilibrium with desires and emotions and social skills. The unified, Aristotelian view of practical knowledge makes the formative thesis far more plausible than it would be for purely non-cognitive capacities.

Do these suggestions threaten the value of autonomy appealed to earlier, in the discussion of democracy? The threat is illusory, for several reasons. First, autonomy should not be conceived as the absence of formative causal influences. If we so conceive it, we make it impossible, hence make fostering and respecting autonomy irrelevant to politics. Secondly, as we have just seen, we do not aim to condition or manipulate, which would threaten autonomy, but rather to form cognitive capacities. The autonomous exercise of cognitive capacities is not threatened by causal influences on their formation. Thirdly, autonomy is a higher-order value, which depends on the capacities of people to reflect and deliberate on appropriate first-order values. The value of autonomy does not depend on the autonomous person's reaching right answers all or even most of the time, but it does depend on his recognizing some basic first-order values as providing *pro tanto* reasons, and on his having the capacity for higher-order reflection and deliberation. The value of autonomy, that is, presupposes a subject with an ethical constitution. We can cultivate basic first-order values, in part via the formative causal influence of punishment (both within families and in political society), while recognizing that these values often conflict and while also fostering and respecting autonomy. In fact, autonomy presupposes such first-order values; in their absence (as in some kinds of mental deficiency) it is ill-defined. The 'autonomy' of a psychopath may for this reason be a sham. There is still plenty of room within these constraints for respecting autonomy, whether or not people reach right answers in exercising it.

But the objection may be reformulated. Suppose someone does recognize the normal range of first-order values, but when in a conflict situation he reflects and deliberates he nevertheless autonomously decides to do an evil act: say, to commit murder. He supposes the evil is somehow overridden by other considerations. If we take an aim of punishment to be to influence the formations of people's characters so that such exercises of autonomy do not occur, do we threaten the value of autonomy?

Here, we face a conflict within the value of autonomy: the evils in question are evils in part because they involve the complete negation of one person's autonomy (the murdered person's, for example) by another person. We can reasonably judge that exercises of autonomy with such evil consequences should be avoided, in the name of autonomy. In such cases, the end of mutual respect for autonomy may be served by means of formative influences that do amount to restrictions on autonomy. But this cost is worth paying, in terms of the value of autonomy itself, since considerations of potential victims' autonomy may outweigh considerations of potential criminals' autonomy. Implicit here is the view that the state cannot properly wash its hands of violations of autonomy merely because they are not the immediate result of state action or because they involve private rather than public acts.

For these reasons a state role may be needed, via penal institutions, in supporting a shared aversion to evil and a cognitively appropriate sense of shame among citizens. These emotional traits do not relate solely to the evil of injustice; they do not respect the boundary between the right and the good. In the absence of such traits, we may doubt that the sense of justice and allegiance to just institutions will be strong enough to sustain respect for justice (cf. Rawls 1993: 142). In this way the communitarian charge that it is sociologically naïve to suppose liberal neutrality will sustain respect for justice echoes the Scandinavian insistence that it is naïve to ignore the formative effects of state punishment as expressing a common sense of shame and aversion to evil. And these traits may be needed to sustain respect for justice and legitimacy even though a shared way of life or politics of the common good are not.

It may be objected that this distinction fails because talk of shame and recognition of evil is a mere correlate of talk of the good. But, while the correlation claim is true, the objection is nevertheless facile. Many ways of life and conceptions of the good overlap in recognizing certain evils. The good that consists in the absence of these widely recognized evils does not define a shared way of life or a distinctive or comprehensive doctrine about the good or the good life. Rather, it provides an important shared presupposition of many such conceptions. Public support for a shared aversion to evil and appropriate sense of shame, fully compatible with reasonable pluralism, may be needed to sustain respect for justice and rights, rather than either a shared sense of justice by itself or a shared conception of the good in the rich sense. We do not need to choose between liberal neutrality and a communitarian politics of the common good; the dichotomy is spurious. A reasonable pluralism may itself require the support of a shared aversion to evil and sense of shame.

Something along these lines may temper a variety of approaches to punishment that in different ways treat the offender too much in isolation from his society and his motivations as too private. We have made great advances in respecting the human rights of individual prisoners, and we should not want to go back on these. But at the same time, we may need to regain sight

206 S. L. Hurley

of the way in which the social context provided by the practice of legal punishment can contribute to making us the persons we are, including the vast majority of us who never venture non-trivially into criminality.

In summary: the practice of punishment may, via long-term formative influences, be among the social conditions of the capacity for practical knowledge, including a shared aversion to basic evils and appropriate sense of shame, which may be needed to sustain respect for justice. There are many ways of distorting this suggestion, and many ways for it to go wrong in practice. But the social consequences of trying to do without the formative role of punishment may be undesirable enough, in the form of widespread violent crime, to warrant focusing attention on how to design penal institutions that harness that formative role to appropriate cognitive standards.

5. CONCLUDING REMARKS

There is scope for cognitivist approaches to other topics in political philosophy, such as the justification of the adversarial legal system and of freedom of speech. Some of the ways in which political cognitivism can internalize liberal concerns have been indicated, though its affinity is with perfectionist rather than neutralist liberalism.

REFERENCES

Andenaes, Johannes (1974), *Punishment and Deterrence* (Ann Arbor: University of Michigan Press).

Bacharach, Michael, and Hurley, Susan (1991) (eds.), *Foundations of Decision Theory: Issues and Advances* (Oxford: Blackwell).

Barry, Brian (1989), *Theories of Justice* (London: Harvester Wheatsheaf).

Churchland, Paul M. (1995), *The Engine of Reason, the Seat of the Soul* (Cambridge, Mass.: MIT Press).

Cohen, G. A. (1989), 'On the Currency of Egalitarian Justice', *Ethics*, 99: 906–44.

——(1992), 'Incentives, Inequality and Community', in Grethe Petersen (ed.), *The Tanner Lectures on Human Values*, vol. 13 (Salt Lake City: University of Utah Press), 263–329.

Condorcet, Marie-Jean-Antoine-Nicholas Caritat, Le Marquis de (1785), 'Essai sur l'application de l'analyse à la probabilité des decisions rendues à la pluralité des voix', in *Sur les elections et autres textes*, ed. Olivier de Bernon (Paris: Fayard, 1986).

Ellsberg, Daniel (1961), 'Risk, Ambiguity, and the Savage Axioms', *Quarterly Journal of Economics*, 643–69.

Feinberg, Joel (1970), 'The Expressive Function of Punishment' in *Doing and Deserving* (Princeton: Princeton University Press), 95–118.

Fiss, Owen M. (1996), *The Irony of Free Speech* (Cambridge, Mass.: Harvard University Press).

Gardenfors, Peter, and Sahlin, Nils-Eric (1982), 'Unreliable Probabilities, Risk Taking, and Decision Making', *Synthese*, 53 (1982), 361–86.

Hampton, Jean (1984), 'The Moral Education Theory of Punishment', *Philosophy and Public Affairs*, 13: 208–38.

Hurley, S. L. (1989), *Natural Reasons* (New York: Oxford University Press).

——(1993), 'Justice Without Constitutive Luck', in A. Phillips Griffiths (ed.), *Ethics, Royal Institute of Philosophy Supplement*, vol. 35 (Cambridge: Cambridge University Press), 179–212.

——(1995), 'Troubles with Responsibility', *Boston Review*, 20/2: 12–13.

——(1999), 'Rationality, Democracy, and Leaky Boundaries', *Journal of Political Philosophy*, 7: 126–46.

Hutchins, Edwin (1995), *Cognition in the Wild* (Cambridge, Mass.: MIT Press).

Kymlicka, Will (1990), *Contemporary Political Philosophy* (Oxford: Clarendon Press).

Lacey, Nicola (1988), *State Punishment* (London: Routledge).

McClennen, Edward F. (1990), *Rationality and Dynamic Choice* (Cambridge: Cambridge University Press).

Mill, John Stuart (1958), *Considerations on Representative Government* (New York: Liberal Arts Press).

Nozick, Robert (1974), *Anarchy, State, and Utopia* (New York: Basic Books).

Nussbaum, Martha C. (1986), *The Fragility of Goodness* (Cambridge: Cambridge University Press).

Raiffa, Howard (1961), 'Risk, Ambiguity, and the Savage Axioms: Comment', *Quarterly Journal of Economics*, 75: 690–4.

Rawls, John (1971), *A Theory of Justice* (Cambridge, Mass.: Harvard University Press).

——(1985), 'Justice as Fairness: Political not Metaphysical', *Philosophy and Public Affairs*, 14: 223–51.

——(1993), *Political Liberalism* (New York: Columbia University Press).

Roemer, John (1985), 'Equality of Talent', *Economics and Philosophy*, 1: 151–87.

——(1986), 'Equality of Resources Implies Equality of Welfare', *Quarterly Journal of Economics*, 101: 751–84.

——(1987), 'Egalitarianism, Responsibility and Information', *Economics and Philosophy*, 3: 215–44.

——(1993), 'A Pragmatic Theory of Responsibility for the Egalitarian Planner', *Philosophy and Public Affairs*, 22: 146–66.

——(1995), 'Equality and Responsibility', *Boston Review*, 20: 3–7.

——(1996) *Theories of Distributive Justice* (Cambridge, Mass.: Harvard University Press).

——(1998) Equality of Opportunity (Cambridge, Mass.: Harvard University Press).

Ross, Alf (1975), *On Guilt, Responsibility and Punishment* (London: Stevens & Sons).

Sandel, Michael J. (1982), *Liberalism and the Limits of Justice* (Cambridge: Cambridge University Press).

Scanlon, T. M. (1982), 'Contractualism, and Utilitarianism', in Amartya Sen and Bernard Williams (eds.), *Utilitarianism and Beyond* (Cambridge: Cambridge University Press), 103–28.

Scanlon, T. M. (1988), 'The Significance of Choice', in S. McMurrin (ed.), *The Tanner Lectures on Human Values* (Salt Lake City: University of Utah Press), 149–216.

Sen, Amartya K. (1970), *Collective Choice and Social Welfare* (San Francisco: Holden-Day).

Strawson, Galen (1986), *Freedom and Belief* (Oxford: Clarendon Press).

Taylor, Charles (1985), *Philosophy and the Human Sciences* (Cambridge: Cambridge University Press).

Waldron, Jeremy (forthcoming), 'Deliberation, Disagreement and Voting', *Working Paper for Shell Center for International Human Rights*.

12

The Central Conflict: Morality and Self-Interest

Joseph Raz

> The most important point to make about the putative dualism of prac-
> tical reason is that deliberation of a sufficiently global scope is not con-
> ducted in terms of 'prudence', 'self-interest' or 'flourishing' on the one side
> and 'morality' on the other. It is conducted in terms of strength of prac-
> tical reasons. . . . values, neither expressly prudential nor expressly moral
> but values . . . are what we appeal to.
>
> (*WB* 161)

Reflection on the nature of morality, the sources of its normativity, and
the motivation people have, or should have, to abide by it, often centres on
the problems posed by the possibility of conflict between morality and self-
interest. It is sometimes said that the central question of morality is: why
is it that we must conform with morality even when doing so involves
significant sacrifice of our own interests?[1] The answer, it is thought, would
explain the normativity of morality. It would explain why it is binding, and
why every person has reason to conform with it. I will follow the same route.
I too will use reflection on the nature of the conflict between morality and

This essay was written during 1996–7. That year earlier versions of it were presented at a
seminar at NYU, at the Scots Philosophical Club, and at a one day conference on well-being at
University College, London. I have learnt much from questions and comments by participants
on these occasions. I am particularly grateful for written comments or long conversations on
the paper to Roger Crisp, Jonathan Dancy, Anthony Duff, Ronald Dworkin, Brad Hooker, and
Tom Nagel.

[1] To simplify I will consider only cases in which the sacrifice morality calls for falls short of
sacrificing one's life, or putting it in grave danger. I will consider only the case of sacrifices of
interests that one has while alive, not the interest, if any, to remain alive. The latter case presents
complications affecting not so much the central conflict as the peculiar nature of one's interest
in remaining alive.

self-interest, but my goal is different. I aim to draw certain lessons about the nature of well-being.[2]

The key to my reflection is in Griffin's statement quoted above, which forms the backbone for all that follows, though my understanding of it and of the issues it raises is not entirely the same as his. I believe that this statement, in the interpretation that I give it, is true only if a common view about the relations between morality and self-interest is mistaken. But my purpose is not to establish that. Rather it is to explore difficulties, apparent or real, in the alternative that I favour, which I will call the classical view, for while not faithful in detail to Plato's or Aristotle's writings it derives from them, and from the philosophical tradition that their writings informed.

I will outline the classical view, contrasting it with some variants of one alternative, a common view about the relations between morality and well-being. I will then turn to the difficulties the classical approach has to face. I will take it for granted (*a*) that morality can call upon one to make sacrifices, and (*b*) that moral requirements can conflict with the well-being of the agent to whom they are addressed. The difficulty is that neither seems possible according to the classical view. All this will take up the first two sections.

The third section will start unravelling the mystery. It explains the character of a central case of self-sacrifice, showing (*a*) that self-sacrifice does not necessarily involve conflict of morality and self-interest, and (*b*) that when making sacrifices we do not necessarily harm our self-interest (or set back our well-being). This will lead to Section 4 and to the central claim of the article— namely, that, while people may reasonably care about their own well-being, a person's well-being is not, for that person, a source of reasons for action. Section 5 will explain how it is that reason may require people to act against their own self-interest, while the final two sections reflect on the character of people's concern for their own well-being.

1. MUST MORALITY CONFLICT WITH SELF-INTEREST?

A common view of the nature of the conflict between morality and the agent's well-being sees the conflict as a natural result of the fact that morality and

[2] To facilitate presentation and avoid monotony I will use 'in one's interest', 'self-interest', and 'well-being' interchangeably. The expressions diverge in meaning. 'Self-interest' is often used to refer to a kind of motive, and I will have nothing to say about the nature of that motive. When talking of a person's interest one commonly refers to the means that facilitate the pursuance of that person's well-being or goals. It is in one's interest to be in good health and to have lots of money. On the other hand, it is odd to say that it is in the interest of a Baroque music lover to listen to a good concert of Baroque music. This would indicate a reason for listening other than his love of the music (e.g. that it will correct some mistaken view he holds, or introduce him to new people). These are just two examples of the many nuances in the language used in this domain. I will ignore all of them and will take well-being in its philosophical sense as my subject.

well-being are two separate, independent (though not entirely unrelated) domains. Each has an internal structure that secures the absence of internal conflicts (at least the absence of serious conflicts), but their independence of each other makes them liable to conflict with each other. Reasons are either prudential or moral (or belonging to some other kind). Prudential reasons have a weight or stringency that is determined by the degree to which they serve the agent's well-being. The stringency of moral reasons is determined from the moral point of view, independently of their contribution to the well-being of the agent. It is not surprising that prudential and moral reasons often conflict. The hard question is what to do when they do, and how to understand the fact that moral reasons have normative force even though they do not serve the agent's well-being.

I have challenged this view elsewhere.[3] But it is necessary to recapitulate in order to launch the discussion and locate some of the views that separate this approach from others. Whenever we act intentionally, we act for a reason or for reasons. That means that we do what we do because, as we see it, the action we perform is more attractive than its alternatives—that is, it appears to possess some characteristic or other that makes it worthwhile, or better than the alternatives. This is where I am in total agreement with Griffin's statement. When we think about what to do, we simply think of the options available and of which of them—if any—is best, and which—if any—is required.

That, understood in a way that is perhaps more radical than Griffin's, has major implications both for morality and for well-being. Regarding morality, it means that moral values and moral requirements may differ in content from other values and requirements, but they do not differ fundamentally in the source of their normativity. I do not mean by this that there is just one explanation, or one master argument, that establishes all values and requirements. Far from it, I believe that many diverse arguments are required, for there are many diverse values and requirements. I mean rather that the diversity affects moral values and requirements as much as non-moral ones, and that there is nothing very special about the moral arguments, which sets them apart from the others. Were moral considerations a class apart, were they derived—as

---

[3] Both issues are discussed in *The Morality of Freedom* (Oxford: Clarendon Press, 1986). More recently I addressed the first in 'On the Moral Point of View', in J. B. Schneewind (ed.), *Reason, Ethics, and Society* (Chicago: Open Court, 1996), 58–83, and 'The Amoralist' in Garrett Cullity and Berys Gaut (eds.), *Practical Reason and Ethics* (Oxford: Clarendon Press, 1997), 369–98. The second is challenged more indirectly. I argued—both in *The Morality of Freedom* and in 'Duties of Well-Being' in my *Ethics in the Public Domain* (rev. edn., Oxford: Clarendon Press, 1995), 3–28—that the reason for promoting one's own well-being is a formal reason, in itself without content, and that desires are not reasons—especially in 'Incommensurability and Agency', in Ruth Chang (ed.), *Incommensurability, Incomparability, and Practical Reason* (Cambridge, Mass.: Harvard University Press, 1997), 110–28. On the second point, see also W. Quinn, *Morality and Action* (Cambridge: Cambridge University Press, 1993), essays 11, 12, 210–55. Griffin shares the first of the assumptions I challenge, and, though his position on the second is more nuanced, our views on it are fairly close.

Kant, for example, thought—from a master argument that determines not only their content, but their character and their stringency, we would not have been able, in practical deliberation, to take our eyes off this fact. It would have determined the outcome of our deliberation. For example, had Griffin, and others, been right in thinking that moral considerations always trump all others, their presence would have put an end to any consideration of any other factor.

I am not making this point as an argument against the special character of morality, or against its special stringency. For one thing, Griffin's statement quoted at the outset can have a sparer meaning, which does not carry this implication. I am simply explaining the sense in which, as I see it, it is true that when we deliberate we consider which reasons are most pressing in a way that transcends and defies the common division of practical thought into moral and self-interested (and other) considerations. The implications of this view for well-being are equally far-reaching. If, when we deliberate, reasons and values feature in our thoughts regardless of their relation to our well-being, then considerations that advance our well-being need not be undertaken with that as our end. How can that be?

Like others I take the notion of a person's well-being as the notion we use in general judgements about how well people's lives went for them—that is, excluding any consideration of their contribution to the well-being of others, or to culture, etc., except in as much as such contributions affected the quality of the life judged from the point of view of the person whose life it was. These are judgements of how good someone's life was, how good it was for the person whose life it was. Clearly this is not the only way in which the concept is used. The following example from an in-flight magazine is probably more typical of its common use: 'You will find Well-being located on Channel 3 . . . This is specifically designed to help you wind down . . . freeing both mind and body of tension and creating a sense of inner calm.' The philosophical use I am following is none the worse for deviating from other ordinary uses. But, as we will see, it is not without problems of its own.

The more successful a person is in his life the better is his life, other things being equal. Other things need not be equal, for there are other factors that affect the quality of a person's life. One's attitude to oneself and to one's life is one of them. The life of people who are consumed by self-doubt, or self-hate, or suffering from very low self-esteem is diminished by these factors. Similarly, success in relationships or enterprises that are demeaning, worthless, or evil does not contribute to one's well-being. But, provided one's success is in something worthwhile, and that one is at peace with oneself and wholehearted about one's life, then well-being depends on the degree to which one is successful in one's relationships and goals.

Both goals and relationships are subject to people's voluntary control in the sense that they maintain and develop or pursue them at will. They can decide to abandon them or let them decline, or decide to let them assume a more or less prominent role in their lives. So people's well-being depends, up to a point, on themselves—on their wisdom and judgement in choosing goals and relationships, and in pursuing them.

As was noted, only the pursuit of worthwhile goals and relationships contributes to a person's well-being (though they may be goals that the person pursues only incidentally to the pursuit of another goal that may be worthless in itself). But are there any other restrictions on the sort of ends that could further a person's well-being? This question brings us to the heart of our subject. If the demands of morality and people's concern for their own well-being are often, perhaps even normally or necessarily, in conflict, then perhaps all possible considerations, all possible goals, etc., divide into at least two distinct classes: one including those pursuit of which advances the agent's well-being and the other consisting of those pursuit of which is morally required, but which by their nature cannot advance the agent's well-being, and sometimes, or often, conflict with the agent's well-being. There may, of course, be other categories. Moreover, the first category may include moral requirements conformity to which (or attempts to conform) necessarily advances the agent's well-being.

Such division of considerations would offer a ready explanation of conflicts between morality and self-interest (or at least of one type of such conflict). They occur when a moral consideration that is essentially unhelpful to one's well-being conflicts with considerations of one's well-being. I think that many believe this to be if not the only then the typical case of conflict between morality and self-interest. However, is there any general theoretical reason to think that such a division exists? One simple thought is that the goods that can be realized in or through action divide into two classes, those that are good for the agents, and those that are good for the recipient(s), for others affected by the action (or at least some of them). I do not wish to endorse the thought that moral considerations include only those that concern the well-being of others. But let us, for the sake of argument, follow the implications of this thought. Everyone would agree, of course, that many acts are good in both ways. They are, when successfully performed, good for those who perform them, and also for others. I have, morally, to look after my ailing mother. I have to visit her, look to her needs, and give her strength and support. But doing all this also cements our relationship, and enhances the quality of my life. Arguably all actions that are intrinsically good or worthwhile, other than some of those whose *sole* intrinsic merit is that they give the agent hedonic pleasure (sun-bathing, eating, etc.), are also at least potentially beneficial to others, either instrumentally (as is the case with many economic activities, such as the work of a bank clerk, a plumber, a nurse, or a production worker), or intrinsically (as with creating or performing works of art or entertainment).

So the question is whether there are classes of action that are morally good, but that by their nature cannot contribute to the well-being of those who perform them. There are beyond doubt some cases that suggest this. For example, possibly one is morally required to kill or harm in some other way very wicked people (for example, brutal dictators set on genocide). Is it plausible to think that one's well-being is served by killing another human being, even such a human being? Are we not inclined to think that we ought to kill while feeling personal discomfort with the act, regret that we have to perform it, and even distress at having to do so? That is indeed so, but it does not support the existence of moral requirements that do not serve the agent's well-being, unless one thinks, erroneously, that only what one takes pleasure in can contribute (non-intrumentally) to one's well-being. Many artists, writers, and others, do not enjoy the process of creation, but the fact that they successfully engage in it contributes to their well-being.[4] Regarding the morally required killing, it is arguable that thus proving oneself in action does, other things being equal, contribute to the goodness of one's life.[5]

Another type of moral requirements that seem to be inherently opposed to one's interest consists of some requirements of toleration, and of respect for the rights of opponents. Some people, pursuing their own interests, propose public measures that are harmful to my interests. I have a moral reason to let them present their case and argue for it within fair democratic procedures even though their doing so is against my interests. Here we need to distinguish two aspects of the situation. We are required to respect the democratic rights of others, regardless of the way their proposals bear on ours. Doing so is, I would claim, other things being equal, a good to the agent. What is against his interest is the use made on some occasions of the rights he protected. I do not have reason to support people's democratic rights because they conflict with my interest, only to support them regardless of whether they conflict with my interest. It is accidental to the moral requirement that it happens on occasion to lead to consequences that put my interest at risk, or that harm it. I will consider such cases below.

---

[4] Whether or not they would have been better off had they enjoyed it is irrelevant to our purpose. Note that their creative activity is part of what makes their life go well for them. It is not (or not merely) a cause of some good.

[5] Moral tragedies are different. A person faces a moral tragedy if all the options open to him, at least all those that are not inferior to some others of those open to him, are morally wrong. Sophie's Choice is a well-known example. In this case, doing what one is required to do cannot advance the agent's well-being. But that is because doing what is morally wrong cannot advance an agent's well-being, not because there are actions that are morally right that cannot advance his well-being. (Some people deny that it is possible for an act that is morally required to be also morally wrong. We need not consider the matter here).

A final example is a requirement, should there be one, to give, let us say, a tenth of my income to charity. Surely, here there can be no doubt that the moral requirement is essentially against my interest. It is a requirement to reduce my resources in favour of others, and reducing my resources is against my interest. Indeed so, unless what I do with my resources is not to reduce them but to use them. I am not acting against my interest when I go to see a film, even though I have to buy a ticket to do so. This is not simply 'reducing' my resources. It is using them. So the description of my tithe example is already loaded. If giving (that sum of) money to charity is an act that benefits me, then the fact that it depletes my resources does not show that it is against my interest. It is just an ordinary case of using my resources.

But how can just signing a cheque, or handing over banknotes, to charity be in my interest? Looking after the poor, teaching, tending the ill, and so on are all activities that can benefit agents. They can give valuable content to their lives and bring satisfaction. But how can a momentary act be good for the agent? I have suggested that the difficulty presented in this case is the difficulty we generally have in understanding how acts, as against activities, can be intrinsically good.[6]

Breaking the world 100 meter sprinting record is an example of such an act. Sprinters may enjoy the running, but they need not. Even if they do not, the act of breaking the record is worthwhile. Its value is, however, in its result: setting a new world record. Those who achieve it cannot complain that they do not enjoy the activity of racing which led to the result as well. Their reward is in the result.[7] The same is true of giving to charity. There need be no intrinsic value in the activity which constitutes the giving. Writing a cheque need not be intrinsically rewarding. The value is in the giving to charity, in doing something which is morally good. That is the reward of the agent, just as setting a new record is the reward of the sprinter.[8] So giving to charity is good for the giver, or at least we have no reason to think otherwise.

Some people may object that by removing the requirement that only what gives pleasure can be good for the agent I removed the subjective element in the notion of well-being. 'And this', they will say, 'is inconsistent with the thought that the notion designates the goodness of the life *from the point of view of the person whose life it is*. If well-being is having a life full of good actions and activities then it is indistinguishable from the morally good life. But we know that people can have a good life even though their lives are not

---

[6] I have in mind here the distinction between acts and activities as drawn by G. H. von Wright in *Norm and Action* (London: Routledge & Kegan Paul, 1963). See also A. J. P. Kenny, *Action, Emotion and Will* (London: Routledge & Kegan Paul, 1963).

[7] Since the result is intrinsic to the act (you cannot break the world record without setting a new one), the intrinsic value of the result makes the act itself intrinsically worthwhile.

[8] 'On the Moral Point of View', 76.

free from moral blemish. Moreover, we know that moral considerations can conflict with a person's self-interest. Hence, well-being must be connected to pleasure. This is its connection to the person's own point of view.'

The objection is based on a misconception. The notion of well-being does indeed have a strong subjective element. It simply need not be through taking pleasure. People's lives go well for them only if, as we saw, they are at peace with themselves, and to the extent that they are whole-heartedly engaged in their relationships and in the pursuit of their goals. Moreover, pleasure is often no more than the satisfaction that is, or is inseparable from, the recognition of one's success in accomplishing what one whole-heartedly wanted to do. In that sense, giving money to charity can give pleasure, and does not contribute to one's well-being unless it does.[9]

Henceforth I will proceed on the assumption that there are no moral considerations pursuit of which cannot serve the agent's own well-being (at least so long as we exclude consideration of the value of one's continued existence, and the possibility that there are moral requirements that necessarily include a requirement to sacrifice one's life). One can profit from, one's well-being can be served by, compliance with, or the attempt to comply with, any moral consideration. There is no conclusive argument to that effect that I know of. But considerations like those recited above, and the absence of successful counter-arguments, give some support to this conclusion. One counter-argument has already been intimated. It informed the objection that I have just dismissed. According to it, there is no way of distinguishing the moral life from the life that is good for the agent. Without this distinction it is impossible for morality to conflict with the agent's well-being. That objection lies at the core of the argument of this article.

2. CAN MORALITY CONFLICT WITH SELF-INTEREST?

The direct implication of the discussion so far is that it is plausible to think that there is no inherent conflict between morality and self-interest. It does not follow that they do not conflict. Whether or not they do may depend on the circumstances, and on the choices people make during their lives. If an earthquake strikes, it may become one's moral duty to abandon everything and dedicate oneself to helping the injured. This may set back one's career, or

---

[9] Recognition of success is not generally a necessary condition of the act, or activity, contributing to one's well-being. In particular, it is not generally the case that one needs to know that one's action had its hoped-for (causal) consequences for the action to contribute to one's well-being. In the example of giving to charity, however, the success involved amounts to no more than realization that the act has been accomplished as intended (that one really did give to charity). One's pleasure in the act is no more than one's whole-hearted commitment to it.

call for other major sacrifices. But if one strikes it lucky one can continue with normal life and never be called upon to make any sacrifice in the name of morality. Perhaps this picture is too optimistic. Perhaps morality is such that in the circumstances of life today all conscientious people have to make sacrifices all the time. I will avoid such issues as they take us into controversial questions about the nature and scope of moral reasons that do not belong to the present topic. The point that matters is that conflict, more or less likely, is contingent, not necessary.

But, as noted above, we are not only in danger of rightly denying that morality and self-interest inherently conflict; we are in danger of denying that morality and self-interest can ever conflict. How can such conflicts arise? If our well-being is determined, other things being equal, by success in our goals, which we can adopt, maintain, or abandon, as well as upgrade or downgrade in importance relative to other goals, and since our well-being can be served by doing what we have moral reason to do, does it not follow that, so long as we choose wisely, we choose in ways that serve both morality and our well-being?

The difficulty results from the combination of the following propositions:

First, our well-being depends on success in pursuing worthwhile options. It does not matter whether they are worthwhile for moral or other reasons.

Secondly, when faced with conflicting considerations, we should conform with those that are more important or more stringent. Doing what we have most reason to do is the rational course of action, and it is also the one that serves our well-being.

Thirdly, when we have most reason to do what moral considerations indicate, that is, when moral considerations outweigh or are more stringent than other considerations, then what we are morally required to do is also what we are rationally required to do, and thus it is what will serve our well-being.[10]

Fourthly, when we have most reason to do what non-moral considerations suggest, even though moral considerations alone indicate a different action, then the moral considerations are overridden, and we are not doing anything morally wrong in not conforming to them.[11] Again, so long as we deliberate and act rationally and succeed in conforming to the best reason, we are serving

---

[10] To simplify presentation I write as if there is only one moral consideration present in each choice situation. It can be understood as the moral reason (or combination of reasons) that outweighs all the conflicting moral considerations that apply to the situation.

[11] I am assuming here what I denied earlier—namely, that moral considerations constitute a class apart—because I am presenting a view that I do not in fact share. The best exploration known to me of the relations between morality and other reasons that assumes that morality is a separate domain is S. Scheffler, *Human Morality* (Oxford: Oxford University Press, 1992). As he explains, there can be other alternative interpretations of the situation described in the fourth proposition. But replacing this proposition with alternative variants will not affect my conclusions.

our well-being, and doing what we are morally required to do at the same time.

There is a second closely related difficulty: the classical conception of well-being makes self-sacrifice impossible. We often feel that moral considerations force us to do what we do not want to do, and that is what is meant by saying that we have to make sacrifices if we are to be moral. But, and this is the difficulty, according to the classical view, *so long as we are whole-heartedly rational,* morality can never be rightly said to impose requirements that force us to do what we do not want to do. What we want we want for reasons, and we choose to do that which we believe is supported by the best reasons. If moral considerations require us to give up something we cherish, we may regret the circumstances that made it so, and we may feel emotional difficulty in adjusting to them, in whole-heartedly endorsing our decision to do the right thing. But, if we overcome them, then in doing the moral thing we do what we want to do and we are making no sacrifices.

To illustrate the difficulty, consider two pairs of cases, one involving a small the other a big decision. I can either use my car to go on a pleasant day trip this weekend or give it to someone—known through friends to be reliable, etc.—who needs it to go to the nearby town to visit his young son who is in hospital seriously ill. Usually in such cases there are questions about the other person's ability to get a car from other sources, or his ability to travel by bus, etc. So assume that it is known that there is no other way he can get to the hospital, and that that is nobody's fault. According to the classical view, it is a straightforward comparison of the strength or stringency of the reasons for and against either option. It does not matter that one of them is a moral reason. If on reflection it turns out to be the strongest reason, then I should lend the car to that person. My action will be a good action and therefore one that makes my life a little better. It is true that I am also denied a pleasant day in the country (we assume, of course, that the best alternative way of spending the day is not as attractive to me). Nevertheless, so the argument above goes, from the point of view of my own well-being it is better to lend the car and stay at home and (for example) listen to music, than to go to the country having refused to lend the car. The fact that the reason for lending the car is better than the reason for using it myself guarantees that my well-being is better served by lending it.

Consider now a big decision: should I become a teacher or a lawyer? I will assume that both will provide a decent level of earning. It is well known, let us further assume, that there is a glut of lawyers but a great need for teachers, and that that is going to remain so for some time to come. This gives me a moral reason to be a teacher rather than a lawyer. Assume that on balance this is what I should do, but that, but for that (moral) reason, the best judgement would have been to become a lawyer. Again, it seems that on the classical view I should become a teacher, and I would not be making any sacrifice by doing so. I would simply be doing what I have reason to do, and my well-being depends on success in what I have reason to do. If so, then considerations of morality and of well-being never conflict. Moral considerations do conflict with non-moral considerations, but they do not conflict with concern for my well-being. That concern is malleable. It is shaped by what I have reason to do, including moral reasons. Well-being cannot conflict with morality, for it embraces it.

So far the difficulties. One weakness of the argument purporting to establish them is obvious. It assumes not only, as I claimed in the previous section, that responding to any moral consideration can contribute to one's well-being (i.e. would contribute in the absence of conflicting considerations), but also that the importance of any moral reason as a moral reason is the same as its importance as a possible contribution to the agent's well-being. Relying on that weakness, we can see how a rebuttal of the argument suggests itself.

Consider a simplified example. I have a moral reason to volunteer as a driver for food convoys in a faraway country afflicted by starvation. According to the assumptions of the classical position, doing so willingly and successfully would contribute to my well-being. Alternatively I could start my university studies. I gained a lucrative grant without which I cannot afford to go to university, but which has to be taken immediately. In other words, if I volunteer as a driver, I will lose my chance of university education for the foreseeable future. What should I do? I should conform with the more stringent reason. Let us assume that the more stringent reason is the moral one. I do not mean that it is more stringent because it is a moral reason. I do not believe that moral reasons always defeat non-moral reasons. It is more stringent because many lives would be saved if I volunteer. The absence of drivers is the bottleneck in the fight against famine in that faraway country. Every week I work there I keep dozens of people alive, and, if they survive a year, the new crops will give them a fair chance to enjoy a life of normal length. For the sake of the argument[12] let us assume that, in the circumstances prevailing, the reason to volunteer easily defeats the very weighty reasons I have to take up the grant and go to university. Does it follow that, according to the classical view, doing what I have, both morally and rationally, to do would serve my well-being better than going to university? Surely it does not. While my volunteer work

---

[12] Various philosophers have argued that, in the circumstances described, the moral reason does not defeat the non-moral one. See, among others, Griffin, *VJ*, and Scheffler, *Human Morality*. I do not wish to take a position on this issue here. I am using this as an example only. So long as it is acknowledged that morality and well-being may conflict, examples that will serve to illustrate the rebuttal can be found.

will contribute to my well-being, it is plausible to assume that it would not do so nearly as much as would a university education. Therefore, so the rebuttal goes, the difficulty suggested above does not arise. The classical view does not lead to the conclusion that morality and the agent's well-being cannot conflict.

How convincing is the rebuttal? There is a doubt about its compatibility with the basic tenets of the classical approach, for it seems to reintroduce the fundamental division between considerations of well-being and of morality, as two distinct classes of normative considerations with their own internal structures, sources, and procedures for ranking the stringency of considerations that may diverge. Only thus, the doubters would say, does it make sense to suppose that one and the same reason would have one weight as a reason of the agent's own well-being and a different weight as a moral consideration.

This doubt is, however, misconceived. The rebuttal does not presuppose the division of so-called prudence and morality. It does not say that the moral consideration has two lives, a life as a 'prudential' consideration, where its weight is determined by its contribution to the well-being of the agent, and a different life, with different weight, as a moral consideration. Rather, the rebuttal assumes, consistently with the classical view, that the consideration is one and its weight or stringency is one. Its weight is determined by its nature, not as being an instance of a class of moral reasons, but as being what it is. And it does not have a different 'prudential' weight. We can say that conforming with it has certain consequences for one's well-being. But that does not imply that we have a separate reason of well-being not to follow it, or not to conform with it.

An analogy may help elucidate the point. Imagine that Mary, a renowned painter, decides to move from Oxford to York. This will impoverish the art community in Oxford, with which Mary has been associated for many years. We can well imagine that both she and Jo, an Oxford art-lover, will be sorry to see this happen. They may agree that Mary's decision is reasonable; perhaps it is even the best decision for her. Yet it results in a loss. Given that Jo knows it is the best, he will not do anything to change Mary's mind. But he, as well as the arts in Oxford, are the losers as a result. The example shows that we are used to carving up the domain of value into smaller domains. We often assess events in terms of their significance to the sub-domains. We recognize that some may care about some sub-domains more than about others. None of this requires attributing independent sources of normativity to the sub-domains. Nor need those who care particularly about a sub-domain think that they should prefer promoting its values over what is best overall.

This explanation is bound to appear very puzzling. It avoids the doubt at the cost of an apparently implausible claim, and quite apart from that it leaves a central question to be answered. The explanation assumes (*a*) that at least normally one's own well-being is not a reason for one's own action. Judgements of well-being, of how good a person's life is or was, are evaluative judgements, but they are not action guiding, at least not for the person whose well-being is in question. It leaves unexplained (*b*) how it can be that, while following all reasons for action contributes to the agent's well-being, the significance of the contribution may be determined by considerations other than the stringency or weight of the reasons. To explain and test this explanation, it is better to consider practical deliberation in cases to which no moral considerations apply.

3. MAKING SACRIFICES AND THE DISRUPTION FACTOR

I will start the process of dissolving the difficulties by considering the case of self-sacrifice. As was implied earlier, while it seems clear that people sometimes do and sometimes have to make sacrifices for moral reasons, I do not believe that we always harm our self-interest, or act against our expectations regarding our self-interest, when we make sacrifices. Once we see that self-sacrifice is not essentially[13] connected to well-being, it will be easier to understand why an agent's well-being is not, normally, a reason for action for that agent.[14]

We need to focus on big decisions. Let us imagine a ballet dancer enjoying a reasonably successful career with a small provincial ballet company, the only one within hundreds of miles. Then dwindling audiences threaten the future of the company. If it is forced to disband, our dancer will have to abandon ballet, to change career and look for something else to do. It does not surprise us that he regards the prospect as a great personal disaster. I think that it would be agreed that it is reasonable for him to try to prevent the collapse: he may urge all the dancers to accept a cut in earnings, and of course accept one himself. He may agree to volunteer some of his time for fund raising in the community, and so on. Let us assume that the company has to close. Our dancer looks for other possibilities and starts a new career as a theatre director with the local theatre company, where he remains until his retirement.

---

[13] This is not a claim about the meaning of the word. It is a normative claim about when it would be right to judge a person to be making a sacrifice. To a degree I accept that some will find claims concerning self-sacrifice, which I reject, convincing, for—as I see it—they have a skewed understanding of values. At the same time, my explanation fails if it does not capture the central elements in the common understanding of self-sacrifice.

[14] I am not claiming that all self-sacrifices can be explained in this way—that is, without invoking the fact that the sacrificing act affects the agent's self-interest adversely. I will briefly comment on other kinds of self-sacrifice below.

He quickly comes to like his new work, enjoying a success comparable to his success in his first career.

It is easy to imagine cases like this in which a person's life loses nothing by a forced change of career, and yet where this person is acting reasonably in trying to stave off the change, being willing to pay a considerable price in the process. Does it mean that people finding themselves in such situations are concerned by something other than their own well-being? There is certainly no suggestion that they are moved by concern for someone else, or for a cause. Their actions are self-regarding. But are they moved by concern for their own well-being? Yes, you may say. At the time they are trying to hang on to the life they have, they are uncertain whether they will be able to find an alternative as good. That is what moves them. And no doubt in the vast majority of cases this is a factor. But it does not fully explain why people try to hang on to the life they have.

One way of bringing out this fact is by imagining an ideal situation: imagine that our dancer knows that a career in the theatre is his for the asking. The director of the theatre company is a friend, all the way back from schooldays, and, remembering how the dancer was directing school plays and knowing of the precarious position of the dance company, he offers him a job as an assistant director, with promotion after a learning period. This no doubt affects the situation, and it affects the type of sacrifice it would be reasonable for the dancer to accept in order to stay with the life he has. But it is still reasonable for him to regard the threat to his dancing career as a disaster for him. He wants to be a dancer not a theatre director. Yes, he knows that if he is forced into the theatre he will come to like it and be reasonably successful. But that is not what he wants and he is willing to try hard to stay with dancing. These admissions of his entail, on the assumption that his feelings and actions are rational,[15] that he is not concerned with his well-being. His concern is to have the life he wants to have, meaning the life he has become committed to.[16]

Here is another example. Jane faces a difficult choice. She has a uniquely challenging and rewarding job, but her employer is moving the business to another place a great distance away. Her partner cannot move. What is she to do? Both she and her partner are attractive people who will find no difficulty in establishing new relationships, should this one end. They know this from past experience, and they are confident, positive sort of people. If they decide

[15] That is, not irrational. I am not implying that he would have been irrational to conclude that it is time to give up and change. We ought to remember that some people change in mid-career just because they feel like a change.

[16] I put the point in this, linguistically somewhat awkward, way in order to underline the fact that what matters is not how he has come to have that career (did he freely choose it?), but what it has come to mean to him.

to break up, the overwhelming odds are that they will have as good a life overall as they would have had had the move not occurred. They may well decide to part. But they may not, or at least not that easily. I suspect that we will have a feeling that something has gone awry if they find it easy to part, on the ground that their well-being is not at stake. This will show that they were not really very committed to each other. If they are, if they love each other deeply, or are very much in love, they will want to continue together, and they will try to find ways to do so, making serious sacrifices to do so, possibly even sacrificing their careers to do so. This is a reasonable, and rational, human response to such situations. But it cannot be explained by their concern for their own well-being.

Familiar as the feelings and conduct I illustrated are, are they really rational? Can they be defended by theoretical considerations? I believe that they can, though 'defending', here as elsewhere, does not mean deriving from first principles. It means explaining the way these feelings fit with other aspects of practical reason, thus showing how they make sense to us. The analysis I suggested for these examples sees them as illustrating the fact that normally our own well-being is not an independent factor in our deliberations.[17] In most cases when people refer to their well-being or their interests, they refer either to their chances of succeeding with worthwhile goals or relationships that they have, or want to have, or to their possession of the means (money, education, etc.) that will enable them to pursue whatever worthwhile goal or relationship they may at some time come to want to pursue. Goals and relationships they have or may want to have are what people have reason to care about, not their well-being as such. That is why it is rational for them to behave in the ways described in the examples.[18]

The classical view, as set out in the previous section, provides a ready explanation of the rationality of this behaviour, and of the correctness of the analysis. We saw that the explanation of how—according to the classical view—agents' well-being can conflict with moral requirements that apply to them depends on the fact that normally agents' well-being is not a factor in their deliberations. The examples above complement the explanation by showing, first, how people may feel torn about following morality on grounds other than the conflict with their well-being; and, secondly, why they feel that

---

[17] Strictly speaking, it illustrates only that well-being is not always an overriding factor. But the phenomenology of such cases does, at least in some of them, point to the absence of any separate weight being given to one's well-being at all.

[18] We mark types, or degrees of sacrifice. Whenever we give up (for what appears a good reason) something that we deeply care about, we are making a sacrifice. Normally this would warrant saying that we are sacrificing the goal or relationship we are giving up (e.g. our career). When we do so with great reluctance, we also sacrifice ourselves or (in slightly different circumstances) our life.

they are making sacrifices to follow morality for reasons that do not depend on the impact of their action on their well-being. Both are explained by the fact that moral requirements may force people to give up goals, careers, and relationships that they care about. Crucial to the explanation is the fact that conflict between moral and non-moral considerations is just like conflict between various non-moral considerations: the demands of one's chosen and happy career may conflict with one's goal of pursuing certain hobbies, or with some of one's relationships, and so on. In such cases we sacrifice careers for family, or the other way round.

Sacrifices for morality's sake are like all sacrifices, like sacrifices where no moral considerations are involved, a matter of giving up something one cares a lot about for the sake of something else one cares about. Both in cases which involve moral considerations, and in those which do not, the fact that one is making a sacrifice does not mean that one's action is setting back one's well-being. It means perhaps that one's life is not going to be as good as it might have been had circumstances been different, had one not been forced by circumstances to make sacrifices, but it does not mean that one's life is less good because of one's decision or action.

Moreover, while it is true that when making a sacrifice one's action may set back one's well-being, that can happen both in cases that involve moral considerations and in those that do not. Acting reasonably, even where no moral considerations are involved, need not serve one's well-being best. Let me develop the dancer's example to illustrate the point. We can imagine that the dancer's efforts to save the dance company are successful. After three or four years of hard struggle the future of the company is made secure. The dancer continues his successful career, but he has paid a price. He is embittered, he lost much of his zest and energy, his *joie de vivre*. Had he recognized defeat, he would have made a relatively painless transition, and would even have taken pride in his ability to change direction. He would have had a better life. Yet his decision to struggle for his life as he had it is not unreasonable.[19]

Let us take stock of the conclusions so far.

My main aim is to defend the classical view against the twin objections that it cannot make sense of (*a*) self-sacrifice, and (*b*) the conflict between morality and self-interest. To reply to the objections, one has to show that the explanation of self-sacrifice and of conflicts between morality and self-interest does not require the assumption that practical reason has (at least) two sources of reasons: morality and the agent's well-being.

---

[19] I am not claiming that no sacrifice would have been too much. There is a point where dedication turns into irrational obstinacy. My claim is only that there are sacrifices it is not irrational of people to make in such situations that in fact diminish their well-being, and where uncertainty about the outcome is not a complete explanation of their actions.

I have argued that the notion of self-sacrifice does not involve essential reference to the agent's well-being. It is simply a special case of conflict of reasons. Reasons conflict when they cannot all be conformed with. Conflict can be said to be the manifestation of scarcity, when this last term is understood broadly and metaphorically. Again to speak metaphorically, the response to scarcity is efficiency. It does not overcome scarcity but it reduces its impact. The efficient solution to a conflict is one in which the loss made inescapable by scarcity is as small as possible, or of as small a significance as possible. The terminology of scarcity, loss, and efficiency is obviously inept for many practical conflicts. I use it to make the point that, while there is something undesirable about every conflict, some regret that it had to happen, there is normally no sacrifice made when one's response to conflicts is reasonable.

Some conflicts do call for sacrifices. A common explanation has it that conflicts between considerations whose normativity derives exclusively from concern for the well-being of the agent do not call for sacrifices. They involve only efficiency in the pursuit of one's well-being. On the other hand, when morality conflicts with the agent's well-being, sacrifices may be called for. I suggested that this view is mistaken on both counts. Sacrifices are involved when the rational response to conflict involves abandoning one of one's cherished goals or relationships. This can happen when the conflict involves no moral considerations (as I tried to show by the examples at the beginning of this section) as well as when one or more of the considerations involved is moral. Either way there is no general reason to think that sacrifice will lead to diminution of the agent's well-being. Disruption, by one's own hand forced by circumstances, of the life one has is the context in which we normally feel forced to make sacrifices. For it is in such contexts that we find it most difficult to adjust to the actions and pursuits that reason imposes on us, when they require us to give up cherished aspects of our life. In this reluctance lies the essence of one central type of self-sacrifice.

The explanation of sacrifice is not yet complete. Before we return to it briefly, we have to address the second objection to the classical view by explaining the possibility of conflict between morality and well-being. For it is true that sacrifices may sometimes make one's life less good than it would have been without them. That possibility is yet to be explained.

4. ACTING AGAINST ONE'S INTEREST

Here is the difficulty. Even allowing that well-being has, for the agent, primarily an evaluative role, since right actions contribute to the well-being of those who undertake them, how is it that they do not contribute to the agents' well-being in proportion to their value? Why does the perspective of well-being deviate from that of right reason?

The answer is very simple, and familiar. One consideration determines the distinct perspective of an agent's well-being. It allows the contribution of options to the agent's own well-being to diverge from the general verdict on their value overall. It is the fact that, in assessing the contribution of actions, or anything else, to the well-being of a person, we take that person's life as a whole as the measure. In assessing the value of actions and activities their ability to fill a span of time in the life of a person with worthwhile content is central. That means that, while the more valuable options should be chosen over those of lesser value, those of lesser value may fill the life of the agent for longer, and thus contribute more to his well-being.

We already saw a simple illustration of the point in my conflict between volunteering to drive famine relief convoys and to go to university next year. While, by hypothesis, the value of my volunteering is greater than the value of going to study (since it will save lives that otherwise would perish), it will occupy me only for a few months. My failure to study in university will affect the rest of my life. That is why doing the right thing is, in the circumstances, against my self-interest. Paradoxically, had the volunteer work been life-long (as in some circumstances it may well be), then volunteering may not have been against my interest. (We need more information to judge this possibility.)

Naturally the short duration of some options, in as much as it reduces their contribution to the well-being of the agent, also reduces their value. But, given that their value does not (at least not entirely) depend on their contribution to the well-being of the agent, that fact cannot restore the coincidence of the perspective of the well-being of the agent with the value of his options over-all.

The dependence of the perspective of the agent's well-being on the temporal dimension explains why we tend to find it natural to think that morally valuable activities, such as tending the sick or teaching the young, do not necessarily detract from the agent's well-being, whereas actions, such as giving to charity, do. Typically, actions have shorter duration than activities, and therefore, other things being equal, contribute less to the agent's well-being. These are, of course, gross generalizations, to which counter-examples are easy to find.

We can now briefly return to complete the analysis of self-sacrifice. It was acknowledged earlier that cases where we are forced to give up the life we have form only one type of self-sacrifice. It is common to regard every case in which a person knowingly acts against his own interest in following what he regards as right reason as a case of self-sacrifice. The analysis of this section and the previous ones explains their nature. It does so without drawing any deep divide between prudential and moral or other reasons. This vindicates the classical view against the objection that it is incapable of explaining self-sacrifice.

Finally, it is important to emphasize that, while cases in which self-interest is at odds with morality provide one context in which reason sometimes requires agents to act in ways detrimental to their self-interest, this is not the only context where this can happen. Part of the reason that some moral considerations can set back one's well-being is that they are categorical. Categorical reasons are those whose weight or stringency is independent of the agent's will. Many of the reasons that apply to us arise out of our goals and relationships, and depend on our will in choosing and wishing to maintain those goals and relationships. That is why David, the composer, has a greater reason to complete a good musical composition this year than I have. Categorical reasons, such as the reason we have not to kill people, have stringency that is unaffected by whether or not they serve our goals.

All categorical requirements have the potential to conflict with well-being. This includes considerations of self-respect, personal integrity, and respect for the shape of meaningful activities and relationships, and others. An example is the requirement to respect what is of value, and this includes the possibility of engaging in valuable activities, including those one does not care for personally (the common example is respect for works of art, for cultural or historical heritage, but I have in mind a wider category, which includes the more abstract respect for the preconditions that make valuable activities possible). On the common use of 'morality', not all these requirements are moral ones. Moreover, I suspect that there is not much common to all categorical requirements. They include requirements of good manners, such as not spitting on the floor (where this is a customary requirement), and common taboos (against adults playing with excrement, etc.). I am not suggesting that conformity with them commonly conflicts with self-interest, though they can conflict. My point is that categorical requirements are a diverse class, and that many of them are not commonly thought of as moral.

To these we should add that even goals and relationships that are voluntarily undertaken or sustained give rise to requirements, which while they apply only to people with those goals or relationships can conflict with those people's well-being. The commitments of loyalty that are the concomitants of friendship can make one liable to anything from inconvenience (having to forgo a pleasant evening to calm down a distressed friend) to torture (having to refuse to betray the friend to the tyrant's police). Other goals potentially have similar consequences. Finally, where circumstances threaten one of our central goals, we may strive to protect it in ways that are not conducive to our well-being, and act reasonably while doing so. This was the burden of the examples in the last section.

5. WELL-BEING AND THE BIFURCATED VIEW OF PRACTICAL REASON

The general account of well-being also supports the analysis of sacrifice and of conflict between morality and well-being. I have argued that both explanations presuppose that normally an agent's well-being is not, for him, a reason for action. In the present section I hope to lend some support to that view by showing that an agent's well-being is not the fountain of that agent's 'self-regarding' reasons for action.

As we saw, one's well-being depends on success in worthwhile and wholeheartedly engaged-in goals and relationships. Other things being equal, so long as one is successful in the pursuit of one's goals and the conduct of one's relationships one's life goes well. That makes judgements of well-being depend on the goals people have. Neither I nor David has ever composed a musical work. This has no bearing on my well-being, since being a composer is not an aim of mine. But it casts a long shadow on David's life, since he resigned his job five years ago to devote himself to musical composition.

Prima facie, and I will start with a simple claim and qualify it later, it follows that, when I deliberate about what goals to have, concern for my well-being cannot guide me. I need to have goals before I can consult my well-being when pursuing them. But in that case pursuing my goals and pursuing my well-being are normally one and the same thing. Cases of disruption, as illustrated above, concentrate on the occasions when the two come apart—when I need to make decisions about abandoning one goal in favour of another. In such cases concern for our well-being cannot help.

I am not saying that there are no reasons to guide us in the choice of goals and relationships whose success will make our life go well for us. First, we are guided by the relative value of the goals that we can choose. Secondly, we are also guided in our choice of goals by the chances that we will be successful in them. Some may argue that these two points show that we are guided by the pursuit of our well-being after all. How can we assess the relative value of two goals save by their contribution to our own well-being? Why should one's success in the pursuit of one's goals and relationships matter except that it matters to one's well-being?

But neither objection is justified. Starting with the second point: there is an obvious reason for preferring an option one is more likely to succeed in than one where the prospect of success is less, a reason independent of any impact of success or failure on one's well-being. The reason is the very same reason we have for pursuing the option at all—namely, that it is good in one way or another. If I have reason to go to the cinema to see a Tarantino film, I have no reason to go to the cinema if I will arrive too late for the film. Failure means failure to realize the reason for the action. So a reason for an option is a reason for the successful pursuit of the option, and not for a failed attempt to pursue it. Consider playing tennis. If my reason for playing John is the value of beating him at tennis, then, other things being equal, I have no reason to play if I am certain that I will lose.[20] If, on the other hand, my reason for playing John is to have a stimulating vigorous afternoon playing good tennis, then I should play even if I lose, but not if, because of an injury, the match will not be good tennis, nor invigorating, and so on. Reasons for action are reasons for successful actions, and they determine what constitutes success.

Turning now to the first point above: far from being able to assess the relative value of options for an agent by their possible contribution to his well-being, we cannot judge their contribution to his well-being except by reference to their value (i.e. their value independently of such contribution), for the more valuable they are the more their successful pursuit contributes to his well-being. If they do not have a value independent of their value to us, how can they be valuable to us? Because we choose them? Can anything we choose be good for us just because we choose it? And how can we choose it except because we believe it to be valuable? I have discussed these matters elsewhere and will not repeat the arguments here. Their conclusion is that we can choose only what we believe to be of value, and that that value is independent of our choice. The contribution of options to our well-being is determined by their value, and by our success in pursuing them.[21]

Therefore, normally considerations of well-being cannot help with choice of goals. Nor can they determine when is the right time to abandon one goal and look for, or adopt, another. The fact that we know that our well-being will not be harmed if we abandon our goal is neither here nor there. We persist with one goal, or abandon another, or take up a new one, because these are attractive to us, and not because of concern for our well-being. That was the main lesson from the examples.

These conclusions are reinforced by the fact that there are independent reasons for allowing that some of the more important reasons people have need have no impact on their well-being. Judgements of well-being are

---

[20] Other things are often not equal. I may have independent reasons to play him even if I lose—e.g. it may improve my game.

[21] These comments about the value of options and of success in them will be qualified when we come to examine the possibility of adopting a goal of pursuing one's well-being. Griffin's analysis (in *WB*) is in general consonant with these points.

judgements of how well a person's life goes. Not everything that happens to a person, or that he does, affects the course of his life. To do so it must be significant for the life as a whole, or for non-negligible parts of it. If I break off from writing and have a cup of coffee, my well-being will not be affected at all. I have suggested elsewhere that only what affects our comprehensive goals and relationships—that is, those within which much of our short-term goals nest—affects our well-being.[22] Some resist this view, saying that the coffee matters a tiny little bit, and we do not notice this because it matters so little. But that misses the point. I may have a strong reason for having coffee now. I may need a break and some hot liquid inside me quite badly. Nevertheless, so long as my having or not having the coffee has no long-term consequences, my having the coffee does not affect my well-being at all.

The point may be clearer if we turn from coffee to pain and physical suffering. We have a very strong reason to avoid pain, but most episodes of pain, even very severe pain, horrible though they are, do not affect our well-being. It is difficult vividly to remember pain, and, while persistent pain is paralysing and affects well-being by reducing a person's ability to function, and while even momentary pain can traumatize a person and thus affect his or her well-being, most pain episodes pass without trace, without affecting a person's well-being. The same is true of hedonic pleasure (that is the pleasures of the senses). We have strong reasons to pursue intense pleasures, but, unless they fit in with our life's goals and ambitions (as they do with Don Juan, and others), they do not affect our well-being.

I have argued in the present section that well-being cannot be the fountain of all our 'self-regarding' reasons. First, what serves our well-being depends on our goals and relationships, and they cannot, normally, be chosen for the sake of promoting our well-being. Secondly, we may have reasons for 'self-regarding' actions that have no bearing on our well-being. It follows that the pursuit of well-being can at best be one goal of several one may have. That possibility has now to be examined.

6. ONE'S WELL-BEING AS AN OPTIONAL GOAL

Several points are fairly straightforward:

1. Subject to the following point, we advance our well-being by succeeding in the worthwhile goals and relationships that we care about, whether or not we aim to serve our well-being by pursuing them.

---

[22] I am relying here on my analysis of well-being in 'Duties of Well-Being', 1.

2. Some, including some of the most important, goals and relationships cannot be successfully pursued with the aim of improving one's well-being. Loving relationships are motivated by mutual love, and one cannot love another because doing so improves one's life. There are other goals and relationships that have to be undertaken for certain motives, that are other-regarding, rather than self-concerned.

3. As was pointed out above, since largely we promote our well-being by succeeding in worthwhile goals and relationships, there is normally no difference between saying 'I want to have a good life' and 'I want to succeed in the goals and relationships that I care about'. But the second statement is close to analytical: if it is my goal, then I want to succeed in it—that is what it means for it to be my goal. The same is true of voluntary relationships, and of all the relationships that are important to us in the sense that we really care about them. Caring about them means, among other things, that we want them to succeed, and that we want to succeed in conducting them. Of course we may have conflicting desires. Some people are unable to want anything badly without being ambiguous about it, and so on and so forth. Still, in most contexts what we want when we want our own good is to succeed with our worthwhile goals and relationships.

Is it not the case, though, that there is more to caring about how good one's life is than that? Is it not the case that we want to succeed in worthwhile goals and relationships because we care how well our life goes, because we want to have a good life? What we basically care about is our life. This dependence of the way goals matter to us on the fact that our life matters to us would suggest that concern for our well-being is rational, and is the foundation of our concern for anything else, including (if the classical view is right) morality.

I believe this view to be mistaken. To make progress here we need to distinguish various 'thick' uses of the expression 'being concerned with how good one's own life is' from its minimal meaning. People may or may not be inclined to engage in reflection about their life and its direction. People who are concerned with the quality of their life in this sense have, if you like, super-projects (i.e. their goals are to pursue other goals simultaneously or in succession). They are not merely dedicated teachers, parents, friends, and so on. They are also pursuing the super-goal of dividing their lives equally between work and pleasure, friends and vocation, or some other super-goal. They may decide to be stockbrokers until they are 30 and duck-farmers later. And so on. Possibly in our culture most people have some super-goals of this kind, mostly of an inchoate and open-ended kind (I want my life to be useful to others, to be honourable, and so on).

Super-goals differ from ordinary goals in degree only. They are marked by having components that are commonly and rationally taken as independent goals. The partial goals involved with ordinary goals are not commonly taken as goals in themselves. Some want to be duck-farmers, others want to be stockbrokers. If you want to be both you have a super-goal. But training every day for the London Marathon and running the Marathon are two components of the goal of winning the London Marathon.

Super-goals do not change the analysis: when deliberating about their life, people are still concerned with their goals and relationships, including super-goals. The existence of super-goals does not remove the need to choose[23] goals, or to decide between goals one has, in ways that are not totally dictated by the super-goals. In part this is a result of the fact that super-goals are themselves subject to rational assessment, and to the vagaries of emotional attachment. For example, a person dedicated to a life of achievement may lose the taste for it and come to prefer a quiet life. They are also as liable to conflict as are ground-level goals. For most people it is also the result of the fact that their super-goals are, as was mentioned above, inchoate and do not provide complete guidance about their ground-level goals.

People sometimes think of their concern for their success with their super-goals as concern with their own well-being. While the two often coincide, and it is therefore tempting not to distinguish between them, they are not the same. Anyone who has super-goals is concerned with their success, but not everyone who has them need be concerned with his own well-being. As the examples of Jane and the dancer show, the two may come apart.

Interestingly, one of the super-goals people may have is the pursuit of their own well-being. How is this possible? Does it not follow from my previous arguments that promoting one's well-being within reason is a by-product of pursuing one's goals and super-goals, and that giving one's well-being any additional weight would be irrational? Not quite.

There is reason to pursue anything of value. People may make it their goal to see that the musical life of Oxford flourishes. It is good that it does, and while, other things being equal, there is nothing wrong in not taking this good to one's heart, it is perfectly reasonable to care about this and make the prosperity of musical life in Oxford one of one's goals. Can one do the same with one's own well-being? But is it not redundant to do so? One's well-being consists in the successful pursuit of one's valuable goals—that is, we already pursue them as goals and there is no more one can do. There is no doubt that many who are concerned with their own well-being give it an unreasonable

---

[23] For the sake of brevity I use 'choosing goals' in a way that may mislead. I do not mean to say that goals we have are always chosen after deliberation. We usually drift into them. The point is that keeping with them depends on holding them to be worthwhile, and, in many cases, on their continued emotional and imaginative appeal.

role in their deliberations. But there are (at least) three or four ways in which making the promotion of one's well-being one of one's goals can affect one's attitude and deliberations without committing one to acting against reason.

First, one will then be concerned that one should have worthwhile goals at all times of one's life and that one should have the means of satisfying them.[24]

Secondly, while one's efforts in pursuit of one's goals need not be motivated by concern for one's well-being, they can be (except—as mentioned above—where this would be self-defeating). Those who make their own well-being one of their goals do tend to think of many of their decisions in this way. It may not make a difference to what they decide nor to what they do, but it makes a big difference to how and why they decide and behave the way they do.

The third way in which having one's well-being among one's goals may affect one's conduct is, from the point of view of my general analysis, an oddity. To the extent that success in one's pursuits depends on one's effort and skills, one will come to give success a greater weight in one's decisions than one would otherwise do. We saw before that having a goal imports the desire to succeed in it, and that the value of one's activities depends on the value both of one's pursuits and of one's success in them. If all the goods involved were impersonal (number of people a doctor heals, etc.), these factors would not be affected by one's concern for one's well-being. But some of them are personal. They involve judgement, effort, dexterity, skill, etc. The overall value of one combination of value of activity plus success in it compared with another (for example, being a good corporate lawyer—i.e. high success in a not very valuable activity—as against a quite but not as good career as a teacher—less success in a more valuable activity) is often undetermined by reason and is a matter of personal preference. I believe that in general we can expect those very much concerned with their well-being to prefer pursuits where they are reasonably confident of success and where that success depends on their efforts and skills over other pursuits. I described this as an oddity for I am aware of this as an empirical generalization, but am unable to provide a rationally compelling explanation of this phenomenon.

Finally, a fourth way in which the goal of pursuing one's well-being can affect one is a consequence of the fact that concern for one's well-being ranges over one's past as well as over one's future. While we cannot change the past, that does not mean that we are indifferent to how well we did in it. Moreover, it is not the case that our concern about the past cannot be action guiding. Some people have the super-goal of shaping their future to suit their past, to

---

[24] In part this concern overlaps the concern for self that will be discussed in the last section. But it goes beyond it.

continue its path, complement it, make up for it, and so on, in order to make their life better as a whole. They may, for example, wish to compensate for past errors or failures by having another go at the same objectives, hoping that future success will redeem past failures.

It is, therefore, possible to have as one of one's goals the advancement of one's well-being. This leaves intact the following conclusions I argued for above:

1. Such a goal is optional. There is nothing wrong in not having it, nor any defect or deficiency in the character of those who do not embrace it.

   This point is most clearly illustrated by the attitude to one's past which pursuit of one's well-being brings. As we know, past commitments, formal or informal, may shape our future. They generate reasons for action through which one's past controls one's future. They may be grounded on nothing more than integrity, the need not to betray oneself and one's past. But these are the exceptions. For the most part there is nothing wrong in turning our back on our past or just not paying much attention to it when charting our future. As we saw, some people are different. But apart from the fact that not all such goals are sensible, none of them is required. There is nothing wrong with a life which does not include such goals. For goals these are. Hence pursuit of one's well-being is only an optional goal.

2. It is not necessary to have that goal in order to have a good life. Those who do not have it are as likely to have a good life as those who do.

3. Certain important human goods such as love and friendship cannot be pursued with the aim of improving one's well-being.

4. One cannot have only the goal of having a good life. One succeeds in it only by succeeding in other goals. But the goal of having a good life does not provide rational guidance in the choice of one's other goals.

5. These are just one aspect of the fact that pursuit of one's own well-being of does not serve the pivotal role that it is assigned both in some philosophical writing and in popular thought.

The pursuit of one's well-being, at least when given prominence in one's life, is not a very attractive goal to have. In general one's well-being should be an unintended (though obviously not unwelcome) result of the way one leads one's life, rather than one's goal or reason for being concerned with whatever one is. This is true not only regarding those activities and relationships whose success depends on being undertaken for a specific motive (see point 2 above). The point is often made regarding activities for a cause: it is unseemly to volunteer to help rescue seals threatened by an oil spill because concern for the quality of one's own life makes one realize that some more time spent working for green causes will improve it. The same is true of most activities, including those one does for 'self-regarding' reasons. Mountaineers climb mountains for the thrill of the climb, for the skill displayed, the challenge overcome, the camaraderie, and for other reasons, but it somehow shows the wrong spirit to do it for the sake of one's well-being. One likes spending time with a friend because she is funny and entertaining to be with, not because laughing or being entertained improves the quality of one's life.

This argument about the unattractive aspect of pursuing goals in order to advance one's well-being in the narrow sense does not extend to showing that the pursuit of the super-goals that are often referred to as the pursuit of one's well-being in the broad sense are also tainted. There is nothing wrong in having super-goals. Wishing to be a stockbroker in the morning, a duck-farmer in the afternoon, and a poet in the evening is no different from wishing to break both the 800 metre and the 1500 metre world records and to win Olympic gold medals in both events four times running. Super-goals are not to everyone's taste, but in principle we judge them in the same way we judge other goals. This means, of course, that generally even when pursuing super-goals one should do so for the sake of the goal and not for the sake of one's well-being. The taint of narcissism does not attach to super-goals as such, but is may attach to them if pursued out of concern for one's well-being.

Nor does it attach to all aspects of the pursuit of one's well-being. In particular, while there is nothing wrong with the carefree attitude of a person who does not bother to provide himself with the wherewithal to pursue goals that he may have in the future, there is equally nothing wrong with someone who does.

7. CARING ABOUT ONE'S WELL-BEING

Those who adopt the goal of pursuing their own well-being can adopt it in part only, and they can give it more or less importance in their lives. At a minimum it is not a goal at all, merely a focus of evaluative concern. In some ways this is the most attractive stance to take towards one's well-being (though this is a matter of individual preference).

It is only when we consider concern for one's well-being as an evaluative attitude that we conceive its full scope. We care, if we do at all, about the well-being of our life as a whole, past, present, and future. As already commented, those who adopt the pursuit of their well-being as a goal very often do not go as far as setting themselves the goal of bending the future to complement or compensate for their past. In the minimal sense saying that people are concerned not merely with their goals but with how good their life is means that they are not indifferent to evaluative assessments of their life as a whole. They are sad or disappointed if their life turned out to be riddled with conflict between them and members of their family, happy if it was basking in the warmth of good friendships, and so on. This in itself does not show that concern for our well-being is the foundation for all other concerns. It may be just one concern among others. Moreover, while it is reasonable for people to care about how well their life goes, this may be merely an evaluative attitude. Parents are familiar with situations in which, while they are anxious that their children will do well on their own, any attempt by them to help their children to do well on their own will be self-defeating.

The point is a delicate one for two reasons. First, since success in worthwhile activities contributes to one's well-being, people who know that know that what they do for pleasure, or for a thrill, will, other things being equal, be good for their life. The point I am making here is merely that that is not normally the motivating thought, nor should it be. Secondly, I am not claiming that it is always wrong, let alone self-defeating, to be motivated by concern for one's well-being (in the minimal sense). Merely that, especially if this is the general attitude one has towards all one's activities and relationships, it shows a defect in one's personality, a form of narcissism that impairs one's ability to be fully engaged with anything other than oneself. For our purpose, the lesson is that concern for one's well-being (in the minimal sense) is indeed primarily evaluative and not action-guiding. Many reasonable people want their life to go well as a result of their success with goals and relationships undertaken for other reasons. A life that is not outward looking, that is entirely inward looking, being ultimately concerned only with itself, is diminished by this fact.

All these explanations make sense, yet something is still missing. For one thing, in saying that 'many reasonable people want their life to go well', I have grossly understated the case. People care a lot whether their lives go well or not. But all I can claim, consistently with the general position I am advocating, is that concern for one's own well-being is just one normative concern one may have, on a par with concern for how well opera as a form of art is doing today. It is no good, the objector will claim, to assign to biology the explanation of why people's concern for their own well-being is nearly universal whereas caring about the state of the opera is a minority taste. In fact, the objection proceeds, concern for one's well-being is part of what makes persons persons.

There is some truth in the objection. Evaluative concern for one's well-being, I will claim, is neither as central as the traditional philosophical understanding of prudence makes it, nor as accidental as a concern about the state of the opera.

There is a concern that is essential to being a person, but it is not a concern for one's well-being. It is a concern for one's self. Agents who are persons are aware of themselves as conscious beings, with a capacity for rational action, and with a body, a character, and a life. A certain (at least minimal) concern for one's functioning as a person is part of being a person. Persons care about their ability to act and lead their life while they are alive. That means, though they need not think of it in these terms, caring about their ability to control and guide their lives in the light of reason. They also care about their success in their actions, for, as we saw, aiming to succeed is part and parcel of being motivated to act. What else is included in the concern of a person for himself that is an essential aspect of being a person? Exploring this question cannot be undertaken here. But two points need to be made.

First, while concern for oneself is essential, its expression is not constant and it varies with ethical or religious beliefs, and with one's general culturally influenced view of what is of value in the world. For some, for example, concern for themselves involves primarily concern that their soul escape eternal damnation. For others, it may lie in perfecting their character as a virtuous character. Concern for one's well-being is just one possible, and culturally conditioned, manifestation of people's concern for themselves. One way in which the fundamental concern for oneself differs from concern for one's well-being is in being manifested in a variety of different ways, not necessarily including caring about well-being, in different people.

Secondly, there is another way in which the fundamental concern for oneself differs from caring about one's well-being. The fundamental concern is not exhausted by caring about one's well-being even in people who do so care. One's concern about one's ability to function as a person, for example, is not exhausted in caring about one's well-being. It is deeper. It may even conflict with one's well-being, in that preserving one's ability to act as a person while one is alive may require action that is detrimental to one's well-being overall.

If so, does concern for the well-being of others encompass all that is morally relevant in one's relations with them? If, as seems likely, it does not, how does it relate to other concerns? In so far as one has reason to be concerned with the well-being of others, how does that concern manifest itself? And, most directly relevant to the theme of this paper, where people's concern with their own goals and relationships is at variance with what is best for their own well-being, does moral concern for others require helping people with their goals and relationships, or is it fashioned by what is needed for their well-being? Scrutiny of these questions is necessary to complete the account of the meaning and normative role of well-being.

As for the question, 'How is it that people sometimes act for moral reasons in ways detrimental to their well-being?', the answer turns out to be simple.

People act for reasons—that is, for what appear to them to be adequate reasons—regardless of whether or not they serve their well-being. Sometimes the reasons that appear to be conclusive, even when conforming with them affects the agent adversely, are moral reasons.

13

Quality of Well-Being: Quality of Being

John Skorupski

It is an old idea that there is quality as well as quantity of well-being—that a distinction (perhaps a number of distinctions) can and should be drawn between higher and lower human goods. The implications of the idea differ according to the wider ethical framework in which one places it. But, since virtually everyone thinks that a notion of individual well-being plays one or another major role in our ethical thought, the questions at stake—whether it makes sense to distinguish between higher and lower goods, and what it might mean to do so—are of wide interest. In this chapter I want first to examine the idea as such (Sections 1–3) and then to consider its place within a moral philosophy that takes the ethical standard to be the well-being of all, impartially assessed (Section 4). We shall find a number of themes from James Griffin's work guiding us on our way.

1. THE MEASURE OF WELL-BEING

In fact a good starting point is a thought-experiment of a kind to which Griffin alludes in his discussion of incommensurability in *Well-Being*.[1] Suppose I am diagnosed as having an illness whose slow development will be imperceptible over many years. At some time in the future, however, it will reach a crisis point that involves no physical discomfort but is almost immediately fatal. There is a cure for this illness—say an operation or a drug—but it has a serious consequence. It will reduce my mental powers and general energy permanently. I will come to have, as the consultant puts it, 'something

I am grateful to the editors and to John Broome and Jonathan Riley for very helpful comments and criticisms.

[1] *WB*, ch. 5, 'Are There Incommensurable Values?'.

like the mental age of a very small child', and I will also be limited in the amount of physical exercise I can take without exhaustion. After the cure, he explains, I may retain a more or less glazed memory—a remembering as through frosted glass—of the greater powers I currently enjoy, and of their exercise, but I will thenceforth only have a limited range of enjoyments, interests, affections. Physical warmth and comfort, food, melody, colour, stories, straightforward human affections, and communication will now be everything to me. I will no longer have the developed forms of recollection and anticipation, reflectiveness and insight, physical powers and active accomplishments that I now have and will continue to have if I do not take the cure.

On the other hand, medical science has progressed to a point at which my life after the cure can be maintained indefinitely. Moreover, I have the resources to maintain it at a level that gives me a constant positive flow of well-being for as long as I like. I will not be a burden on others. By setting up contracts with an insurance company and a firm of solicitors that will act as my legal guardians, I can so invest my assets as to produce a cash flow that will cover the costs of care for as many years as I want. The only catch is that, if I decide to have the cure, I must have it straightaway. I cannot delay.

So I have a choice. I can choose not to have the operation. Or I can choose to have it, in which case I will be able to live an enjoyable life for as long as I like. Is it unreasonable to refuse the cure?

One might argue that it is, in this way. If I do not have the cure, I will lead a life that achieves a certain overall amount of well-being. It is, however, a finite amount—it could have been greater if I had lived a little longer, had another packet of popcorn, and so on. By hypothesis, if I have the cure, I will be able to live as long as I like, receiving a constant flow of well-being. So it seems that I will be able to live long enough to exceed the amount of well-being I achieve in the life without the cure. And it is surely unreasonable to prefer the lesser amount of well-being in one's life over the greater.

However, many feel that it is not unreasonable to refuse the cure; I am one of them. (If it is unreasonable not to have the cure, is it reasonable to have the operation or take the drug anyway, even if one is not ill?) This view could be defended in a number of ways, of which the following are three (a fourth, the 'perfectionist' response, will be discussed in Section 2).

(1) It may be said that it is reasonable at any given time to discount future benefits in proportion to their futurity—that is, their distance into the future from that time. That being so, the present value of a flow of well-being at a given level may always sum, however long the flow goes on for, to less than

the present value of the finite amount of well-being achieved in my life without the cure. So the principle that it is unreasonable to prefer the lesser amount of well-being in one's life over the greater will not show that I should have the cure, since the assessment of amount must be applied to the present value of the alternatives before me.

(2) It may be said that the person who survives the cure is not really me. So at any rate the *prudential* principle that it is unreasonable to prefer the lesser amount of well-being in one's life over the greater cannot be applied to show that I should have the cure.

(3) It may be said that the notion of amount of well-being is being used equivocally.

I will not consider the first response, which appeals to the rationality of pure time preference. To my mind pure time preference can seem rational only on certain desire-satisfaction models of well-being that are themselves indefensible.[2] The second response raises issues that we shall have to come back to. However the response that will mainly concern us is the third.

Let us distinguish between *measure* and *quantity*. The measure of well-being for a being over a period of time in a possible situation will be a code that represents where the well-being in that possible period stands in an ordering; whether it is greater than, less than, or equal to well-being in another possible period. Whenever it is meaningful to consider whether the well-being of some being in a possible stretch of life is to be preferred, dispreferred, or regarded as indifferent to its well-being in another possible stretch (assuming no considerations other than its well-being to be at stake), it is also meaningful to attach codes to the two stretches of its life representing the comparative measure of well-being in them.[3] With 'measure' thus understood, the principle that it is unreasonable to choose for oneself a lesser measure of well-being is unchallengeable.

But the argument above does not show that I can achieve a greater measure of well-being by having the cure. The measure of well-being need not be

---

[2] Pure time preference affirms the rationality of discounting future benefits by their very futurity, rather than by the greater riskiness that may be associated with their futurity. Perhaps it is programmed into us by evolution, since it is a simpler survival programme than explicit discounting for risk. But *that* explanation of pure time preference undermines its rationality, since we can and do explicitly discount for risk. See Nozick (1997: §IV).

Our thought-experiment assumes that no greater risk attaches to life after the cure than to life without it. (It may indeed be less.) One may, of course, question whether such a thought-experiment is not affected by worries about the risk involved in placing oneself in other people's hands, however reputable the insurance company and the firm of solicitors. But I believe that we can reasonably put this issue to one side.

[3] The codes may be real numbers, but that does not mean that the ordering is representable by a real-valued utility function, for we are allowing the possibility that it contains lexically discontinuous preferences.

additive; it may be incorrect for that reason to assume that the measure of well-being in a period can be represented as the sum of measures of well-being in its sub-periods.[4] And there is one particular possibility here that we must consider further: that the well-being achieved in my uncured life may be *discontinuously* greater than that achievable in any life in which I have had the cure. Discontinuity of this kind, lexical superiority in an ordering, is one of the forms of so-called incommensurability that Griffin (*WB* 85–9) distinguishes in his consummate clarification of that subject, which I referred to earlier. In discussing it Griffin notes as plausible that

> fifty years of life at a very high level of well-being—say, the level which makes possible satisfying personal relations, some understanding of what makes life worth while, appreciation of great beauty, the chance to accomplish something with one's life— outranks any number of years at the level just barely worth living—say, the level at which none of the former values are possible and one is left with just enough surplus of simple pleasure over pain to go on with it.   (*WB* 86)

He describes this as a situation in which 'enough of *A* [those higher contributors to well-being] outranks any amount of *B* [a surplus of "simple pleasure"]' (*WB* 86). There are two problems with this description.

In the first place this thought-experiment, like the thought-experiment with which we started, does not show that *any* life containing this amount of the various higher contributors to well-being outranks any life containing only 'simple pleasure'. We are told that the fifty-year life includes satisfying personal relations, some understanding of what makes life worth while, appreciation of great beauty, and the chance to accomplish something with one's life—but not how much surplus of simple pleasure it contains. Suppose the surplus is reduced and starts to go negative. Is it obvious that the resulting lives, however richly endowed with those contributors to well-being (*A*), continue to outrank any number of years of simple pleasure (*B*) alone—even as they come to have very small and then negative amounts of *B*: perhaps many years of pain following on the fifty years of very high well-being?[5] It is surely far from obvious.

On the other hand, so long as there is *enough* simple pleasure in one's life

---

[4] It may be incorrect anyway: is not obvious that summing the well-being of sub-periods of a life, even if that were possible and even within a single life, would be the right way to assess the measure of well-being in that life—for example, if the well-being in its sub-periods varied immensely (see Skorupski 1992). However, the distributive issues this raises do not, I think, affect the example we are considering, since we are assuming that life after the cure will produce a *constant* flow of well-being.

[5] I may be reading Griffin unfairly here. He characterizes discontinuity on the previous page in this way: 'so long as we have enough of *B* any amount of *A* outranks any further amount of *B*; or . . . enough of *A* outranks any amount of *B*' (*WB* 85). Perhaps the phrase 'so long as we have enough of *B*' should be read as having the second disjunct in its scope as well as the first.

and not too much pain, it is still possible that a sufficient amount of the higher contributors to well-being (*A*) produces a combination good enough to outrank *any* further surpluses of simple pleasure (*B*) if those surpluses are combined with big-enough reductions of *A*. But now the second point is that it does not immediately follow that there is a discontinuity. Another possibility to be considered is that, as simple pleasure increases, its marginal value, measured by the rate at which it is rational to substitute it against the higher contributors of well-being, decreases. If that is a real possibility, then Griffin's thought-experiment does not establish a discontinuous preference for higher well-being.

However he also describes the case as one in which 'we have a positive value that, no matter how often a certain amount is added to itself, cannot become greater than another positive value . . .' (*WB* 85). In talking here about adding a certain amount to itself, he must be referring to an amount of *well-being*. And it is for this additive metric of well-being that I want to reserve the term 'quantity'. Consider the amount of 'simple pleasure' I get from eating a particular bar of chocolate, and suppose you find by asking me that I get an equal amount of pleasure from eating a similar bar of chocolate the following day. If that is so, we should also conclude that the quantity added to my *well-being* by the pleasure of eating the two bars is exactly twice that contributed by the pleasure of eating one bar. Even if such pleasure is only one constituent of well-being why should equal amounts of *it*, as against equal amounts of that which gives it, have diminishing marginal utility? We can see why successive units of chocolate consumption may produce diminishing quantitites of pleasure. In contrast, the suggestion that I get twice as much pleasure, but not twice as much well-being, from eating the two bars would take some explaining. Thus, in this particular case we can legitimately shift to talking about the quantity of well-being contributed by consumption of a bar of chocolate and compare it with that contributed by the consumption of two or three. In this local case you *can* 'tot up' well-being, in Griffin's phrase.[6] Nor does the point apply only to uncomplicated pleasures like eating bars of chocolate. Suppose you are a person to whom great painting matters deeply. If the satisfaction you get from spending an hour looking at Michelangelo's work in the Sistine Chapel is equal to that which you get from an hour looking at Tintoretto's in the Scuola di San Rocco, then going to both Rome and Venice and seeing both makes (other things being equal) twice as great a contribution to your well-being as seeing just one of them. And saying that it makes twice as great a contribution to your well-being has an implication. It means that you should be willing to make twice as great a sacrifice of well-being to seeing both. The rate at which you substitute quantities of well-being from other sources to achieve

---

[6] Thus I agree with Griffin that additive talk about a person's well-being can make sense independently of assessments of that person's subjective probabilities (*WB* 98–102).

constant increases of well-being from this source should not fall. In general, to say that the quantity of well-being generated by some particular activity or state *A* increases at a constant rate is to say that its contribution to well-being does not diminish at the margin, as measured by the rate at which it is rational to substitute it against quantities of well-being derived from some other activity or state *B*.

In describing the thought-experiment with which we started I said that life after the cure would afford a constant positive flow of well-being for as long as one likes. What this means, then, is that the *quantity of well-being* accrues at a constant rate day by day. It is perfectly imaginable that it should do so—in my post-cure state I will experience each day as neither more nor less satisfying than the last; nor will anything other than my experienced satisfaction any longer make a difference to my well-being. And now we are indeed forced to say that our preference for life without the cure implies that we hold a life without the cure to be discontinuously or lexically superior to any life after it. We cannot equal the measure of well-being in life without the cure by adding constant quantities of well-being to life after the cure.

So the measure of well-being is a function of the quantity of well-being derived from various sources and of some other feature of those sources—perhaps the 'quality' of well-being derived from them? That fits, at least roughly, the picture that John Stuart Mill had in mind in his famous discussion of the issue—which is why I have used the word 'quantity' in the way I have. Jonathan Riley has noted the point (1988, 1993). 'The most straightforward way to capture the quality/quantity distinction', he says, 'is in terms of a lexical hierarchy of . . . aggregation procedures, one procedure for each kind or quality of pleasure' (1993: 295). On this most straightforward interpretation, the measure of ethical value for the Millian utilitarian will be pleasure—but with any quantities of higher-quality pleasures outranking any quantities of lower-quality pleasures.[7]

This is *too* straightforward in that it implies that the smallest decrease in higher 'pleasure' always outweighs any increase in lower 'pleasure' (that is, whatever one's existing 'consumption' of the two may be). If, in our thought-experiment, we prefer life without the cure, that does indicate the presence of some lexicality or discontinuity in our preferences but not, so far, of a lexical hierarchy as simple as that. Still, the straightforward model suffices to show the coherence of distinguishing between quantity of well-being and some other aspect of it, also relevant to its measure; I shall not be concerned with how the model might be made more realistic. My main concern will be

---

[7] One should not say that in this interpretation a unit of higher pleasure is equal to an infinite amount of lower pleasure, for the notion of a 'lexical' preference implies that it is reasonable to prefer a unit of higher pleasure combined with *more* rather than *less* lower pleasure. But adding units to a countable infinity still gives you only a countable infinity.

with what it is to think of this other aspect of well-being as a matter of its *quality*.

In distinguishing quantity and measure of well-being we have not yet shown that any notion that deserves the name 'quality' of well-being is required. Does our thought-experiment show that my actual life is higher in 'quality' than life after the cure? Why not content ourselves with saying that the measure of well-being cannot be represented additively? Why should a discontinuity indicate that something turning on 'quality' is at stake, where difference of quality does not just mean difference of kind or sort, but implies assessment in terms of a normative notion of 'higher' and 'lower'? Suppose that below a certain level of consumption of X, Alpha discontinuously prefers X to Y, while above some other level he switches over to a discontinous preference for Y over X. Which enjoyment is superior in quality—X or Y? One might say that, if there are such lexical switchovers, qualitative superiority is simply undefined. But even if switchovers never take place, even if Riley's model of a lexical hierarchy fits people's preferences tolerably well, why should that sustain talk of quality of pleasure? Suppose that Alpha discontinuously prefers heroin to poetry at certain levels of heroin and poetry consumption, and that he never discontinuously prefers poetry to heroin. Suppose indeed that this is true of all those who have sufficient experience of both heroin and poetry. Does this show that taking heroin is qualitatively superior to reading poetry, or does it just show that heroin is addictive?

It may not show that taking heroin is qualitatively superior, because the lexical preference for taking heroin may not be rational. It may simply signify addiction. So, in examining how a normative notion of quality of well-being works, we must look in particular at how it is connected with the rationality of preference. Having done that, we shall be able to reconsider in Section 4 how qualitative distinctions enter into the measure of well-being and what discontinuities in it they may generate.

2. QUALITY OF WELL-BEING

We do think and talk about well-being, contentment, happiness, and pleasure in qualitative terms. For example, notions such as purity, elevation, depth, refinement, sublimity, and their opposites enter into our assessments of a person's enjoyments (including their pleasures).[8] We can easily understand

---

[8] Enjoyment versus pleasure: in this chapter I use the term 'enjoyment' technically, to mean receipt of well-being. I do not use it to refer to an experienced state of pleasure, contentment, or satisfaction. The truth or falsehood of hedonism is not at issue in the present discussion. I do not mean to exclude accounts of well-being that make it possible that one is well-off in some

what it means to say that *A* has more enjoyment in life than *B*, but that the enjoyment involved is a pretty shallow, simple-minded, low, crass, or even base kind.

A person who is satisfied with such kinds of enjoyment is thought to be undiscerning or lacking in finer feeling. It seems that the higher forms of well-being are those that require higher capacities or powers of discernment and sensibility. Their full measure is not accessible to someone who does not have those powers.

The powers involved are rational and moral powers, capacities of reason, imagination, and sensibility and thus of character. It does not follow that higher enjoyments must be of an intellectual or a moral kind in the normal sense. Take the pleasure of an omelette and a glass of white wine on a radiant Mediterranean morning. It offers no deep human insight. Nevertheless to enjoy it to the full one must have active capacities—of attention, concept-formation, discrimination, imaginative synthesis, and recollection. Full enjoyment involves—for example—the idea of perfection in omelettes, dis-criminating attention paid to the look, taste, and smell of this particular omelette, a synthesizing grasp of how perfect omelette, glass of wine, and radiant morning come together into a greater whole. The same can be said for higher enjoyments that involve physical activity such as sport or dance. Whether one enjoys these as participant or observer, they involve the same powers. They may also involve moral insight into qualities of character or indeed the possession of these qualities. Exercise of these mental and moral powers is infused into the sheer animal enjoyment of physical movement and competitions and transforms it, in the way that full enjoyment of the omelette involves an infusion of higher awareness into the animal enjoyment of sen-suous life. Again, when a mother plays with her baby son, the kernel of her enjoyment is a simple animal pleasure: she responds to a small other that, in the most primitive sense, stands to her as 'mine'. Seeing another as 'mine' in this sense is a thing some non-human animals can do, just as competing is. Mental and moral powers transform that kernel—infusing it with the awareness that this is in some fuller sense my son, my responsibility, and to some extent my creation, that he has a life ahead of him, much to discover, perhaps to suffer as well as to enjoy, and so on. In particular, they infuse it with an ethical sense of the innocence and humanity of the relationship involved, of its situatedness in time, of projects from which it came and to

respect without being aware that one is. Indeed, anything like a correct substantive account of well-being seems to me to have that consequence. Hence, in the technical sense of 'enjoyment' adopted in this chapter one can *enjoy* an element of well-being, such as the respect of people one respects, without realizing that one has it. Equally, one can take pleasure in the false belief that one enjoys it. This technical sense can certainly diverge from ordinary use—for example, it is odd to talk of *enjoying* the sorrowful recollection of a death, even if (as I would agree) it can be an intrinsic part of one's well-being to mourn.

which it will lead. So, too, in the case of the omelette, come to that—it can include an ethical-aesthetic sensibility of transience, of the location in time of an experience and a self.

The general pattern, then, is one in which a variety of simple animal enjoyments, enjoyments open to human animals, is transformed or sublimated by developed intellectual and moral powers. This is not to intellectualize higher enjoyment, or moralize about it. But neither should one deny that there are hierarchies of quality in enjoyment, in which enjoyments involving forms of intellectual, spiritual, or moral insight come high. We spend a lot of time discussing how worthwhile particular kinds of enjoyment are and in the same spirit we spend a lot of time discussing the relative worth of various human achievements—here, too, the same considerations, about the range and impressiveness of the powers involved in the achievement and the enjoyment it affords, enter in.

Does this count, one might now ask, in favour of a 'perfectionist' view? Is talk about the quality of well-being really talk about the quality of the being whose well-being it is? Is it that we want to raise ourselves in the qualitative scale of beings, even at the cost of a reduction to the quantity of our well-being?

We should distinguish two points. On the one hand, there is the epistemological truism that the criterion of higher well-being is what people who have, in developed form, the relevant powers of mind prefer. On the other, there is the ethical claim that human development is something that matters in itself, an intrinsic goal in its own right, that there is an ethical imperative to become a person of developed higher powers: to 'raise oneself in the qualitative scale of beings'.

The truism is the inevitable starting point of any discussion of qualitative distinctions in well-being. It is what brings the notion of quality in. A criterion of quality in well-being is the criterion of what persons of greater discernment can enjoy and those of lower discernment cannot. I will come back to the questions this raises in Section 3.

The second thought is a version of perfectionism. I agree with Thomas Hurka's proposal to make it a defining characteristic of perfectionism that it takes excellence to have ethical value as such, irrespective of the contribution excellence makes to well-being.[9]

Thought-experiments like the one from which we started may well suggest

---

[9] See Hurka's very clear discussion and defence of perfectionism in Hurka (1993). 'Mixed perfectionism' attaches ethical value to things other than excellence, such as well-being, as well as excellence. I say it is a 'version' of perfectionism, since a perfectionist may focus (as Hurka does) on excellence of achievement rather than the standing or status of the achiever. But it is hard to keep these separate. If excellence of achievement is not to be valued for the quality of well-being that it brings, is it not valued for the quality of being it brings—the standing of the achiever in the qualitative scale of beings, as measured by ideals of being?

248 *John Skorupski*

it. In fact we can now see, in this version of perfectionism, a fourth response distinct from the three considered in Section 1: one should not have the cure because it lowers one in the qualitative scale of beings. It is better to be Socrates—or Elizabeth David—dissatisfied than a fool satisfied. Would one want to be the kind of person for whom a bag of crisps and a diet Coke would be just as good as a perfect omelette on a crisp morning, because the discriminating capacity and power of attention were lacking? Would one want to be that kind of person even if perfect omelettes and radiant mornings were very hard to come by? If not, is that not because one wishes not to sink to a lower level of being?

To be able to experience higher enjoyments at their full value is to feel the banality of a life without them. In their absence, lower enjoyments leave a sense of dissatisfaction or frustration. That being so, does the welfarist, for whom well-being is all, not have to argue that, if higher enjoyments are not available, then it is positively unreasonable to develop the capacities for their enjoyment? Must he not deny that it is better to be Socrates dissatisfied?

To say that Socrates is dissatisfied is not to say that he is bereft of enjoyments. Many particulars of life may strike him as frustratingly mediocre, it is true; but the mental and moral powers that produce higher enjoyment work holistically. Their development—so long as they are being exercised—sublimates the whole experience of life.[10] It does not follow that such development is worth buying at any price. If, for example, a side-effect of developing them was chronic incapacitating pain that made their exercise impossible it would not be worth it. If we amend our thought-experiment in this way, it becomes much more difficult. It is not obvious that possession of such powers in a condition of personal suffering that makes their exercise impossible is to be preferred to life after the cure. The latter life is still worth living and in these circumstances it may well be that it makes sense to live it.

We are now better placed to see how discontinuity comes in. There is no *conceptual* connection between the idea of a higher enjoyment and the idea of a discontinuous preference. Our criterion of a higher enjoyment is that beings of greater discrimination show a greater preference for it than beings of lesser discrimination—it is not required that they prefer it *lexically*. Does a more discriminating person *lexically* prefer a perfect omelette to any amount of salt and vinegar crisps? Not necessarily. The point is only that the discriminating give it a degree of preference that the undiscriminating do not.

But neither is discontinuity an irrelevant notion. If the exercise of higher powers sublimates experience holistically, then a whole life in which they are

---

[10] This is a version of what John Rawls called the 'Aristotelian principle' (Rawls 1971: §65), but my emphasis here is on the qualitative difference in enjoyment that development brings (and, to repeat, I do not assume that 'enjoyment' must be understood hedonistically).

exercised may be discontinuously preferred to one in which they are not. The reason is that, if I have developed powers and am able to exercise them, my experience and sense of myself is transformed as a whole. What is lexically preferred is a life in which I have those higher powers and can attain the enjoyments they open up to me to a life in which I do not or cannot.

So we can explain why it may be reasonable to eschew the cure without appealing to perfectionism. But another point lends perfectionism some plausibility. Higher powers, and achievements requiring them, call forth admiration and respect. They have a value in their own right: they are admirable in themselves. That is true; on the other hand, it is also true that the value they have has no *direct* implication for action, other than in giving one reason to applaud.[11] To deem something admirable is to see reason to admire it: to find a certain affective response, that of admiration, reasonable and justified. It does not directly entail that there is reason to achieve this thing ourselves, or to put resources towards other people's achieving it. Consider a brilliant violin performance (say). It has aesthetic value whether or not it contributes to well-being and its aesthetic value is independent of the well-being it generates. There is reason to admire it; but only if it contributes to well-being is there reason to seek to emulate it, to allocate resources towards maintaining the skills required for such performance, and so on. It may connect with well-being in more than one way. Excellent achievement may be itself, as Griffin suggests, a part of well-being. And whether or not it is, there is pleasure in being that which one admires and displeasure in failing to be. And obviously achievement can benefit others. But these connections between the admirable and reasons for action work via well-being; while perfectionism short-circuits the connection.

So it seems to me that what is admirable in character and achievement generates reason for action only through the effect it has on well-being. Mill seems to take an even more strongly anti-perfectionist line—holding that the very constitution of the admirable is a matter of its effect on well-being:[12] 'I hold that the very question, what constitutes . . . elevation of character, is itself to be decided by a reference to happiness as the standard.' That is too strong: what there is reason to admire in a particular field turns on the criteria internal to the judging of excellence in that field and does not necessarily refer to

---

[11] I discuss the relation between affective and practical reasons more extensively in Skorupski (1997). The proposition that if there is reason to admire there is reason to applaud is a special case of an important general principle that I there call the 'Feeling/Disposition Principle': if there is reason to feel ϕ then there is reason to do that which ϕ disposes to. Thus, if I have reason to fear, I have reason to flee, if I have reason to admire, I have reason to applaud, and so on. These reasons to act may be overridden by other reasons, of course.

[12] He did not have to. A utilitarian needs only to hold that all reasons for action derive from facts about well-being—he does not also have to hold that reasons to feel derive from the same source. They can have their own, *sui generis*, rationale.

the happiness produced. (Unless of course the happiness produced is itself one of the criteria of excellence in it.) The passage continues, however, with a weaker statement:

The character itself should be, to the individual, a paramount end, simply because the existence of . . . ideal nobleness of character, or of a near approach to it, in any abundance, would go further than all things else towards making human life happy; both in the comparatively humble sense, of pleasure and freedom from pain, and in the higher meaning, of rendering life, not what it now is almost universally, puerile and insignificant—but such as human beings with highly developed faculties can care to have. (*System of Logic*, vi. xii. 7 (*Collected Works*, viii. 952))

The statement may also seem to indicate a departure on Mill's part from hedonism; however, though it would indeed (to my mind) be right to reject hedonism, I do not believe that that is what Mill is doing here, any more than his preference in *Utilitarianism* for the life of Socrates dissatisfied over that of the satisfied fool is a rejection of hedonism. But, be that as it may, there is certainly in this passage a rejection of perfectionism. And whether or not one agrees with hedonism, one can hold, with Mill, that quality of being matters ethically (i.e. to reasons for action) only in as much as it makes a difference to the measure of well-being.[13]

3. TWO VIEWS OF WELL-BEING

The passage from Mill also embodies our earlier criterion of qualitatively superior enjoyment. It is what 'human beings with highly developed faculties can care to have'—but human beings with less highly developed faculties do not care to have as much or at all.[14] What is being suggested is a *criterion*— in other words, the suggestion is at the epistemological, not the definitional, level. This difference of levels should be kept in mind when we examine the notion of well-being as I want to do now. Let us consider two broad approaches to well-being; call them the *ideal-preference* view and the *reason-to-desire* view.

---

[13] Mill discusses the value of nobility of character in similar vein in *Utilitarianism* (*Collected Works*, x. 213–14). Compare his explanation of what he means by 'higher natures' in a paper he wrote for Harriet Taylor, 'On Marriage' (*Collected Works*, xxi. 37–9): 'I mean those characters who from the combination of natural and acquired advantages, have the greater capacity of feeling happiness, and of bestowing it.'

[14] In *Utilitarianism* the 'test of quality, and the rule for measuring it against quantity' is 'the preference felt by those who, in their opportunities of experience, to which must be added their habits of self-consciousness and self-observation, are best furnished with the means of comparison' (*Collected Works*, x. 214).

The ideal-preference view is actually a genus of views. The idea is that to characterize well-being one must start with preference—or with desire, or with contentment—and then idealize it by attaching some condition, C. Characterizing well-being then consists in producing some a priori true equivalence of the form 'ϕ promotes x's well-being if and only if x would choose to ϕ—or desire to ϕ, or be content with the result of ϕ-ing—in condition C. Or again: 'g is an ingredient of (human) well-being if and only if human beings would choose g, desire g, be content with g, in condition C'.

In contrast, the reason-to-desire view holds that an individual's well-being consists in whatever that individual has non-instrumental reason to desire, reason to desire for itself. In talking of reasons to *desire* we are dealing with affective reasons, reasons to feel, not with practical reasons, reasons to act. Indeed, this characterization of individual well-being relies on distinguishing between reason to desire and reason to pursue,[15] for it would otherwise obliterate the distinction between good in general and individual good. If there is such a thing as the good in general at all, it is not a priori that the good in general is equivalent to one's own good—but it *is* a priori that, if there is a good in general, then there is reason to pursue whatever forms part of it. It does not follow that the good in general must also form part of one's own good, since one's own good is defined in terms of what one has reason to desire, not what one has reason to pursue. Note also that to characterize the individual's good in terms of what that individual has reason to desire is not to endorse a desire-satisfaction model of practical reasons. This characterization of individual good, unlike the desire-satisfaction model of practical reasons, leaves open the possibility that there can be reason to do something that does not satisfy one's desires (however idealized) and that recognition of such a reason can lead one to act simply *from* recognition of it. (I may have no particular reason to *desire* your good but I still have some reason to lend it a helping hand.)

Henry Sidgwick held the reason-to-desire view of well-being:[16]

Putting aside the conceivable case of its being my duty to sacrifice my own good, to realise some greater good outside my own existence, we may say that my good on the whole is what I 'ought' to desire: but—since irrational desire cannot be dismissed at once by voluntary effort—we cannot say this in the strictly ethical sense of 'ought'. We can only say it in the wider sense, in which it merely connotes an ideal or standard,

---

[15] By the Feeling/Disposition principle if I have reason to desire g then I have reason to pursue g. But the principle leaves the truth of the converse open.

[16] I quote the *Methods of Ethics* from its fifth edition. However, the whole section from which these passages come (ch. x, sect. 3) was thoroughly revised for the sixth edition. Reading the revised version of the section and then rereading the fifth-edition version, I am now not sure that the 'reason to desire' view of well-being can be attributed to Sidgwick, even in the fifth edition.

divergence from which it is our duty to avoid as far as possible, though, even when it is distinctly recognized, we may not always be able to avoid it at will.   (Sidgwick 1893: 111)

But, as the first clause shows, Sidgwick does not distinguish firmly enough between reason to desire and reason to pursue. As we have just noted, the fact that I may have reason to pursue something other than my good does not entail that I have reason to desire something other than my good. Thus we do not need to put the 'conceivable case' aside. This is not the only infelicity: Sidgwick is quite right to say that the notion of 'ought' involved is not the 'strictly ethical [that is, moral] sense'; but, having made the point, he re-confuses it by suggesting that our good on the whole is a standard divergence from which it is our *duty* to avoid.

After a passage comparing the reason-to-desire view with a 'full-information' version of the ideal-preference view—hedging his bets about the latter's a priori correctness but dismissing it as a strict analysis—Sidgwick offers a reformulation:

I conclude, then, that '*my* ultimate good' must be taken to mean in the sense that it is 'what is ultimately desirable *for me*', or what I should desire if my desires were in harmony with reason, assuming my own existence alone to be considered,—and is thus identical with the ultimate end or ends prescribed by reason as to what ought to be sought or aimed at, so far as reason is not thought to inculcate sacrifice of my own ultimate good.   (Sidgwick 1893: 112)

Again a conflation of reason to desire with reason to pursue is strongly suggested, if not positively endorsed. Setting that aside, there is also an ambiguity in Sidgwick's 'what I should desire if my desires were in harmony with reason'.

To say that my desires are in harmony with reason may simply mean that I desire what there is in fact reason for me to desire. In that case, saying that what is desirable for me is what I should desire if my desires were in harmony with reason is simply a circuitous way of saying that it is what there is reason for me to desire. It makes no improvement on the simple statement that y is desirable for x, good for x, part of x's well-being, just if x has reason to desire y. On the other hand, 'x's desires are in harmony with reason' may mean something rather different: that x's desires are not such as to lay x's reasonableness open to criticism, show some rational failing on x's part. Understood in this way, we would have a version of the ideal-preference view, a normative, not a reductive, version but still a version. It would offer the following as an a priori equivalence: what there is reason for me to desire is what I should desire if my rationality could not be faulted and I was equipped with all relevant information.

We need to know the aim of this counterfactual account. What I have reason to desire depends on the facts. That is, the relation I consider when I reflect on what there is reason for me to desire is of the form *the fact that* p *gives* x *reason (of degree* d *at time* t*) to desire* ϕ. (Call it the 'reason-to-desire' relation.) Now, in the counterfactual account, is rationality so defined as to include the ability to recognize the truth of statements of that form? Alternatively, does the notion of relevant information invoked by the counterfactual account include information about which statements of that form are true? If the answer to either of these questions is affirmative, then the account can throw no light on what it is for a fact to give a person reason to desire something. So, if that is its aim, it is redundant. But the answer is unlikely to be affirmative, because the idea that underlies the counterfactual is likely to be this: what one has reason to want is determined by one's actual underived wants (perhaps subject to some rational systematization) and the facts. Now counterfactual facts about how it would be rational to systematize one's wants presumably supervene on facts about one's actual underived wants (and about other things). So, if this *is* the aim, then again why should one bother with a counterfactual account? If one accepts this underlying idea, then what is actually needed is more direct: a theory showing how facts about *x*'s underived wants, together with other relevant facts, determine conclusions about what *x* has reason to desire.

This is a better route in any case, since there are well-known general problems for such counterfactual explications—problems that arise even when they are proposed not as strict analyses but as a priori equivalences. In the present case, the difficulty may be put thus. What there is reason for *x* to desire in a particular case may be opaque or hidden from *x* in a whole variety of ways—even if *x* is perfectly rational in the sense of incurring no criticism on that score. The counterfactual account attempts to deal with this by idealizing *x*'s information. But now we encounter the following systematic problem: it is logically possible that there is reason for *x* to desire *g* only because *x* is ignorant of some of the facts in virtue of which there is reason for *x* to desire *g*. In this logically possible case, the set of facts on which 'there is reason for *x* to desire *g*' supervenes, $F_1 \ldots F_m$, is such that *x* does not know every single one of $F_1 \ldots F_n$ to hold. Yet when we add to the set the further fact that *x* knows every single one of $F_1 \ldots F_n$ to hold, we find that 'there is reason for *x* to desire *g*' does not supervene on the new set of facts—that is, relative to this new set of facts it is not the case that there was reason for *x* to desire *g*. Now what does the counterfactual account imply in this case? It implies that, if *x* knew every single one of $F_1 \ldots F_n$ to hold and reasoned properly, *x* would desire *g*. But, *ex hypothesi*, there would in this case be no *reason* for *x* to desire *g*. This is already odd. But further, on the counterfactual account, to say that there would in this case be no reason for *x* to desire *g* is to say that, if *x* *knew* that he knew every single one of $F_1 \ldots F_n$ to hold and reasoned properly, he would *not* desire *g*. To avoid contradiction, the proponent of the counterfactual account must respond that knowing does not entail knowing that one knows (presumably he would also need to argue that believing does not entail believing that one believes). He can then try to develop a notion of relevant information in which one can fail to have the *relevant* information by having *more* information that that, as well as *less*. But why bother? Why not just go directly to an account of what facts give x reason to desire what objects?

An ideal-preference account of the reason-to-desire relation looks no more promising than an ideal-belief account of the reason-to-believe relation. What is needed is a *direct* theory of the reason-to-desire relation—of when it is that a given being has reason to desire something, of the facts on which reasons for that being to desire supervene. This is a substantive task for ethics, as a theory of the reason-to-believe relation is a task for epistemology. One may well suspect, then, that ideal-preference accounts of well-being will either turn out to presuppose the reason-to-desire relation or fail.

In contrast, the reason-to-desire view seems to me to offer not only an a priori equivalence but a strict analysis, or definition, of personal good or well-being. There is, indeed, an obvious difficulty: what about the well-being of animals not able to reason? Can they be said to have reason to desire anything?

We have a notion of flourishing or well-functioning: in terms of that notion we can characterize a notion of good for some kinds of entity—as whatever makes an entity of that kind a flourishing or well-functioning specimen of its kind. Fertilizing is good for the lawn and oiling for the saw. It makes no sense to say that lawns have reason to desire fertilization, or saws oiling. But, while this is clearly right, it does not seem to me (perhaps contrary to some Aristotelians) that *that* notion of good is the notion of well-being with which we are here concerned: the ethically significant notion with respect to which one can talk of quality. It does not seem unreasonable to say that well-being in this ethically significant sense is a notion that applies only to beings that can be said to have desires.

But can all such beings be said to have *reasons* to desire? One response is to answer in the negative and then suggest that we can nevertheless form the notion of what there is reason to do for their sake, on their behalf, in their interests, as their trustee. But these notions implicitly invoke the good or well-being of the being in question. For example, what there is reason to pursue on x's behalf is just what there is reason to pursue with the good of x in mind.

However, the negative answer is too intellectualistic about reasons. Animals can be said to have reasons. The cat may have reason to wait by the hole—it is a mousehole. The fox wants to find the chicken coop and it has good reason to want that. One can say without strain or metaphor that the cat's or fox's well-being consists of what it has non-instrumental reason to desire.

More needs to be said. But suppose we allow that the reason-to-desire account can be defended as a *definition* of individual good.[17] That does not mean that it gives us a substantial *criterion*, or defeasible warrant, for judgements about what human good and its ingredients are. And here is where the notion of an ideal preference has its proper place. The primitive criterion of what there is reason to desire is what one does desire—the primitive criterion of what there is reason to feel in general is what one feels. One does not simply have a feeling; one experiences it in the normal case, in the absence of defeating considerations, as a *reasonable* feeling, a *correct* response. But, of course, the primitive criterion is also a crude criterion, since, although what one desires is a warrant for judgements about what one has reason to desire, it is an easily defeasible one. What one would desire after experience and self-examination and discussion with others would provide a less easily defeasible—but still in principle defeasible—warrant. Yet defeasibility does not stop reflection on what one desires, or what competent judges desire, from being an indispensable tool of enquiry in deliberation about one's good.

It is in this sense that Mill's 'what human beings with highly developed faculties can care to have' is a criterion of higher well-being. The relevant faculties are attention, concept formation, discrimination, imaginative synthesis, recollection, insight . . . And to say that they are more highly developed in a person is to say that that person is better at making qualitative judgements, in particular, qualitative judgements about what constitutes and what contributes to well-being, and how. This is no vicious circle, however; it is a perfectly innocent epistemic interaction between judgements about well-being—about what there is reason to desire—and judgements about who is a good judge of well-being. The interaction is made possible by two general conditions of objectivity for discourse about the rationality of feeling and desire—namely, that feelings themselves should be primitive criteria of what there is reason to feel and that an assertion or judgement incurs a commitment to convergence of judgements. Conditions of these two kinds, involving the spontaneity of a particular kind of normative response, and a convergence commitment, characterize the dialogical epistemology (the epistemology of self-examination and discussion) that is proper to all normative judgements.[18]

[17] In general, the point of view adopted here is that the good should be defined in terms of reasons: individual good in terms of reasons to desire, general good in terms of reasons to promote or pursue. So an individual's good is part of general good just if what there is reason for an individual to desire there is reason for all to promote or pursue.

[18] Obviously this is no more than gestural. I say more about what role primitive normative responses and the commitment to convergence play in the epistemology of the normative (though still only sketchily) in Skorupski (1997: §§7, 8). In the terminology used in that paper (and in Skorupski 1993) I am taking it that 'well-being' is a *purely affectively determined concept* that can be defined in terms of what there is reason to desire. In contrast I suggest in those papers that 'morally wrong' is not a purely affectively determined concept and hence that one cannot *define* it, as against characterizing it a priori, in terms of what there is reason to blame, the blameworthy. The criteria of personal good are purely internal or hermeneutic in a way that the criteria of the morally wrong are not.

To sum up. A being's good is defined as what there is reason for that being to desire. More or less refined criteria of its good can be given in terms of what it desires, what it would desire in certain conditions, what beings of that kind do or would desire. Such criteria, however, being defeasible, cannot provide a characterization or explication *in terms of a priori equivalence* of the concept of personal good. Likewise, the criteria governing the concept 'qualitatively higher good of a being of kind K' are given in terms of what beings of kind K, in whom capacities relevant to judging what there is reason to desire are developed, desire or would desire—more than K-beings in whom these capacities are less developed. The more well-informed and cognitively or affectively equipped for the judgements in hand these K-beings are, the less is their judgement open to defeat.

In chapter II of *Value-Judgement* Griffin contrasts two models of judgements about what he calls 'prudential value': a 'taste' and a 'perception' model. 'The perception model gives priority to a judgement of value: desired *because* valuable . . . The taste model reverses the priority: valuable *because* desired' (*VJ* 20). Griffin thinks that both are false pictures and I agree. I also agree with Griffin that particular objects are desirable because they fall under 'prudential values', or categorial ends (as I would call them) under which we reflectively acknowledge objects as *worth* wanting—ends such as pleasure, say, or knowledge of one's situation, or perhaps accomplishment. One can say a bit more about these two models. The notion of a spontaneous normative response—what one acknowledges as worth wanting, as reasonably desired, when the clutter of delusive self-images and distorting ideals is cleared away—belongs to the epistemology of judgements about well-being, not their semantics. If one believes that concepts are patterns of epistemic norms, then it belongs also to an account of the epistemic norms that constitute the concept of well-being. At this level, the taste model is wrong because it ignores the primitively normative element in desire or in any feeling, its criterial role in judgements about what there is reason to feel, and the defeasibility of these judgements by non-convergence. However, the perception model, I am inclined to say, is more wrong, because it imports a quite irrelevant epistemology. That it is reasonable to desire one's happiness, for example, any reasonable person will acknowledge; but this acknowledgement in no way derives from 'perception' or 'non-perceptual intuition' of some special non-natural domain of fact.

4. QUALITY AND IMPARTIALITY

We can return now to our questions about the quality of well-being and its measure.

The criterion of higher goods is that they are what beings of highly developed faculties would, under certain conditions, care to have. Does it follow that they are goods for beings of less developed faculties? That there is reason for beings of less developed faculties to desire them?

Let us say that a good is *accessible* to a person x if x has the personal capacities required to enjoy that good to the full. It is *available* to x if x could obtain it. If a good g is both available and accessible to x, then certainly there is reason for x to desire it: it is a good-for-x. Is there reason for x to desire g if it is accessible but not available? Suppose x is a fine pianist to whom a very high ratio of the potential enjoyment offered by piano playing is accessible. But suppose that enjoyment is unavailable because he is up a creek without a piano. Is it then reasonable for him to want to play the piano? Apparently it is. His desire to play the piano is not unreasonable. It may, indeed, also be reasonable for him to desire to diminish or eliminate this desire, since it makes him unhappy and it is quite reasonable to desire to avoid unhappiness. None the less, a case like this provides no counter-example to the principle that, if a higher good g is accessible to x, then there is reason for x to desire g.

Suppose, on the other hand, that I am thoroughly unmusical. The enjoyment of piano playing is not accessible to me at all. Is there intrinsic reason for me to want to play the piano? No. Piano playing is in this case no part of my good. But what if it is possible for me to overcome my lack of musicality by undergoing some training? It remains the case that there is no intrinsic reason for me to want to play the piano—but there may now be an instrumental reason for me to want to undertake the training whose result will be that I acquire such a reason. A Butlerian desire for one's own well-being in the abstract, so to speak, is a reasonable desire to have. If this training will make a superior form of enjoyment, that of piano playing, accessible to me—and if the opportunity to play the piano will be available to me in circumstances that produce a net gain to my well-being—there is instrumental reason for me to want to undertake the training.

This further condition may not be satisfied, though. A good may be accessible to me without being available to me, or without being available to me on beneficial terms. If it is accessible but unavailable, its unavailability may well make me miserable and dissatisfied. Thus it is does not follow from the fact that I *can* do something to make it accessible to me that I should want to do so. The absence of any such desire on my part may be quite reasonable. A higher good g may not be a part of my good and it may not even be rational to want it to be. Equally, a good g may be a part of my good as things actually stand, even if a more developed version of me would not be content with g. It may even be unreasonable to want to develop myself in such as way as to make myself dissatisfied with g—if there is no net benefit to me in doing so.

These points having been made, we can finally consider how the distinction between quality and quantity of well-being fits into a certain conception of ethical value—one that equates it with the well-being of all, impartially assessed. One may think of the broad class of views that fit this description— of which classical, aggregative and hedonistic, utilitarianism is just one— as *generically* utilitarian. They all make the ethical value of a state of affairs a positive and impartial function of the well-being of all individuals in it and of nothing else. By an 'impartial function' I mean one that expresses an impartial distributive principle, and by that in turn I mean a principle that is both agent-neutral and universalizable.[19] Impartiality in this sense is compatible with giving the well-being of some beings greater weight than that of others, so long as that weight supervenes on some agent-neutrally characterizable property of them. In other words, it is a more inclusive concept than that expressed in the classical utilitarians' 'Everybody to count for one, nobody for more than one'. And this leads me to the final question I want to consider.

It can be introduced by asking how, in an account of general good, we should measure the ethical value of animals' well-being. Do we or should we give the well-being of animals less weight than the well-being of humans? Or should we think of the criterion of general good as a measure in which everybody, including animals, counts for one: but into which judgements about the *quality* of animal well-being are fed?

How should qualitative judgements about well-being feed into the function from individual to general good? To fix ideas, consider an example. Suppose that beings of highly developed faculties place the pleasures of scientific discovery or artistic creation so far higher than those of material well-being that (above a certain threshold of physical comfort and security) they would not give up a certain amount of the former for any amount of the latter, however large. Suppose, however, that beings of considerably less developed faculties do not share this assessment. We now ask, how much of the enjoyment of the less developed beings may be sacrificed to maintain more highly developed beings' higher enjoyments?

On the account we have given, the verdict of the more highly developed beings is the one on which to rely in assessing the relative value of higher and lower enjoyments. It provides the criterion, though a criterion is always of course defeasible. By hypothesis, these beings would be prepared to sacrifice

---

[19]   For a fuller account of my use of these terms—'impartiality', 'agent-neutrality', and 'generic utilitarianism'—see Skorupski (1992, 1995, 1996). ('Welfarist' is a possible alternative to 'generically utilitarian', but it perhaps has as many misleading implications as 'utilitarian' does.) Note that affirming impartially conceived well-being as the final ethical standard is one thing, putting forward some particular account of personal or political justice or public policy is another. They are related, but not straightforwardly. What one takes as the distributive structure of general good will have a bearing on one's account of justice, but it may not be a simple one.

any amount of the lower enjoyment, down to a threshold of physical comfort and security, for a certain amount of the higher. Does it then follow that general good is increased by sacrificing all the lower enjoyment of less developed beings, down to that threshold, so long as that releases that amount of the higher enjoyments to beings able to access them at their full measure?

Obviously the answer depends on what distributive principle one builds into the criterion of general good. On a number of such principles, including plausible descendants of classical aggregative or average utilitarianism, ethical value will be measured by a function whose effect is that value is maximized against increasing resources (in our hypothetical case) *first* as sub-threshold levels of well-being are eliminated, *then* as lexically preferable higher-quality enjoyments are made fully available to those who have access to them, and, finally, as lexically inferior lower-quality enjoyments are made fully available to those who have access to them. But this will not hold for all positive and impartial functions. It will not hold, for example, for a distributive principle that requires that maximization be constrained by a leximin principle.

Of course this thought-experiment makes a substantial assumption about what lexical preferences highly developed beings may be expected to have. Still, in the related example with which we started, many of us prefer not to take the cure—and this is best explained and justified as a discontinuous preference for a superior quality of life, irrespective of the quantity of qualitatively lower enjoyment available in another. Or so I have argued.

What then of our ethical view of animals? Does it illustrate a related lexical discontinuity? It is not easy to say. However, a case for that interpretation can be made. Some fairly common moral assumptions go vaguely like this: in so far as we raise animals and have responsibility for them, we should ensure that they have a pleasant life. But it is not wrong to kill them humanely for a wide range of human purposes, including eating. And we seem to envisage no clear limit to the number of animals that can be slaughtered to safeguard the certainty or even the risk of a small number of human deaths. These common assumptions seem to assume that the well-being of animals has ethical value. On the other hand, they give animals a very different moral standing from human beings.

The moral rights and wrongs of killing cannot be straightforwardly derived from considerations of ethical value, even in a (sensible) teleological ethics. And, further, it is at least a grave possibility that common views about the morality of killing animals are wrong. However, those views, as they are, are consistent with something like the following underlying conception. Many animals are capable of enjoying well-being. But the enjoyment that they can experience is not sufficiently transformed by higher capacities to be fused into a single life—that is, a life-for-oneself as against a more or less contented succession of experience, with nothing to bring the experience together into experience for-a-self. This view of animal experience may, of course, be wrong for some animals—but arguments to that effect seem to be arguments for revising our view about the rights and wrongs of killing them.

There are other possible accounts of these common moral conceptions. Let me consider just one. Jeff McMahan (1995) distinguishes between *the value of a life* and the *worth of the individual* whose life it is.[20] The former refers to the measure of well-being in a life; it is 'the extent to which the life is worth living'. The latter 'is determined by the nature of the subject of the life—by the particular properties and capacities that make that individual the kind of thing that he or she is' (McMahan 1995: 10, 11). McMahan is concerned with the morality, that is the rightness or wrongness, of killing. And, invoking the superior worth of human individuals, he envisages a two-tiered account that distinguishes between a morality of interests that applies to animals and a morality of respect that applies to humans.

I want to ask a rather different question about this distinction between the value of a life and the worth of an individual. How does it affect the measure of ethical value? May it be the case that in assessing general ethical value the well-being of individuals of greater worth should be given greater weight than that of individuals of lesser worth?

That would infringe the principle that every being capable of enjoying well-being is to count for one. But it could still be impartial, so long as differences of worth supervene on properties of the individuals that give rise to agent-neutral reasons for discrimination. What then might these properties—the bases of the worth of an individual—be? McMahan mentions 'capacities for rationality, autonomy, free choice, imagination and creativity, the use of language, deep personal and social relations, empathy, and so on' (1995: 12). So this looks very much like the list of capacities required for enjoyment of qualitatively higher forms of well-being. And the question to ask is why this should give greater weight to the well-being of the individuals who have them, as against giving them access to forms of well-being that already and intrinsically have greater weight in the sense of being qualitatively higher. Would this not be a sort of double counting?

Certainly we admire such capacities. But even if someone deserves greater respect, does that mean that his or her well-being should be given greater weight in the assessment of general good? It might, on certain forms of mixed perfectionism (depending on the distributive criterion the perfectionist used). But we have rejected perfectionism.

So it seems to me that we can stick to narrow impartiality. The appearance that our moral views give animals lesser weight as beings can be explained

---

[20] McMahan says that a similar distinction is drawn in Regan (1983).

away. What we in fact believe is that they have lesser capacity for enjoyment. We believe (perhaps wrongly for some species) that their capacity is so much lower as to make it a mere reaction of contentment or otherwise to the stream of experience. Suppose we go back to our original thought-experiment and ask what attitude to take to a 'cure' that would reduce us to such low level of capacity for enjoyment—even with the enjoyment indefinitely guaranteed. This would be a much more dramatic decline than the possibility originally presented, the possibility of being reduced to the 'mental age of a very small child'. In that original case, one survives the cure in a full sense. One retains a sense of self and of a life extended in time that is one's life. But in this new thought-experiment one cannot be said to retain any such sense. If I have this new cure, what survives is still me; I have not ceased to exist. But there is no longer a life that is mine in the sense of being for-me. In this case, and in this latter sense, the response that said 'this is no longer me' does seem appropriate: it is not literally true that I no longer exist but it is true that there is no longer a life-for-me. It does not seem to matter how brief or long this succession of experience is. All that seems to matter is that, if it takes place at all, it should be an experience of contentment rather than suffering. But, since it does not matter how brief or long it is, it does not matter whether it takes place at all.

REFERENCES

Hurka, Thomas (1993), *Perfectionism* (New York: Oxford University Press).

McMahan, Jeff (1995), 'Killing and Equality', *Utilitas*, 7: 1–29.

Nozick, Robert (1997), 'On Austrian Methodology', in R. Nozick, *Socratic Puzzles* (Cambridge, Mass.: Harvard University Press), originally in *Synthese*, 36 (1977), 353–92.

Rawls, John (1971), *A Theory of Justice* (Oxford: Clarendon Press).

Regan, Tom (1983), *The Case for Animal Rights* (London: Routledge & Kegan Paul).

Riley, Jonathan (1988), *Liberal Utilitarianism* (Cambridge: Cambridge University Press).

——(1993), 'On Quantities and Qualities of Pleasure', *Utilitas*, 5: 291–300.

Sidgwick, Henry (1893), *The Methods of Ethics* (5th edn., London: Macmillan).

Skorupski, John (1992), 'Value and Distribution', in M. Hollis and W. Vossenkuhl (eds.), *Moralische Entscheidung und rationale Wahl* (Scientia Nova, Munich: Oldenbourg), 191–207.

——(1993), 'The Definition of Morality', in A. Phillips Griffiths (ed.), *Ethics: Philosophy Supplement*, 35 (Cambridge: Cambridge University Press), 121–44.

Skorupski, John (1995), 'Agent-Neutrality, Consequentialism ... A Terminological Note', *Utilitas*, 7: 49–54.

—— (1996), 'Neutral versus Relative: A Reply to Broome, and McNaughton and Rawling', *Utilitas*, 8: 235–48.

—— (1997), 'Reasons and Reason', in Garrett Cullity and Berys Gaut (eds.), *Ethics and Practical Reason* (Oxford: Clarendon Press).

14

An Abortion Argument and the Threat of Intransitivity

Larry S. Temkin

Many years ago, I had the pleasure of house sitting for James Griffin while he was on holiday. Throughout the days, and into the nights, I would work in his study, papers—and cats—strewn across his large desk, surrounded by his magnificent library. As a young philosopher, labouring over the initial draft of my book *Inequality*, the setting was not merely conducive to work, it was inspirational. Sitting in James Griffin's study in Oxford, I realized how fortunate I was to be a philosopher.

Over the years, I have profited both from discussions with Griffin and from his work. So I am proud to contribute a chapter to a volume honouring him. In addition, I am especially pleased to acknowledge my long-standing personal debt. My own study, where I write these words, is not nearly so grand, but it was inspired by Griffin's. Correspondingly, when, as before, I sit in my study and contemplate my good fortune in being a philosopher, my thoughts often turn—with gratitude and fondness—to James Griffin.

Much of this chapter was written while I was a Fellow in the Program in Ethics and the Professions at Harvard University. I am most grateful to the Program, and especially Dennis Thompson, for providing a nearly ideal research environment. I am also grateful to numerous audiences for their reactions to this chapter's ancestors, including those at Brown University; Harvard University; New York University; the University of Massachusetts at Amherst; the Program in Economics, Justice and Society at the University of California at Davis; and the Society for Ethics and Legal Philosophy in Cambridge. My memory is too faulty properly to acknowledge all those who have given me useful comments about intransitivity, but they include Baruch Brody, John Broome, Tyler Cowen, Roger Crisp, Keith DeRose, Fred Feldman, Charles Fried, David Gauthier, Shelly Kagan, F. M. Kamm, Liam Murphy, Thomas Nagel, Ingmar Persson, John Roemer, Tim Scanlon, Amartya Sen, Ernest Sosa, Peter Unger, Peter Vallentyne, and J. David Velleman. Stuart Rachels deserves special mention. He commented extensively on earlier drafts, and buttressed my views with his own powerful arguments against transitivity. Derek Parfit inspired my work on intransitivity, and has been both my biggest source of encouragement and my most penetrating critic. Finally, I would like to thank this volume's editors for their patience and helpful comments.

1. INTRODUCTION

In *Well-Being: Its Meaning, Measurement and Moral Importance*, James Griffin considers, as all consequentialists must, whether there are incommensurable values. He discusses various purported forms, or sources, of incommensurability, and dismisses most of them. Thus, he denies the *incomparability* of different values—'values can at least be ranked', argues against some values *trumping* others—'no value, no matter how little is at stake, outranks another, no matter how much is at stake', claims that *weighting* 'is a distraction', and suggests that *pluralism* is a red herring— 'the monism–pluralism issue is not especially central to the issue of incommensurability' (*WB* 75–92, at 85 and 90). However, Griffin believes there are incommensurabilities of the form: enough of *A* outranks any amount of *B*. According to Griffin, such incommensurabilities reflect *discontinuity* between values, which involves 'the suspension of addition . . . we have a positive value that, no matter how often a certain amount is added to itself, cannot become greater than another positive value, and cannot, not because with piling up we get diminishing value or even disvalue . . . but because they are the sort of value that, even remaining constant, cannot add up to some other value' (*WB* 85).

To exemplify his view, Griffin imagines a scale of art ranging from the very best Rembrandts, Vermeers, and de Hoochs all the way (down!) to contemporary kitsch. Griffin suggests that though the 'kicks' of kitsch are real, they are different from the genuine appreciation of beauty; so much so that, other things being equal, it would be rationally defensible to prefer fifty years appreciating the beauty of Rembrandt, Vermeer, and de Hooch to any number of years of enjoying the kicks of kitsch. For Griffin, then, we might have a 'basic preference' for 'a life with beauty' over 'a life with only lots of kitsch', and this reveals a discontinuity of value between the extreme ends of the art scale. The judgement that enough 'high' art would outweigh any amount of kitsch implies that one cannot plausibly apply an additive scale of value across the whole range of art.

Although Griffin suggests that there is a discontinuity of value *between* the extreme ends of the art scale, he notes that 'we should not expect to find sharp discontinuities at either extreme of the scale' (*WB* 86). More generally, his discussion suggests that we should not expect to find discontinuities between artworks of similar quality. Thus, Griffin writes:

Fifty years at a very high level—say, with enjoyment of a few of the very best Rembrandts, Vermeers, and de Hoochs—might be outranked by fifty-five years at a slightly lower level—no Rembrandts, Vermeers, or de Hoochs, but the rest of the Dutch School. And then fifty-five years at that level might be outranked by sixty years at a slightly lower level—no Dutch School but a lot more of the nineteenth-century revival of the Dutch School. And so on. . . .   (*WB* 86)

So, given a scale of art, ranging from 'high' art to kitsch, one should expect continuity between artworks that are similar in quality, and hence near each other on the scale, even though there is discontinuity between works that are radically different in quality, and hence at the extreme opposite ends of the scale.

Griffin acknowledges an apparent problem for his views. Suppose there is an art scale ranging from *A*, high art, to *Z*, kitsch, such that *B* is only slightly lower quality than *A*, *C* only slightly lower quality than *B*, and so on. If, as seems plausible, we might prefer fifty-five years of *B* to fifty years of *A*, sixty years of *C* to fifty-five years of *B*, and so on, then it might seem we are committed to preferring a 'sufficiently' large number of years of kitsch, *Z*, to fifty years of high art, *A*. As Griffin notes, 'This step-by-step approach seems irresistible. Yet it presents us with two embarrassments: a Sorites Paradox and a slippery slope' (*WB* 87). Griffin 'put[s] the Sorites problem to the side', but argues that here, as elsewhere, we should reject the seemingly 'irresistible' conclusion of the step-by-step approach. On his view, even if we have a 'basic preference' that would lead us to consistently value greater number and more variety in art over 'somewhat' higher quality art that is fewer in number and less varied, we might also maintain a 'basic preference' for a certain amount of art at a very high level over any amount of art at a very low level. Thus, as I interpret Griffin, we can retain our basic preference for fifty years of high art over any amount of kitsch, even if we accept that there is a range of art from *A*, high art, to *Z*, kitsch, and have a basic preference for fifty-five years of *B* to fifty years of *A*, sixty years of *C* to fifty-five years of *B*, and so on.

As indicated, Griffin offers his argument in support of the conclusion that there are 'incommensurabilities of the form: enough of *A* outranks any amount of *B*' (*WB* 89), and suggests that this reflects discontinuities along our scale of values. Of particular importance for Griffin is the view that there may be 'discontinuities in the addition of well-being' (*WB* 89) that reflect a basic preference, 'when informed, to rank a certain amount of life at a very high level above any amount of life at a very low level' (*WB* 87).

Griffin's arguments are interesting and his conclusions important. But, as stated, they may seem innocuous. The claims that values are incommensurable and that there may be discontinuities along our scale of values have a familiar and comfortable ring. Many find such claims intuitively plausible, perhaps even obvious. But I think arguments of the sort Griffin offers *suggest* a conclusion that is wildly counter-intuitive and deeply problematic. They suggest that 'all-things-considered better than' is not a transitive relation.

Most people accept the *axiom of transitivity*: that, for any three alternatives *A*, *B*, and *C*, if, all things considered, *A* is at least as good as *B*, and, all things considered, *B* is at least as good as *C*, then, all things considered, *A* is at least as good as *C*.[1] Many believe the axiom of transitivity *must* be true, as a matter of logic, or conceptual necessity. Others believe it is intuitively 'obvious', even if they reject the notion of analytic truths. For many, the axiom of transitivity is intimately bound up with our conceptions of consistency and rationality, so that to reject transitivity would require radical revision in our understanding of practical reasoning. Moreover, expected utility theory relies on transitivity, as does much of economics, game theory, and decision theory. Finally, we implicitly rely on transitivity throughout our lives, for example, whenever we choose between a set of alternatives on the basis of a sequence of pair-wise comparisons. That is, in choosing between a set of options, we typically consider the first and second, and remove the second from further consideration if we think the first is better. But this approach depends on transitivity, since we cannot remove the second from further consideration if it might be better than another option that itself is better than the first. It is the axiom of transitivity that rules out such a possibility.

Thus, rejecting transitivity is a radical move with far-reaching implications. In most people's minds it is far more disturbing than 'merely' acknowledging incommensurability or discontinuity among values. Yet, arguments of the sort Griffin presents seem to support the former conclusion if we think they establish the latter conclusion. Suppose, for example, that at least for some people it would be rational, or right, or better, for them to have the basic preferences Griffin describes. More particularly, suppose we say that for some people fifty-five years of *B* would be *better*, all things considered, than fifty years of *A* (high art), sixty years of *C* would be *better*, all things considered, than fifty-five years of *B*, and so on. Transitivity then *requires* that, for the people in question, 'enough' years of *Z* (kitsch) would be *better*, all things considered, than fifty years of *A* (high art). But to accept Griffin's claims about incommensurability and discontinuity is to reject the necessity of accepting such a conclusion. The idea is that, *even if*, for some people, fifty-five years of *B* would be better, all things considered, than fifty years of *A* (high art), sixty years of *C* would be better, all things considered, than fifty-five years of *B*, and so on, it might *still* be true for those very people that *no* number of years of *Z* would be better than fifty years of *A*. But this seemingly contradicts the axiom of transitivity.

---

[1] More generally, any relation *R* will be transitive, if and only if, for any *a*, *b*, and *c*, if *aRb* and *bRc*, then *aRc*. 'Taller than' is a standard example of a transitive relation, since, if Andrea is taller than Becky, and Becky is taller than Claire, then Andrea is taller than Claire. By contrast, 'being the birth mother of' is clearly not a transitive relation, since Andrea's being the birth mother of Becky, and Becky's being the birth mother of Claire, does not entail—and in fact is incompatible with—Andrea's being the birth mother of Claire.

No longer do Griffin's arguments for the apparently plausible conclusions about incommensurability and discontinuity seem innocuous. Rather, they threaten a fundamental principle of practical reasoning, the axiom of transitivity.

Griffin may resist the move from claims about 'basic preferences' to 'all-things-considered better than' judgements or rankings. And perhaps he could successfully defend the view that his argument does not, in fact, entail the rejection of transitivity. I shall not pursue this issue here. But, as indicated, I think arguments similar to Griffin's do threaten transitivity. In this chapter, I shall present one such argument. Specifically, I shall discuss an apparent counter-example to transitivity that involves a new interpretation and understanding of an old argument from the abortion debate. This chapter's aim is not to convince the reader that transitivity must be rejected, but to raise doubts about transitivity that are not easily vanquished.

One preliminary terminological point. Elsewhere, I noted that the kind of argument I will be presenting 'might appropriately, albeit a bit dangerously, be called a continuum argument'.[2] Unfortunately, as I feared, some find this nomenclature confusing, since my use of 'continuum' corresponds with a common-sense use of the term that is looser than its strict mathematical meaning. So, in this chapter, I shall refer to my argument as a *spectrum* argument for intransitivity. I am, of course, concerned not with what we *call* such arguments, but with their implications for transitivity or practical reasoning.

2. A SPECTRUM ARGUMENT FOR INTRANSITIVITY: FROM INFANT TO ZYGOTE

In her classic article, 'A Defense of Abortion', Judith Thomson quickly summarizes and dismisses a standard conservative argument against abortion. She writes:

We are asked to notice that the development of a human being from conception through birth into childhood is continuous; then it is said that . . . to choose a point in this development and say 'before this point the thing is not a person, after this point it is a person' is to make an arbitrary choice, a choice for which in the nature of things no good reason can be given. It is concluded that the foetus is, or anyway that we had better say it is, a person from the moment of conception. But this conclusion does not follow. Similar things might be said about the development of an acorn into an oak tree, and it does not follow that acorns are oak trees, or that we had better say they

[2] Larry Temkin, 'A Continuum Argument for Intransitivity', *Philosophy and Public Affairs*, 25 (1996), 176.

are. Arguments of this form are sometimes called 'slippery slope arguments'—the phrase is perhaps self-explanatory—and it is dismaying that opponents of abortion rely on them so heavily and uncritically.[3]

Following Thomson, and many others, I have long thought the argument in question a bad argument. In charitable moods, I described it as weak; more commonly, I disparaged it as silly. Like Thomson, I believed the argument was exactly as strong, and hence as weak, as those line-drawing arguments purporting to prove that acorns were oaks, heaps of sand were the same as grains, and hairiness was the same as baldness. However, I now think I was deeply mistaken. In fact, I now think that, if it is presented carefully, the conservative argument is a good argument, even a *sound* argument, *if* transitivity holds. If I am right, then those who continue to believe, as I do, that this particular conservative argument is not sound, have reason to worry about transitivity.

To illustrate this, I will first detail one version of the conservative argument. I will then show how reflections on this argument naturally suggest why one might give up transitivity. Next, I will consider an objection to the argument that seemingly preserves transitivity. However, I will argue that the argument can be revised to meet the objection, as long as transitivity holds.

I begin with some background. Suppose John decides that Jim's dying would be better than Joe's. When asked why, he notes that Jim is taller, heavier, hairier, is missing a leg, has blue eyes rather than brown, and so on. Many believe that, by themselves, such purely physical differences are morally irrelevant.[4] They think that the moral demands of impartiality or equality preclude our attaching greater value to one being over another on the basis of purely physical differences. Next, suppose that John defends his preference by pointing out that Joe is smarter, more musical, has a better memory, more complex beliefs, more developed desires, and so on. Once again, many believe that, by themselves, such psychological differences provide *no reason at all* to attach greater value to Joe's life than Jim's. Certainly, our confidence in the 'equal worth' of all human beings might be shaken if the psychological gaps were enormous—if, perhaps, Jim lacked consciousness, or most of the capacities we regard as distinctively human. But, in general, we do not attribute individual moral worth on the basis of psychological differences that lie within a normal, and fairly large, range.

The first version of the conservative argument can now be put as follows. Suppose the death of a newborn infant, *A*, is *very* bad. Suppose, for example,

---

[3] Judith Jarvis Thomson, 'A Defense of Abortion', *Philosophy and Public Affairs*, 1 (1971), 47.

[4] If Joe's being shorter, or lighter, enabled him to save ten people who would otherwise die, that might give us an indirect reason to think Jim's death would be better than Joe's, but that is another matter.

that for moral, and not merely cultural, reasons infanticide should be treated as roughly on a par with murder.[5] Then consider the foetus one day before birth, *B*. Since human development is a gradual process from conception until death, presumably there are physical and psychological differences between *A* and *B*. However, these differences are very slight. Such physical and psychological differences will be insignificant compared to those obtaining between Jim and Joe. Correspondingly, since the relatively large physical and psychological differences between Jim and Joe give *no reason at all* to value Joe's life more than Jim's, it seems the much smaller physical and psychological differences between *A* and *B* lack moral significance. That is, we admit that there are small differences between *A* and *B*, but we deny that they are morally relevant to our assessment of the value of the two lives. Thus, considered by themselves, *B*'s death would be as bad as *A*'s.

It is clear how the argument runs from here. *C* is compared with *B*, *D* with *C*, and so on. Eventually, one is comparing *Z*, the newly fertilized ovum, with *Y*, the one-day old zygote. With each comparison, there will be some physical or psychological differences, but these differences will lack moral significance. Specifically, at any stage of its development, we should be indifferent between the death of an embryo or foetus at that stage, and the death of the embryo or foetus one day later. Considered just by themselves, there would be no morally relevant reasons to think the latter outcome worse than the former.

So, the argument is that *B*'s death is as bad as *A*'s, *C*'s death as bad as *B*'s, *D*'s as bad as *C*'s, . . . , and *Z*'s as bad as *Y*'s. But, then, transitivity entails that *Z*'s death must be as bad as *A*'s. The death of the newly fertilized ovum is as bad as the death of a newborn infant.

Importantly, this argument does *not* hinge on the obviously false claim that *A* is identical to *B*, *B* identical to *C*, . . . , and *Y* identical to *Z*, in order to ground, via transitivity and Leibniz's Law,[6] the dubious claim that if *A* is a person then *Z* is a person, or 'anyway that we had better say it is'. To the contrary, the argument clearly recognizes that there are small physical or psychological differences between adjacent members of the spectrum from *A* to *Z*. The key to the argument is simply the plausible premiss that the differences between *adjacent* members of the spectrum are not *morally* significant. That is, differences between adjacent members of the spectrum are not large enough, or the right kind of differences, for the adjacent members to have a

[5] There are powerful reasons to doubt this claim, but they need not concern us here. I assume, for simplicity, that it is seriously wrong to kill a newborn infant. A similar argument could be run for those who think it is seriously wrong to kill a 2-year-old, but not a newborn.

[6] Leibniz's Law states that *A* is identical to *B* if and only if every property of *A* is a property of *B* and vice versa. For reasons familiar from philosophy of language, it does not hold for modal or intensional properties.

different moral status. It is this, quite plausible, premiss that, *combined with transitivity*, yields the conservative's conclusion that the fertilized ovum's *moral* status must be the same as the infant's. Thus, the conservative might insist that, if we should treat an infant as a person, we should also treat a fertilized ovum as we would a person—because the two have the same moral status. But this is not the same as claiming that, if the infant *is* a person, then the fertilized ovum is too. (Perhaps we should treat an advanced Dolphin as we would a person, but that does not mean that an advanced Dolphin actually *is* a person.[7])

Many might grant the premiss that there is a spectrum between *A* and *Z* such that there are no *morally* relevant differences between *adjacent* members of the spectrum. However, they would deny the conservative's conclusion. They would insist that, from the fact that there are no morally relevant differences between *adjacent* members of the spectrum, it does *not* follow, and is simply not true, that there are no morally relevant differences between the end points of the spectrum. There are large differences between the fertilized ovum and the infant, and some are clearly of moral relevance. For example, the infant, but not the fertilized ovum, is sentient, feels pleasure and pain, experiences satisfaction and frustration, and is capable of forming attachments and expectations.

The preceding suggests a natural way of resisting the axiom of transitivity. One might urge that an entity's moral status is a function of its natural characteristics. One might then point out that, while small changes in an entity's natural characteristics will not affect its moral status, large changes can. Thus, considering each pair in turn, the natural differences between them may be so small that perhaps we *should* be morally indifferent between *A*'s death and *B*'s, *B*'s death and *C*'s, *C*'s death and *D*'s, and so on. However, we need not be indifferent between *A*'s death and *Z*'s. Instead, we can reject the axiom of transitivity, pointing out that *together* the small changes along the spectrum—each of which, by *itself*, is morally irrelevant—add up to large changes that are morally relevant.[8]

The preceding suggests a general explanation for failure of transitivity. How two outcomes compare *all things considered* depends on how they compare in terms of the relevant and significant factors for making that comparison.

---

[7] I here follow common usage, where 'person' means 'human being', which itself can be interpreted in various ways. Many philosophers use 'person' as a technical term, for example, to mean an entity with a serious right to life. On that usage, if two beings have the same moral status, and one is a person, so is the other.

[8] Cf. Derek Parfit, *Reasons and Persons* (Oxford: Clarendon Press, 1984), ch. 3, and especially his fascinating discussion of 'The Harmless Torturers' (78–82). Parfit shows that, given a certain belief many hold, one ought to accept the kind of position discussed here. However, Parfit's own view differs from the one noted here, and is the model for an alternative position I discuss next. See n.10 below.

Thus, if *different* factors were relevant and significant for comparing different outcomes, it could be true that even if *A* were better than *B*, and *B* better than *C*, in terms of the relevant and significant factors for comparing *those* alternatives, *A* might *not* be better than *C*, in terms of the relevant and significant factors for making *that* comparison. Notice, even if there is substantial overlap in the factors for comparing alternatives, as long as there is *some* difference intransitivity may arise. For example, suppose that factors *x* and *y* are each significant when comparing *A*, *B*, and *C*, but that another factor, *z*, is significant *only* when comparing *A* and *C*. Then it might be that, all things considered, *A* is better than *B* (regarding *x* and *y*), and *B* is better than *C* (regarding *x* and *y*), but *C* is better than *A*. This could be so if *C* were sufficiently better than *A* regarding *z* to outweigh the extent to which it was worse than *A* regarding *x* and *y*. So, the crucial question arises, can the factors that are relevant and significant for comparing different outcomes, all things considered, vary with the outcomes being compared? As our example illustrates, the answer seems to be 'yes'.

For many, the spectrum from fertilized ovum to infant exemplifies the fact that *together* a sufficient number of differences in degree can sometimes amount to a difference in kind. But then, it should not be surprising that transitivity fails along this spectrum, since the relevant factors for comparing alternatives merely differing in degree may differ from those for comparing alternatives differing in kind. So, if there is a spectrum from *A* to *Z*, such that *A* and *B*, *B* and *C*, . . . , *X* and *Y*, and *Y* and *Z* merely differ in degree, while *A* and *Z* differ in kind, then there may be good reason for being indifferent between *A* and *B*, *B* and *C*, *C* and *D*, and so on, yet for not being indifferent between *Z* and *A*. After all, the relevant and significant factors for comparing 'distant' alternatives *A* and *Z* may differ from those for comparing the intervening 'adjacent' alternatives.

I have shown how one could respond to the conservative's argument by rejecting transitivity. Alternatively, one might respond by disputing the argument's key premiss that the physical or psychological differences between adjacent members of the spectrum are of *no* moral significance. This response might be put as follows.

Grant that there is a spectrum from fertilized ovum to infant such that the physical or psychological differences between adjacent members of the spectrum are smaller, in absolute terms, than the physical or psychological differences between Jim and Joe. Still, such differences can have moral weight when comparing embryos or foetuses, even *if* they lack moral weight when comparing adult humans.[9] Specifically, although, phenomenologically,

---

[9] Note, one need not grant the 'if' clause. Perhaps small physical or psychological differences always have *some* weight, but the weight is negligible, or lexically outranked by other factors, in the case of normal adults.

it *seems* that, for any stage of development, we should be indifferent between the death of that stage, and the death of the stage obtaining one day later, in fact, the small differences in development must have *some* moral significance. Unfortunately, the moral significance is so small as to be intuitively imperceptible, and this explains our willingness to mistakenly accept the claim that, considered just by themselves, we should be indifferent between whether an embryo or foetus dies one day earlier or later.

On this view, an entity's moral status is a function of, or supervenient on, its natural characteristics in such a way that even small, seemingly trivial, differences in natural characteristics can make a difference to an entity's moral status. But, not surprisingly, if the natural differences are small enough, the difference in moral status will not be intuitively noticeable. This explains how the key premiss of the conservative's argument can seem so plausible, yet still be false.

The crux of this response is to argue that B's death really *is* worse than A's, though, unfortunately, imperceptibly so. Similarly, C's death is imperceptibly worse than B's, D's is imperceptibly worse than C's, and so on. This, then, explains the widely held judgement that Z is clearly worse than A. After all, together, a series of small imperceptible changes can add up to a quite significant, and easily perceptible, change.[10] So, just as a sequence of relatively small developmental changes from Z to A eventually results in major physical and psychological differences, a sequence of imperceptible moral changes from Z to A eventually results in major differences in moral status between the fertilized ovum and the infant.

The preceding seems to support both transitivity and the view that an infant's death is much worse than a fertilized ovum's. However, ultimately, I think such a response fails; for, as we shall see next, the conservative's argument can be recast to avoid this response.

Suppose one grants that the moral status of an embryo or foetus is constantly changing throughout development. So, we suppose, even for *adjacent* members of the spectrum from A to Z, the death of the later member will in fact be worse than the death of the earlier one. Surely, the difference in moral status between adjacent members of the spectrum is slight. It is *so* slight, in fact, that it is intuitively imperceptible. This is why we thought, wrongly we are now supposing, that B's death is as bad as A's.

But, then, let us not simply compare A's death to B's. Let us compare

---

[10] My discussion here is indebted to Parfit, *Reasons and Persons*, ch. 3, esp. §29. Parfit notes the natural, but deeply mistaken, tendency to treat small or imperceptible benefits, harms, or chances as if they were *no* benefit, harm, or chance. He then illustrates that serious consequences can result from this mistake, since, together, many small or imperceptible benefits, harms, or chances can add up to very large benefits, harms, or chances.

A's death to the combination of B's death and another event that is perceptibly bad; one, let us say, that is clearly of some significance, though still relatively minor. Suppose, for example, one of two outcomes will occur. If A' occurs, a particular individual will die as a newborn infant, but there will be no other bad consequences. If B' occurs, the same individual will die one day before birth and, in addition to this, a student in a class will be accidentally misled about the timing of an exam. This will result in the student failing, ultimately causing both her and her parents significant aggravation and worry. Which outcome, if either, would be worse, A' or B'?

Considering the death of the individual by itself, there is little reason to prefer A' or B'. As noted previously, most would intuitively think that there is *no* difference between the moral status of the individual's death in A' or B'. But even granting, for the sake of argument, that the individual's death would be better in B' than A', since the extent to which it is better is so slight as to be imperceptible, it seems we should grant that A'—which is *clearly* better than B' with respect to the plight of the student and her parents—would be better than B', *all things considered*. The moral loss involved in postponing the individual's death by one day—assuming there is any—would be more than offset by the moral gain involved in the student's not being misled about the exam.

Next compare C' with B'. C' stands to B' as B' stands to A'. Specifically, C' involves the death of the foetus one day earlier than would occur in B'; it also involves the same student being misled with the same consequences as would occur in B', together with a second student being misled with analogous consequences. All things considered, B' would be better than C'. Grant, if one wants, that the death of the foetus in B' would be slightly—even if imperceptibly—worse than its death in C'. Still, if the same foetus is going to die anyway, and it is just a question of whether it is *one* day earlier or later, there is precious little to choose between B' and C' on that account. On the other hand, B' is clearly better than C', in terms of its sparing one student and her parents significant aggravation and worry. So here, as before, it seems the moral loss involved in postponing the foetus's death by one day—assuming there is any—would be more than offset by the moral gain involved in avoiding the extra aggravation and worry.

It is clear how this argument proceeds. D' is compared with C', E' with D', and so on. Eventually, Z' is compared with Y'. With each comparison the later member of the spectrum stands to the earlier one as B' stands to A', and C' stands to B'. With each comparison the extent to which the earlier member of the spectrum is clearly better than the later one outweighs the extent to which it is (imperceptibly) worse. Correspondingly, it appears that, all things considered, A' is better than B', B' better than C', ..., and Y' better than Z'.

Suppose we accept the pair-wise rankings of the spectrum from A' to Z'. Transitivity then entails that A' is better than Z'. But this is hard to accept. A' is an outcome involving the death of a newborn infant. Z' is an outcome involving the death of a fertilized ovum, together with the aggravation and worry of 270 students and their parents.[11] I think A' is much worse than Z', and I think most people share this view.

One can see how this revised argument supports the conservative's position. Most believe that human life is enormously valuable. It is so valuable that the sort of aggravation and worry that accompanies failing an exam—however real and significant in its own way—counts as virtually nothing in comparison with a human life. So, the fact that 270 (or 2,700!) students and their parents might suffer aggravation and worry gives us very little reason to think Z' worse than A'. Correspondingly, the only reason we might think Z' worse than A' is if we thought the death of the fertilized ovum was as bad, or at least *almost* as bad, as the death of the infant. If we thought that, then we might think the extra aggravation and worry could 'break the tie' or 'tip the balance' between two alternatives that were otherwise virtually on a par. I suggest, then, that, if transitivity commits us to the view that Z' is worse than A', we should admit that the moral status of a fertilized ovum is (roughly) on a par with that of a newborn infant.

As already indicated, I believe a fertilized ovum's moral status is *not* on a par with a newborn infant's. Correspondingly, I believe Z' is much better than A'. Those sharing these views must respond to the recast version of the conservative's argument in one of three ways.

First, one might deny the premiss of imperceptibility. Specifically, one might claim that the difference of even one day in the development of a foetus clearly makes a much larger moral difference to the goodness of an outcome than does the aggravation and worry caused by failing an exam. So, one might claim that, even intuitively, A' is worse than B', B' is worse than C', and so on. On this view, transitivity entails that A' is worse than Z', exactly as those rejecting the conservative conclusion believe.

Secondly, one might deny that imperceptible differences in the moral status of two beings can be outweighed by perceptible moral differences of the sort in question. Perhaps the sort of reasons connected with the basic moral status of a being are so much weightier than those connected with aggravation and worry that even imperceptible differences in the former kind of reason count much more than large perceptible differences in the latter. On this view,

---

[11] I here assume a normal gestation period of 270 days.

reflection reveals that A' is worse than B', B' worse than C', and so on, even if it is not intuitively apparent that this is so.

Finally, one can reject transitivity. One can grant that A' is better than B', B' better than C', and so on, but deny that A' is better than Z'.

I favour the third response. The first is implausible. It simply is not the case that intuitively A' is worse than B'.[12] The second response bites the bullet prematurely. Do we really believe that one day makes a significant difference in the moral status of an embryo or foetus? And, if we think there are a few key days of rapid, morally relevant, physical or psychological development, then recast the argument in terms of hours, or minutes, for those crucial days. Surely, there will be *some* spectrum from A to Z, such that, morally, we should be virtually indifferent between adjacent members of the spectrum. But, if we are virtually indifferent between adjacent members of the spectrum, then should not we rank outcomes that would affect adjacent members the same on the basis of other moral factors present in those outcomes?

But how can we give up transitivity? As we have seen, we can give it up, and should give it up, if the factors that are relevant and significant for comparing different alternatives all things considered vary depending on the alternatives being compared.

Since the moral status of *adjacent* members of the spectrum from A to Z is roughly on a par, one might, other things being equal, just flip a coin to rank alternatives that affect adjacent members equally. Consequently, it would not take much in terms of other things not being equal to tip the balance one way or the other. But the end points of the spectrum seem radically different. The difference between A and Z is, seemingly, not merely one of degree, but one of kind. Correspondingly, we may think that the moral status of an infant is *so* much greater than that of a fertilized ovum that only the most serious of moral factors could lead us to rank an alternative involving an infant's death as better than one involving a fertilized ovum's death— factors that must themselves be morally on a par with human life. Thus, as we have seen, factors that might be perfectly relevant and significant for the first kind of ranking—such as aggravation and worry—might not be relevant or significant for the latter kind of ranking. Hence, there is no reason for transitivity to hold.

Let me conclude this section by considering one further response to my argument. Some may try to block the revised conservative argument by appealing to Frances Kamm's 'Principle of Irrelevant Alternatives'.[13] Kamm

---

[12] Perhaps one day our intuitions will sufficiently change in the light of philosophical argument and theory that the first response will no longer seem implausible. But that day is not yet here and I, for one, do not expect it to arrive soon.

[13] My discussion here draws on F. M. Kamm, *Morality, Mortality*, vol. i: *Death and Whom to Save from It* (New York: Oxford University Press, 1993). Quotes are from 146–8.

suggests that, if we can only save Jim or Joe, treating them as equals requires that we 'use a random decision procedure to select between them'. She further suggests that, even if saving Jim were the only way also to 'save a patch of beautiful flowers, which gives pleasure to a great many people', so that saving Jim would maximize utility, 'it would be wrong to decide against Joe and for Jim solely for the sake of this extra utility'. Kamm believes that the moral requirement to treat people as equals precludes our appealing to 'irrelevant utilities' in deciding whom to save.

Similarly, some might argue that, if we had to choose between saving one embryo or foetus, and another that was only one day older, we could not do so on the basis of an 'irrelevant utility', such as whether saving one would enable some student and her parents to avoid aggravation and worry. Hence, it might be argued, if we should choose alternatives without regard to irrelevant utilities, we should choose between A', B', C', etc., solely on the basis of the moral status of the embryos and foetuses themselves. Thus, we could favour B' over A', C' over B', and so on, on the view that, for any stage of development, it would be imperceptibly better for an embryo or foetus at that stage to die than for one that was a day older to die.

Many questions could be raised about the notion of an 'irrelevant utility'. But I am sympathetic to Kamm's point. It expresses a powerful deontological position. Still, it is important to recognize that the point is *not* relevant to my recast conservative argument. Kamm's point rests on a distinction between the right and the good. My recast argument rests on claims about the good, not claims about the right. Perhaps we should not *choose* between two embryos or foetuses on the basis of 'irrelevant utilities' such as aggravation and worry from a failed exam. But this does not mean that the extra utility is irrelevant regarding which outcome is *better*.

Kamm, herself, is clear about this. She notes that 'we may permissibly decide against tossing an ordinary coin to select between Jim and Joe and in favor of tossing a *magic extra-utility* coin that causes extra utility when it is tossed— it might, for example, cause flowers to grow wherever it lands'. Kamm's fundamental concern is that we be sure to treat Jim and Joe as equals by giving them an equal chance. But she clearly recognizes that an outcome where one of them is saved *and* there are beautiful flowers would be better than an outcome where one is saved and there are no beautiful flowers. Indeed, she would produce the former outcome, rather than the latter, as long as she could do so consistently with treating both Jim and Joe as equals.

I conclude that the Principle of Irrelevant of Utilities may be important for how we can permissibly *choose* between outcomes such as A', B', C', etc. But the principle is not relevant to the ranking of those outcomes. A' is better than B', even if we could only permissibly bring about A' with the help of a magic-utility coin.

3. CONCLUSION

Elsewhere, I have argued that examples like the preceding one cannot be simply dismissed as yet another Sorites Paradox.[14] They require a different analysis and response from those typically given to Sorites Paradoxes. I have also argued that such examples are much more worrisome than examples of intransitivity commonly discussed by psychologists, economists, and game theorists. I shall not repeat those arguments here. Instead, let me conclude with a few brief observations.

Some people find my arguments plausible, but continue to insist that 'all-things-considered better than' *must* be transitive. They believe the axiom of transitivity is a logical, or conceptual, truth. On their view, my arguments may establish the intransitivity of some *other* notion, and this other notion may itself be of central concern for moral and practical reasoning. However, my arguments must fail to establish its purported conclusion, as *no* arguments could succeed.

I have three reactions to this position. First, even if one grants that it is part of the meanings of the words that 'all-things-considered better than' is transitive, this would not show that my arguments necessarily fail. My arguments may succeed, if the wider lesson to be drawn from them is that the notion of 'all-things-considered better than' is incoherent.[15] Perhaps my arguments demonstrate that, while certain elements of the notion entail transitivity, others support intransitivity. We would then be compelled to reject, or revise, our notion of 'all-things-considered better than'.

Secondly, a conceptual defence of the axiom of transitivity can result only in a hollow victory. Such a defence succeeds only by robbing the axiom of its force. If there is no way the axiom could fail to be true—by definition or as a matter of 'logic'—then I fear it lacks substance. A linguistic truth that is unfalsifiable is trivial, and not a useful substantive principle for guiding and assessing actions or beliefs.[16]

Thirdly, I have little interest in terminological disputes. The crucial question is whether a central element of moral and practical reasoning

[14] See my 'A Continuum Argument for Intransitivity'. That article was originally joined with this chapter as a single piece, but, since the combined work was too long for this volume, I divided it into separate parts. Correspondingly, some of this chapter's issues are dealt with further in that article. In addition, this chapter's conclusion is taken from that article, as that article's conclusion was originally written to go with this material.

[15] This lesson of my arguments against transitivity was first suggested to me—though not necessarily endorsed—by my colleague Baruch Brody. Many others have since echoed this suggestion.

[16] I raise a similar worry about John Broome's defence of the sure-thing principle in 'Weighing Goods: Some Questions and Comments', *Philosophy and Public Affairs*, 23 (1994), 350–80.

involves an intransitive relation. If my arguments lead us to recognize that this question's answer is 'yes', it matters not what we *call* this element. If people want to use 'all-things-considered better than' solely to express a transitive relation, so be it. We then need another expression to refer to the relation obtaining between my example's outcomes.

Derek Parfit has suggested the notion of *choiceworthiness*.[17] 'Choiceworthiness', unlike 'all–things–considered better than', is an (essentially comparative) intransitive relation. According to Parfit, my example seemingly illustrates that *A* is more choiceworthy than *B*, *B* more choiceworthy than *C*, . . . , and *Y* more choiceworthy than *Z*, yet *Z* is more choiceworthy than *A*. What are the implications of this seeming intransitivity? *Given what these outcomes involve*, which outcome is *most* choiceworthy? Which of these outcomes ought we to choose or prefer morally, or rationally? As Parfit recognizes, these questions are just as pressing whether we are using the terminology of 'choiceworthiness' or 'all-things-considered better than'. Thus, how we choose to *describe* my example will not affect its substance or the significance of its claims.

Some find my arguments compelling, and in the face of them express a willingness, or even eagerness, simply to abandon transitivity. More generally, they are prepared to abandon outcome comparisons *tout court*, and with it consequentialist reasoning in both the moral and practical realms. I am pleased with the first half of this response, but stunned at the second. For reasons briefly indicated in my introduction, I am convinced that those making this response have not thought seriously enough about what is involved if we make such moves.

Derek Parfit believes that I substantially misrepresent and understate my arguments, in so far as I focus on them as arguments for intransitivity. On his view, my arguments are not merely a threat to the axiom of transitivity; they are amongst the most powerful arguments yet produced for scepticism about practical reasoning. The idea is *roughly* the following. Rational choice involves responding to reasons. Positive or desirable features of an alternative provide reasons for promoting that alternative. Negative or undesirable features provide reasons for avoiding that alternative. To choose rationally between alternatives is to respond 'appropriately' to the alternatives' positive and

---

[17] In discussion. I have worries about this expression, but they need not concern us here. Roger Crisp has made the interesting observation that this notion of 'choiceworthiness' comes from Aristotle's *Nicomachean Ethics*. I, myself, think there are interesting similarities between Parfit's views and Aristotle's—for example, both involve a rational principle—but also important dissimilarities—for example, for Aristotle the notion of choiceworthiness only ranges over alternatives that we can produce or prevent, whereas for Parfit the notion of choiceworthiness might allow us to rank alternatives over which we have no control. A detailed analysis of the relation between Aristotle and Parfit's conceptions of choiceworthiness would be instructive, but lies beyond this chapter's scope.

negative features, giving each their 'due' weight. The rational choice will be the one for which, overall, there are the best, or strongest, reasons (taking *all* of the relevant features into account). But the notion of best, or strongest, reasons seems to presume a scale for which transitivity holds. How can we choose between *A*, *B*, and *C* on the basis of which has the best, or strongest, reasons, if *A* is better, or more choiceworthy, than *B*, *B* is better, or more choiceworthy, than *C*, and yet *C* is better, or more choiceworthy, than *A*?

Parfit believes that rational choice involves responding to the best, or strongest, reasons. His worry, I think, is that my argument ultimately threatens the notion that there even are, or could be, 'best' or 'strongest' reasons to underlie, and justify, rational decisions.

Parfit wants to resist scepticism about practical reasoning. So do I. The question is how best to do this. Perhaps my arguments can be refuted. If not, perhaps their scope can be carefully circumscribed so as to quarantine their implications.

Because so much is at stake in this debate, I am acutely aware that here, as elsewhere in philosophy, *no* arguments can force a conclusion that we are unable or unwilling to accept.[18] But, unfortunately, while I am aware of several ways of defending transitivity against my arguments, each requires abandoning views that many care about deeply.

---

[18] I am reminded here of, and sympathetic to, Thomas Nagel's methodological remark in the preface to *Mortal Questions* (Cambridge: Cambridge University Press, 1979), p. x. 'Given a knockdown argument for an intuitively unacceptable conclusion, one should assume there is probably something wrong with the argument that one cannot detect.' But I take some comfort in his immediately following qualifying remark 'though it is also possible that the source of the intuition has been misidentified,' as well as in his preceding comment, 'I believe one should trust problems over solutions, intuition over arguments, and pluralistic discord over systematic harmony. Simplicity and elegance are never reasons to think that a philosophical theory is true: on the contrary, they are usually grounds for thinking it false.'

REPLIES

James Griffin

When I first arrived in Oxford, I went to a meeting of a student society addressed by G. R. G. Mure, then the Warden of Merton College and the last representative of early twentieth-century idealism in the University. His subject was Gilbert Ryle's book *The Concept of Mind*, and Ryle replied. Mure thought that Ryle's hidden assumptions were where the trouble began. 'Tell us your assumptions, Gilbert,' Mure at one point said. As near as I remember, Ryle replied, 'I think that assumptions are like halitosis. Better without them. Though your best friends won't tell you, your enemies might.'

In the new style Festschrift your best friends are invited to tell you. I am immensely grateful to all of the contributors to this volume, those who tell me and those who do not. But the new style Festschrift has its consequences. In fairness the honorand is also invited to have a say, while being provided with almost irresistible motive to accept. But to keep my say within reasonable bounds I have had to impose some restrictions upon myself. I have decided to comment only on the chapters that discuss my views. To the authors of the rest of the chapters I want to express not just my gratitude but also my gratification that so much good work is being published between these two covers.

1. WELL-BEING

I can see now that I made an expository blunder in my book *Well-Being*. I called the view about well-being that I was advancing there a 'desire account'. I openly hesitated over the label, but in the end I used it. Its inappropriateness then misled some of my readers, through no fault of theirs, and occasionally, far less excusably, misled me too.

I thought that there was an important truth in desire accounts that needed

championing. My thought ran like this. We cannot plausibly explain prudential values in terms of *actual* desires; the explanation would have to be in terms
of *informed* or *rational* desires. That being so, the crucial question is, *informed*
or *rational* in exactly what sense? Not in the sense that the desires are formed
merely without errors of facts or logic. A mad man who wants to count the
blades of grass in various lawns (to taken John Rawls's example) may make
no factual or logical mistakes, but the satisfaction of those desires of his need
by no means enhance his well-being (*VJ* 22–3).[1] The relevant desires have to
be 'informed' or 'rational' in a particularly strong sense—namely, formed in
proper appreciation of the nature of their object (*WB* 14).

It is here that I hesitated. If one puts the standard of 'informed' or 'rational' as high as that, does one any longer have a *desire* account (*WB* 26)? My
account seems to shift the real explanatory weight from the mere occurrence
of a desire and of its satisfaction onto the features or qualities of the objects
of desire. Then I give prominence to only a certain range of features or qualities (for example, accomplishment, enjoyment, certain kinds of understanding, and so on—the list of prudential values that I later compiled) (*WB* 67–8).

My point in *Well-Being*—and more emphatically and more clearly in *Value
Judgement*—was that the informed-desire account, fully worked out, effectively becomes a list account. What I mean by a 'list account' is very close to
what these days is more commonly called an 'objective list account'; the prudential values on the list form a general profile of the good-making features
that human life can characteristically realize (*WB* 114–15, 117–19). I do not
myself call it an *objective* list account because I think, along with many others,
that judgements about prudential values have both objective and subjective
features (*WB* 32–3; *VJ* 32–6). I record in *Well-Being* the journey that desire
accounts must take. The best account of welfare

has to move from an actual-desire to an informed-desire account; and it has to set the
standards for a desire's being 'informed' in a place not too distant from an objective
list account. This is a stiffer standard for 'informed' . . . than other writers have wished
to adopt, so much so that it might seem that I should use a different label.   (*WB*
33–4)

I was foolish not to.

Why didn't I? For two reasons. First, I thought that the venerable question,
'Valuable because desired, or desired because valuable?', was to be answered,
'Neither'. Not only is there no priority between value and desire; the nature
of the one is not independent of the other. If something is valuable, we must
be able to cite a feature it has that makes its desirability intelligible; otherwise,
the notion of value loses hold. And the cited feature has to be generally intelligible as one that makes things desirable. One cannot make something desir-

---

[1] Rawls used the example in *A Theory of Justice* (Oxford: Clarendon Press, 1972), 432–3.

able just by adopting it as one's own personal aim (*WB* 27). Still, understanding something, such as accomplishment, to be valuable is not without a
motivational component. There is no adequate explanation of accomplishment's being a *desirability* feature without appeal to a normal human desire
to go for what has that feature (*WB* 29).

My second reason was that not every value on the list is valuable to everyone. Any account of prudential values has to accommodate the important
fact of individual differences. Great accomplishment makes a characteristic
human life better. But, if an uncharacteristic person can accomplish great
things only at the cost of extreme anxiety, then that person may, if informed,
rightly desire to forgo great accomplishments.

So, what I saw as the advantage in keeping the label 'desire account' was
the stress it put on the essential role of desire in explaining prudential value:
that something's being prudentially valuable embodies characteristic human
desire, and that prudential values must always be valuable to a (possibly idiosyncratic) individual. Neither reason now seems to be enough to justify using
a label that in other ways is so misleading.

These reflections are prompted by Wayne Sumner's chapter. I think that the
fusillade that he directs at standard desire accounts is deadly accurate, but my
own informed-desire account in *Well-Being*, which is his chief target, is so
non-standard that it comes through the fire slightly wounded but still very
much alive. I think my label, 'desire account', has misled him.

Let me start, though, with how it misled me too. Sumner rightly observes
that I meant my informed-desire view as a formal, not a substantive, account
of well-being. I meant it to explain not what actually contributes to a good
life but what it is for something to be prudentially valuable for someone. But
a list account is, in an important way, a *substantive* account of well-being; the
list consists of components of a good life. More standard desire accounts, in
contrast to my non-standard one, are best understood, I still think, as *formal*
accounts. What was not clear to me in *Well-Being*, obscured by my wish to go
on calling my view an informed-desire account, was how the development
that I thought a desire account had to go through in order to make it more
plausible also made it less formal. It remains formal in the marginal sense that
it says that what makes a life prudentially valuable is given in a list of substantive values (to be specified). And, of course, a list account leaves room for
metaethical explanations of how we know what those values are, and of what
their metaphysical status is. But what it does not leave room for is any further,
merely formal, account of 'what it is for something to be valuable for
someone', of the sort the standard desire accounts supply.

I think that my label 'desire account' misled Sumner, too. It is common
ground between Sumner and me that not all desires, when satisfied, increase
well-being. Sumner therefore presses the question: 'Which do?'. He presses it

against desire accounts generally, mine included, because he thinks that no satisfactory answer is forthcoming. I said in *Well-Being* that only those desires count that enter our lives in certain ways, and my description of those ways Sumner finds, understandably, 'pretty vague and undeveloped'. As my account is a kind of list account, there is another, and more helpful, answer available to me: only those desires count the satisfaction of which is subsumable under one or other of the value notions on the list. This, of course, constitutes a radical shift of importance from desire to its objects, but that I admitted in *Well-Being* is what my non-standard account makes.

Take Sumner's example of the brother I want cured of his debilitating disease. As my brother breaks off contact with me when he sails to Papua New Guinea in search of a cure, how can the fact that he is indeed cured there make me any better off? It satisfies my keen desire. But can it possibly be thought thereby to enhance my well-being? I, like Sumner, think not. But on a plausible list account it would not enhance my well-being. As I do not hear about the cure, I can get no pleasure from it (an item on the list). As I had no hand in it, it is no accomplishment of mine (another item on the list). And so on.

This reply will not meet quite all of Sumner's objections. I think that he will want to re-aim one or two of his rifles at my sort of list account. For instance, his point about posthumously satisfied desires could simply be turned around into a point about posthumous accomplishments. In *Well-Being* I said that it would not be absurd for Bertrand Russell to think that, if his work for nuclear disarmament had, after his death, actually reduced the risk of nuclear war, his last years would have been more worthwhile, and his life more valuable prudentially, than if it all proved futile. I still think that a posthumous accomplishment can enhance the prudential value of a person's life. Sumner does not. He allows that, seen from a perfectionist point of view, a posthumous accomplishment might make a life better, *but* without the person's being made better off by it. After death, he says, 'Nothing can ever again go badly (or, alas, well) for us.' True enough. But what we *have* done may not fully have worked itself out or fully have emerged into the light of day until after our deaths. But, Sumner insists, even if it eventually emerged that Russell had indeed reduced the risk of nuclear war, Russell himself would not have been made better off. But the form of words 'made him better off' is not a neutral one here; it suggests something that the person is aware of. It fits comfortably with what I called the Experience Requirement, which may be why Sumner chose the expression. But the expressions 'well-being' and 'the prudential value of a life' do not have this strong suggestion. Posthumous accomplishments might sit more comfortably with them.

This raises important issues. Perhaps my list account and Sumner's own happiness account are not clear-cut competitors, but accounts of somewhat different things. Perhaps we are not clear precisely what either is meant to be an account of. The terms 'well-being', 'the prudential value of a life', 'the quality of a life', and so on do not pick out a known subject about which we then turn out to agree or disagree. What we say about 'well-being' (and the rest) will partly fix the subject we think important to elucidate as well as offer an elucidation of it. What is more, there may be several notions here that our present vocabulary fails to discriminate but that different ones of us think important to elucidate. We find one sort of fracture of the notion of the quality of life in medical ethics; different conceptions are appropriate to different kinds of decision, some decisions served best by mere indicators of well-being (and some by only a selection of such indicators) and others by the fundamental notion itself (see DB). But what I have in mind here is a different sort of fracture—into several different fundamental notions. This is a subject that needs more said about it, but unfortunately I have no more now to say. In any case, it is only the first of several questions that will emerge in the course of these comments that I shall have simply to hope to return to some other time.

2. THE INCOMMENSURABILITY OF VALUES

Thirty years ago the discussion of the incommensurability of values was in a poor state. There was disagreement, and sometimes confusion, about what was at issue. And there was little argument or investigation: many of the protagonists thought that the truth was obvious and had merely to be asseverated, perhaps with an example or two. Things are better now. There is a measure of agreement that the important issue is about the *incomparability* of values (see I 35–6).[2] And there seems to be greater acceptance that the truth is far from obvious.

John Broome and I largely agree about this subject. We agree on what the important issue is and in many of our conclusions about it. None the less, Broome's present paper shows that we approach the subject from rather different angles, and this itself produces some confusion. It seems to me to lead Broome at times to misunderstand what I am about. Broome defines the 'incommensurability' of values as their 'incomparability'. I certainly have no quarrel with that. But I deliberately start, not from this sensible stipulative definition, but from the much broader and confused use of the term 'incommensurability' in recent philosophy. Compared to that, Broome narrows the subject. He narrows it first by confining attention to incomparability,

---

[2] See also Ruth Chang, 'Introduction', in Ruth Chang (ed.), *Incommensurability, Incomparability, and Practical Reason* (Cambridge, Mass.: Harvard University Press, 1997).

ignoring other senses that philosophers have attached to the term (*WB* 83–92). Then he narrows it still further by interpreting incomparability in connection with what he calls the 'standard configuration'. The 'standard configuration' is the comparison of the value of one option taken as a stand- ard (say, a certain career in the army) with a continuous range of values of options of another kind (say, various possible careers in the church), which yields division of the church careers into those worse than the standard army career, those better than it, and either a single option neither better nor worse or an 'intermediate zone' of several such options. Broome shows that, if there is a single option, it is equal to the standard; if there are several, none is equal to it. Broome's concentration on the standard configuration reduces the ques- tion whether there are incommensurable values to the question whether there is only a single option between the better group and the worse group (hence comparability) or an intermediate zone of several options (hence incompa- rability). But this approach rules out those who, while accepting that incom- mensurability is incomparability, wish to deny that any value of a certain *type* can be compared to a certain other type (see e.g. *WB* 81–5)—the rather crude 'chalk-and-cheese' sort of incomparability that some think appears at type level. (Broome could, of course, accommodate type incomparability in his standard configuration by allowing the limiting case in which the intermedi- ate zone contains all possible options of the value-type in question, but as he actually defines the standard configuration this case is ruled out.) I say in *Well- Being* that the chalk-and-cheese sort of incomparability is implausible; it is hard to find two values such that no amount of one can be compared to any amount of the other (*WB* 80). Broome says that this is beside the point. So it is if one believes, as Broome does, that the only interesting question is about comparability between tokens. But not everyone does, so it is not beside *their* point. Also, Broome says that I seem not to have recognized clearly enough that it is value-tokens not value-types that need to be ordered. I wanted to talk about both.

But these are minor misunderstandings of intention. Let me come to Broome's important question. Both he and I think that there are cases—his example of careers in the army and the church is a plausible one—in which, to put it in his terms, there will be an intermediate zone. There will be a church career that we cannot rank as better or worse than a certain army career. There will be other church careers of which the same is true, although we can still rank the church careers against one another (*WB* 80–1). These cases consti- tute a breakdown in comparability, and a breakdown in comparability threat- ens a breakdown in practical rationality. If we cannot rank two such options as to better, worse, or equal, we seem to have lost any rational basis for choos- ing between them. In *Well-Being* I did not take this threat very seriously. This phenomenon appears, I thought, only when the options get close to one another in value. They are, I said, 'roughly equal'; so for nearly all practical purposes they can be ordered (*WB* 96–8). Rough equality can, as far as choice goes, be regarded as equality. There are intermediate zones, but they are narrow.

Why did I think so? All the cases that I could think of, including the sort of example that Broome uses, seemed to me intuitively to be narrow enough zones to justify my label 'rough equality'. Broome suggests that I offer one argument for my conclusion: namely, that incommensurability is vagueness. What, in fact, I say is that rough equality is vagueness (*WB* 81, 96–8), and, as I do not restrict incommensurability to the intermediate zone, I do not think that incommensurability itself is vagueness. In any case, it was not a logical feature of these cases, vagueness, that moved me, but, for better or worse, my intuitions about them. The intermediate zone, my impression was, is narrow. My 'argument' was no weightier than that.

I am grateful to Broome for showing me that my assumption is less than obvious. And if the intermediate zone turns out to be wide, there is after all a serious threat to practical rationality. Broome's own intuition is that the zone is likely to be narrow when we compare similar types of thing (say, joining the Northumberland Rifles versus the Fifth Lancers), but wide when we are comparing different kinds of thing (a church career versus an army career). The nub of his argument is this: 'A mediocre career in the church may not be definitely worse than a career in the army, and a successful career in the church may not be definitely better than a career in the army. But a successful career in the church is much better than a mediocre one. It follows that not all careers in the incommensurate zone are roughly equally as good as a career in the army.'

He challenges me to show otherwise: 'we need from Griffin an argument why this [intermediate] zone should be narrow.' Fair enough. I did not give one; what moved me were my intuitions about examples. But, of course, what moves Broome is his intuition about the example he presents. We must be wary of intuitions. They can be induced by trivial matters such as the rhetorical flourishes in the description of the case; the identification of, and deliberation with, prudential values is unfamiliar territory to us, and we therefore do not have rich experience about them to fall back on. Could we actually encounter a case of the sort Broome describes—with the church careers, though not better or worse than the army career, very different in value from one another?

We are not confined to comparing a church career and an army career on that fairly high level of generality; we can break them down into a series of more manageable comparisons. On the level of generality of whole careers, their comparison does indeed look uncomfortably close to chalk and cheese. That, no doubt, is why Broome chose this example. But as a good life can be broken down into various prudential values (*WB* 64–8; *VJ* 29–30), so can a good career. A career will be good, or not, as it realizes certain goods—enjoyment, accomplishment, autonomy, and so on. Suppose, to start with a simple case, we can compare the army career and the two church careers along a single dimension of value: namely, how enjoyable they would be. Of course, we are often uncertain as to how careers will actually work out. But let us, as Broome does, put this familiar kind of uncertainty aside: suppose we can predict how each career will progress. All that we then have to do is to compare the value of outcomes that we can safely predict. How fine can our judgements about amounts of enjoyment in the outcomes be? No doubt, often they can be only fairly rough. The things we enjoy fall into radically different kinds, and that will sometimes present problems of comparison. But is it plausible to think that, with this full knowledge of outcomes, we might finally decide that the two church careers were neither more nor less enjoyable than the army career but that one church career was *much* more enjoyable than the other? That seems to me far from clear.

Of course, that was a simplified case, so let us take a more complex one. Suppose that two dimensions of value are relevant: enjoyment and accomplishment. Does that change the scene radically? Suppose that the army career would be more fun but, as we are in a time of domestic and foreign peace, offers little scope for contributing to the good of others. And suppose that the two church careers would be less fun but offer great scope for this sort of contribution. Many-valued comparisons are likely to be more difficult than single-valued ones. But why? No doubt, it is *partly* because trade-offs between very different values, such as enjoyment and accomplishment, are difficult to make. But we must not exaggerate the difficulty; that would just be to manipulate our intuitions in the direction of incomparability. When we first judge that, say, accomplishment is valuable, we also, as part of that judgement, acquire the ability to recognize to some extent how valuable various of its instances are. Similarly for enjoyments, or any other prudential value. Belief that something is prudentially valuable runs into belief about why it is valuable, which runs into belief about how valuable various instances of it are (see *MV* 107–8). And there is a single standard behind these judgements about prudential value: how much they contribute to the quality of a life. We can, on this basis, go quite far in comparing instances of enjoyment with instances of accomplishment. It is by no means clear, I think, what the limits of these comparisons are. If that is so, then it is by no means clear how wide the intermediate zone will turn out to be. And sometimes, no doubt, many-valued comparisons are especially difficult because we have such an inadequate understanding of prudential values. Enjoyment (pleasure, happiness) presents difficulties that have received some attention in the course of the history of philosophy. Accomplishment is unclear in definition and controversial as to importance. These shortcomings in our understanding are likely to present problems to single-valued comparisons, but the problems might be especially acute in many-valued ones. But these difficulties are not necessarily permanent; they are not inherent in values or in our thought about them. They could be mitigated by improved understanding. So they cannot be the basis for a judgement about the breadth of the intermediate zone.

These remarks are well short of a defence of my rough-equality view. They are instead reasons to hold back from endorsing either Broome's hunch that the intermediate zone is wide or mine that it is narrow. I have not changed my hunch. But I am less confident about it, and I owe this Socratic improvement to Broome's powerfully reasoned chapter.

3. RECOGNITION AND REACTION

In some sense we *recognize* values; yet values also involve a motivationally coloured *reaction* of ours to the world. So much is obvious. But the central debate in metaethics is about how to explain the precise role of recognition and reaction. I think that, for the most part, philosophers have distinguished them far too sharply (*VJ* 36).

Jonathan Dancy is willing to grant that, on this subject, my heart is in the right place. It is just that I am faint-hearted. I aim merely to 'blur' the distinction 'a bit', while what is needed is 'transcending' it altogether.

I have, he says, various ways of blurring the distinction, all of which fail because they show at most that in real life recognition and reaction can get quite complexly tangled together. That is obviously not enough, because what gets tangled can still in principle be disentangled. Recognition and reaction survive my arguments still separable from one another. According to Dancy, I claim that to understand something as valuable is to grasp certain desirability features that it has, which owe their status as such to normal human desires and motivation. Yet, he replies, this claim does nothing to undercut the distinction between recognition and reaction; it is compatible with their being essentially distinct. I also offer the argument, he says, that desires can be rationally evaluated—for instance, by appeal to whether their object is worthwhile. But this, he again replies, is too weak a claim for my purposes; it could be made equally well by those who sharply distinguish recognition and reaction, but favour one side of the distinction.

I do not dispute the particular claims that Dancy attributes to me here, but I do want to dispute his belief that these are my 'arguments' for why recognition and reaction are in principle inseparable. My arguments are stronger.

Dancy is wrong that my aim is merely to 'blur' the distinction 'a bit', that it is merely to show that in real life recognition and reaction are 'mutually intertwined'. On the contrary, I say explicitly that the role of neither can, in itself, be understood without the other (*VJ* 32); the one is essentially involved in the other. 'It is not that the recognitional and reactive components are there in this complex mix as separable, still independent parts. That separation itself is what seems impossible to maintain' (*VJ* 56). Recognition is not itself reaction free, and vice versa (*VJ* 56). Recognition and reaction are 'inseparably mixed' (*VJ* 57). So my aim is considerably stronger than Dancy allows.

But aim is one thing, achievement another. If my arguments are stronger than Dancy allows, are they strong enough to justify the 'inseparability' conclusion? Why is reaction (say, desire) not recognition-free? Because, I say, not any desire is relevant to the nature of prudential values. The relevant sort of desire is the sort that is characteristic of intentional actions: these desires aim at the good (*VJ* 27). Furthermore, they are 'informed' or 'rational' desires, where (as I have said already) 'informed' or 'rational' has to be understood as representing an especially strong constraint: they are desires formed in proper—that is to say, correct—appreciation of the nature of their object (*VJ* 22–3). So the relevant sort of desire incorporates the recognition of something as valuable. What it incorporates is the *recognition* of a value, not just some sort or other of value *judgement*. The requirement that the relevant sort of desire be 'rational' has to be understood in a way that rules out, say, Hume's understanding of what it is correctly to judge something to be valuable. Recognizing a value is not just a matter of getting our beliefs about the natural world full and correct and then responding to the natural world, so understood, in a certain way. It is a matter of identifying a prudential value, which is something more than what Hume would regard as part of the natural world; and the identification need not appeal to a pre-existent, independent motivational set (*VJ* 24–5). It would be pointless to repeat the whole argument; I have said all that I now can in *Value Judgement*. The point here is that the content of this argument does not allow the response that Dancy imagines. Defenders of the separability of recognition and reaction cannot any longer appeal to a reaction that is recognition free. And they cannot fall back on an explanation of prudential value in terms of pure recognition, thereby preserving separability, because of the following consideration.

One cannot isolate valued objects in purely natural terms—at least on Hume's understanding of the domain of the natural—and then independently react to them (*VJ* 25). In this I am moved by arguments of Wittgenstein, McDowell, and others. The act of isolating the object is not itself neutral. 'One cannot here distinguish the identification of the object to be responded to and the response to it' (*VJ* 25). Pains, for instance, have both a phenomenological side to them and a reactive side (avoidance, alleviation, and so on). One learns the word 'pain' through grasping both their experienced side and their place in human life—that we want to avoid them, alleviate them, and so on. 'With pains, we do not recognize something to which we also, independently, react. Our reaction is a constituent of our recognition. The way pain fits into human life is part of the criterion for its being pain' (*VJ* 72). I argue the same point at some length about other prudential values—for example, accomplishment (*VJ* 24–7, 55–7). So defenders of separability cannot evade my point by evincing 'a preference for one side of the distinction', as Dancy puts it. They cannot say that prudential values are the object of pure recognition. There is no plausible form of recognition with such purity.

Those are my chief arguments in *Value Judgement* for inseparability, and they nowhere appear in Dancy's account of my views. And they do indeed address 'the core of the distinction'. Dancy drains the red blood from my arguments and then diagnoses anaemia. But he is examining the wrong body.

It is hard, I say, to get the role of recognition and reaction quite right. I attack the taste model and the perception model because they both make recognition and reaction too independent of one another. But Peter Railton thinks that I have not given the taste model its due, particularly not Hume's version of it. I have just paraded the anti-Humean strands of my thought in responding to Dancy, and it is precisely these that worry Railton.

I do not know of a more attractive account of a Humean taste model than Railton's. I am satisfied that a lot of what I want can be supplied by, or would work in harmony with, a Humean account. A Humean need not keep recognition and reaction sharply separate from one another. Our beliefs and desires need not be linguistically encoded and consciously present to the mind; many of them have a presence in our life only as dispositions. Understanding can sometimes be available only to someone with certain motivations, as when empathy is needed for understanding what others are feeling. Motivation can sometimes be available only to those with a certain understanding; for example, one first has to understand what autonomy is before one can aspire to it. And one of my central claims in *Value Judgement* can be fitted into the taste model. I claim that 'to see anything as prudentially valuable . . . we must see it as an instance of something generally intelligible as valuable . . .' (*VJ* 29). Hume too, Railton says, has his own way of accounting for 'the inherent generality of the value concepts'. It is the subject of his essay 'On the Standard of Taste'. To have authority, taste must be good, developed, educated. I can always announce, however feeble my powers of discrimination, which wine strikes my fancy. But, if I claim that a wine is good, I make a different kind of judgement. I make a judgement with inherent generality: I am claiming that there are things about the wine that anyone with an educated palate, working normally on the day, would also find makes it good. And, just as there can be correct, authoritative judgements about the quality of a wine, there can be correct, authoritative judgements about the quality of a life. The inherent generality of judgements of taste is to be found also in judgements of prudence.

Still, the question is not whether the Humean taste model can explain a lot but whether it can explain enough. It explains value, Railton says, in terms of a match or fit: a match, or fit, between features of the world (for example— the taste of a wine) and one's capacities and situation (an educated palate, though, as Railton would certainly agree, we need not be too highbrow here: some good things about wine are accessible to the capacities of an uneducated palate too). But the idea of a 'fit' between features of the world and capacities of conscious beings is, in itself, too general to tell us much about value, and Hume is more specific. The 'fit' is between features of the natural world, on the one side, and one's desires or attitudes or motivations, on the other. And our value judgements have standards that they must meet because our understanding of the natural world can, in various and subtle ways, be defective.

But this is one place where I worry that Hume has not given us enough. A person's understanding of the natural world can be without defect, and his logic flawless too, yet what he wants be without value. That is the point of the example of the unfortunate person who wants to count blades of grass. This is where I think we need to strengthen Hume. To repeat, values have to be accounted for in terms of desires formed in *proper* appreciation of the nature of their objects—an appreciation that involves the recognition of something valuable in characteristic lives of the beings making, or about whom others are making, a judgement. That is why my claim about the inherent generality of value concepts went on beyond what I just quoted. I said, 'to see anything as prudentially valuable . . . we must see it as an instance of something generally intelligible as valuable *and, furthermore as valuable for any (normal) human*' (*VJ* 29). It is that additional clause that Railton objects to. He finds it too limiting because it excludes *non-normal* humans—for example, the unfortunate person who wants to count blades of grass. (He finds it too limiting also because it excludes the *non-human*, but I shall come to that in a moment.) 'Would a severely retarded human among us', Railton asks, 'whose intrinsic interest in the activity of counting is one of the organizing themes of his life, not realize any prudential value in doing so?' Railton thinks he would; we can see this repetitive counting 'as an object of intrinsic concern and a source of prudential value'. If that were so, it would support Railton's more liberal *matching* account rather than my more restrictive account. I would not deny that we can understand this repetitive counting as an object of intrinsic concern; that is just a matter of understanding a certain kind of extreme abnormality. But can we understand mere counting *also* as being of value? Would it make the person better off? Well, yes, if it avoids distress, or brings contentment, or is enjoyed. But these are all values of characteristic human life. And, yes, if we give a certain interpretation to what seems to me the crucial part of Railton's description of the case. Perhaps this is 'one of the organizing themes of his life', because this crazy project of counting blades of grass is one thing that holds his life together. Described like that, then counting is indeed valuable; the alternative to keeping one's life together is its falling apart, and that is clearly bad for humans generally. We seem to need some such element in the story, some element that allows us to bring the case under one of the items on the list of prudential values for humans generally. If we were to take away all such elements, if we were to be left with nothing but an unelaboratable desire to count blades of grass, why should we think that the person is made better off by its fulfilment?

I suggested a moment ago that we not only need, but can also have, more than Hume gives us. This brings us to the heart of the matter. How are we to understand what goes on when we bring our critical resources to bear on our beliefs about the quality of a life? I use a familiar example that Railton comments on in his chapter. Suppose that I am a fool-like sort of person living for day-to-day pleasures but I am struck that you, a Socratic sort, seem to have a life with a point or weight that mine lacks (*VJ* 24–5). So I try to figure out what it is about your life that prompts my envy. It is not just a matter of your achieving things, because some achievements strike me as not the sort to give life point or weight. Nor is it just achieving things that are of themselves of some value, because not all values are the sort that endows their achievement with this particular weight-giving effect. I should be in search of a possible value. At all stages of this search I should have to use more than just factual description—at least on Hume's understanding of the boundaries of the factual. I should have to use notions such as giving life a *point*, stopping a life from being *wasted*, notions that are already heavily evaluative. I proposed in *Value Judgement* that this search has a successful outcome—the value I label 'accomplishment' (*VJ* 19–20). What seems to be going on here has more the character of a *recognition* of a human interest than merely a refined motivational *reaction* to something factually delineated. And this sort of recognition, I propose in the book, has its own standards of success, which may even confer a kind of realist status on interests such as accomplishment (*VJ* 59–66). We do seem to have more critical powers than Hume allows.

'But', Railton rightly insists, 'if my motivational set contained no potential positive sentiment that could be "recruited by" the information I gave about the Socratic life, then how could my novel exposure to the Socratic have any tendency to engage me . . . ?' The positive sentiment is there all along: we come to understand *accomplishments* by exploiting sentiment-laden notions such as what it is to *waste* one's life. That is just the point of the inseparability claim about recognition and reaction. But the Humean taste model talks simply about a match between factually correct desires and the object of the desires. It says nothing about other things that do indeed seem to be going on here: the recognition of something more than a fact, the recognition of a value or interest. This further recognitional element restricts the desires that can plausibly explain values and should not be left out of the story.

I have another worry, though it may be more a worry about Hume's taste model than the potentially subtler Humean taste model that Railton is developing. Hume's own version of the taste model, at any rate, assumes that we can isolate a valued object, such as accomplishment, in purely natural terms and then, independently, respond to it with approval or disapproval. But I doubt that we can (*VJ* 25–7), for reasons that I have already rehearsed in connection with Dancy's chapter.

I said that I would return to the second way in which Railton finds my account too limited: it excludes the non-human. To see anything as prudentially valuable, I do indeed say, one must see it as valuable for any (normal) human being. Railton's 'matching' account does not restrict prudential values to humans, and so seems to recognize a greater inherent generality in our value concepts than mine does. Railton attributes to me the view that normal human interests are built into the concept of prudential value. I see now that I have said many things that suggest that. But I did not *mean* that. In the book I was interested exclusively in *human* prudential values—so interested, perhaps, that I failed to make those chosen limits clear. What I meant was that to see anything as prudentially valuable to an individual human being one had to see it as valuable for any (normal) human being, that one had to be able to subsume it under one or other item on the list of prudential values for human beings. Of course, the list of prudential values for Martians or Venusians is likely to be different. I never intended to suggest that normal human interests are part of the very concept of prudential value.

This brings me to the large measure of agreement between Railton and me. Our views are very close. I still stand by the passage from *Well-Being* that Railton quotes at the end of his chapter: 'We have to find some mode of deliberation about values that sees them as they fit into particular lives. The manifestation of these objective values in particular lives is the deepest measure of value' (*WB* 55). People differ. What is good for one may not be for another. But this sovereignty of the individual is compatible with many different accounts of prudential value. Where Railton and I differ is in my wanting to put a few further restrictions on what he calls 'matching'. I am still attracted by my somewhat more restrictive account.

What I say about recognition and reaction has implications for the objectivity of prudential values. The dualism of 'objective' or 'subjective' values has its heuristic uses but is based, I say in *Value Judgement*, on a distinction between recognition and reaction that in reality is not really as sharp as the dualism needs it to be. Andrew Moore, however, thinks that my doubts about the dualism are exaggerated and that some of the implications I have drawn are *non-sequiturs*.

Moore applies the terms 'objective' and 'subjective' not only to prudential values themselves but also to what it is that makes them values. My interest in *Value Judgement* was in the latter. The taste model says that what makes something prudentially valuable is that it is desired. In contrast, the perception model holds that what is prudentially valuable is so independently of desire—typically, it is so simply in virtue of what it is, which we can 'perceive', and which will then prompt desire. As I understand him, Moore thinks that I move from the premiss that recognition and reaction, perception and desire, cannot be sharply separated in explanations of the nature of prudential goods (in short, from claims about how the objective/subjective duality applies to prudential values themselves) to the conclusion that they cannot be sharply separated in an account of what makes them good (in short, to claims about how the duality applies to the good-maker), which is a *non-sequitur*. I agree; it is a *non-sequitur*. Moore rightly says that simply from the assumption that perception and desire cannot be sharply separated it does not follow that desire has any role in making something good, and that from the mere claim that a prudential value has a desire-dependent nature one cannot infer that it has a desire-dependent good-maker. That seems right, because desire could enter into the nature of a value in many ways and its entering so as to make it valuable is only one of them. I should indeed have to say more to show that it enters in that particular, value-making, way. As Moore puts it, 'Griffin needs at least one additional premiss to get him . . . to non-objectivism about the good-maker.'

I think that I have supplied it. I do not just claim that desire enters into the nature of a prudential value, but say a great deal about the particular way in which it does. I use several examples, one of which, pain, I have already mentioned (*VJ* 34, 72–5). I say not only that the reactive element in pain is not

entirely separable from the recognitional element, but also that its inseparability comes from the fact that our standard of sameness in the sensations that
we group together under the concept 'pain' is partly that they are characteristically to be avoided, alleviated, and so on. Our reaction is a constituent of
our recognition. So part of the criterion for its use involves characteristic
human desire. Is that enough for desire to be part of what makes pain a disvalue, part of what gives it value status? I think it is. And I use the same argument with other examples (*VJ* 24–7, 54–9).

Moore characterizes prudential objectivism in these terms: 'goods are made
so by features or properties of theirs that are independent of whether they are
or would in certain circumstances be objects of desire.' But what my 'additional premiss' seeks to call into question is whether the crucial features or
properties *are* independent in this way. The property 'painful' does not seem
to be so.

I think that we should abandon the dualism of objective/subjective. Moore
does not. He continually expresses what is at issue between us in terms of these
two notions. My own conclusions about prudential goods (as opposed to
good-makers) are, he says, 'generally subjectivist'. And he sees me wanting
to argue for 'non-objectivism about the good-maker'. This is not, of course,
the way I see what is at issue between us, nor the way I should want to formulate my conclusion. And I give reasons for scepticism about the dualism—
my reasons constitute, in a way, the 'additional premisses' to my conclusions
that Moore demands. We cannot talk about 'desire' and 'understanding' in
these contexts without some further explanation of what they are. There are,
for example, many sorts of desires. But the desires that are relevant in this
context, so I contend, are the kind of desire characteristic of intentional
action—desires that essentially involve beliefs about human interests (*VJ*
32–3). Desires in the relevant sense, I say, are therefore not blind—they have
an eye for the good. And the further account of understanding that we need
would show, so I also contend, that understanding in the relevant sense is not
inert (*VJ* 33–4). It is these 'additional premisses' that are essentially at issue
between us, and Moore's chapter leaves me wondering what he would say
about them.

4. THE SUPERVENIENCE OF THE EVALUATIVE
ON THE NATURAL

Any two objects identical in their natural features will also be identical in their
evaluative features. So the supervenience thesis says. In *Value Judgement*
I express doubt about it; I say that I find it 'unclear' whether supervenience

holds (*VJ* 46). Smith vigorously defends it. 'How can I possibly doubt?', he asks; it is a conceptual truth.

The supervenience thesis, thus baldly stated, needs various clarifications and constraints added to it. Smith adds several, some of which I too add and all of which I accept. The conflict between us arises because I add a further constraint, a relevance constraint, that he rejects. There is a way of working out the relevance constraint that raises doubts about the thesis itself (*VJ* 45–6). It is a constraint that applies to supervenience theses generally, not just to the thesis of the supervenience of the evaluative on the natural. My reason for adding it was this. When we speak of the supervenience of the mental on the physical, say, a relevance requirement is implicit. We would not accept that the mental supervenes on the physical if it turned out merely that there were always differences at some deep subatomic level that are irrelevant to differences at the physiological level. Nor would we if it turned out that there were physiological differences in the epidermis unconnected to anything that is happening in the brain and nervous system. That would trivialize the supervenience relation. In the case of mental states, we consider whether they supervene on a particular kind of physical state, namely, brain states. And we consider whether they supervene not just on any state of the brain (for example, perhaps not deep subatomic states), but states of the sort (and at a level of grossness) that affect mental states. We specify the base level in the way we do because we believe that there are certain sorts of connections between it and the supervening level. That comes over, I think, in the language that philosophers use to express their intuitive understanding of the relation that we are trying to specify further; they use such words as 'dependence', 'underlying', 'consequential property'. The same goes on, I think, in the supervenience of the evaluative on the natural. We do not have in mind *anything* in the domain of the natural—say, the state of deep subatomic particles. Rather, we have in mind a subclass of the natural—namely, the natural features relevant to something's being valuable, features that help make it the case that the thing is valuable. Although it is not easy to specify the subclass, I thought, for these reasons, that we should accept a relevance restriction. It is not an eccentric suggestion; many moral philosophers accept one (*VJ* 45).

Smith correctly sums up my position like this: with the relevance restriction, the supervenience thesis is doubtful; without it, it is uninteresting.

Why, with it, is the thesis doubtful? Because, once we add the relevance requirement, it looks likely that some evaluative features will be relevant, will be among the features necessary for making the object valuable. That is, it looks likely that the remaining relevant non-evaluative features will, on their own, be insufficient to make the object valuable; they might all be present both in objects with a certain valuable feature and in objects without it. And that, of course, would rule out supervenience. To this Smith responds: 'I do not see how Griffin thinks that [the possibility that other evaluative features are relevant] can be embraced by someone who accepts his official definition of what it is for a property to be relevant. According to his official definition the relevant properties are a *subclass of the natural*. But it follows immediately from this that *only* natural properties can be relevant. Nothing can be a member of a subclass of the natural, after all, that is not a member of the class of the natural.'

This gets me wrong. Of course, a member of a subclass is a member of the parent class. I was merely imposing a restriction on the natural properties to which the supervenience thesis referred—namely, to relevant properties. But that my restriction is to *natural properties* does not mean that there cannot be non-natural properties that are *also* relevant to whether something has a certain evaluative feature. I nowhere 'define', officially or not, the term 'relevant' in a way that rules that out.

Why, without the relevance requirement, is the supervenience thesis uninteresting? Because we can always, though uninterestingly, produce *some* natural difference between any two objects with different values. It is altogether too easy. Jack and Jill both write poetry. Jill's is first-rate and Jack's is mediocre. So there must be a difference in the natural features of their poetry. All too many: the poems were written in different colour ink, by persons with different genes, and so on. Smith responds: 'why does Griffin think that the supervenience thesis puts any constraint at all on our relative assessments of the value of [their] poetry . . . ?'. Perhaps I am right, he concedes, that their poetry, in the actual world, will not have the same naturalistic features. But it does not follow that the inter-world supervenience thesis that Smith is advancing is thereby made uninteresting. There is some possible world in which there is poetry with all the natural features of Jill's poetry, including the colour of the ink with which it was written and the entire genetic make-up of the person by whom it was written. The supervenience thesis survives: if Jill's poetry has a certain value, then this possible person's poetry has the same value.

True, the supervenience thesis survives, but not without acquiring a certain oddity. Why have a supervenience thesis that applies so rarely to the real world? It is not that the comparisons central to the supervenience thesis need to have anything approaching direct practical import; they are used to make, not an ethical point to help us out in the real world, but a metaphysical point about the nature of value. But that is why Smith's proposal becomes odd. It is counter-intuitive that we have to reach so far to get at the features that make things valuable. 'If the life of the Socratic sort of person is good, then so is the life of any person in any other possible world whose life is an exact duplicate in every naturalistic respect.' But do we need sameness in *all* natural features, without a single exception, down to the deepest subatomic level, before we strike the sameness in natural features that requires sameness in evaluative features? Do we really need a *doppelgänger*? This is just the point about relevance again, but from an angle that gives it some further force. Smith concludes that, once we see that the supervenience thesis has an inter-world scope, my claim that, without a relevance restriction, the thesis is uninteresting lapses. I do not think it does. Is Smith's the thesis we are interested in?

There are many possible interpretations of the supervenience of the evaluative on the natural, as Smith acknowledges. Given our acute uncertainties about the nature of the relation, it is neither surprising nor undesirable that we philosophers should be looking at quite a few different versions of the thesis. I think that Smith does not sufficiently clearly mark the fact that he and I are talking about substantially different versions. It can hardly be a criticism of my view that the supervenience thesis does not have all of the features that it has in his view—for instance, that it is not a conceptual truth. It was no aim of mine that it should be.

Why, anyway, does Smith insist that it is a conceptual truth? We are interested in the supervenience relation because we think that, in some form or other, it will tell us something—not much, actually, but something—about several relations that puzzle us: how the mind is related to the body, how evolutionary phenomena are related to micro-biological phenomena, how these puzzling things that we talk about, evaluative features, are related to much less puzzling natural features of the world, and so on. It represents an unclear, undeveloped, but modestly promising idea about these relations. But the idea needs a lot of clarification. What precisely is the sort of supervenience that illuminates these puzzling relations? The most useful clarification of the idea, it would seem, would be one with such power of illumination. But why then start by imposing a restriction that the supervenience thesis be conceptually true? It cannot be because most moral philosophers are in search only of a supervenience relation with that restriction; they are, for the most part, more open-minded. What, then, motivates it?

For Smith, the conceptual truth at work here is that evaluative claims cannot be *barely* true. That is, they must be made true by other claims. If evaluative truths are always made true by other claims, then, when all the claims that make an evaluative claim true are true of two objects, the same evaluative claim is true of those objects. Hence, supervenience.

This shows us a bit more about how we are to understand Smith's crucial notion of 'barely true'. It is clear that evaluative claims cannot be true independent of *some* other claims: for instance, and quite trivially, a life cannot be good unless there is someone living the life, someone who acts or is acted upon. That would be a necessary condition for the truth of this particular evaluative claim, and something comparable would be necessary for any other evaluative claim. But Smith's point is stronger: the truth of the other claims *make* the evaluative claim true in the sense of being sufficient for its truth. Smith says: 'all of those non-particular features objects have which are such as to figure in empirical regularities [i.e. universal natural features] are supposed to be sufficient for whatever evaluative features they have.' We should have a better grasp of what 'barely true' means if we had an example of a claim that *is* barely true. Perhaps the claim, 'That's blue', is an example. The question, 'What *makes* it blue?' is odd. In this context the 'What makes it . . . ?' question is not, I suppose, after the physics and physiology of vision. It is to be understood as a question about those truths accessible to anyone capable of identifying the feature in question that allows them to make successful identifications. And here the appropriate response would seem, at least on some occasions, to be, 'It's just blue'.

Why, then, is it *incoherent* that any evaluative truths could be barely true? Smith gives an example. Suppose that I say that a certain person's life is good. 'What makes it good?', I am asked. 'You don't understand,' I respond. 'It isn't made good by *other* features; it's just good.' Smith says that my response violates the rules for the use of the word 'good'. I agree. But is that because of features about the rules for the use of the word 'good' in particular or because of features present in the rules for the use of value terms universally? The rules for the use of the word 'good'—at least, the uses we are interested in here—require that it be used against a background of interests that can be met or not met. So anyone who uses the word 'good' in these contexts must be prepared to make claims about the interests that are the bases for the evaluation. But bases eventually come to an end. It is not a requirement of coherence that one can go on supplying bases for ever. Why might we not come to an end with a claim that is still evaluative?

Let us see how the conversation would go on. What makes the life good? It has certain interest-satisfying features: enjoyment, deep personal relations, accomplishment, and so on. Suppose the life is good because it is a life of accomplishment. Accomplishment is still an evaluative notion. So we apply the iterative question: 'What *makes* it a life of accomplishment?' The answer would have to be along the lines of the person's having done things with the sort of importance that give life weight or point. But these are still evaluative notions. So we try the iterative question again: 'What *makes* those things have the sort of importance that gives life weight or point?' But here, to my mind, it becomes hard to answer the question as it is meant. One can certainly describe the things that were done that *had* this sort of importance. They, so described, are what is important. But the claims that they have the natural features that appear in the description are not jointly sufficient (in the sense that has been in use so far) to make the claim that they are important itself true. A good life just *is* a life that answers to certain central human interests, and that is why it would be incoherent to claim that a life is good that has no concern with whether interests were met. A life of accomplishment just *is* a life in which one has done things of an importance that gives life weight or point. And that is why it would be incoherent to claim that something was an accomplishment that had no concern with whether it had that sort of importance. But the road of conceptual analysis that we are now travelling down certainly has an end, and the end may not be totally outside the territory of the evaluative. And the requirement that one must be able to provide descriptions of the things that were done that had this sort of importance is just the weaker requirement that we started with: that an evaluation has an object—for example, that a life cannot be good unless there is someone living the life. Why can one not eventually reach a point with the iterative question where one just recognizes the presence of a value, rather as one recognizes a colour? Is there an incoherence in asserting that one can? I must admit that I do not find it entirely clear what the proposition that an evaluation cannot be 'barely true' amounts to, so I am unsure what the content of Smith's proposed conceptual truth is. But I doubt that he has made out his case that this supposed conceptual truth actually is one.

This brings me straight to the major point of contention between us and to an important matter on which I think that Smith is right and I am wrong. I said in *Value Judgement* that there *are* cases (for example, Jack's and Jill's poetry) in which we find the same relevant natural properties but different evaluations, at least on a certain interpretation of relevance. Let us see in more detail where Smith and I disagree. Jill's poetry, I say, is an accomplishment and Jack's is not. Jill's poetry shows understanding on important matters. But perhaps here, Smith proposes, by use of the iterative question, we have broken through a crucial barrier; perhaps now we have reached a characterization in non-evaluative terms of what Jill did. Jill had the thoughts she did; she wrote the words she did; she gave them the arrangement she did. They carried the sense that showed the understanding that had the sort of importance that made the poetry an accomplishment. None of what Smith says here do I want to deny. What I want to deny is what I denied a moment ago: that these purely non-evaluative claims about thoughts and words are, on their own, sufficient to make the evaluative claim about importance true. All that one must, and should, admit is that the truth of the evaluative claim is not independent of the claims about thoughts and words. For one to accomplish anything, one has to do something, which can be described in non-evaluative terms. That is the weaker and undeniable claim. It is the denial of the sufficiency of the non-evaluative that I wanted to make in *Value Judgement* and that I still want to make.

But I also made a stronger claim that now seems to me wrong. I said that the particular words that Jill used, for example, could have been different, and may have been different in earlier drafts, and the important understanding could still remain. This led me to think that the particular words Jill used were no more part of the set of relevant non-evaluative features than the colour of the ink she used. If the set of relevant non-evaluative features is as exclusive as this, then it is not unreasonable to think that the set of claims needed to make the evaluative claim true would have to include some evaluative claims.

There are a number of doubts about this line of thought, but the central one now is that this seems to be an unreasonably exclusive interpretation of the relevance requirement. And, once I admit that, then I am vulnerable to another of Smith's arguments, which uses, as I shall come to in a moment, a different standard for sufficiency from the one we have spoken of so far. What makes Jill's poetry good is that it contains important understanding. The understanding that is important is embodied in these thoughts of hers, which can be described in non-evaluative terms. The same thoughts, had Jack been lucky enough to have them, would also have constituted important understanding. One does not need to add any further non-evaluative features to the situation in order for it to constitute important understanding. It constitutes, simply as already described, an object that has the evaluative feature, important understanding. In that sense, the non-evaluative features are sufficient for the presence of the evaluative feature. And, if two objects have all of the same non-evaluative features, then they will have the same evaluative feature. Once my over-exclusive interpretation of the relevance requirement goes, my reasons to doubt supervenience go.

But this sort of sufficiency is not, I think, the sort that Smith appeals to when he argues that the supervenience thesis is a conceptual truth. That is the sort of sufficiency that implies that, if one made an evaluative claim and denied that it needed the truth of non-evaluative claims to make it true, in the way discussed earlier, then one would be violating the rules for the use of the evaluative term. But we could find no reasons to think that this is true. The two different standards of sufficiency are then: first, such-and-such (described in non-evaluative terms) is all that this object needs to be in order to be important; and, secondly, such-and-such (described in non-evaluative terms) is all that importance itself amounts to. The first standard seems to me acceptable, the second not.

I am not attracted to Smith's account of supervenience; it lacks a relevance requirement and it makes supervenience conceptually true. But I no longer altogether like mine: the interpretation I gave of the relevance requirement no longer seems to me defensible. Once I correct my interpretation, one of Smith's main criticisms goes through. And it is interesting that it goes through both on his interpretation of supervenience, without a relevance requirement, and on mine, with one. In the end, it is not the relevance requirement that importantly divides us. It is the issue about conceptual truth. I do not think that either of us has got the supervenience of the evaluative on the natural quite right yet.

5. CONSEQUENTIALISM

Towards the end of *Value Judgement* I risk some strong, contentious, incon-clusively argued-for opinions (*VJ* 103–16). Consequentialism, deontology, and virtue ethics—at least, the common forms of them—are unrealistically ambitious. They take too little notice of what human beings and their envi-ronment are really and recalcitrantly like. They assume that whatever powers of rationality or whatever plasticity of will their theories might turn out to require are available. They display an unexamined and largely indefensible optimism, which from time to time in the history of philosophy has provoked a minority into an answering pessimism. In *Value Judgement* I wanted to locate myself on the optimism–pessimism spectrum. I did not do it clearly enough.

For instance, I am not as pessimistic as Roger Crisp thinks I am. I can see how the misunderstanding arose. In my desire to distance myself from (as I see it) the prevailing over-optimism of much philosophical ethics, I seem to have overdone the pessimism—at any rate, the pessimistic rhetoric. In fact, I see my answer to the central question of *Value Judgement*—'How, and how much, can we hope to improve our ethical beliefs?'—as being fairly optimistic. But that 'fairly' needs specification.

Our critical powers are, I say, considerable. We have available to us a large group of beliefs of high reliability: beliefs about prudential goods, about certain basic moral norms, about certain facts about human nature and the nature of society. They then allow us to criticize our ethical beliefs by appeal to utilities, to these basic moral norms, and to the feasibility of the standards that we are told we should judge and live by. We thus have resources to refine our current common-sense ethics. In fact, most of the refinements that Crisp presses in the course of his chapter I find irresistible—for example, that we should be much less biased towards ourselves and those close to us than most of us now are, that many instances of our letting people die are far worse morally than we are prepared to admit, and that a still much invoked notion of the sanctity of life makes people suffer senselessly.

So, much of what Crisp says does not confront my worry, which is this. Our critical powers, which we can turn against common sense, can also be turned against some of the ambitious, systematic ethical views produced by philosophy. Our critical powers, I say, are quite considerable, but only *quite*. Much philosophical ethics has tended to exaggerate them. Crisp often speaks as though my complaint were against the pretensions of *philosophy*. Here too I am less pessimistic than he may take me to be. I see philosophy as having a large role to play in establishing just what our critical powers in ethics are; establishing them is the aim of *Value Judgement*. Crisp attributes to me the view that philosophy has taken us to the wrong place, to (as I put it) 'a spare landscape in which . . . ethics . . . will not grow'. The term I used, however, was not 'philosophy' but the much more specific 'modern moral philosophers' (*VJ* 136). My term was, I confess, even a bit too specific. By 'modern' I meant seventeenth century and later. Ancient philosophers— for example, Aristotle and some of the Stoics—paid more attention to human character and its recalcitrances than most modern philosophers, but it seems to me that many of them too were over-optimistic about the powers of human rationality (*VJ* 112–16). Still, extending my complaint so that it also includes some ancient philosophers leaves it well short of a complaint against philosophy itself.

Crisp thinks that philosophical ethics, at any rate utilitarianism, survives my worries substantially intact. But I do not see from his comments why he is not more worried himself.

My view is that considerations about the good life and the limits of the human will suggest that the most plausible form of utilitarianism is a highly indirect one. It will propose that we act in accordance with certain norms and dispositions and ways of feeling that it will justify by appeal to the higher level principle of utility. My worry—hardly new—is whether we can do the necessary calculations to a reliable degree of probability. Nearly everyone would agree that some utility calculations are within our capacity and some are not. Clearly, some are. As I have said, Crisp contends that the loss to most of us in the affluent world of becoming a little less wrapped up in ourselves and those close to us would be less than the gain to the abjectly poor of the world from our being a little more concerned about them. I agree. But some utility calculations are beyond us. I doubt that we can answer, even to a reliable degree of probability, the question that some rule utilitarians make the pivotal one in ethics: what set of rules and dispositions would, if it were the dominant one in our society, produce most utility over the society at large and in the long run. Crisp agrees: 'this calculation is beyond us.' So we are both members of the majority who think that sometimes we can do the calculations and sometimes we cannot. The crucial question therefore is: 'How often would we fail, and how central to ethical life would the failures be?' If utility calculation is beyond us fairly often and in fairly central parts of ethics, then utilitarianism is in jeopardy.

The issue is immensely complex, the outcome by no means obvious. My worry is that there would indeed be enough failures at the centre of ethical life to jeopardize utilitarianism. I tried to explain that worry in *Value Judgement*, and there is no point in my repeating it here (*VJ* 103–7).

What *is* central to ethics? Well, distributive justice is certainly one thing that is. So is the sort of respect for life that morality requires, which is the example I discuss at some length in chapter VII of *Value Judgement*. So are the many obligations generated by what seem to us worthy social institutions such as property, which I discuss in chapter VI. In all of these cases modifications to certain of our common-sense beliefs can be justified by appeals to utilities. But in all of them a point is reached at which we can no longer do calculations of utilities to a reliable degree of probability, and beyond this point we shall still often need moral guidance.

I should stress the phrase 'to a reliable degree of probability', which I used in my book. Crisp attributes to me the view that, if we cannot be *sure* what maximizes utility, then the principle of utility has no application. It is no wonder that he speaks of my suspect 'stringency'. But that is not my view. We do not need to be sure in order to have good reasons for action. But, when we do not have even probability on which it is reasonable to base action, then our utilitarian thought runs out of practical value.

So how frequent and how central are the failures in calculation? It does not advance the argument to cite a few cases in which we *can* do the calculations. Crisp, of course, does much more than that. He presses distinctions that he thinks I have not sufficiently appreciated: the distinction between the *practical* and the *intellectual* roles of moral philosophy, or between a theory of *practical reason* and a theory of *morality*, or between a *decision procedure* and a *criterion* in ethics. I accept that the most plausible form of utilitarianism will make some such distinctions central. But I see a problem to its doing so: a criterion for ethics cannot become too remote from our capacities without losing its standing even as a criterion, and the principle of utility is too remote (*VJ* 105–6). To my mind, there are knowledge constraints not just on a decision procedure but also on a criterion in ethics. But 'How remote is remote?', Crisp asks. He says that often—with restrictions on harming or killing others, with principles of justice, with certain virtues—we can amend our views by appeal to utilities. But this just brings us back to where we were a moment ago. Surely sometimes we can and sometimes we cannot. The crucial question is: 'How frequent and how central are our failures?' Crisp replies that, in one sense, the utilitarian can say that such calculation *never* fails. 'For any justification must ultimately refer to the advancement of well-being, and if that reference is unavailable then so is the justification.' But what if the reference is often and importantly unavailable? We still have to decide what to do. There is no need, he says, to think 'that such reference will be rare'. It is here that Crisp does indeed address my worry. Will it be available often enough and centrally enough? Crisp, in effect, reassures me, Yes, it will. But I should be happier with some grounds for the reassurance.

Crisp does offer one consideration in support of it. I said a moment ago that the most plausible form of utilitarianism will make central some such question as: 'What set of rules and dispositions will most promote utility, given agents of such-and-such nature and a society that works thus-and-so, over society at large and in the long run.' Crisp and I agree: this calculation is beyond us. But Crisp thinks that this does not matter, as the central question is not this, but rather: 'What improvements can we make to the rules and dispositions that guide our lives at present?' But could this be the central question of utilitarianism? No doubt we can often make improvements by calculating the utilitarian *pros* and *cons*; that is the common ground again. But there are rules and dispositions that guide our lives at present—for instance, some of the rules and dispositions concerning respect for life such as 'Don't deliberately kill the innocent', with the reservations and qualifications we attach to it—for which the calculation of the utilitarian *pros* and *cons* for it and for its very many possible alternatives seems to me beyond us (*VJ* 98–102, 116–21). Yet this is a part of our life where we certainly need guidance. Crisp, I take it, would himself not want to say that what gives our rule its normative status is its being part of our current common sense. That sits uncomfortably with his uncompromising view that the justification of norms 'must ultimately refer to the advancement of well-being, and if that reference is unavailable then so is the justification'. And there are current rules—say, the ones generated by our institution of property—which we may be able to improve by appeal to utilities, but the improved rules will still be part of one particular institution of property among a wide range of possible other ones that we cannot rank against one another (*VJ* 95–6). Crisp cannot say that what justifies our (improved) rule is that it is generated by *our* institution: 'the mere existence of an institution speaks neither in favour of nor against acting in accord with it.' Quite right; some institutions are atrocious. What I have claimed is, rather, that when we think that an institution is working tolerably well (perhaps only after amendment), when we therefore have much more than its mere existence, then we accept the obligations that it generates, and rightly so. We are not able to say that this is the best of all the possible institutions of property in the wide band of alternatives. Our justification is that it is what our institution requires. If I am right that the band is broad, and that we enter it at a fairly early stage in our moral life, and that a similar band appears in the case of many norms at the centre of our ethical life, then in a large and central part of our moral life utilitarian justification is unavailable, and we must conduct our lives on a different basis. It is not that I think that the different basis will always be, as in the case of property, an appeal to the contingent fact of what *our* institutions are. There are many different bases. I shall come back to this matter soon. But, if that is in fact the outcome, if we do indeed need some non-utilitarian norms, then utilitarianism loses one claim to being systematic—namely, that it covers something close to the whole moral domain.

Would Crisp say that if indeed utilitarianism came up with no answer over much of the centre of the ethical domain then there simply was no answer? Would he say that there is a truth of the matter about ultimate ethical reasons for action, that the principle of utility states it, and that, if it follows from the truth that we are bereft of answers in much of the centre of the ethical domain, then we must simply accept that unwelcome fact? The truth, he might say, need not be comfortable. But what would be the source of his confidence in this truth? My guess is that here he sides with Sidgwick. He says that Sidgwick was right to think that philosophy has a purely intellectual as well as a practical aspect. Perhaps he would agree with Sidgwick that we know the principle of utility by intuition. Perhaps that is why he is anxious to insist that Sidgwick's foundational principle 'can be seen as resting on a substantive view of well-being, and thus to be as "thick" as any of Griffin's foundational beliefs'. I doubt that the principle of utility is anything like as thick as a list of basic human interests. But thickness is not the issue. The issue is how we are supposed to know that the principle of utility is true. I set out a case in *Value Judgement* for our having a sensitivity to what is in our interest. But one is not entitled to speak of a sensitivity to a certain kind of thing unless one can explain what it is for the sensitivity to work well, and what to work badly. What is more, one has to explain how we have access to what shows whether on some particular occasion it is working well or badly. I spent much time (chapters II–IV) doing this. My foundational beliefs and Sidgwick's are not on all fours. I doubt that there is anything like as plausible an account of how an intuition works well or badly that has as its object such complex practical standards as the ones that Sidgwick is concerned with, the egoistic principle and the principle of utility.

Brad Hooker is more sympathetic to my worries than Crisp is. He accepts that they do indeed undermine some versions of indirect consequentialism. But, he adds, they undermine neither all versions, nor the best. Two or more codes of rules, he allows, may be, as far as we can tell, equal bests in utility. (This is his concession to my doubts about our powers of calculation.)

Indirect consequentialists must, therefore, 'make their theory even more modest'. The suitably more modest—and best—version will hold that, 'of these codes with unsurpassed expected value, the one closest to conventional morality determines which kinds of acts are wrong'.

This more modest version of consequentialism does not still my old worries, and it raises a fresh one. The fresh one is about Hooker's use of the notion of a 'conventional morality'. He makes it a benchmark, and for it to serve as such it would have to be a fairly full, identifiable set of beliefs. But conventional morality is much vaguer, more fragmentary, and less consistent than this use of it suggests. For Hooker the key question is: 'Would a change in some conventional norm(s) result in better consequences overall?' If the answer is a fairly confident 'Yes', then we change the norm(s); if 'No', then we stick to the conventional norm(s).

It is true that we philosophers often speak of 'common-sense morality', but we do not, or should not, think that it consists of a compatible set of beliefs covering pretty much the whole of ethical life. It consists of some widely distributed moral intuitions, a few of which—such as that cruelty is wrong—are among the most secure ethical beliefs we have. It consists also of obligations generated by institutions that command widespread acceptance—such as property and the obligation not to steal. But in our present society there is deep disagreement about respect for life—about suicide, abortion, and euthanasia. There is no 'conventional morality' about them. And on other ethical matters, such as our behaviour towards the environment, there never has been. The environment has only recently been let into the ethical domain. We are now trying to develop plausible ideas about it that might eventually graduate to being conventions. I think that abortion, for example, is a matter about which a very large number of norms could be formed, all of which would fall into Hooker's category of 'unsurpassed expected value'. But we could not then choose just one by determining which is closest to conventional morality. On this matter there is no such thing.

But my main worry about Hooker's suitably modest indirect consequentialism is still my old one. What if, as I think and Hooker may think too, there are in fact very many codes with unsurpassed expected value. What if the resulting area of uncertainty includes many major ethical questions—questions, for instance, about what distributive justice requires, what respect for life requires, what respect for ownership requires? Utility calculation, *ex hypothesi*, has done what it can for us. We have to find other ways of proceeding. I doubt that we can successfully proceed by invoking Hooker's formula: now choose the code closest to conventional morality. Conventional morality is especially thin on what distributive justice requires and especially unsettled on what respect for life requires. Very many codes would still remain. I think that we should (and most of us do actually, whatever our official positions in moral philosophy are) proceed differently. We appeal to one kind of consideration on one occasion and another on another. The considerations we introduce have no systematic connections with one another, but despite that we do what we can to make the results harmonious. In short, we muddle through, carried along by our genetic make-up, natural sentiment, social change, and piecemeal exploitation of ideas that seem to us good on their own ground but start giving bewilderingly bad results when we try to squeeze more advice out of them than they were made to give.

I do not deny that *sometimes* the right thing to do is, as Hooker proposes, to appeal to convention. I said a moment ago that, if our own institution of property does not seem obviously seriously flawed, we should work within it. It would not then matter that there is in fact a very large number of differently constituted institutions of property that doubtless have different consequentialist values though we are unable to determine reliably enough what they are. The arbitrary fact that this one is *our* institution, good enough to be getting on with and not decidedly worse than the others, is enough for us. And it is enough for us to live by the obligations that it generates.

This reliance upon convention is one of the ways in which we proceed, but only one. Hooker thinks that it is my central proposal for how we arrive at sufficiently determinate norms for action, but that is not what I intended. Another case that I discussed in chapter VII of *Value Judgement* is respect for life. I gave my reasons there for doubting that consequentialist calculation will pick out for us the very large set of norms that define respect for life—for example, the norm prohibiting deliberately taking innocent life, its domain of application restricted by the norm permitting some euthanasia, the norm permitting certain acts to limit overall loss of life, and so on. There will be many differing sets of such norms that we shall not be able to rank in consequentialist terms. But we do not need that ranking. We arrive at our norm, 'Don't deliberately kill the innocent', in a much more direct way. We greatly value human life and have erected an important moral norm in its protection. And, because the norm is so important, we require any restriction on its application—say, for some sorts of euthanasia—to have an especially strong justification. It is not that, given the embarrassing variety of sets of norms that we are left with after consequentialist calculation has done its best, we appeal to convention. This is an area in which there is none to appeal to. I said in *Value Judgement* that there are many, heterogeneous, unsystematic considerations that shape our norms. This is an example of how basic values themselves sometimes directly shape norms: the norm 'Don't deliberately kill the innocent' is non-consequentialist because it is justified not by appeal to what most pro-motes the good but by a more direct, non-maximizing appeal to the value of life (*VJ* 101–2, 118).

In some parts of our lives consequentialist calculation is just what is needed. But in other parts we have rightly worked out different approaches. Certain basic values give rise to central moral norms, without reliance upon conse-quentialist calculation. Our conception of the limits of the human will and human understanding also shapes these norms. The norm against deliberately killing the innocent is one example. Human rights are another. We value highly our status as self-determiners, and the values of autonomy and liberty (along with others) attract the protection of a special kind of norm, human rights. These various norms, and what they are grounded in, can be used to criticize and amend our traditions and conventions.

Hooker is hopeful that what seem to me various piecemeal, unsystematic forms of criticism reduce, on scrutiny, to consequentialist reasoning. He can allow that these norms may in fact have arisen independently of conse-quentialist calculation, and that they may be used in our deliberation without explicit reference to consequentialist calculation. But, still, what justifies them in the end is that they are sanctioned by consequentialist calculation. In *Value Judgement* I mentioned human rights as one of our grounds for amending our traditions and conventions, and he takes me up on this. He points out that, according to me, human rights are grounded partly in the protection of autonomy, and that autonomy is a component of well-being. Therefore rights, he concludes, have a fundamentally consequentialist grounding. But here he seems to me to be too quick. Not all interest accounts of rights have to be consequentialist. They will be consequentialist only if what justifies the selection of a certain set of human rights is that they would produce the best consequences over the society at large and in the long run. But that is just the sort of calculation that I doubt can be done to a reliable degree of probability.

6. AN ETHICS UNDISTORTED BY OVER-AMBITION

I have left visible loose ends throughout these comments. I have just touched on the way in which I think utilitarianism has too ambitious a picture of prac-tical rationality. In *Value Judgement* I make similar cases about deontology (*VJ* 107–12) and virtue ethics (*VJ* 112–16). All the cases are too quick. But if they were true, where would that leave us? What would an ethics undistorted by over-ambition look like?

It is not enough just to make the negative case against these highly systematic ethics, even if the negative case is subtle enough also to make the positive point that our ethical life can get on quite well without them. It is not enough because it leaves an inescapable question unanswered, 'What *are* our critical powers?' The answer cannot be anything as simple as an instruction to be ever-increasingly sensitive to the fine features of particular situations. Some extreme forms of virtue ethics, especially ones that make the fiction of 'the perfectly virtuous person' basic to practical thought, are as much exercises in fantasy as the most confident conceptions of the utilitarian calculator. Nor may we just remain silent. Our critical powers are not negligible, and we do not have to be left to flounder quite as badly as we do now with our confused sense of what they are and how best to deploy them. The difficulty is obvious: a highly systematic ethics can give a snappy answer to the question, 'What are our critical powers?'; a non-systematic ethics cannot. Part of its point is that there is no snappy answer.

It is a nice reversal of roles when I, who think that much philosophical ethics is unrealistic and over-ambitious, am accused of being unrealistic and over-ambitious myself. Amélie Rorty reminds us eloquently that decision-making in the real world falls far short of autonomy. Collective decision-making is, she says, a drama: we adopt, or are forced into, roles; what happens in the early acts of a drama can then change our roles in later acts; we often exaggerate our agreements or disagreements with opponents; chance occurrences can deflect us in entirely new directions. Individual decision-making, she says, should be seen on the same model: what goes on inside one person's head is a kind of drama—different voices, often attached to different ancestral players, and happenstance upsetting the dialogue. And the same model applies to our decisions in ethics, to our choice of ends and norms.

In Rorty's chapter I seem to be locked in a dramatic dialogue with her, in which she gets to write both parts. She assigns me a role: that stock figure of fun, the Ivory Tower academic. I am 'the philosopher within: the Griffin-minded philosopher' with illusions of 'philosophy as a strong normative enterprise', with 'Olympian pretensions' to a purely rational form of decision-making, for whom her conclusions will prove 'embarrassingly deflationary'. I am assigned such lines as: Once having acknowledged all of these heteronomous forces at work in decision-making, should we not still aim at the old ideal of autonomous, rational choice? Rorty thinks that, given our actual psychology, we are not best served 'earnestly attempting to approximate that idealized model for decision-making'. I am meant to illustrate the importance of not being earnest. Norms remain, she says, 'but they have neither the form of a confident calculation, nor a set of guidelines for deliberative evaluation, with fixed ends or set rules of procedure'.

I am not as opposed to Rorty's positive views as she thinks, which another dialogue involving the mythical 'Griffin' will serve to show. 'Griffin's answer might be: A comprehensive ethical theory should provide an ideal to which we should attempt to approximate . . .' Take just the first four words she puts into my mouth: 'A comprehensive ethical theory'. I think (and clearly say) that a person's moral outlook, even a reflective person's, is an assemblage of norms arrived at in piecemeal fashion, to which the word 'theory' is inapposite (*VJ* 132). And contrary to thinking that a person's moral outlook can be 'comprehensive', I say that this assemblage of norms is unsystematic and incomplete (*VJ* 14–16, 103–19, 132). My views are closer to hers than she thinks.

But I do not know quite how close because I do not know quite where she stands. Rorty's conclusion wavers between a modest truism and a pretty Olympian edict of her own. She says that the retreat to modesty that she counsels would encourage philosophers to present their 'weightiest arguments' but at the same time to acknowledge that their arguments have 'limitations' and 'lacunae'. But what moderately sane philosopher would gainsay that? Rorty supposes that there are those who will be embarrassed by this deflationary truism. But who? Presumably the 'Griffin' of her drama, but also, I think, many others who aspire to fairly ambitious critical powers in ethics. According to Rorty, 'Griffin . . . brackets the influence of context and history on the formulation and evaluation of ethical standards and concentrates instead on a fundamentally contextless normative philosophical question: "How are we to refine our standards?"' I do not 'bracket' (that is, ignore) the influence of context and history. My question is asked from a position embedded in our own present situation: 'How, and how much, can we hope to criticize and change our ethical standards?' One way we can criticize them (*only* one of many piecemeal forms of criticism available to us) is by considering their feasibility, given some realism about what agents and society are actually like. Are the ambitions that I harbour here, or that the mythical 'Griffin' and certain other philosophers are supposed to harbour, immodest? To say so is not simply to utter the truism again. It is an Olympian edict. Exactly (or even roughly) how modest do we have to be? Nothing that Rorty says tells us. To say that there are all sorts of non-rational influences on our decisions tells us nothing about what in the end our critical powers in ethics are or how best to exploit them. Our understanding of that would be helped along by someone's doing well the project I set myself in *Value Judgement*. Part of the project would be to describe a sane ethics—an ethics for the likes of us, living and deciding together, in our actual circumstances—an ethics undistorted by over-ambition or (one probably needs now to add) under-ambition either.

As for the question, 'What would an ethics undistorted by over-ambition look like?', I said what I could in *Value Judgement* (*VJ* 116–19), but hardly enough. Here too, there is no quick answer, and it is expecting too much to think that we should ever get anywhere near a complete answer. Of all the questions I am leaving open, that is the one to which I am most anxious to return.

Index